TRANSITIONAL JUSTICE IN THE ASIA-PACIFIC

The question of how the human rights violations of previous regimes and past periods of conflict ought to be addressed is one of the most pressing concerns facing governments and policy makers today. New democracies and states in the fragile post-conflict peace-settlement phase are confronted by the need to make crucial decisions about whether to hold perpetrators of human rights violations accountable for their actions and, if so, the mechanisms they ought to employ to best achieve that end. This is the first book to examine the ways in which states and societies in the Asia-Pacific region have navigated these difficult waters.

Drawing together several of the world's leading experts on transitional justice with Asia-Pacific regional and country specialists, the book provides an overview of the processes and practices of transitional justice in the region as well as detailed analysis of the cases of Cambodia, Sri Lanka, Aceh, Indonesia, South Korea, the Solomon Islands, and East Timor.

Renée Jeffery is an Associate Professor of International Relations at the Australian National University. She is the author of *Amnesty and Accountability: The Persistence of Amnesties from Athens to Aceh, Indonesia* (scheduled for 2014), *Reason and Emotion in International Ethics* (scheduled for 2014), *Evil and International Relations: Human Suffering in an Age of Terror* (2008), and *Hugo Grotius in International Thought* (2006) and the editor of *Confronting Evil in International Relations: Ethical Responses to Problems of Moral Agency* (2008).

Hun Joon Kim is a Senior Lecturer at Griffith University. His PhD dissertation, *Expansion of Transitional Justice Measures: A Comparative Analysis of Its Causes*, was the winner of the 2009 American Political Science Association Best Dissertation Award (Human Rights Section). He is the author of *The Massacres at Mt Halla: Sixty Years of Truth-Seeking in South Korea* (scheduled for 2014).

Transitional Justice in the Asia-Pacific

Edited by

Renée Jeffery

Australian National University

Hun Joon Kim

Griffith University

CAMBRIDGE
UNIVERSITY PRESS

CAMBRIDGE
UNIVERSITY PRESS

32 Avenue of the Americas, New York, NY 10013-2473, USA

Cambridge University Press is part of the University of Cambridge.

It furthers the University's mission by disseminating knowledge in the pursuit of education, learning, and research at the highest international levels of excellence.

www.cambridge.org
Information on this title: www.cambridge.org/9781107040373

First published 2014

Printed in the United States of America

A catalog record for this publication is available from the British Library.

Library of Congress Cataloging in Publication Data
Jeffery, Renée.
Transitional justice in the Asia-Pacific / Renée Jeffery, Australian National University; Hun Joon Kim, Griffith University, Brisbane.
pages cm
Includes bibliographical references and index.
ISBN 978-1-107-04037-3 (hardback)
1. Transitional justice – Asia. 2. Transitional justice – Pacific Area. 3. Political crimes and offenses – Asia. 4. Political crimes and offenses – Pacific Area. 5. Rule of law – Asia. 6. Rule of law – Pacific Area. I. Kim, Hun Joon, 1975– II. Title.
K5250.J44 2014
340'.115–dc23 2013019591

ISBN 978-1-107-04037-3 Hardback

Contents

Contributors

Kirsten Ainley is a Lecturer in the Department of International Relations at the London School of Economics and Political Science. She is the coauthor, with Chris Brown, of *Understanding International Relations*, 4th edition (2009), as well as several book chapters and articles on aspects of international criminal law.

Edward Aspinall is a Professor of Politics in the Department of Political and Social Change at Australian National University, Canberra. He is the author of *Islam and Nation: Separatist Rebellion in Aceh, Indonesia* (2009); *Opposing Suharto: Compromise, Resistance and Regime Change in Indonesia* (2005); *The Helsinki Peace Agreement: A More Promising Basis for Peace in Aceh?* East West Center, Policy Paper series (2003 and 2005); and *The Peace Process in Aceh: Why It Failed* (coauthored with Harold Crouch), as well as the editor of *Problems of Democratisation in Indonesia: Elections, Institutions, and Society* (coedited with Marcus Mietzner) (2010) and *Local Power and Politics in Indonesia: Decentralisation & Democratisation* (coedited with Greg Fealy) (2003).

Renée Jeffery is an Associate Professor of International Relations at the Australian National University. She is the author of *Amnesty and Accountability: The Persistence of Amnesties from Athens to Aceh, Indonesia* (forthcoming); *Reason and Emotion in International Ethics* (forthcoming); *Hugo Grotius in International Thought* (2006); and *Evil and International Relations: Human Suffering in an Age of Terror* (2008) and the editor of *Confronting Evil in International Relations: Ethical Responses to Problems of Moral Agency* (2008), as well as the author of numerous articles.

Lia Kent is a Postdoctoral Research Fellow with the State, Society and Governance in Melanesia Program at the Australian National University. She has worked in, and conducted research on, East Timor, since 2000. Dr. Kent received her PhD in 2010 for a thesis entitled *Justica Seidauk Mai (Justice Is Yet to Come): Rethinking the Dynamics of Transitional Justice in East Timor*. She is the author of *Transitional Justice and Local Realities: East Timor and Beyond* (2012), as well as of several articles and book chapters.

Hun Joon Kim is a Senior Lecturer in the Griffith Asia Institute and Centre for Governance and Public Policy at Griffith University. Dr. Kim received his PhD in 2008 for a dissertation titled *Expansion of Transitional Justice Measures: A Comparative Analysis of Its Causes*, which was the winner of the 2009 American Political Science Association Best Dissertation Award (Human Rights Section). He is the author of several journal articles published in *International Organization*, *International Studies Quarterly*, *Human Rights Quarterly*, the *Journal of Peace Research*, the *International Journal of Transitional Justice*, *Global Governance*, and the *Journal of Human Rights*. He is the author of *The Massacres at Mt Halla: Sixty Years of Truth-Seeking in South Korea* (forthcoming).

Leigh A. Payne is Professor of Sociology (Latin American Societies) and a Fellow of St. Antony's College at the University of Oxford. She is also a faculty affiliate at the University of Minnesota Law School and was a Visiting Professor in the Political Science Department at the University of Minnesota (2008–2011). She is the author of *Brazilian Industrialists and Democratic Change* (1994), *Uncivil Movements: The Armed Right Wing and Democracy in Latin America* (2000), and *Unsettling Accounts: Neither Truth nor Reconciliation in Confessions of State Violence* (2008). Her most recent coauthored book is *Transitional Justice in Balance: Comparing Processes, Weighing Efficacy* (2010). She has edited other volumes and written various book chapters and articles on human rights and transitions from authoritarian rule in Latin America and South Africa.

Kathryn Sikkink is Regents Professor and holds the McKnight Presidential Chair in Political Science at the University of Minnesota. She is the author of *The Justice Cascade: Human Rights Trials and Global Change* (2011), *Mixed Signals: U.S. Human Rights Policy and Latin America* (2004), and *Activists Beyond Borders: Advocacy Networks in International Politics* (with Margaret Keck) (1998); coeditor of *Restructuring World Politics: Transnational Social Movements, Networks, and Norms* (with Sanjeev Khagram and James Riker) (2002) and *The Power of Human Rights: International Norms and Domestic Change* (with Thomas Risse and Stephen Ropp) (1999); and author of more than forty book chapters and articles.

Chandra Lekha Sriram is Professor of International Law and International Relations at the University of East London. She is author and editor of various books and journal articles on international relations, international law, human rights, and conflict prevention and peace-building. She is the author of three monographs: *Peace as Governance: Power-Sharing, Armed Groups, and Contemporary Peace Negotiations* (2008); *Globalizing Justice for Mass Atrocities: A Revolution in Accountability* (2005); and *Confronting Past Human Rights Violations: Justice versus Peace in Times of Transition* (2004). In 2010, the book she coedited with Suren Pillay, *Peace versus Justice? The Dilemma of Transitional Justice in Africa* (2010), won an Outstanding Academic Title award from *Choice*, of the American Librarian Association.

Fajran Zain is a PhD student in the Department of Political and Social Change at the Australian National University, doing research on transitional justice and reconciliation in Aceh. He works with the Aceh Institute, a public policy research institute based in Banda Aceh, as political analyst, and was a consultant for International Center for Transitional Justice (ICTJ).

Acknowledgments

This volume of essays is the product of a two-day workshop, hosted by Griffith University and funded by an Area of Strategic Investment workshop grant in the winter of 2011. The workshop, titled "Transitional Justice in the Asia-Pacific," brought together several of the world's leading scholars of transitional justice as well as experts on transitional and post-conflict justice processes in the Asia-Pacific cases of Cambodia; East Timor; the Solomon Islands; Aceh, Indonesia; South Korea; and Sri Lanka. This volume is, in large part, the result of two days of vibrant and intensive discussions and debates about transitional justice in a region of the world that largely had been ignored by scholars of transitional justice. Without that concentrated effort, this volume would have been greatly diminished. We therefore thank all of the participants who presented papers at the Brisbane workshop, particularly those who traveled around the world to get there. We thank them for their generosity, of both time and intellectual engagement, and for making the workshop so enjoyable. In addition we thank our discussants and observers for their keen critiques and contributions to both the individual papers that appear in this volume and the framing of the book as a whole. In particular, we would like to thank Tim Dunne, Jason Sharman, Liane Hartnett, and Sri Lestari Wahyuningroem. Thanks also go to Pat Weller, Andrew O'Neil, Angela McDonald, Paula Cowan, and the staff at the Ship Inn for their support throughout the planning stages and during the workshop.

Introduction

New Horizons: Transitional Justice in the Asia-Pacific

Renée Jeffery and Hun Joon Kim

THE QUESTION OF HOW THE HUMAN RIGHTS VIOLATIONS OF previous regimes and past periods of conflict ought to be addressed is one of the most pressing concerns facing governments and policy makers today. New democracies and states in the fragile post-conflict peace-settlement phase are confronted by the need to make crucial decisions about whether to hold perpetrators of human rights violations accountable for their actions and, if so, the mechanisms they ought to employ to best achieve that end. Since the 1980s, post-transitional states have increasingly opted in favour of accountability for human rights violations and have used a wide range of measures from prosecutions and punishment to truth telling, lustration of police and security forces, reparations, and judicial reforms, to reconciliation processes, apologies, forgiveness ceremonies, exhumations and reburials, memorialization projects, traditional and indigenous justice practices, and other guarantees of non-repetition.[1] In doing so, they have contributed to the emergence of what has variously been termed 'the justice cascade' or as a 'revolution in accountability.'[2]

1 Naomi Roht-Arriaza, 'Civil Society Processes of Accountability' in M. Cherif Bassiouni (ed.), *Post-Conflict Justice*, Ardsley, NY: Transnational Publishers, 2002, p. 97.

2 Ellen Lutz and Kathryn Sikkink, 'The Justice Cascade: The Evolution and Impact of Foreign Human Rights Trials in Latin America,' *Chicago Journal of International Law*, Vol. 2, No. 1 (2001), pp. 1–34; Chandra Lekha Sriram, 'Revolutions in Accountability: New Approaches to Past Abuses,' *American University International Law Review*,

The purpose of this book is to provide an in-depth analysis of the practices, processes, and problems of transitional justice in the Asia-Pacific region. Although the practice of transitional justice is global in its reach, scholarship concerned with theorizing and analyzing the practice has focused on cases in Latin America, Africa, and Eastern Europe. The reasons for this are largely historical. During the 1980s and 1990s large numbers of states in Latin America, Africa, and Eastern Europe experienced transitions to democracy and, in doing so, pioneered efforts to hold state officials accountable for past human rights violations. For example, exemplary truth commissions were established in the 1980s and 1990s in Argentina and South Africa, and foreign and international criminal prosecutions were carried out in response to human rights violations that occurred in Chile, the former Yugoslavia, and Rwanda throughout the 1990s. Although the use of transitional justice mechanisms to address past human rights violations has been similarly prevalent in the Asia-Pacific, however, this region has attracted decidedly less scholarly attention than Latin America, Africa, and Eastern Europe.

A simple comparison of the number of publications reveals this unbalance. As the Transitional Justice Database Project reveals, of the 1,520 country-specific studies of transitional justice published in recent years, only seventy-eight (5 percent) are on countries of the Asia-Pacific region. By contrast, 629 studies (41 percent) have appeared on transitional justice in Africa, 474 (31 percent) on Europe, and 336 (23 percent) on Latin American cases.[3] The imbalance is not caused by the number of new democracies in the region because the Asia-Pacific region, with twenty-four new democracies since 1980, ranks second, following Africa (twenty-nine countries), and followed by Europe (twenty-one countries) and Latin America (seventeen countries). More strikingly, studies of

Vol. 19, No. 2 (2003), pp. 310–429; Hunjoon Kim, *Expansion of Transitional Justice Measures: A Comparative Analysis of its Causes*, PhD Thesis (2009), University of Minnesota.

3 Transitional Justice Database Project, at http://sites.google.com/sites/transitionaljustice database/home (accessed 20 May 2011).

Japan, Cambodia, and East Timor make up almost 90 percent of all regional research. This suggests a lack of interest in those cases which do not get much attention from the international media. This is a significant oversight. The Asia-Pacific, as the region that has most recently embraced the practice of transitional justice, following, developing, and modifying practices employed in the rest of the world, has shaped many of the most innovative, dynamic and, at times problematic, processes. Examining the practices and processes of transitional justice in the Asia-Pacific will thus provide not only sorely lacking regional analysis but also broader insights into the theory and practice of transitional justice.

The remainder of this introductory chapter thus explains our understanding of transitional justice in the twenty-first century. By expanding the conceptual horizons of what constitutes a 'transition' and what the term 'justice' means, we provide a broad understanding of transitional justice that encompasses the range of contexts within which states and other actors pursue accountability for past human rights violations as well as the various means by which they seek that end. In order to situate our work within the development of transitional justice scholarship over the past three decades, we then provide an overview of the three key debates that have shaped the sub-field: prosecution versus pardon, retributive versus restorative justice, and bottom-up versus top-down approaches. In doing so, we suggest that a new trend in transitional justice is emerging and consolidating in the Asia-Pacific, where previous dichotomous divides are no longer relevant and synthetic and holistic approaches that combine different transitional justice mechanisms and notions of justice have taken hold. This provides the basis on which we explain the selection of cases included in this book before outlining its structure and content.

Redefining Transitional Justice in the Twenty-First Century

Transitional justice has traditionally been defined as 'the conception of justice associated with periods of political change, characterized by legal responses to confront the wrongdoings of repressive predecessor regimes.'[4] In this book, however, we adopt a broader understanding of transitional justice that extends both the constitutive elements of transition and justice beyond their original conceptualizations. By redefining its parameters, we hope to reflect developments in both the practice and study of transitional justice that have seen its contours significantly expanded over the past three decades.

Although transitional justice has been practiced since at least the time of the ancient Greeks and found form in the aftermath of World War II with the Nuremberg and Tokyo Trials, the origins of the contemporary study and practice of transitional justice are most commonly associated with the 'third wave' of democratic transitions from authoritarian rule in the 1980s in Latin America.[5] Democratization in this context commonly referred to the movement from a repressive and closed regime, such as military, authoritarian, and one-party dictatorships, or communist regimes, to more open and decentralized government marked by free, fair, secret, and direct national elections for major government offices including head of state.[6] Reflecting this, transitional justice was primarily focused on 'justice associated with periods of political change', specifically the 'movement from repressive regimes to democratic societies.'[7] Justice, in this context, was generally conceived in terms of the establishment of trials and truth commissions to address past human rights violations.

4 Ruti G. Teitel, 'Transitional Justice Genealogy,' *Harvard Human Rights Journal*, Vol. 16 (2003), p. 69.

5 Jon Elster, *Closing the Books: Transitional Justice in Historical Perspective*, Cambridge: Cambridge University Press, 2004, p. 1; Neil J. Kritz (ed.), *Transitional Justice: How Emerging Democracies Reckon with Former Regimes*, Washington D.C.: United States Institute of Peace, 1995; Paige Arthur, 'How "Transitions" Reshaped Human Rights: A Conceptual History of Transitional Justice,' *Human Rights Quarterly*, Vol. 31, No. 2 (2009), pp. 329–331.

6 Samuel Huntington, *The Third Wave: Democratization in the Late-Twentieth Century*, Norman: University of Oklahoma Press, 1991, p. 7.

7 Richard H. Solomon, 'Preface' to Neil J. Kritz (ed.), *Transitional Justice: How Emerging Democracies Reckon with Former Regimes*, Vol. 3, Washington D.C.: United States Institute for Peace, 1995, p. xxiii.

Starting from the mid-1990s, however, the parameters of the 'transitions' included within the scope of transitional justice began to expand into areas that had traditionally been demarcated in scholarly terms as the concerns of conflict resolution and peace building. With this, movements from conflict to peace (or some other sort of post-conflict state) associated with the end of civil wars and periods of violent instability came to also be viewed as transitions. In these types of contexts, political transitions were primarily brought about by one party to a conflict inflicting a decisive victory over their adversaries or by the signing of a peace accord, often mediated by international actors. Significantly, these types of transition have not always accompanied movements from authoritarian rule to democracy, but also occurred within established democracies like Northern Ireland. In large part, this spillover of the study of transitional justice into conflict resolution and peace building reflected changing practices in world politics. In particular, in the face of new ethnic and civil conflicts in Yugoslavia and Rwanda, diplomats, peace negotiators and international organizations considered and actually adopted trials and truth commissions before, during, and after conflict resolution. In scholarly terms, what followed was not simply the encroachment of transitional justice into conflict resolution and peace building, but the simultaneous redefinition of peace building to include the pursuit of justice as a key priority.[8] The result was the establishment of this second type of transition from conflict to peace as a key concern of transitional justice along with justice associated with transitions from authoritarian rule.

At the same time, the concept of justice embedded in traditional understandings of transitional justice has also been expanded beyond its original focus on 'legal responses . . . to the wrongdoings of repressive predecessor regimes' to reflect broader notions of justice.[9] Although some

8 John Paul Lederach, *Building Peace: Sustainable Reconciliation in Divided Societies*, Tokyo: UNU Press, 1994, p. 14; Michael Barnett, Hunjoon Kim, Madalene O'Donnell, and Laura Sitea, 'Peacebuilding: What Is in a Name?,' *Global Governance*, Vol. 13, No. 1 (2007), p. 44.

9 Teitel, 'Transitional Justice Genealogy,' p. 69.

scholars and practitioners hold firm to the view that criminal prosecutions remain the 'unrivaled' means of addressing past human rights violations, a dramatic increase in other formal and official responses such as truth commissions, reparations, vetting procedures, and amnesties, as well as in informal and customary practices, has taken place.[10] What unites these different approaches to transitional justice, however, is that each seeks to achieve accountability for serious crimes, including human rights violations, committed in the past. Accountability, in this sense, denotes being held responsible or blameworthy for an action or set of actions. In minimal terms, accountability requires 'actors to accept' whether forcibly or through their own volition, 'responsibility for the impact of their action or inaction on human rights.'[11] Accountability thus means that 'some actors have the right to hold other actors to a set of standards, then judge whether they have fulfilled their responsibility and to impose sanctions if they determine these responsibilities have not been met.'[12] Accountability may be pursued through trials and punishments or through the provision of compensation or restitution, the issuing of apologies, truth telling, expressions of guilt and repentance, and requests for forgiveness.[13]

However, these different approaches to transitional justice are not only united in their common pursuit of accountability but in their attempts to right the wrongs of the past. They do this in different ways by pursuing retribution, restoration, reinterpretation, rectification or reparation. Retribution, which is often understood as the most traditional notion of justice – 'an eye for an eye' – seeks to establish blame for wrongs committed and administer punishment.[14] It is primarily, although not exclusively,

10 Mark Freeman, *Truth Commissions and Procedural Fairness*, Cambridge: Cambridge University Press, 2006, p. 10.

11 United Nations Human Development Report, 2000, p. 89, at http://hdr.undp.org/en/media/hdr_2000_ch5.pdf (accessed 3 March 2011).

12 Robert Keohane and Ruth Grant, 'Accountability and Abuses of Power in World Politics,' *American Political Science Review*, Vol. 99, No. 1 (2005), p. 29.

13 Rachel Kerr and Erin Mobekk, *Peace and Justice: Seeking Accountability After War*, Cambridge: Polity, 2007, p. 4.

14 Howard Zehr, 'Restorative Justice: The Concept,' *Corrections Today*, Vol. 59, No. 7 (1997), p. 68.

manifested in judicial activities such as criminal and civil proceedings and the punishments, which exact certain costs on the perpetrator that followed them.[15] Transitional justice may also attempt to right the wrongs of the past by reinterpreting that past, re-establishing suppressed facts, reconceiving distorted ideas, and rewriting official narratives in sanctioned documents and history textbooks. At its most basic, reparative justice seeks to repair damage or harm that has been unjustly inflicted on an individual, group, or state. In its ideal extreme it is 'designed to re-establish the situation prior to . . . [a] wrongful act or omission' and, in doing so, 'wipe out all consequences of the illegal' or, indeed, immoral act.[16] Reparative justice may be administered through a formal legal system with current efforts concentrated on recovering stolen assets from former dictators for redistribution to victims, or through informal community or grass-roots processes.[17] Similarly, restorative justice aims to 'create peace in communities by reconciling the parties and repairing the injuries caused by the dispute.'[18] It commonly does so through truth telling, reconciliation processes, apologies, forgiveness ceremonies, the payment of compensation, and participation in traditional dispute reconciliation practices. Finally, rectification is the restoration of the prior social and political status of the victims of human rights violations and their family members. It seeks to specifically address the injustice of 'direct physical violence suffered by people during conflict' by providing

15 Many traditional, customary, and indigenous justice practices also incorporate retributive elements alongside those commonly deemed 'restorative'.

16 Louis B. Sohn and R.R. Baxter, 'Responsibility of States for Injuries to the Economic Interests of Aliens,' *American Journal of International Law*, Vol. 55 (1961), pp. 545–546; Jo M. Pasqualucci, 'Victim Reparations in the Inter-American System: A Critical Assessment of Current Practice and Procedure,' *Michigan Journal of International Law*, Vol. 18, No. 1 (1996–1997), p. 25.

17 Ruben Carranza, 'Plunder and Pain: Should Transitional Justice Engage with Corruption and Economic Crimes?,' *International Journal of Transitional Justice*, Vol. 2, No. 3 (2008), pp. 310–330.

18 Burt Galaway and Joe Hudson, 'Introduction' to Burt Galaway and Joe Hudson (eds.), *Restorative Justice: International Perspectives*, Monsey: Kugler, 1996, p. 2; Allison Morris, 'Critiquing the Critics: A Brief Response to Critics of Restorative Justice,' *British Journal of Criminology*, Vol. 42, No. 3 (2002), pp. 596–615.

restitution or rehabilitation.[19] Of course, these represent ideal types of justice that, in reality, are often pursued in combination with one another. Nonetheless, all, in their different ways, seek to address the wrongs of the past and attempt, as far as is possible, to put those wrongs right.

With this we arrive at our broad understanding of transitional justice as the pursuit of accountability for, and attempts to make right, the wrongs of human rights violations committed in the past associated with major political shifts, including movements from authoritarian rule to democracy, or ruptures, such as those that mark the end of violent conflicts. This understanding, as we will see, not only reflects the changing nature of transitional justice over the past thirty years or so, but provides a starting point for examining the actual dynamics of transitional justice as it is practiced in the Asia-Pacific region.

Three Debates in Transitional Justice

Developments in the theory and practice of transitional justice have also been reflected in three main debates that have preoccupied scholars and practitioners since the 1980s. The historical development of these debates is important for our purposes for it serves to further underpin our broad understanding of transitional justice and helps to further establish the context in which new developments in transitional justice have taken place in the Asia-Pacific. The three key debates in question emerged around three sets of dichotomous extremes:

(1) prosecution versus pardon, also referred to as trial versus amnesty, or justice versus peace;
(2) retributive versus restorative justice, variants of which included 'justice versus truth, perpetrator-focused versus victim-centered approaches, and backward-looking versus forward-looking approaches; and,

19 Rama Mani, *Beyond Retribution: Seeking Justice in the Shadows of War*, Cambridge: Polity, 2002, p. 7.

(3) top-down versus bottom up, or state led versus civil society initiated approaches, or international versus local approaches.

Prosecution versus Pardon

In the early years of scholarship concerned with transitional justice, a fault line emerged between international lawyers and social scientists over questions of the morality, legality, and efficacy of pursuing criminal proceedings against former state officials. At their core, these 'major debates' concerned whether or not new democracies should 'prosecute or punish . . . [or] forgive and forget' crimes committed by members and supporters of past authoritarian regimes.[20] In the main, the lawyers who engaged this question endorsed the criminal prosecution of the perpetrators of human rights violations on both deontological and utilitarian grounds.[21] They argued that criminal prosecutions were either necessary moral and legal responses to criminal offenses or were useful means of endorsing the criminal justice system, upholding the rule of law, and preventing future abuses through the effects of deterrence, or both. These scholars explicitly opposed the main alternative to prosecutions – amnesties – and questioned their ability to serve the instrumental function of bringing peace and stability to transitional countries with which they had been readily associated.[22]

By contrast, scholars of democratization viewed the rising demand for accountability that had accompanied the Latin American transitions as a fad that would pass with the passage of time. For example, in

20 Huntington, *The Third Wave*, pp. 211, 213.

21 Aryeh Neier, 'What Should be Done About the Guilty?,' *New York Review of Books*, Vol. 37, No. 1 (1990), pp. 32–35; Diane F. Orentlicher, 'Settling Accounts: The Duty to Prosecute Human Rights Violations of a Prior Regime,' *Yale Law Journal*, Vol. 100, No. 8 (1991), pp. 2537–2615; Naomi Roht-Arriaza, 'State Responsibility to Investigate and Prosecute Grave Human Rights Violations in International Law,' *California Law Review*, Vol. 78, No. 2 (1990), pp. 449–514.

22 Gary J. Bass, 'War Crimes Tribunals' in Keith E. Whittington, R. Daniel Keleman, and Gregory A. Calderia (eds.), *The Oxford Handbook of Law and Politics*, Oxford: Oxford University Press, 2008, p. 237.

accordance with his view that transitional justice is 'shaped exclusively by politics', Huntington observed that no effective criminal prosecution and punishment occurred in most transitional countries before concluding that '[i]n new democratic regimes, justice comes quickly or it does not come at all.'[23] His guidelines for democratizers thus advised that only when it is both 'morally *and* politically desirable' should the leaders of past authoritarian regimes be prosecuted.'[24] Similarly, O'Donnell and Schmitter predicted that such prosecutions would become less likely as 'the bitterness of memories attenuated with the passage of time' in transitional societies.[25] These scholars openly supported the positive function of amnesties in bringing democratization and raised concerns that pushing new democracies to prosecute still-powerful members of former regimes might derail transitions and precipitate renewed violence.

The punishment versus pardon debate came to a head in 1993 with the creation of the International Criminal Tribunal for the Former Yugoslavia (ICTY). In this instance, the 'Security Council voted to create' an ad hoc international tribunal 'while the fighting and atrocities still raged.'[26] Skeptics of criminal prosecutions vehemently criticized the tribunal for obstructing the ongoing peace process and thus prolonging a war that brought great human suffering.[27] As one anonymous analyst famously wrote, one of the lessons of the former Yugoslavia was that the 'quest for justice for yesterday's victims should not be pursued in such a manner that it makes today's living the dead of tomorrow.'[28] Lawyers and human rights activists responded to these criticisms and supported the

23 Huntington, *The Third Wave*, pp. 215, 231.
24 Huntington, *The Third Wave*, p. 228.
25 Guillermo A. O'Donnell and Philippe C. Schmitter, *Transitions from Authoritarian Rule: Conclusions about Uncertain Democracies*, Baltimore: Johns Hopkins University Press, 1986, p. 29.
26 David Forsythe, *Human Rights in International Relations*, Cambridge: Cambridge University Press, 2006, p. 97.
27 Anthony D'Amato, 'Peace vs. Accountability in Bosnia,' *American Journal of International Law*, Vol. 88, No. 3 (1994), p. 500.
28 Anonymous, 'Human Rights in Peace Negotiations,' *Human Rights Quarterly*, Vol. 18, No. 2 (1996), p. 258.

tribunal by arguing that the 'enforcement of international law' was 'an immediate priority, subordinate to neither political nor military imperatives.'[29]

With the signing of the Rome Statute in July 1998 and the arrest of the former Chilean president Augusto Pinochet in October of the same year, the prosecution versus pardon debate continued and intensified.[30] Both events instigated debate over the legitimacy and efficacy of invoking the principle of universal jurisdiction and raised questions about the international status of amnesties granted at the domestic level.[31] While proponents of trials heralded their ability to deter future human rights violations,[32] others voiced concerns that pursuing international prosecutions through bodies such as the ICC 'could initiate prosecutions that aggravate bloody political conflicts and prolong political instability in

29 David Scheffer, 'International Judicial Intervention,' *Foreign Policy*, No. 102 (1996), p. 38; See also Payam Akhavan, 'Justice in the Hague, Peace in the Former Yugoslavia? A Commentary on the United Nations War Crimes Tribunal,' *Human Rights Quarterly*, Vol. 20, No. 4 (1998), pp. 249–458; Felice D. Gaer, 'UN-Anonymous: Reflection on Human Rights in Peace Negotiations,' *Human Rights Quarterly*, Vol. 19, No. 1 (1997), pp. 1–8; Juan E. Mendez, 'Accountability for Past Abuses,' *Human Rights Quarterly*, Vol. 19, No. 2 (1997), pp. 272–275.

30 Naomi Roht-Arriaza, 'The New Landscape of Transitional Justice' in Naomi Roht-Arriaza and Javier Mariezcurrena (eds.), *Transitional Justice in the Twenty-First Century: Beyond Truth versus Justice*, Cambridge: Cambridge University Press, 2006, p. 7.

31 Chandra Lekha Sriram, 'Revolutions in Accountability: New Approaches to Past Abuses,' *American University International Law Review*, Vol. 19, No. 2 (2003), pp. 301–429; John Dugard, 'Dealing with Crimes of a Past Regime: Is Amnesty Still an Option?,' *Leiden Journal of International Law*, Vol. 12, No. 4 (1999), p. 1007; Leila Nadya Sadat, 'Redefining Universal Jurisdiction,' *New England Law Review*, Vol. 35, No. 2 (2000–2001), pp. 241–263; Darryl Robinson, 'Serving the Interests of Justice: Amnesties, Truth Commissions and the International Criminal Court,' *European Journal of International Law*, Vol. 14, No. 3 (2003), pp. 481–505; Anja Seibert-Fohr, 'The Relevance of the Rome Statute of the International Criminal Court for Amnesties and Truth Commissions,' *Max Planck Y.U.N.L.*, Vol. 7 (2004), pp. 553–590.

32 Kenneth Roth, 'The Court the US Doesn't Want,' *New York Review of Books*, Vol. 45, No. 18 (1998), p. 47; M. Cherif Bassiouni, 'The Universal Model: The International Criminal Court,' in M. Cherif Bassiouni (ed.), *Post-Conflict Justice*, Ardsley, NY: Transnational, 2002, pp. 820–821.

the affected regions.'[33] For example, Snyder and Vinjamuri presented a strong argument based on empirical data that human rights trials can actually increase the likelihood of future atrocities, exacerbate conflict, and undermine efforts to establish democracy.[34] In particular, they argued that insurgents engaged in civil conflicts will not sign peace agreements if they fear they will be held accountable for past abuses, even going so far as to accuse '[p]roponents of legalistic justice who underrate the centrality of... political considerations' of causing 'more abuses than they prevent.'[35]

In response, proponents of prosecutions have increasingly turned to large-scale empirical studies to determine whether prosecutions or pardons produce the most favorable sets of outcomes for peace, democracy, and human rights. Sikkink and Booth Walling thus conducted a comprehensive study of the impact of human rights trials in Latin America and found that in these cases prosecutions did not 'undermine democracy and lead to military coups', lead to more atrocities, or extend or exacerbate conflict.[36] More recently, in a study involving 100 cases from around the world, Kim and Sikkink have confirmed not only that human rights trials have a deterrent effect on human rights violations in the country in which they are held, but 'have a deterrence impact beyond the confines of the single country.'[37] In contrast Meernik, Nichols, and King argue that 'while human rights trials and international tribunals do not exercise

33 Jack Goldsmith and Stephen D. Krasner, 'The Limits of Idealism,' *Daedalus*, Vol. 132, No. 1 (2003), p. 55.

34 Jack Snyder and Leslie Vinjamuri, 'Trials and Errors: Principle and Pragmatism in Strategies of International Justice,' *International Security*, Vol. 28, No. 3 (2003/2004), pp. 5–44.

35 Leslie Vinjamuri and Jack Snyder, 'Advocacy and Scholarship in the Study of International War Crimes Tribunals and Transitional Justice,' *Annual Review of Political Science*, Vol. 7 (2004), p. 353.

36 Kathryn Sikkink and Carrie Booth Walling, 'The Impact of Human Rights Trials in Latin America,' *Journal of Peace Research*, Vol. 44, No. 4 (2007), pp. 434, 438, 440.

37 Hunjoon Kim and Kathryn Sikkink, 'Explaining the Deterrence Effect of Human Rights Prosecutions for Transitional Countries,' *International Studies Quarterly*, Vol. 54, No. 4 (2010), p. 939.

any negative effects, they do not appear to contribute to reducing the recurrence of civil war or improvements in human rights practices.'[38] The debate thus continues.

Retributive Justice versus Restorative Justice

At the same time as scholars were initially debating the relative merits of prosecuting and pardoning the perpetrators of human rights violations, a new and potentially powerful alternative to criminal prosecutions began to emerge in the form of the truth commission. As early as 1988, an international group of experts unanimously agreed on 'the central importance of establishing and acknowledging the truth about past violations.'[39] As Alice Henkin noted, 'There was common agreement that the successor government has an obligation to investigate and establish the facts so that the truth be known and be made part of the nation's history. Even in situations where pardon or clemency might be appropriate there should be no compromising of the obligation to discover and acknowledge the truth.'[40] Over time, truth commissions became a frequently used feature of post-transitional states in Latin America and, with this, scholars began to assess their efficacy, recording some encouraging results.[41]

This new demand for the establishment and acknowledgment of the truth precipitated a further scholarly divide characterized in terms of

38 James D. Meernik, Angela Nichols, and Kimi L. King, 'The Impact of International Tribunals and Domestic Trials on Peace and Human Rights after Civil War,' *International Studies Perspectives*, Vol. 11, No. 4 (2010), p.1.

39 Diane F. Orentlicher, '"Settling Accounts" Revisited: Reconciling Global Norms with Local Agency,' *International Journal of Transitional Justice*, Vol. 1, No. 1 (2007), p. 12.

40 Alice H. Henkin, 'State Crimes: Punishment or Pardon (Conference Report)' in Neil J. Kritz, *Transitional Justice: How Emerging Democracies Reckon with Former Regimes*, Vol. 1: General Considerations, pp. 184–188.

41 David Weissbrodt and Paul W. Fraser, 'Report of the Chilean National Commission on Truth and Reconciliation,' *Human Rights Quarterly*, Vol. 14, No. 4 (1992), pp. 610–622; Thomas Buergenthal, 'The United Nations Truth Commission for El Salvador,' *Vanderbilt Journal of Transnational Law*, Vol. 27, No. 3 (1994), pp. 497–544; Mark Ensalaco, 'Truth Commission for Chile and El Salvador: A Report and Assessment,' *Human Rights Quarterly*, Vol. 16, No. 4 (1994), pp. 656–675.

truth versus justice. Its emergence coincided with debate over how South Africa ought to address its violent past as part of its transition to democracy. The course of action chosen in the end for South Africa was posed as a deliberate '"third way", a compromise between the extreme of Nuremberg trials and blanket amnesty or national amnesia' that came in the form of the South African Truth and Reconciliation Commission before which individual perpetrators could tell the truth about their actions in exchange for amnesty.[42] By criticizing criminal prosecutions and eschewing wholesale impunity, the South African model added another dimension to the prosecution versus pardon debate. In particular, it helped to shift the focus of debate away from the simple peace versus justice and truth versus justice dichotomies to concentrate on the question of the particular types of justice that ought to be prioritized. As truth became acknowledged as an instrument of justice, what was initially framed as the 'truth versus justice' debate gave way to debates over retributive versus restorative justice.[43]

As noted above, retributive and restorative justice are not wholly opposed but characterized by overlapping goals and common practices. They can, nonetheless, be distinguished by their different understandings of who the subjects of crimes are and who constitutes the focus of justice.[44] Retributive justice conceives crime as a 'violation of the law' of which the state or the international community is the victim. The aim of justice, by this view, is therefore 'to establish blame' and administer punishment.[45] Critics of punitive justice thus point out that criminal prosecution is 'a struggle *against perpetrators,* rather than an effort *on behalf*

42 Desmond Tutu, *No Future without Forgiveness*, New York: Doubleday, 1999, p. 30.

43 Elizabeth Kiss, 'Moral Ambition Within and Beyond Political Constraints: Reflections on Restorative Justice' in Robert I. Rotberg and Dennis Thompson (eds.), *Truth v. Justice: The Morality of Truth Commissions*, Princeton: Princeton University Press, 2000, p. 86.

44 Kieran McEvoy, Harry Mika, and Barbara Hudson, 'Introduction: Practice, Performance, and Prospects for Restorative Justice,' *British Journal of Criminology*, Vol. 42 (2002), p. 469.

45 Howard Zehr, 'Restorative Justice: The Concept,' *Corrections Today*, Vol. 59, No. 7 (1997), p. 68.

of victims.'[46] By contrast, restorative justice conceives crime as 'a violation or harm to people and relationships.'[47] That is, crime is primarily viewed as 'a conflict between individuals that results in injuries to victims, communities and the offenders themselves, and only secondarily as a violation against the state.'[48] Justice conceived in this way thus focuses on repairing injuries and reconciling communities and draws on a range of mechanisms including truth telling, apologies, forgiveness, compensation, reparations, and participation in traditional dispute resolution practices. Proponents of restorative forms of justice thus argue that victim-centered justice and the forward-looking restoration of social relationships ought to take precedence over backward-looking measures that focus on the perpetrators of human rights violations.[49]

However, there is a still unresolved issue of whether amnesties could be constituted as a justice or accountability mechanism. Amnesties are 'official state declarations that individuals or groups accused or convicted of committing human rights violations will not be prosecuted or further prosecuted or will be pardoned for their crimes and released from prison.'[50] Amnesties can take different forms depending on beneficiaries. Olsen, Payne, and Reiter divide the amnesty according to the four sets of beneficiaries: armed non-state actors; state forces in armed conflicts;

46 Pablo de Greiff, 'Repairing the Past: Compensation for Victims of Human Rights Violations' in Pablo de Greiff (ed.), *Handbook of Reparations*, Oxford: Oxford University Press, 2006, p. 2; Rosemary Nagy, 'Traditional Justice and Legal Pluralism in Transitional Context: The Case of Rwanda's Gacaca Courts' in Joanna R. Quinn (ed.), *Reconciliation(s): Transitional Justice in Postconflict Societies*, Montreal: McGill-Queens University Press, 2009, p. 166.

47 Zehr, 'Restorative Justice,' p. 68.

48 Galaway and Hudson, 'Introduction,' p. 2; Allison Morris, 'Critiquing the Critics: A Brief Response to Critics of Restorative Justice,' *British Journal of Criminology*, Vol. 42, No. 3 (2002), pp. 596–615.

49 Laurel E. Fletcher and Harvey M. Weinstein, 'Violence and Social Repair: Rethinking the Contribution of Justice to Reconciliation,' *Human Rights Quarterly*, Vol. 24, No. 3 (2002), pp. 573–639.

50 Tricia D. Olsen, Leigh A. Payne, and Andrew G. Reiter, *Transitional Justice in Balance: Comparing Processes, Weighing Efficacy*, Washington D.C.: United States Institute of Peace, 2010, p. 36.

domestic political opposition for crimes against state; and state agents for actions committed against non-state agents (i.e. state repression).[51] Here, the first and last categories are most controversial because it is difficult to discern these types of amnesties from either impunity or blanket amnesty. Some scholars further note that even these kinds of amnesties have an element or a hint of accountability by 'acknowledging the past human rights violations' and 'generating a larger discussion of transitional justice' but these arguments are still highly controversial.[52]

Top-down versus Bottom-up

With the global expansion of transitional justice marked, most notably, by the establishment of the ICC in 2002, came a further set of debates about whether transitional justice ought to be directed or imposed from above, or whether it should be encouraged to emerge from the grass-roots. As more and more countries have come to adopt transitional justice mechanisms, so too have international organizations increasingly adopted and promoted transitional justice as one of their policy goals. For example, new international nongovernmental organizations, such as the International Center for Transitional Justice (ICTJ), have emerged, while older NGOs, such as Amnesty International and Human Rights Watch, have begun to frame much of their work in terms of transitional justice. In 2004, the United Nations secretary general issued a report on the rule of law and transitional justice in conflict and post-conflict societies, thus officially launching transitional justice as a policy tool to promote and protect human rights.[53] Although the UN clearly states that it tries to avoid imposing a 'one-size-fits-all' approach, the UN Office of the High

51 Olsen, Payne, and Reiter, *Transitional Justice in Balance.*

52 Olsen, Payne, and Reiter, *Transitional Justice in Balance.* Charles Villa-Vicencio, 'Why Perpetrators Should Not Always Be Prosecuted: Where the International Criminal Court and Truth Commissions Meet,' *Emory Law Journal*, Vol. 49, No. 1 (2000); see also Renée Jeffery, *Amnesty and Accountability: The Persistence of Amnesties from Athens to Aceh, Indonesia*, Philadelphia: University of Pennsylvania Press, forthcoming.

53 United Nations, 'Report of the Secretary-General on the Rule of Law and Transitional Justice in Conflict and Post-Conflict Societies,' (UN Doc. S/2004/616), 2004.

Commissioner for Human Rights (OHCHR) and the United Nations Development Program have, in conjunction with the ICC and donor states, started to standardize the practice and demand the acceptance of fixed norms and practices in transitional and post-conflict countries.[54] Transitional justice has thus become something that is 'normal, institutionalized, and mainstreamed', and transitional and post-conflict states are now 'expected, encouraged, or even coerced' to adopt transitional justice by 'the international justice industry.'[55] As recent works suggest, the impact of the top-down imposition of criminal tribunals and truth commission is already beginning to be felt in places such as Sierra Leone, Rwanda, East Timor, and Cambodia.[56]

At the same time, in places like East Timor, Rwanda, and Northern Uganda, local leaders, often supported by international activists, began to promote the use of traditional, customary, and indigenous justice measures to address past atrocities.[57] Proponents of these types of bottom-up approaches have argued:

> However well-intentioned, transitional justice needs to more deeply grapple with the messiness of global and transnational involvements and the local, on-the-ground realities with which they intersect,

54 For examples, see the OHCHR, *Rule-of-Law Tools for Post-Conflict States: Truth Commissions* (2006).

55 Kieran McEvoy, 'Letting Go of Legalism: Developing a "Thicker" Version of Transitional Justice' in Kieran McEvoy and Lorna McGrgor (eds.), *Transitional Justice from Below: Grassroots Activism and the Struggle for Change*, Oxford: Hart Publishing, 2008, p. 16; Jelena Subotic, *Hijacked Justice: Dealing with the Past in the Balkans*, Ithaca: Cornell University Press, 2009, p. 21.

56 Rosalind Shaw, 'Rethinking Truth and Reconciliation Commissions: Lessons from Sierra Leone,' *United States Institute of Peace Special Report* 130, (2005), p. 8; Nagy, 'Traditional Justice and Legal Pluralism,' p. 86; Elizabeth Drexler, 'The Failure of International Justice in East Timor and Indonesia' in Alexander Laban Hinton (ed.), *Transitional Justice: Global Mechanisms and Local Realities after Genocide and Mass Violence*, New Brunswick: Rutgers University Press, 2011, pp. 49–66.

57 Joanna R. Quinn, 'What of Reconciliation? Traditional Mechanisms of Acknowledgment in Uganda' in Joanna R. Quinn (ed.), *Reconciliation(s): Transitional Justice in Postconflict Societies*, Montreal: McGill-Queen's University Press, 2009, pp. 174–206; Renée Jeffery, 'Forgiveness, Amnesty, and Justice: The Case of the Lord's Resistance Army in Northern Uganda,' *Cooperation and Conflict*, Vol. 46, No. 1 (2011), pp. 78–95.

> complexities that are too often glossed over, due in part to the privileging of a cluster of liberal normative goods, such as the rule of law, peace, reconciliation, civil society, human rights, combating impunity, and justice.[58]

Thus international efforts are often referred to as transitional justice 'from above' and posed as being in opposition to the efforts made by 'grass-roots actors.'[59]

Debate about the relative merits of top-down versus bottom-up or international and state-led versus civil society-led accountability processes resonates strongly with similar debates about liberal-international versus local peace-building approaches. In large part this is a function of the blurring of practical and, now scholarly, distinctions between transitional justice and peace building. In accordance with its antecedents in peace management and peacekeeping, the practice of peace building tends toward state-oriented, top-down processes.[60] Perjoratively termed the 'liberal peace' by critics, this approach to peace building favors the promotion of democracy and the establishment of a liberal market economy as the means of attaining self-sustaining peace.[61] Within this frame, the optimal functioning of the rule of law is conceived as a key component of democracy and, as such, a strengthened criminal justice system (or, failing that, an international criminal tribunal) is viewed as the best place to pursue accountability for human rights violations.

58 Alexander Laban Hinton, 'Introduction: Toward an Anthropology of Transitional Justice' in Alexander Laban Hinton (ed.), *Transitional Justice: Global Mechanisms and Local Realities after Genocide and Mass Violence*, New Brunswick: Rutgers University Press, 2011, p. 1.

59 McEvoy and McGregor, 'Transitional Justice from Below: An Agenda for Research, Policy and Praxis,' p. 5.

60 Oliver P. Richmond, 'A Genealogy of Peace and Conflict Theory' in Oliver P. Richmond (ed.), *Palgrave Advances in Peacebuilding: Critical Developments and Approaches*, Basingstoke: Palgrave Macmillan, 2010, pp. 21–22.

61 This idea is, of course, based on the central tenets of the democratic peace thesis. On this, see Michael Doyle, 'Three Pillars of the Liberal Peace,' *American Political Science Review*, Vol. 99, No. 2 (2005), pp. 463–466.

In recent years, however, scholars from within the critical theory tradition have, as is their modus operandi, criticized the 'creeping neo-imperialist tendencies of peace promoted by hegemonic forces.'[62] That is, they have opposed the imposition of Western liberal approaches to peace building on non-Western societies and the apparent marginalization of local, indigenous processes that have accompanied them. Embedded within these critiques is the assumption that marginalized local forms of justice are inherently 'good' and thus deserving of protection against the 'bad' imperialist justice imposed by intervening forces. However, just as MacGinty cautions us against the tendency to 'romanticize' indigenous and traditional approaches and to assume that they are '"good" or [of] higher normative value', so too we must avoid automatically demonizing the liberal approach.[63] Both have strengths, and both are susceptible to criticism, based not on ideology but on evidence of the justice outcomes they produce.

In recognition of this and in response to recent practice, some scholars have begun to discuss the emergence of 'liberal-local hybrid' forms of peace building. Also termed 'post-liberal' peace, liberal-local hybridity 'represents a transmutation of both the liberal and the local' whereby the two approaches 'meet each other on the ground, react and modify each other.'[64] Where justice is concerned the assumption inherent in the very notion of a 'liberal-local hybrid' approach is that both liberal international and local forms of justice will be transformed by their interactions with one another – that is, that a symbiotic relationship exists between state-led and civil society transitional justice projects.[65]

62 Roger MacGinty, 'Indigenous Peace-Making Versus the Liberal Peace,' *Cooperation and Conflict*, Vol. 43, No. 2 (2008), p. 143.

63 MacGinty, 'Indigenous Peace-Making Versus the Liberal Peace,' pp. 139, 149.

64 Oliver P. Richmond, 'De-romanticising the Local, De-mystifying the International: Hybridity in Timor Leste and the Solomon Islands,' *The Pacific Review*, Vol. 24, No. 1 (2011), pp. 115, 117.

65 David Backer, 'Civil Society and Transitional Justice: Possibilities, Patterns, and Prospects,' *Journal of Human Rights*, Vol. 2, No. 3 (2003), pp. 297–313.

Emerging Trends in Transitional Justice and the Asia-Pacific

As hinted at in the discussion above, the dichotomous extremes that once defined the key debates have softened with far more nuanced accounts of transitional justice dominating contemporary thought. As a recent UN OHCHR report notes, 'the assumed tension between justice and peace has gradually dissolved.'[66] In its place is the widespread recognition that '[i]n reality the choice is seldom simply "justice" or "peace" but rather a complex mixture of both.'[67] A new trend has thus emerged where a range of diverse transitional justice mechanisms are applied simultaneously or in sequence with one another, thus allowing transitional and post-conflict states to pursue prosecutions and amnesties, truth commissions and justice measures, and international, state, and local initiatives at the same time. In accordance with this development, the UN now endorses the pursuit of 'comprehensive' approaches to transitional justice, while the ICTJ, which initially focused on promoting the South African model of truth commissions, now favors holistic solutions to transitional justice.[68] This approach has garnered some degree of support from scholars who have found empirical evidence that transitional justice approaches that combine trials and amnesties, or trials, amnesties, and truth commissions provide the best sets of outcomes for democracy, peace, and human rights.[69] This approach was not entirely new; the ICTJ, the 2005 revision

66 UN OHCHR Report, 'Analytical Study of the HC – Human Rights and Transitional Justice – Addendum' (UN Doc. A/HRC/12/19), 2009.

67 Chandra Lekha Sriram, 'Transitional Justice and Peacebuilding' in Chandra Lekha Sriram and Suren Pillay (ed.), *Peace versus Justice? The Dilemma of Transitional Justice in Africa*, Scottsville: University of KwaZulu-Natal Press, 2009, p. 1.

68 Report of the Secretary-General, 'The Rule of Law and Transitional Justice in Conflict and Post-Conflict Societies,' United Nations Security Council, 23 August 2004, S/2004/616, Summary, p. 1, at http://daccess-dds-ny.un.org/doc/UNDOC/GEN/N04/395/29/PDF/N0439529.pdf?OpenElement (accessed 6 June 2011); Christine Bell, 'Transitional Justice, Interdisciplinarity and the State of the "Field" or "Non-Field,"' *International Journal of Transitional Justice*, Vol. 3, No. 1 (2009), p. 8; see the vision and mission section of the ICTJ's Web site, http://ictj.org/about/vision-and-mission.

69 Olsen, Payne, and Reiter, *Transitional Justice in Balance.*

of the Principles to Combat Impunity by Diane Orentlicher,[70] and the 2004 report of the UN Secretary-General upheld the holistic and comprehensive approach in principle.[71] However, the application of these principles and promotions in the field and serious academic engagement came more recently.

It is within the Asia-Pacific, in particular, that many of these recent developments in transitional justice have occurred. We have to make it clear that this new development in transitional justice is not exclusively confined to the experience of the countries in the Asia Pacific. Certainly, many combined and holistic approaches have been taken in places such as Chile, Guatemala, Peru, Sierra Leone, Rwanda, and Uganda. However, as mentioned earlier, compared to these cases, the country cases in the Asia Pacific have not fully explored either by international practitioners and scholars so far. In this book we define the Asia-Pacific as a contiguous region of the world that includes East Asia, Southeast Asia, South Asia, Melanesia, and Oceania (primarily Australia and New Zealand). In one sense this is a narrower understanding of the Asia-Pacific than that adopted by the Asia-Pacific Economic Cooperation (APEC) which also includes states that reside on the Pacific Rim such as Russia, the United States, Chile, Peru, and Mexico. In another sense, by excluding the states of Central Asia and the Middle East, it also represents a narrowing of the normal geographical boundaries of Asia.[72]

Addressing the past wrongs is not a new theme for countries in the Asia-Pacific. Although much less mentioned compared to the Nuremberg counterpart, the Tokyo international military tribunal was set up

70 United Nations, 'Report of the Independent Expert to Update the Set of Principles to Combat Impunity, Diane Orentlicher on Promotion and Protection of Human Rights' (UN Doc. E/CN.4/2005/102), 2005.

United Nations, 'Report of the Secretary-General on the Rule of Law and Transitional Justice in Conflict and Post-Conflict Societies,' (UN Doc. S/2004/616), 2004.

71 We thank an anonymous reviewer for reminding us of this valid point.

72 This narrowing is largely represented in our selection of case studies. However, in their chapter Payne and Sikkink include the states of Central Asia in their analysis of the Asia-Pacific region to allow for a comprehensive, global analysis of transitional justice mechanisms.

immediately after the end of the World War II to address war crimes and crimes against humanity, and more than 5,000 Japanese nationals were brought to the court. Moreover, the legacy of Japanese colonialism left a deep chasm between Japan and its neighbors, especially China and two Koreas, over issues such as sex slavery and forced labor, apologies and reparations, territorial ownership, the content of Japanese history textbooks, and Japanese state officials' visits to the Yasukuni Shrine.[73] On the other side of the equator, human rights violations perpetrated by Western settlers in Australia and New Zealand have also left emotionally-charged tensions between new settlers and aborigines, issues that their respective governments continue to address.[74]

In the past decade or so, however, the Asia-Pacific region has experienced a significant increase in the use of transitional justice mechanisms to address past human rights violations. In this it has lagged behind Latin America, Eastern Europe, and Africa where the pursuit of transitional justice gained momentum in the 1980s and 1990s. Coming to transitional justice relatively late, however, the approaches pursued in the Asia-Pacific reflect the range of mechanisms available, both individually and in combination with one another and the contemporary challenges faced by transitional justice more broadly.

Table 1 illustrates the overall trend of adopting three main transitional justice mechanisms – trials, truth commissions, and amnesties – in the Asia-Pacific region. Although this data measures only the existence of these mechanisms in the country within a given year, it is still useful to get the bigger picture of the general trend. Notably, all the cases

73 For more details, see Gi-Wook Shin, Woon-Won Park, and Daqing Yang (eds.), *Rethinking Historical Injustice and Reconciliation in Northeast Asia: The Korean Experience*, New York: Routledge, 2007. See also Renée Jeffery, 'When Is An Apology Not An Apology? Contrition Chic and Japan's (Un)Apologetic Politics,' *Australian Journal of International Affairs*, Vol. 65, No. 5 (2011), pp. 607–617.

74 However, we do not include these measures addressing historical injustices since it is outside the scope of our definition of transitional justice, which requires democratization of a peace process, which is a widely accepted definition in the literature of transitional justice.

Table 1. *Transitional Justice Mechanisms in the Asia-Pacific, 1980–2010*

Country/Case	Trials	Truth Commissions	Amnesties
Afghanistan	1980, 2004	1986	1979–1981, 1986, 1992, 1997, 2003, 2007
Bangladesh	1988, 1995, 2000		1983, 1989, 1991, 1997–1998
Bougainville, Papua New Guinea	2000		1995, 1998
Burma			1980, 1988
Cambodia	**1993, 2006–ongoing**		**1994, 1996**
East Timor	**2002–2006**	**2002–2007**	**2001, 2005**
Fiji			2000
India			1986, 1991, 2004–2005
Indonesia	1992, 1999, 2002–2004	1999–2007	1998, 2005
(Aceh)			**2005**
Laos			1991, 2004
Nepal	2007, 2008	1990–1991	1998–1999, 2001, 2003, 2005–06
Pakistan	1981, 1995		2006
Philippines	1988, 1990	1986–1987	1985, 1987, 1992, 1994–1996, 2000, 2007
Solomon Islands	**2005**	**2009–ongoing**	**2000, 2001**
South Korea	**1996**	**2000–2004, 2005–ongoing**	**1981, 1997**
Sri Lanka		**1994–1997, 2001–2002, 2006**	**1987–1988, 1995**
Thailand	1985, 1998, 2009	2001–2004	1980–1981, 1988, 1991–1992, 2004, 2006
Vietnam			1987

Note: The table is based primarily on Olsen, Payne, and Reiter, *Transitional Justice in Balance*, pp. 181–188, with some updates.

of transitional justice in the Asia-Pacific since the 1980s have involved the granting of amnesties. Rather than simply choosing impunity over accountability, however, most have also instituted human rights trials at the domestic or international level. Significantly, it was in the Asia-Pacific case of Cambodia that the idea of instituting hybrid international-domestic criminal tribunals to prosecute the perpetrators of human rights violations was first developed. Although it did not come into operation until 2006, the genesis of the Extraordinary Chambers in the Courts of Cambodia gave rise to what has become known as the 'Cambodia model', replicated in the East Timor Serious Crimes Special Panels, the Kosovo Courts' 'Panels 64', and the Special Court for Sierra Leone.[75] In addition, truth commissions have also found form in the Asia-Pacific, particularly from 2000 onward. Also significant about the implementation of transitional justice in the Asia-Pacific is that the vast majority of cases listed in Table 1 have implemented more than one mechanism.

Of the nineteen cases of transitional justice in the region since 1980, only six have instituted just one mechanism and, in each case, this was an amnesty. More common has been the implementation of two or more mechanisms either simultaneously, as in the case of East Timor, or in sequence, as in the case of the Solomon Islands in which amnesties in 2000 and 2001 were followed by trials in 2005, and then a truth commission which began in 2009 and is still conducting its investigations. As such, the Asia-Pacific provides fertile ground for examining the practices, processes, and problems associated with the newly endorsed comprehensive or holistic approach to transitional justice. The cases examined in this book are highlighted in bold in Table 1 and constitute a representative sample of the combinations of transitional justice mechanisms used in the region: amnesty only (Aceh, Indonesia); amnesty and trials (Cambodia);

75 John D. Ciorciari, 'Introduction,' in *The Khmer Rouge Tribunal*, Phnom Penh: Documentation Center of Cambodia, 2006, p. 18; Tom Fawthrop and Helen Jarvis, *Getting Away with Genocide? Elusive Justice and the Khmer Rouge Tribunal*, London: Pluto Press, 2004, p. 181; Renée Jeffery, 'Beyond Repair? Collective and Moral Reparations at the Khmer Rouge Tribunal,' *Journal of Human Rights*, forthcoming.

amnesty, trials, and truth commissions in combination (East Timor); amnesty, trials, and truth commissions in sequence (Solomon Islands and South Korea); and truth commissions and amnesties (Sri Lanka).

Considered in political terms, the Asia-Pacific also brings together two major contexts in which transitional justice is instituted: transitions from authoritarian rule to democracy and from conflict to peace. Since 1980, twenty-eight states in the region have experienced some form of political transition. Of these, eleven have undergone at least one transition to democracy.[76] During the same period, East Timor has gained independence from Indonesia while Aceh and Bougainville have been granted autonomy from Indonesia and Papua New Guinea, respectively. At the same time, some sixteen states in the region were engaged in violent civil or, less commonly, interstate conflicts.[77] Of these, seven also involved a transition from authoritarian rule while two involved a transition to autonomous democratic rule within another state (Bougainville/Papua New Guinea, and Aceh/Indonesia).

Table 2 provides an overview of the political transitions that have taken place in the various sub-regions of the Asia-Pacific in which at least one of the transitional justice mechanisms included in Table 1 (trials, truth commissions, and amnesties) have been used. This means that political transitions in which no transitional justice mechanisms were employed have not been included. Dividing the Asia-Pacific into its various sub-regions is also significant because it is within the sub-regions that the

76 Bangladesh (1991), Cambodia (1993), Indonesia (1999), Mongolia (1992), Nepal (1990), Pakistan (1988), Philippines (1987), South Korea (1988), Taiwan (1992), and Thailand (1992).

77 Philippines (1967–ongoing; 1970–ongoing (Mindanao)), Cambodia (1967–1998), Thailand (1974–1982; 2003–ongoing), Indonesia (1975–1998 (East Timor); 1990–1991, 1999–2005 (Aceh)), Pakistan (1990–1996, 2007; 2004–ongoing (Baluchistan)), Nepal (1996–2006), Bangladesh (1975–1992), Malaysia (1981), Burma (1948–1994; 1949–ongoing (Karen), 1959–ongoing (Shan); 1992–1996, 2005 (Karenni), 1997 (Wa)), Laos (1989–1990), East Timor (1975–1998), Afghanistan (1978–ongoing), India (1990–2007; 1978–2006 (Tripura); 1982–ongoing (Manipur); 1983–1993 (Punjab/Khalistan); 1989–ongoing (Kashmir); 1990–ongoing (Assam); 1992–ongoing (Nagaland)), Sri Lanka (1989–1990, 1984–2009), Solomon Islands (1998–2003), Papua New Guinea (1989–1996).

Table 2. *Political Transitions Involving Transitional Justice in the Asia-Pacific, 1980–2010*

Sub-Regions	Transition from Authoritar-ianism	Transition from Authoritar-ianism and Civil War	Transition from Civil War	No Transition
Northeast Asia	**South Korea**			
Southeast Asia		Philippines, **Cambodia**, Thailand, **Indonesia (Aceh)**	Burma, Laos, **East Timor**	Vietnam
South Asia		Pakistan, Nepal, Bangladesh	Afghanistan, India, **Sri Lanka**	
Oceania			**Solomon Islands**, Papua New Guinea (Bougainville)	Fiji

greatest commonalities in historical, cultural, and linguistic terms lie and the influences of the great powers of the region are felt. Thus while China and Japan exert influence over Northeast Asia, India looms large over the politics of South Asia, China over Southeast Asia, and Australia over the small island states of Oceania.[78] As we will see in the case studies to follow, these influences have in some instances had great bearing on the contexts in which transitional justice has been pursued in the region and the choice of mechanisms according to which it has been implemented. In order to provide a representative sample of cases across the sub-regions of the Asia-Pacific and the three major types of transition the cases highlighted in bold have been selected for individual consideration. Note that neither of the cases listed under the heading of 'No Transition' have been

78 This is not to suggest that Australia is a great power, only that it exerts significant influence over a small cluster of Pacific Island states.

included. This is because each of these is a case of an amnesty being instituted in isolation (as addressed in the case of Indonesia/Aceh).[79] In addition, Fiji is something of an anomaly for in this case, an amnesty was granted to those engaged in a military coup in 2000 but was followed by another military coup in 2006, the leaders of which are still in power. Together the cases selected are emblematic of the contexts in and mechanisms by which transitional justice is pursued across the various sub-regions of the Asia-Pacific.

Certainly, this volume does not aim at collecting a comprehensive list of all transitional countries in the Asia-Pacific region. We chose a representative sample of cases from the Asia-Pacific region rather than aiming for comprehensiveness. The main reason for the choice is because, as many of the cases are relatively unknown, we believe that in-depth analysis of these cases is required to delve further into the historical contexts in which transitional justice have taken place and explain some detailed processes and practices that have been undertaken.

The Collection

Chapter 1, by Kathryn Sikkink and Leigh Payne, serves two main purposes, the first empirical and the second theoretical. First, it serves to situate the study of transitional justice practices and processes implemented in the Asia-Pacific region in a global context. Drawing on transitional justice database projects undertaken at the Universities of Minnesota and Wisconsin, it presents global and regional transitional justice trends from 1980 to 2010 and compares transitional justice practices in the Asia-Pacific region to those of other regions. In doing so, the chapter seeks to highlight what is distinctive about the practice of transitional justice in the Asia-Pacific. Second, the chapter also considers the impact that trials, truth commissions, and amnesties have on human rights and democracy.

79 Renée Jeffery, 'Amnesty and Accountability: The Price of Peace in Aceh,' *International Journal of Transitional Justice*, Vol. 6, No. 1 (2012), pp. 60–82.

It demonstrates that when trials and amnesties are used together, with or without truth commissions, they have a positive impact on both human rights and democracy. In doing so, this chapter provides a further theoretical framework to be utilized in the case study chapters of the book.

The remainder of the book is devoted to the detailed analysis of the cases of Sri Lanka, Aceh, Cambodia, East Timor, South Korea, and the Solomon Islands. In Chapter 2, Chandra Lekha Sriram puts the current situation in Sri Lanka in historical and comparative perspective. She discusses earlier commissions of inquiry and prosecutions that have taken place for human rights abuses in Sri Lanka before considering options for domestic and international accountability in the current domestic political climate. She notes that to date, the only proposed response to human rights abuses committed during Sri Lanka's civil conflict is a commission of inquiry created by the government to examine the crimes committed by the Liberation Tigers of Tamil Eelam (LTTE), thus leaving the widespread human rights violations committed by government forces unaccounted for. From an international perspective, the possibilities for accountability are similarly limited. Although there is some international interest in potentially pursuing the case of Sri Lanka at the International Criminal Court, Sri Lanka is not a state party to the Rome Statute and thus this option seems unlikely. The case of Sri Lanka, it seems, it marked by the absence of serious transitional justice practices and appears likely to remain so for some time to come.

In the case of Aceh, Indonesia, examined by Edward Aspinall and Fajran Zain in Chapter 3, transitional justice has taken a markedly different path although there too it has failed to meet the expectations of many. In this case, the Memorandum of Understanding (MoU) for peace in Aceh provided for a wide range of transitional justice mechanisms, including the granting of amnesties to former combatants, the establishment of a Truth and Reconciliation Commission and the establishment of a Human Rights Court. As Aspinall and Zain argue, however, despite this promising start, transitional justice has stalled in Aceh with virtually no progress in any justice-related area. In particular, the proposed establishment of a TRC for Aceh has faced stiff opposition and obstacles at every turn. They thus conclude that in the absence of strong political support for transitional justice it is likely that Aceh will become like several other post-conflict societies, such as Mozambique, where ongoing peace processes continue but without truth or reconciliation.

By contrast, the case of East Timor, examined by Lia Kent in Chapter 5, has experienced a wide range of transitional justice mechanisms, from the establishment of the Serious Crimes Special Panels, a hybrid tribunal to prosecute human rights violations, to the Commission for Reception, Truth, and Reconciliation (CAVR) and the joint East Timorese/Indonesian Commission for Truth and Friendship (CTF), as well as various grass-roots initiatives. As Kent argues, however, despite implementing such a wide range of transitional justice mechanisms, 'there remains a profound sense of community disappointment with the lack of justice in relation to the violence of the past.' In particular, she notes that the failures to prosecute senior members of the Indonesian military, to provide material assistance to survivors, and to assist in the recovery of bodies, coupled with a disjuncture in local and international understandings of 'justice' have significantly limited the success of transitional justice in East Timor. However, the story she tells is not an entirely negative one. Rather, Kent demonstrates that 'new and unforeseen possibilities are emerging from the CAVR and CTF' processes and within local justice initiatives that are helping to redefine how justice is being pursued in East Timor.

In Chapter 4, Kirsten Ainley examines the other example of a hybrid domestic-international tribunal operating in the Asia-Pacific, the Extraordinary Chambers in the Courts of Cambodia (ECCC). She argues that although the ECCC was ostensibly set up to help 'heal' the trauma inflicted by the Khmer Rouge, its establishment 'represents less a victory for advocates of transitional justice than . . . a reflection of the interests of the Cambodian government.' In particular, Ainley argues that the ECCC represents the coincidence of power and principle, where the power of the domestic government has come together with international principles surrounding the pursuit of accountability for serious human rights violations. Thus, despite the efforts of its offices devoted to victim participation and outreach, the ECCC's activities have fallen well short of the expectations of the victims in whose name it was established.

In Chapter 6, Renée Jeffery turns to the case of the Solomon Islands, a case in which amnesties, domestic human rights trials, and a truth and reconciliation commission have operated. She notes that in the aftermath of the civil conflict in the Solomons, two dominant approaches to post-conflict justice emerged. The first, implemented by the Regional Assistance Mission to the Solomon Islands (RAMSI), favored a rule of law approach according to which large numbers of militants on both sides were arrested and processed through the criminal justice system resulting, in many cases, in the imposition of lengthy periods of imprisonment. The second, 'reconciliation' approach, favored local, grass-roots, traditional, and indigenous justice processes and were routinely implemented by community groups, women's organizations, and churches. Jeffery argues that in the absence of a formally planned transitional justice process, these two approaches to post-conflict justice have come into serious tension with proponents of each accusing the other of hampering their justice efforts. She examines those tensions and analyzes the extent to which the Solomon Islands' Truth and Reconciliation Commission, designed in part to provide a bridge between the rule of law and reconciliation approaches, has been able to quell this new set of tensions.

In contrast to the negative or, at best, mixed, appraisals of the transitional justice mechanisms implemented in Sri Lanka, Cambodia, Aceh, East Timor, and the Solomon Islands, the story of South Korea Hun Joon Kim tells in Chapter 7 is one of success. He notes that since democratization in 1987, South Korea has adopted three types of transitional justice measures: criminal prosecutions, truth commissions and investigatory committees, and reparations. Focusing on three of South Korea's ten truth commissions, Kim argues that 'truth commissions have had a positive impact on Korean society as a whole by improving human rights and enhancing democracy.' He notes key changes in Korean society that have followed the truth commissions, including the issuing of formal apologies, the revision of history textbooks and official histories, and the excavation and reburial of victims. Kim concludes that by pursuing this course of action, South Korea has served to strengthen the core values of democracy: justice, human rights, and the rule of law.

In the Conclusion, we turn to questions of success and failure in implementing transitional justice mechanisms. We note that, with the exception of the case of South Korea, the assessments made of the pursuit for accountability for past human rights violations in the region make for sobering reading. Failures of design, capacity, and, in particular, political will, appear to mark efforts at transitional justice in the Asia-Pacific far more than stories of successful outcomes. We consider whether this is a fair assessment by providing a comparative overview of the successes and failures of transitional justice in the cases examined in the book. We argue that although there are grounds on which to be critical of the pursuit, or lack thereof, of accountability for human rights violations in the region, the Asia-Pacific has made significant efforts to address the wrongs of the past. These efforts have brought a measure of justice, however imperfect it may be, to bear on human rights violations committed in the region. We argue that this is a significant and positive outcome that provides the foundations on which further attempts at transitional justice might be built in the future.

1 Transitional Justice in the Asia-Pacific

Comparative and Theoretical Perspectives[1]

Leigh A. Payne and Kathryn Sikkink

THIS VOLUME SEEKS TO DESCRIBE AND ANALYZE THE PREviously unexplored processes of transitional justice in the Asia-Pacific region. In so doing, it not only fills a geographical void in the study of state responses to past atrocities, it contributes to our understanding of patterns of transitional justice processes, diffusion of those processes, and their impact on human rights and democracy outcomes.

In the 1980s and 1990s, when studies of transitional justice began, transitional justice had penetrated less deeply in Asia than in other regions, such as Latin America and Eastern Europe. As a result, there were fewer scholarly studies of transitional justice in the Asia-Pacific region and less evidence to evaluate the impact of transitional justice mechanisms there. In recent years such mechanisms have started to be used with greater frequency in the region, thereby offering a unique setting for testing theoretical arguments about their emergence and spread. Likewise, evidence

1 The data presented in this chapter are partially based on research supported by the National Science Foundation (Grant No. 0961226) and the Arts and Humanities Research Council (Grant No. 0AH/I500030/1) relating to the project titled "The impact of transitional justice on human rights and democracy." Any opinions, findings, and conclusions or recommendations expressed in this material are those of the authors and do not necessarily reflect the views of the National Science Foundation or the Arts and Humanities Research Council. We wish to thank our NSF/AHRC research teams for their assistance with data for this article, and in particular, Emily Braid and Tricia Olsen (for preparation of Figure 2), Geoff Dancy (for preparation of Figures 1 and 3–7), Megan Geigle, Pierre Louis Le Goff, Francesca Lessa, and Gabriel Pereira.

of the impact of transitional justice from other regions may be useful as scholars, policy makers, and practitioners debate what kinds of accountability mechanisms to adopt in the Asia-Pacific region. This chapter aims at contributing to these debates.

In this chapter we begin with an analysis of what we have learned from our cross-national studies of transitional justice and apply the lessons to the Asia-Pacific region. We first present an overview of the historical background and global trends on transitional justice to situate the Asia-Pacific region in the context of these global trends. We then explore various theoretical explanations for the origins, spread, and impact of transitional justice mechanisms and their implication for the Asia-Pacific experience.

Historical Background and Global Trends

This brief discussion aims to place current debates about accountability for past human rights violations in the Asia-Pacific within a global history of past practices. Prior to WWII, countries virtually never held state officials accountable for past human rights violations.[2] At the international level, various pre-WWII attempts at accountability for war crimes and mass atrocities failed to set up the necessary institutions.[3]

Beginning after WWII and continuing through the second half of the twentieth century, states negotiated and produced a series of human rights treaties. Although an individual criminal accountability model was used in the Nuremberg and Tokyo trials, most of these human rights treaties reflected instead the state accountability model. In this model, the state as a whole was held accountable for human rights violations and was expected to take action to remedy the situation. This continues

2 There were isolated examples of accountability in ancient Greece and in revolutionary France, but no sustained attempts at domestic transitional justice until after WWII. See the historical narrative in Jon Elster, *Closing the Books: Transitional Justice in Historical Perspective* (New York: Cambridge University Press, 2004).

3 Gary Jonathan Bass, *Stay the Hand of Vengeance: The Politics of War Crimes Tribunals* (Princeton: Princeton University Press, 2000).

to be the model used by virtually the entire human rights apparatus in the United Nations, including almost all of the treaty bodies. It is also the model employed by the regional human rights courts, the European Court of Human Rights, the Inter-American Court of Human Rights, and the African Court of Human Rights. The actual individuals who carried out human rights violations were not affected.

In the 1970s, the individual criminal accountability model began to emerge. The main differences between the state accountability model and the individual criminal accountability model involve *who* is being held accountable and *how* these actors are held accountable.[4] Under a state accountability model, the state provides remedies and pays damages, whereas under a criminal model, the convicted individuals go to prison. In the period from 1990 to 2010, the individual criminal accountability model gained momentum and became more embodied in international law, in international and domestic institutions, and in the global consciousness.[5]

The distinction between state accountability and individual criminal accountability can also be used to categorize transitional justice mechanisms. As part of a broader global trend toward accountability for past human rights violations, states are not only initiating trials but also increasingly using multiple transitional justice mechanisms including truth commissions, reparations, lustration or vetting, customary justice, apologies, museums and memory sites, archives, and oral history projects to address past human rights violations.[6] Reparations, apologies, museums, memorials, and many truth commissions emphasize state accountability, and the state as a whole tries to provide some kind of remedy for the damages inflicted by past human rights violations. Prosecutions,

4 Steven R. Ratner and Jason S. Abrams, *Accountability for Human Rights Atrocities in International Law: Beyond the Nuremberg Legacy* (New York: Oxford University Press, 2001), 15.

5 See, for example, Ellen L. Lutz and Caitlin Reiger, eds., *Prosecuting Heads of State* (New York: Cambridge University Press, 2009).

6 Elizabeth Jelin, *State Repression and the Labors of Memory* (Minneapolis: University of Minnesota Press, 2003).

customary justice, and vetting or lustration, on the other hand, tend to focus on individual accountability, where specific individuals responsible for repression are punished. This difference has often been thought of as a difference between restorative and retributive justice, but may just as usefully be seen as a difference in who is held accountable and how they are held accountable.

For years scholars were unaware of the magnitude of the move toward accountability because no global dataset on transitional justice existed. Without data, it was difficult to detect the growth of the new norms and practices. Separately, each of the authors of this chapter worked with a team to create datasets on some transitional justice mechanisms. These database projects blossomed into a major joint research initiative that received financial support from the National Science Foundation (NSF/U.S.) and the Arts and Humanities Research Council (AHRC/U.K.). In addition to analysis from our earlier separate data projects, this chapter presents initial data for our joint project on transitional prosecutions, truth commissions, and amnesties. We are currently engaged in a subsequent project that will produce global data on reparations, civil trials, vetting and lustration, and customary justice.

Figure 1 presents an overview of data on trends in verdicts and convictions in human rights prosecutions and the adoption of new amnesty laws. The figure shows the number of countries in any given year with at least one verdict or conviction in a human rights prosecution as well as the number of countries adopting a new amnesty law.

The increasing use of prosecutions resulting in convictions attests to the existence of a broader accountability norm. A clear shift away from amnesties, however, has not accompanied the global accountability trend. Although the data in Figure 1 show a decline in the adoption of *new* amnesty laws for human rights violations, existing amnesty laws have remained in place throughout the world alongside the increased use of prosecutions. Figure 2 shows the results of our analysis of amnesty laws that have legal standing over the same time period.

This may seem puzzling because amnesty laws are designed to block prosecutions. The combination of amnesty with prosecutions was

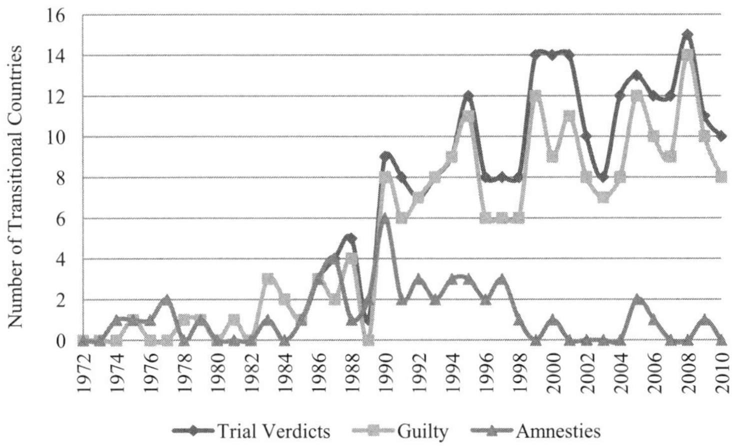

Figure 1. Trends in amnesty and domestic accountability, 1972–2009. *Note:* This is the number of countries in any given year adopting or using at least one of each mechanism.

possible, first, because each amnesty law was different with some exempting certain actors or actions. These partial amnesty laws coexist with prosecutions and are thus consistent with individual criminal accountability. Second, blanket amnesty laws sometimes faced challenges in courts that

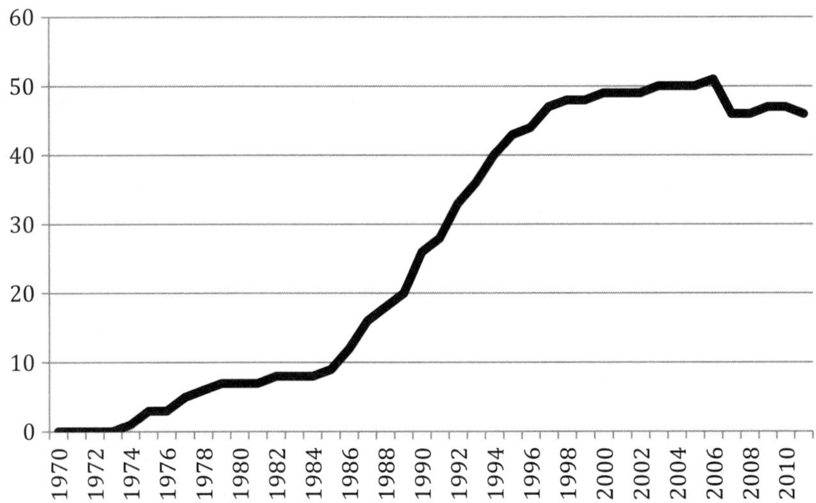

Figure 2. Amnesties for human rights violations with legal standing

led to circumvention of amnesty laws and sometimes to their erosion or reversal in practice, if not on the books.

Human rights prosecutions are occurring simultaneously at the domestic and international levels. The domestic level involves trials for individual criminal accountability conducted in a single country for human rights abuses committed in that country or committed elsewhere in the world by a national of that country. For example, the trials in Indonesia for human rights violations in Indonesia are domestic trials, but the prosecutions in Indonesia for human rights violations in East Timor can also be considered domestic trials because they held Indonesian nationals accountable (see Chapter 3 by Edward Aspinall and Fajran Zain in this volume). International trials also involve trials for individual criminal responsibility for human rights violations in a particular country or conflict and result from the cooperation of multiple states, typically acting on behalf of the United Nations. Examples include the International Criminal Tribunal for the former Yugoslavia (ICTY) and the International Criminal Tribunal for Rwanda (ICTR). The international trials category also includes hybrid criminal bodies defined by their mixed character of containing a combination of international and national features, as seen, for example, in Cambodia and East Timor (see Chapters 4 and 5 by Kirsten Ainley and Lia Kent in this volume).

Despite the global trend toward expanded prosecutorial activity, there is significant variation in the frequency of human rights prosecutions in different regions of the world. As the pie chart (Figure 3) indicates, the trend toward domestic human rights prosecutions has been most pronounced in Latin America and in Central and Eastern Europe. Prosecutions are underway in Asia and Africa, but to a lesser extent than in Europe and the Americas. However, the percentage of prosecutions in Asia is the third largest, after Europe and the Americas, and the number of domestic human rights prosecutions in Asia now appears to be increasing more than in other regions.

International prosecutions are also unevenly distributed across different regions in ways that don't simply reflect where the worst human

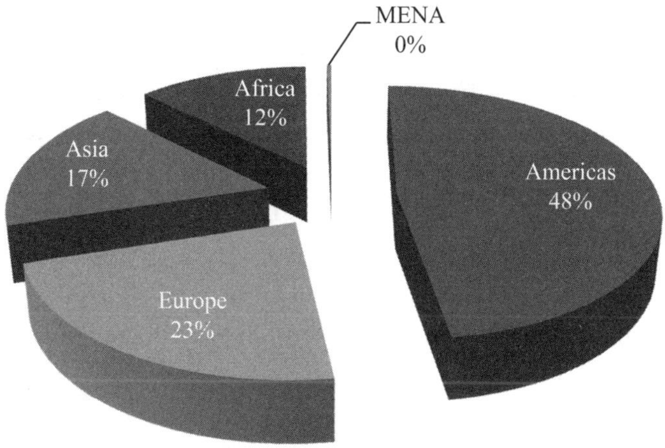

Figure 3. Regional distribution of domestic transitional prosecutions, 1970–2009 (year start)

rights violations in the world have occurred. Figure 4 records the regions of the countries whose nationals have been subject to outside efforts to achieve justice through international tribunals, not the countries where the tribunals are located.

As Figures 3 and 4 demonstrate, marked differences exist between the regional distribution of domestic and international tribunals. For example, Latin America accounts for the greatest number of domestic human rights prosecutions, but no international tribunals have been set up to

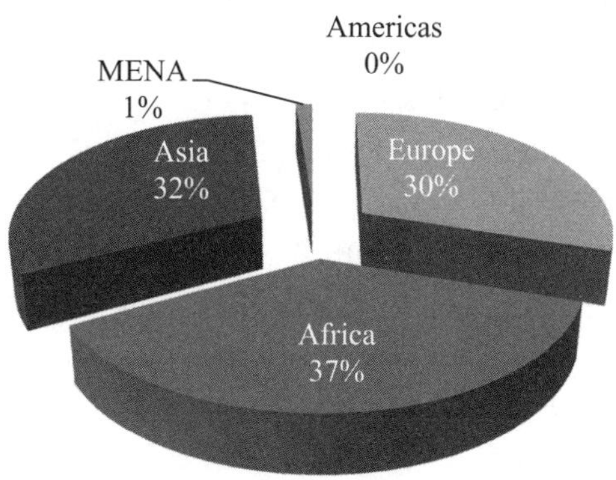

Figure 4. International human right prosecutions, 1970–2009

deal with human rights situations in Latin America. Asia accounts for 17 percent of the total number of domestic human rights prosecution activity from 1970 to 2009 and 32 percent of international prosecutions during the same period. These international prosecutions include a small number of trials at the hybrid tribunal in Cambodia, the Extraordinary Chambers in the Courts of Cambodia (ECCC). The rest are made up entirely of prosecutions at the East Timor hybrid tribunal, the Dili Special Panel for Serious Crimes (SPSC). This hybrid tribunal has received less scholarly attention than other international tribunals and has often been considered relatively ineffective. Our coding process nevertheless reveals a very large number of prosecutions and convictions there. The criticism of the SPSC is largely due to its inability to bring suspects residing outside of East Timor to trial. As a result, mainly low-level East Timorese militia members rather than higher level Indonesian officials were prosecuted. Even given these criticisms, the SPSC's relatively high number of prosecutions and convictions is nevertheless notable.

According to Figures 3 and 4, Asia has a lower level of domestic transitional prosecutions compared to Europe and the Americas and a lower level of international prosecutions than Europe and Africa. These figures may be slightly misleading, however, because they do not control for the number of transitional countries in the region. Because we are comparing prosecutions only in transitional countries, the total number of transitional countries in the region will clearly affect the total number of trials.

Using changes in Polity II scores to generate a list of transitional countries, we consider fifteen Asia-Pacific transitional: Bangladesh, Bhutan, Cambodia, East Timor, Fiji, Indonesia, Kyrgyzstan, Malaysia, Mongolia, Nepal, Pakistan, Philippines, South Korea, Taiwan, and Thailand. Some of these countries experienced multiple transitions.[7] The Solomon Islands is not on this list because it is not listed as transitional in the Polity II data. Renee Jeffrey's chapter in this volume shows nonetheless that the

7 Our NSF/AHRC dataset includes Central Asia as part of the Asian region.

Solomon Islands experienced an important disruption in democracy and afterwards used mechanisms to address human rights violations during that period. Thus for the purposes of this volume, we include the Solomon Islands in the transitional category and speak of sixteen cases of transition in the large Asia-Pacific region. This is a lower number of transitional countries than we find in many other regions of the world, which may influence the number of transitional mechanisms used.

The NSF/AHRC project used the U.S. State Department annual country reports to initially identify human rights prosecutions for their database. We then gathered additional information about each prosecution using diverse primary and secondary sources. In order to be characterized as a transitional human rights prosecution, a case had to involve judicial processes in countries that have experienced a transition to democracy, holding current or former state officials accountable for human rights violations that occurred *prior to*, *during*, or *between* the transition(s) with a trial *between*, *during*, or *after* the transition(s). This is thus an exacting definition that is quite difficult to code, as for every prosecution, coders have to check when the human rights violation and the prosecution occurred in relation to the transition in that country.

Given this definition, and including the Solomon Islands in the group of transitional countries, eleven of the sixteen transitional countries in the Asia-Pacific region held human rights *domestic* prosecutions: Bangladesh, Cambodia, Indonesia, Kyrgyzstan, Nepal, Pakistan, the Philippines, the Solomon Islands, South Korea, Taiwan, and Thailand. In this sense, the fact that 69 percent of the transitional countries in the region held prosecutions is significant and suggests a higher level of accountability than indicated by Figure 3. This level is higher than the levels of accountability in Africa and Europe, but still lower than levels in Latin America (see Figure 5). If we include the international prosecutions in East Timor, the level of accountability is even higher. Although our definition of Asia-Pacific encompasses more countries than this volume covers, the trend toward accountability is evident in the chapters on Cambodia (Chapter 4), Indonesia (Chapter 3), and South Korea (Chapter 7).

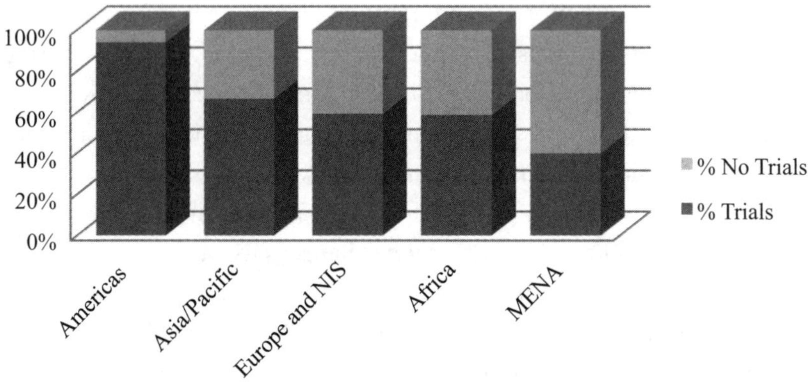

Figure 5. Percentage of transitional countries in each region with trials, 1970–2009

In this sense, a high number of transitional countries in the Asia-Pacific region have had either domestic or international/hybrid prosecutions. Even if we set a somewhat higher standard of evaluation and look only at countries that have experienced at least three transitional human rights prosecutions, we still find that the Asia-Pacific region is second among regions with the highest number of prosecutions as a percentage of transitional countries (see Figure 6).

A look at human rights prosecutions in non-transitional countries suggests that accountability in the Asia-Pacific region has not been limited

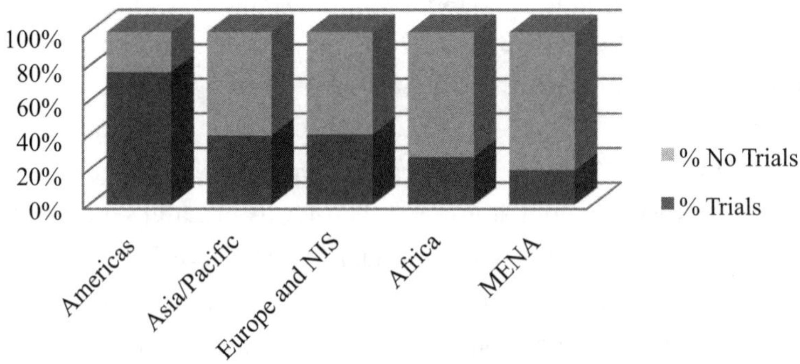

Figure 6. Percentage of transitional countries in each region with more than three trials, 1970–2009

to countries making transitions to democracy. In addition, human rights prosecutions have also occurred in non-transitional countries such as the Federated States of Micronesia, India, Japan, New Zealand, Palau, Papua New Guinea, Samoa, Singapore, and Sri Lanka (see Chapter 2 on Sri Lanka).

Our data on amnesties do not find that Asia, or the Asia-Pacific countries in particular, are more likely than other regions to adopt amnesty laws to protect perpetrators of past human rights violations. Of the seventy-six transitional countries in the database, thirty (40 percent) adopted amnesty laws for human rights violations by state agents. Asia as a whole included a smaller percentage of these amnesty laws than other regions (four countries or 13 percent compared to Europe with five countries or 17 percent, Africa with 10 countries or 33 percent, and Latin America with 11 countries or 37 percent). In terms of the numbers of amnesty laws, Asia is also as low as Europe: six amnesty laws or 11 percent of the fifty-six total number of such laws compared to fifteen amnesty laws in Africa (27 percent) and twenty-nine in Latin America (51 percent). Importantly, all of the countries and amnesty laws for past human rights violations in Asia are in the Asia-Pacific subregion: Bangladesh, Cambodia, South Korea, and Thailand. In addition, some scholars and human rights advocates have raised concerns about de facto amnesties that block prosecution in other parts of the region[8] (see Chapter 3).

Finally, we turn to truth commissions. Among the transitional countries in Asia-Pacific, there are eight countries with truth commissions: the Philippines, Nepal, South Korea, Indonesia, East Timor, Pakistan, the Solomon Islands, and Thailand. Some of these countries, such as South Korea, have made multiple use of truth commissions. If we include all truth commissions, both in transitional and non-transitional countries, the number is higher and includes Sri Lanka (1994, three commissions of

8 Patrick Burgess, "De Facto Amnesty? The Example of Post-Soeharto Indonesia," in *Amnesty in the Age of Human Rights Accountability: Comparative and International Perspectives*, edited by Francesca Lessa and Leigh A. Payne (Cambridge: Cambridge University Press, 2012): 263–290.

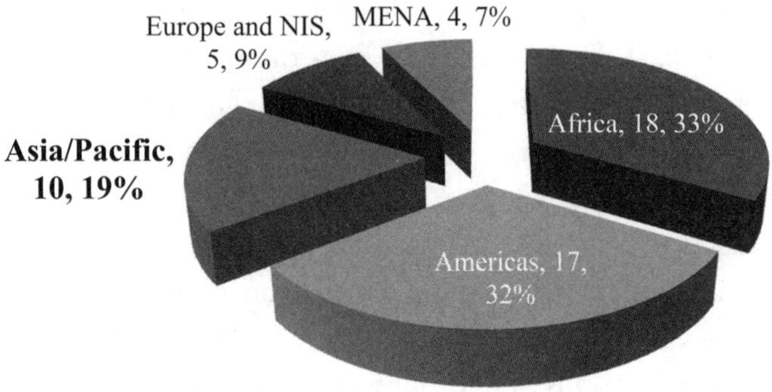

Figure 7. Number and percent of truth commissions by region, 1970–2009

inquiry) and India (1977). Thus while numbers of truth commissions in the Asia-Pacific are smaller than the numbers in the Americas and Africa, they are significantly higher than in Europe and are also increasing at a more rapid rate compared to other regions. For example, the Americas used to account for more than 50 percent of truth commissions, but they now account for only 40 percent, in large part due to the growth of truth commissions in the Asia-Pacific region.

In sum, in terms of global rankings, the Asia-Pacific region ranks third for the number of truth commissions, domestic prosecutions, and international prosecutions, and fourth for the number of amnesties. However, if we rank prosecutions in terms of the percentage of transitional countries that have used domestic human rights prosecutions, Asia ranks second. Regardless of how one counts, and including all the mechanisms considered here, these new data suggest that the Asia-Pacific region has had a significant amount of transitional justice, and generally a higher level than often assumed by scholars of transitional justice. This is all the more reason a volume such as this is a welcome addition to the literature.

Theoretical Arguments about the Origins and Diffusion of Transitional Justice Mechanisms

The transitions in the third wave of democracy are a necessary factor to explain both the emergence and diffusion of the norm of individual criminal accountability.[9] However, democracy alone is not in any sense a sufficient condition because the earlier second wave of democratization was not accompanied by human rights trials. Even in the third wave, fewer than half of the countries that transitioned to democracy held human rights trials. Because transitional justice has followed the global wave in democratization, however, it will not extend to regions of the world where democratic transitions have not taken root, for example, in the Middle East, or where democratic reversals are occurring, as in Russia and Central Asia. Because the Asia-Pacific region has experienced somewhat fewer transitions to democracy than other regions such as Latin America and Eastern Europe, by definition, it will not have had the same opportunities to adopt transitional trials and truth commissions.

One explanatory factor for the use and diffusion of transitional justice is the degree to which relevant international legal regimes and institutions are in place to make accountability possible. Those states that have ratified international and regional human rights law with provisions for accountability are more likely to use human rights prosecutions.[10] International human rights institutions exist at both the global level and in some regions. Thus there is considerable regional variation in human rights law, regarding the degree to which different countries in the region have ratified international human rights treaties and have set up regional human rights institutions. Three regions have full-fledged regional human rights regimes: Europe, the Americas, and Africa. These international and regional human rights institutions provide crucial legal doctrines that have facilitated human rights prosecutions, particularly in the Americas. For example, in the Americas, the Inter-American Court of Human Rights has increasingly ruled that countries have an obligation to provide remedies to victims of human rights violations, and these remedies need

9 Samuel P. Huntington, *The Third Wave: Democratization in the Late Twentieth Century* (Norman, Oklahoma: University of Oklahoma Press, 1991).

10 Geoff Dancy and Kathryn Sikkink, "Ratification and Human Rights Prosecutions: Toward a Transnational Theory of Treaty Compliance," *New York University Journal of International Law and Politics*, Vol. 44, No. 3 (2012), 751–790.

to include provisions for legal accountability. In addition, the international legal doctrine that crimes against humanity that are not subject to statutes of limitations gave invaluable legal tools for human rights litigation in the Americas. It is interesting that the Asia-Pacific region, however, has achieved relatively high levels of accountability without the support of a regional human rights institution.

More recently, the International Criminal Court (ICC) with its doctrine of complementarity has provided a powerful impetus for individual criminal accountability. Under complementarity, the ICC can take action against perpetrators of war crimes, genocide, or crimes against humanity if states are unwilling or unable to hold them accountable. But the ICC can act only if states have ratified the Rome Statute of the ICC, or if a case is referred to it by the UN Security Council. Of the current 121 States Parties to the ICC, 16 are from the Asia-Pacific region.[11] While not an inconsiderable number of ratifications, the ICC can act only in the cases of gross violations of core human rights that occur after ratification, so most of the human rights episodes considered in this volume are not subject to ICC jurisdiction.

Research on the origins of transitional justice mechanisms suggests that early norm adoption is the result of domestic political struggle and norm entrepreneurs. Domestic human rights organizations with transnational linkages were especially important in promoting the adoption of human rights prosecutions as well as truth commissions. It is noteworthy that those Asia-Pacific countries that have adopted transitional justice mechanisms most fully, such as South Korea and Indonesia, are among the countries in the region with the most active civil society organizations (see Chapters 3 and 7).

How countries respond to demands from civil society is also relevant to understanding when transitional justice mechanisms were adopted.

11 These include: Afghanistan (2003), Bangladesh (2010), Cambodia (2002), Cook Islands (2008), Fiji (1999), Japan (2007), Marshall Islands (2000), Mongolia (2002), Nauru (2001), New Zealand (2000), Philippines (2011), Republic of Korea (2002), Samoa (2002), Tajikistan (2000), Timor Leste (2002), and Vanuatu (2011).

In order to pursue transitional justice in some counties, civil society groups first had to work to challenge amnesty laws that blocked prosecutions. Without political or judicial leadership to attempt to circumvent or displace amnesty laws, trials become less likely. Our database thus coded not only the existence of amnesty laws, but also legal challenges to those laws. We found 161 challenges to fifty-six amnesties from 1970 to 2011. In relative terms, Asian countries have had slightly more challenges to their amnesty laws than Europe and Africa: five (3 percent) of challenges in Asia compared to four (2 percent) in Europe and seven (4 percent) in Africa. None of the regions compare, however, with the high number of challenges in Latin America 145 or (90 percent), which have resulted in innovative mechanisms for bypassing or overturning amnesty laws and thus allowed for prosecutions. The high proportion of challenges reflects the degree to which social movements have effectively demanded accountability and the capacity of the legal system to respond to those demands. Civil society activity in the Asia-Pacific transitional countries is reflected in the legal challenges to amnesty laws in four countries: Bangladesh, Cambodia, South Korea, and Thailand. In addition, the challenges in Bangladesh led to the repeal of the 1976 amnesty law, making it one of only three countries in the world to do so.[12]

Once practices of individual criminal accountability had emerged and were starting to spread, the most important predictor for adoption of prosecutions was the actions of neighboring countries. Hun Joon Kim has found, for example, that the single most important determinant for whether a country will use a truth commission or human rights prosecutions is the number of other states in that region that have previously used a truth commission or prosecutions.[13] Early norm adoption is the result

12 The other two cases are Argentina and Uruguay.

13 Hun Joon Kim, "Structural Determinants of Human Rights Prosecutions after Democratic Transition," *Journal of Peace Research*, Vol. 49, No. 2 (2012), 305–320; and Hun Joon Kim, "Why and When Do Countries Seek to Address Past Human Rights Violations after Transition? An Event History Analysis of 100 Countries Covering 1980–2004" (presentation, Annual Meeting of the International Studies Association, Chicago, Illinois, February 28–March 3, 2007).

of domestic political struggle and norm entrepreneurs, but later adoption is the result of a combination of internal demands and external diffusion of models. Norms emerge and diffuse first within regions and only later jump from one region to another and globally. For this reason, the spread of the justice norm has been, and will continue to be, regionally uneven. Regional diffusion patterns lead to a kind of snowball effect; regions in which transitional justice started early are likely to see rapid diffusion while regions with initially few early examples of transitional justice will lag behind.

In summary, because Asia experienced relatively fewer democratic transitions during the third wave and does not have a regional human rights law system or institution, we would have expected the process of accountability to be slower in Asia than in Europe, Latin America, and Africa. The level of transitional justice in the region, however, is somewhat higher than anticipated. The increase in the use of various forms of transitional justice mechanisms in the region as documented in this chapter and in the entire edited volume may be the result of the active role of civil society organizations in key countries and regional diffusion effects that have multiplied the use of transitional justice in the region.

Theoretical Arguments on the Impact of Transitional Justice

We consider three approaches to explain the impact of transitional justice: *deterrence*, *normative socialization*, and *accountability-with-stability*. While these hypotheses could be competing, they could also be complementary. The deterrence hypothesis derives from both the international relations compliance literature, involving a rationalist assumption that an increase in enforcement should lead to an increase in cooperation,[14] and the literature on deterrence in domestic legal systems[15] that an increase in

14 George W. Downs, David M. Rocke, and Peter N. Barsoom, "Is the Good News about Compliance Good News about Cooperation?," *International Organization*, Vol. 50, No. 3 (1996), pp. 379–406.

15 Ross L. Matsueda, Derek A. Kreager, and David Huizinga, "Deterring Delinquents: A Rational Choice Model of Theft and Violence," *American Sociological Review*,

the likelihood or probability of arrest and punishment can deter crime.[16] The normative socialization hypothesis sees transitional justice mechanisms as high-profile symbolic and performative events that communicate and dramatize norms and socialize actors to accept those norms. These processes of communication and socialization in some cases can lead to behavioral change without the use of material sanctions or punishment.[17]

Our previous research has produced some evidence for each of these hypotheses. Sikkink's book, *The Justice Cascade: How Human Rights Prosecutions are Changing World Politics*, in particular, stressed the importance of both deterrence and normative socialization as theories that help explain why trials have a positive impact on human rights practices. In addition, Payne's research with Olsen and Reiter[18] and Sikkink and Kim[19] have found that the use of trials is associated with improvements in human rights, lending some support for the deterrence hypothesis that an increase in enforcement or punishment can lead to a decrease in crime. In addition, new research using the NSF/AHRC data on convictions also suggests that prosecutions that end in convictions have a more significant impact on human rights practices than prosecutions that do not

Vol. 71, No. 1 (2006), pp. 95–122; Bill McCarthy, "New Economics of Sociological Criminology," *Annual Review of Sociology*, Vol. 28 (2002), pp. 417–442; Daniel S. Nagin, "Criminal Deterrence Research at the Outset of the Twenty-First Century," *Crime and Justice: A Review of Research*, Vol. 23 Edited by Michael Tonry (Chicago: University of Chicago Press, 1998), pp. 1–42.

16 Bruce Bueno de Mesquita and Lawrence E. Cohen, "Self-Interest, Equity, and Crime Control: A Game-Theoretic Analysis of Criminal Decision Making," *Criminology*, Vol. 33, No. 4 (1995), pp. 483–518; McCarthy (2002); Nagin (1998).

17 Thomas Risse, Stephen C. Ropp, and Kathryn Sikkink, eds., *The Power of Human Rights: International Norms and Domestic Change* (Cambridge: Cambridge University Press, 1999); Ryan Goodman and Derek Jinks, "How to Influence States: Socialization and International Human Rights Law," *Duke Law Journal*, Vol. 54, No. 3 (2004), pp. 621–703.

18 Tricia D. Olsen, Leigh A. Payne, and Andrew G. Reiter, *Transitional Justice in Balance: Comparing Processes, Weighing Efficacy* (Washington D.C.: United States Institute of Peace Press, 2010).

19 Hun Joon Kim and Kathryn Sikkink, "Explaining the Deterrence Effect of Human Rights Prosecutions for Transitional Countries," *International Studies Quarterly*, Vol. 54, No. 4 (2010), pp. 939–963; Hun Joon Kim and Kathryn Sikkink, "How Do Human Rights Prosecutions Improve Human Rights after Transition?" forthcoming in the *Interdisciplinary Journal of Human Rights Law*, Vol. 7 (2012–2013).

end in convictions.[20] This provides support for the deterrence argument, in which an increased likelihood of retribution or punishment is the factor contributing to human rights improvements. At the same time, Kim and Sikkink (2010, 2012–2013) have found that truth commissions and prosecutions that do not result in convictions continue to be associated with improvements in human rights, providing some support also for the normative communication hypothesis. Olsen et al. (2010), on the other hand, have found that the use of truth commissions alone is not associated with improvements in human rights, but rather a deterioration of those scores, which calls into question the normative socialization hypothesis.

On the surface, the use of amnesties does not appear to be consistent with either the deterrence or the norms and socialization explanation. However, our joint research project suggests that amnesty laws and accountability efforts set in motion dramatic and public debate, establishing a new justice norm to replace the prior culture of impunity. Payne's research with Olsen and Reiter has revealed a set of pathways used around the world to circumvent amnesties and allow for trials and improvements in human rights and democracy.[21] Indeed, some evidence suggests that where amnesties exist, mobilization to undermine them leads to trials, a pathway to accountability and deterrence that is less likely where no amnesty law exists to condemn domestically or internationally.[22] Moreover, trials and truth commissions reveal the lack of legitimacy of amnesties, suggesting that normative socialization may contribute to undermining the effectiveness of amnesties in preventing accountability.

20 Kim and Sikkink (2012–2013).

21 Olsen et al. (2010); Tricia D. Olsen, Leigh A. Payne, and Andrew G. Reiter, "Conclusion: Amnesty in the Age of Accountability," in *Amnesty in the Age of Human Rights Accountability: Comparative and International Perspectives*, eds. Francesca Lessa and Leigh A. Payne (Cambridge and New York: Cambridge University Press, 2012).

22 Patrick Burgess, "De Facto Amnesty? The Example of Post-Soeharto Indonesia," in *Amnesty in the Age of Human Rights Accountability: Comparative and International Perspectives*, eds. Francesca Lessa and Leigh A. Payne (Cambridge and New York: Cambridge University Press, 2012).

Payne's research with Olsen and Reiter in particular develops the *accountability-with-stability* approach. In their 2010 book, *Transitional Justice in Balance: Comparing Processes, Weighing Efficacy*, they tested the assumptions in the existing literature regarding the impact of transitional justice on human rights and democracy. They found that they could not confirm the theoretical approaches that assume that single mechanisms are likely to bring improvements in human rights or democracy. Neither trials nor truth commissions nor amnesties – by themselves – produced positive statistically significant findings for those outcomes.[23] They found, however, that certain combinations of mechanisms produced positive and statistically significant results for human rights and democracy.

Two specific combinations produced those results: (1) trials and amnesties or (2) trials, amnesties, and truth commissions. The "justice balance" approach that they derived from this analysis contends that trials and amnesties complement each other. Trials enhance the institutional strength and legitimacy of courts by showing that previously untouchable perpetrators of state violence can be held accountable. By punishing perpetrators, moreover, trials attach a cost to committing atrocity, thereby eroding the previously prevailing culture of impunity. Amnesties, on the other hand, allow for stability during the early vulnerable period of transition in which trials might catalyze former perpetrators and jeopardize the nascent democracy and its protections of human rights. Amnesties might also protect against "show" and "sham" trials that are likely to occur in the early transition period before the old regime's legal community is replaced with prosecutors and judges trained after the democratic opening. In addition, amnesties might offset the cost of expensive trials by first allocating scarce public funds to resolve economic crises in the early years of the transition before adopting trials during a more secure economic moment. The balance, hence, involves stability on one side and accountability on the other, together increasing the likelihood of

23 In their quantitative study, Olsen et al. found that truth commissions, by themselves, produced statistically significant but negative findings for human rights measures.

positive results for human rights and democracy. The assumption behind the justice balance is that accountability might not have a positive result without stability, enhanced by amnesties, and that amnesties will not likely advance human rights and democracy without accountability mechanisms. Truth commissions contribute to the balance by enhancing the stability-accountability function of transitional justice and addressing the specific needs of victims.

This approach draws on existing scholarship on transitional justice. It concurs, for example, with those who advocate trials as essential to human rights improvements.[24] It also concurs with those who consider amnesties a "necessary evil," an undesirable but often crucial ingredient to successfully ending violence and promoting democratic transitions.[25] These approaches are often viewed as incompatible. Those advocating trials tend to consider amnesties a form of impunity that jeopardizes human rights advances. Those advocating amnesties tend to view trials

24 See for example: Hun Joon Kim and Kathryn Sikkink, "Explaining the Deterrence Effect of Human Rights Prosecutions for Transitional Countries," *International Studies Quarterly*, Vol. 54, No. 4 (2010), pp. 939–963; Juan E. Méndez, "Accountability for Past Abuses," *Human Rights Quarterly*, Vol. 19, No. 2 (1997), pp. 255–282; Diane F. Orentlicher, "Settling Accounts: The Duty to Prosecute Human Rights Violations of a Prior Regime," *Yale Law Journal*, Vol. 100, No. 8 (1991), pp. 2537–2615; Naomi Roht-Arriaza, "State Responsibility to Investigate and Prosecute Grave Human Rights Violations in International Law," *California Law Review*, Vol. 78, No. 2 (1990), pp. 464–465; M. Cherif Bassiouni, "International Crimes: *Jus Cogens* and *Obligatio Erga Omnes*," *Law and Contemporary Problems*, Vol. 59, No. 4 (1996), pp. 66–68; Naomi Roht-Arriaza, ed., *Impunity and Human Rights in International Law and Practice* (New York: Oxford University Press, 1995); Michael Scharf, "The Letter of the Law: The Scope of the International Legal Obligation to Prosecute Human Rights Crimes," *Law and Contemporary Problems*, Vol. 59, No. 4 (1996), pp. 41–61.

25 See, for example, Jack Snyder and Leslie Vinjamuri, "Trials and Errors: Principle and Pragmatism in Strategies of International Justice," *International Security*, Vol. 28, No. 3 (2003), pp. 5–44; Leslie Vinjamuri and Jack Snyder, "Advocacy and Scholarship in the Study of International War Crimes Tribunals and Transitional Justice," *Annual Review of Political Science*, Vol. 7, No. 1 (2004), pp. 345–362; Jon Elster, *Closing the Books: Transitional Justice in Historical Perspective* (New York: Cambridge University Press, 2004); Mark Freeman, *Necessary Evils: Amnesties and the Search for Justice* (Cambridge and New York: Cambridge University Press, 2009).

as undermining the transition process. Indeed, advocates of truth commissions see them as negotiating the space between the potentially destabilizing trial process and the impunity associated with amnesties and, therefore, a better alternative to both trials and amnesties. The justice balance approach suggests that these three sets of mechanisms are not trade-offs, or alternatives, to each other, but rather are complementary. Together they bring the stability and accountability that advances human rights improvements.

Olsen et al. draw the conclusion that the existing literature exaggerates the presumed trade-off between trials, amnesties, and truth commissions. This analysis suggests that human rights and democracy improvements depend on trials and amnesties, with or without truth commissions, suggesting that the mechanisms complement one another in a justice balance of accountability combined with stability.

Since the publication of their book, Olsen et al. have begun researching alternative explanations for their results. Some scholars argue that the coexistence of trials and amnesties may result from historical and sequenced outcomes, rather than a functional relationship. In particular, when trials and amnesties coexist to improve human rights, trials may have succeeded in overcoming the limitations on accountability that amnesties impose. Latin America provides the most compelling example of such a process. Thus, sequencing, timing, type of amnesty, context, and region may suggest that trials alone, without the need for amnesties, improve human rights. The researchers have considered these alternative explanations in their recent work.

Sequencing. Some scholars, including Payne's research team, assume that the positive outcome from combining trials and amnesty results from their adoption sequence. In some cases, however, scholars suggest that where trials follow amnesties, they render amnesties ineffective and irrelevant. Trials therefore drive the improvements in human rights – not amnesties or combinations. Payne's team contends, in contrast, that if trials were doing all of the work for improvements in human rights, then trials on their own would have produced positive outcomes for human rights. Payne's research team suggests that amnesties play an important role in establishing stability. Thus sequencing trials after the initial vulnerable period of transition would allow for amnesties to play the stabilizing role that allows for the transition and subsequent trials allow for the accountability function of strengthening judicial institutions and raising the cost of committing human rights violations.

Timing. Deterrence and normative socialization arguments suggest that increased enforcement mechanisms in the international system and the spread of norms in favor of accountability, rather than amnesties, have led to an improvement in human rights. The stability-with-accountability approach suggests that increased enforcement mechanisms and the spread of norms must be combined with amnesties in order to have a positive effective. This is supported by the evidence that a clear shift away from amnesties has not accompanied the global accountability trend. Figure 1 shows that the use of amnesties has fluctuated: while the numbers of new amnesty laws reached their highest level in the early 1990s, and have declined ever since, existing amnesty laws continue to be in effect in many countries as shown in Figure 2. Very rarely have amnesty laws been repealed, though they have been circumvented in many cases. To date, therefore, we do not have incontrovertible evidence that trials have replaced amnesties and played a role by themselves in bringing improvements in human rights on their own. A compelling argument that could be made regarding timing, however, is that human rights advocates may not mobilize behind early trials, understanding that without a generational shift in the judiciaries these trials may render unjust verdicts. Political and judicial leadership behind trials is likely to emerge over time and unlikely to be present in the early years of the transition.

Types of Amnesties. Another explanation for the findings involves the types of amnesties that states implement. For example, recent amnesties may be more likely to be compatible with international law to avoid the International Criminal Court, ad hoc tribunals, or domestic legal challenges. They might exclude particular crimes absolutely prohibited by treaties, such as genocide, crimes against humanity, and torture. In the interest of stability, they might limit their scope to include only top officials behind the crimes, to prevent catalyzing the entire military against them, or only lower ranking officials to protect against mobilization by the former top leaders. The challenge to the justice balance approach, therefore, is that not all amnesties will effectively work with trials to bring about improvements in human rights. The analysis of the justice balance cases, however, suggests a different explanation for the compatibility between trials and amnesties.

First, strong evidence supports the assumption that amnesty laws provide some form of stability in the early years of transition. In some cases, self-amnesties allowed for extrication of the authoritarian regimes, paving the way for transition (e.g., Argentina, Chile, and Peru). Democratic governments subsequently accepted these amnesties through executive decree or legislation (although not before a trial of the regime leaders in the case of Argentina). In other cases, peace accords with amnesties ended civil conflict and permitted the transition to peace and democracy (e.g., El Salvador and Guatemala). In a third set of cases, democratic governments adopted decree laws that prevented prosecution or pardoned convicted authoritarian leaders in the interest of "national reconciliation" or "political stability" (e.g., Greece, South Korea, and Uruguay). While perhaps unnecessary, based on an exaggerated fear of authoritarian reversal, or designed as a façade to protect political alliances, amnesty laws gave fragile democratic governments flexibility to negotiate the transition.

More importantly, amnesties did not block subsequent trials. Civil society groups and courts challenged the amnesty laws, finding legal loopholes to circumvent them (i.e., Chile, El Salvador, Guatemala, Honduras, and Peru) or overturning them (i.e., Argentina, Bangladesh, and Uruguay) to bring perpetrators to trial for past human rights abuses. In other words, trials often played a key role in challenging and weakening and ultimately undermining amnesty laws. Indeed, in many cases amnesty laws continue to have legal standing or remain de facto, even when some trials continue to hold perpetrators accountable. There are only three known cases in which amnesty laws have been annulled. Two of them are in Latin America (Argentina, Uruguay); the third one is in the Asia-Pacific (Bangladesh). Thus, evidence suggests that despite the prevalence of amnesties, and even blanket amnesty laws, trials may still provide the necessary accountability to improve human rights.

Context. Improvements in human rights may also be due to other contextual factors associated with the transitional state and not the specific transitional justice choices that these states make. Some scholars view the improvements in human rights associated with transitional justice as endogenous. Particular factors may drive transitional justice choices *and* improvements in human rights. In other words, human rights improvements may not result from the transitional justice mechanism adopted, but rather from some other factors that also shape transitional justice decisions. In statistical language, transitional justice may be correlated with the error term.

An additional means to address this question is to track the changes in human rights measures of the countries that utilized trials and amnesties to examine key patterns. Initial findings do not confirm any clear patterns. The team did confirm, however, that amnesties and trials are not implemented only in states where human rights improvements have already occurred. In addition, the use of amnesties does not bring lower scores for human rights. Indeed, more often than not, human rights improvements occur at the time of amnesties. Amnesties cannot be assumed to have brought about those improvements, but the pattern shows that they have not harmed the process of improving human rights.

In short, regardless of the context, or starting point in terms of level of human rights violations, amnesties coupled with trials tend to be associated with improvements. Those improvements do not occur exclusively in countries with low levels of human rights protections or in those countries with already high levels of human rights improvements, as some scholars might assume.

Region. The regional explanation focuses on a potential bias in the results due to a prominence of Latin American cases that utilize amnesties and trials. Eight out of thirteen of the countries that have the trial-amnesty combination and improvements in human rights are Latin American. When the team analyzed those countries qualitatively, it observed that trials have occurred despite the authoritarian regimes' self-amnesty and early democratic governments' acceptance of those or adoption of other blanket amnesty laws. Amnesties seemed to offer new democracies a means by which they could protect themselves from potential threats from the old authoritarian forces. Amnesties also provided the means to negotiate peace in the Central American wars. Amnesties, however, did not prevent accountability in most of these cases. Our initial analysis of these cases show that a combination of factors allowed for trials to occur even in the context of far-reaching amnesty laws. Components that facilitated trials include mobilized victim-survivors and human rights communities, lower court decisions that tested the strength of the amnesty law, and Supreme Court decisions. The Inter-American Court of Human Rights has also played a much more significant role than the other regional courts around the world in adjudicating the amnesty laws of member countries.

In sum, the justice balance approach shows that despite domestic and global pressure and their success in increasing the number of human rights trials around the world, amnesties continue to exist. These amnesties have not prevented accountability, however. Indeed, the justice balance findings suggest that where amnesties and trials coexist, with or without truth commissions, countries are likely to experience improvements in human rights.

The Asia-Pacific in Comparative Perspective

What do these theoretical approaches offer to an understanding of transitional justice in the Asia-Pacific region, and how do patterns in the Asia-Pacific region help advance our theoretical and empirical understandings?

Regarding the adoption and diffusion of trials, our work suggests that compared to other regions, Asia has made less use than Latin America of the transitional justice mechanisms considered here: transitional human rights trials, truth commissions, and amnesties. This is in large part the result of the fewer number of transitions to democracy in the region rather than any particular reluctance to carry out transitional justice. When we include human rights prosecutions and truth commissions in non-transitional countries in Asia, an important accountability trend seems underway in the Asia-Pacific region – a trend that has increased in importance in recent years. This new data and the chapters in the volume reveal that many more and diverse transitional justice responses are happening in the region than previously understood.

How do we account for these developments? First, many of the transitional justice experiences in the region are relatively recent and thus few previous studies have been published. Second, much of the work on transitional justice in the region has focused on single studies of countries rather than on comparative studies within the region or among regions. Single-country studies, or studies of single tribunals, may focus on the many ways in which such experiences fall short of the ideals of justice held by scholars or civil society organizations. For example, the problems with the Dili Special Panels for Serious Crimes (SPSC) in East Timor were significant. Nevertheless, when compared to the very few prosecutions in the related hybrid tribunal in Cambodia, the SPSC appears to have been a very active tribunal, in terms of the number of indictments, prosecutions, and convictions. On those counts, it compares positively to international tribunals in other regions. But, if we evaluate it in light of whether or not high-level officials who planned the human rights violations were held accountable, it would be seen as less successful. Some of the transitional justice cases are happening in particular subregions of countries (such as Aceh, Indonesia) and thus may not be recorded in the sources examining national-level phenomena. Third, many interesting transitional justice activities are taking place in the small Pacific Island countries with populations too small to usually be coded in global databases (such as the Solomon Islands; see Chapter 6). Finally, Asia Pacific countries are making use of other types of transitional justice mechanisms – such as customary justice – that have not been studied systematically. Indeed, in our recent study of twelve countries identified as having adopted customary justice to address past human rights violations, four of the countries are in Asia Pacific: East Timor, Fiji, Papua New Guinea, and the Solomon Islands.[26]

In other words, transitional justice in the Asia-Pacific region has been moving ahead. It has done so even when some of the theoretical explanations for the advance of accountability are absent from the region. In particular, the Asia-Pacific region lacks the regional human rights regimes and courts that have been important in Latin America, Europe, and Africa for furthering processes of transitional justice and accountability. A number of Asian Pacific countries have ratified the Rome Statute, but most of the human rights violations considered in this volume took place before ratification, so the International Criminal Court is not able to play a role in these cases, as it has in Africa. But, because diffusion processes happen first within regions, and the single biggest predictor of the adoption of human rights prosecutions and truth commission is their use by neighboring countries, it is likely that these diffusion processes have also led to some snowball effects in Asia. The important innovations in countries such as South Korea, Indonesia, and East Timor (see Chapters 3, 5, and 7) may have served as regional models that were

26 Of these countries, only Papua New Guinea, a non-transition case, has used customary justice to adjudicate human rights violations. The other three transitional countries used customary justice as part of their restorative justice or reconciliatory processes. The data presented on customary justice are based on research supported by the National Science Foundation (Grant No. 0961226) and the Arts and Humanities Research Council (Grant No. AH/K502856/1) relating to the project titled "Alternative Accountabilities for Past Human Rights." Any opinions, findings, and conclusions or recommendations expressed in this material are those of the authors and do not necessarily reflect the views of the National Science Foundation or the Arts and Humanities Research Council. We thank our NSF/AHRC research team working on customary justice for gathering this material, particularly Laura Bernal-Bermúdez, Pierre Louis Le Goff, Francesca Lessa, Gabriel Pereira, and Marcela Villarazzo.

later emulated by other countries in the region. If so, we should expect to see more accountability in the future in the region, as the diffusion processes continue.

In terms of the impact of the transitional justice mechanisms already in use, there is not yet systematic evidence for analysis in the Asia-Pacific region. Based on our previous research, we would expect that countries that have made use of prosecutions to see more improvements in their human rights situation than countries that have not used such prosecutions. The accountability-with-stability approach would expect improvements in human rights measures if the countries also adopt amnesty laws. We are still uncertain about the effects of truth commissions, when used alone, although we expect that, if used together with trials and amnesties, they are likely to be more effective than when used on their own. Only with time and future research will we be able to determine whether the combinations that have brought positive outcomes for human rights elsewhere will have a similar impact in the Asia-Pacific.

2 Sri Lanka

Atrocities, Accountability, and the Decline of Rule of Law

Chandra Lekha Sriram

IN MAY 2009, THE BRUTAL 26-YEAR CONFLICT IN SRI LANKA between the government and the Liberation Tigers of Tamil Eelam (LTTE) was brought to a close. Estimates of casualties during the conflict vary, but may be as high as 100,000, and during the final government offensive from January to May 2009, the UN expert report estimates that as many as 40,000 civilians may have been killed.[1] During the course of the conflict, widespread human rights violations were committed by forces of the government and the LTTE alike. The LTTE engaged in acts of terrorism, including suicide bombing, and also attacked civilians and recruited child soldiers. Government forces, both the army and other security forces, engaged in attacks including shelling on civilians and hospitals and other humanitarian installations, involuntary disappearance, torture, arbitrary arrests, killings of noncombatants and combatants attempting to surrender, and denial of food and medical supplies to civilians.

1 United Nations, *Report of the Secretary-General's Panel of Experts on Accountability in Sri Lanka* (31 March 2011), p. 41. REDRESS Trust, 'Comments and Recommendations to the Secretary-General's Panel of Experts on the Issue of Accountability with Regard to Alleged Violations of International Human Rights and Humanitarian Law during the Final Stages of the Conflict in Sri Lanka' (15 December 2010), at www.redress.org; Anonymous, 'Against the Grain: Pursuing a Transitional Justice Agenda in Postwar Sri Lanka,' *International Journal of Transitional Justice* Vol. 5 (2011).

The International Crisis Group (ICG) and a range of other international human rights NGOs have thoroughly documented abuses on both sides and highlighted what they deem widespread acts tantamount to war crimes committed by government forces during their final offensive. However, the only proposed response to abuses during the conflict is a commission of inquiry created by the government, designed to examine only crimes alleged to have been committed by the LTTE. The government has been resistant to external scrutiny of its activities and loudly condemned both NGO and UN reports regarding alleged war crimes.

A close examination of the situation in Sri Lanka is merited in any comparative study of transitional justice in Asia, even though accountability measures that address violations committed by both the LTTE and the government throughout the conflict and during the brutal final months of the conflict seem unlikely at this time. Despite the limited prospects for accountability at this time, closer examination is merited because Sri Lanka has in fact utilized accountability measures for past abuses previously (largely during the 1990s), the country is and has almost continuously been a democracy since independence, and until recently a vibrant civil society has issued frequent calls for accountability.

The resistance of the government to discussions of accountability seems peculiar, in the context of developing scholarship suggesting that past transitional justice measures help engender better human rights and democracy records given that the country has experienced a range of such measures, yet the quality of democracy, human rights, and rule of law appear to have been progressively degraded.[2] Thus, Sri Lanka's experience is important per se, but also because it seems to run counter to predictions from recent large-N studies.

This chapter will discuss the conflict in Sri Lanka, its earlier experiments with accountability, and the concomitant decline of rule of law

2 Tricia Olsen, Leigh Payne, and Andrew Reiter, *Transitional Justice in Balance: Comparing Processes, Weighing Efficacy* (Washington, DC: United States Institute of Peace Press, 2010); Kathryn Sikkink, *The Justice Cascade: How Human Rights Prosecutions Are Changing the World* (New York: Norton, 2011).

there. It will then turn to the end of the conflict, alleged abuses, and the failure to address them, and posit that perhaps the prior accountability measures served as cover, intentional or not, for the broader undermining of rule of law. It will, finally, consider options for accountability outside of Sri Lanka, and whether they have any prospect of affecting the domestic landscape.

History of the Conflict

At independence, Sri Lanka was a functioning democracy with universal suffrage. However, colonial practices providing preferential treatment to the Tamil minority in education and other areas were resented by the Sinhalese majority, and post-independence governments developed increasingly restrictive and discriminatory laws with regard to Tamils, pushing some to define themselves ethnically and increasingly stridently, eventually leading to a call for an independent Tamil homeland. In particular, Tamil access to higher education was progressively restricted, and debates over textbooks intensified controversies over language. Thus in 1977 the Tamil United Liberation Front (TULF) called for a separate *eelam* or homeland for Tamils.[3] In the same year, J.R. Jayewardene came into power, promising a Buddhist revival with little concern for the status of the Tamil minority.[4] Meanwhile, the Liberation Tigers of Tamil Eelam – formed in 1972 as the student wing of the TULF – grew in strength, eventually breaking off from the TULF. Following anti-Tamil riots in 1977, the LTTE escalated military activity, and, in 1978, the LTTE was officially banned and centralization of power increased with a new constitution enshrining an executive presidency.[5] This was followed by

3 Sumantra Bose, *States, Nations, Sovereignty* (New Delhi: Sage Publications, 1994), pp. 46, 68–72; Bruce Matthews, 'Devolution of Power in Sri Lanka,' *The Round Table*, No. 330 (1994), p. 223.

4 Steven Kemper, 'J.R. Jayewardene, Righteousness, and *Realpolitik*,' in Jonathan Spencer, ed., *Sri Lanka: History and the Roots of Conflict* (London: Routledge, 1990), pp. 191, 200–201.

5 Bose, States, Nations, Sovereignty, pp. 74, 94.

the Prevention of Terrorism Act in 1979 and emergency regulations and a constitutional amendment in 1983 which further limited freedom of speech and rights of those under arrest.[6]

These actions set the stage for the anti-Tamil riots in Colombo in 1983. The immediate cause of the riots was ostensibly the killing of thirteen Sinhalese soldiers by the LTTE near Jaffna in July 1983. The bodies were brought to the capital by fellow soldiers, sparking violence against Tamils by both local civilians and the soldiers themselves. The result was widespread and systematic destruction of Tamil-owned homes, businesses, and factories. Accurate estimates of fatalities are difficult to obtain: the government ultimately offered reparations to 937 persons, whereas others place the number at 2,000 to 3,000.[7] At least 80,000 to 100,000 Tamils were displaced to refugee camps in the Colombo area alone; other estimates place the number of Tamils made homeless at 150,000.[8] At the same time there was a rise in Sinhalese extremist Janatha Vikmuthi Peramuna (JVP)-perpetrated violence in the south, as the group accused the government of being India's pawn and failing to deal firmly enough with Tamils.[9] Not only did the military and police

6 Prevention of Terrorism Act, *Gazette* (1979), No. 48, and Prevention of Terrorism, Amendment to the Prevention of Terrorism Act, *Gazette* (19 March 1982), pt. 2, supp. Bose, *States, Nations, Sovereignty*, pp. 74, 79; S.J. Tambiah, in *Sri Lanka: Ethnic Fratricide and the Dismantling of Democracy* (Chicago: University of Chicago Press, 1991), pp. 42–45, argues that the Act has progressively generated the very militancy and separatist sentiments it was meant to repress.

7 See Sarath Kumara, 'Sri Lankan President Offers Empty Apology for 1983 Pogrom,' *World Socialist Web Site* (6 August 2004), at http://www.wsws.org/articles/2004/aug 2004/sril-a06.shtml. Accessed 13 June 2013.

8 Bose, *States, Nations, Sovereignty*, p. 73; S.J. Tambiah, *Sri Lanka: Ethnic Fratricide and the Dismantling of Democracy* (Chicago: University of Chicago Press, 1991), pp. 15, 22; S.J. Tambiah, *Leveling Crowds: Ethnonationalist Conflict and Collective Violence in South Asia* (Berkeley: University of California Press, 1996), [pp. 94–100; Robert A. Denemark, "Democracy and the World System: The Political Economy of Sri Lanka's Vicious Electoral Cycle," in Chronis Polychroniou, ed., *Perspectives and Issues in International Political Economy* (Westport: Praeger Publishers, 1992), p. 206]; Marshall R. Singer, 'Sri Lanka's Ethnic Conflict: Have Bombs Shattered Hopes for Peace?' *Asian Survey*, Vol. 36, No. 11 (1996), p. 1149.

9 Austin, *Democracy and Violence in India and Sri Lanka* (London: Chatham House, 1995), p. 74.

fail to restrain the riots; in some cases they actively encouraged them. Civilians and members of the military also rioted in the east, near Trincomalee Harbor. On 25 and 27 July, some fifty-three Tamil 'terrorists' were killed in a Colombo jail, presumably with at least the collusion of their jailers.[10] Following the riots, the LTTE's military activities, and the conflict, escalated.

The conflict's intensity varied over the decades, with a reduction in violence following a ceasefire and the creation of the Sri Lankan Monitoring Mission in 2002. However, peace negotiations failed, and fighting escalated in 2006, with the ceasefire ending formally and the mission closing in 2008; the conflict escalated and ended with military victory by the state in 2009.

Abuses throughout the Conflict

The conflict in Sri Lanka took a heavy toll on civilians, through everyday restrictions on liberties, particularly those of the Tamil population, and through violence and abuses. The repeated invocation of states of emergency by various presidents limited freedom of association and movement, and Tamils in particular were subjected to detention and harassment at government checkpoints.

Abuses were committed by the government and the LTTE, as well as splinter groups of the LTTE, throughout the conflict. The LTTE engaged in extensive recruitment of child soldiers, as did the government and the splinter wing of the LTTE, led by Colonel Karuna and collaborating with the government. The LTTE also engaged in extensive use of suicide bombers. The government and the LTTE engaged in forced disappearances, torture, and extrajudicial executions. Throughout the conflict, internal displacement was rife, with more than half a million persons displaced in all, some 75,000 to 90,000 by the LTTE in 1990 alone.[11]

10 Tambiah, *Sri Lanka*, pp. 16–26.

11 Sri Lanka Democracy Forum, 'Submission to the Universal Periodic Review of Sri Lanka.'

Since the end of the conflict, the lives of civilians in the north and east have remained grim. Rather than withdrawing, the military has increased its presence and control over the north and east of the country. It retains control over many administrative decisions, is the body which approves or rejects plans for religious ceremonies and private gatherings, and often attends private functions for intelligence-gathering. The military has prevented public grieving over losses at the end of the conflict and similarly prevented local dialogue. Further, at least 3,000 Tamils continued to be detained in 2012, some 3 years after the end of the conflict as suspected LTTE, and the authorities first restricted and then eliminated ICRC access to these prisoners. Some 2,000 individuals detained and awaiting trial under the Prevention of Terrorism Act are being held for extended periods in 'rehabilitation' centres, and many Tamils are regularly detained and harassed, released, and re-arrested without charge.[12] Attacks on Tamils, including sexual assaults on Tamil women by members of the military, have been frequent. Although the majority of civilians displaced at the end of the conflict have returned home, they often lack the most basic services.[13] Outside the north and east, opposition politicians, critical media outlets, and local and international NGOs are subject to harassment and attack.[14]

Earlier Accountability Mechanisms

Numerous Commissions of Inquiry

It bears remembering that Sri Lanka has conducted numerous inquiries into abuses and disappearances and even prosecuted a small number of perpetrators, even as the war raged during the 1990s. This is not to

12 International Crisis Group, 'Reconciliation in Sri Lanka: Harder than Ever,' *Asia Report* No. 209 (18 July 2011), pp. 17–18, at http://www.wsws.org/articles/2004/aug2004/sril-a06.shtml.

13 Charu Lata Hogg, 'Sri Lanka: Prospects for Reform and Reconciliation,' Chatham House Asia Programme Paper ASP PP 2011/06 (October 2011); International Crisis Group, 'Reconciliation in Sri Lanka.'

14 International Crisis Group, 'Reconciliation in Sri Lanka,' p. 19.

overstate the success or impact of previous efforts, and these earlier commissions have been criticized for limited mandates and the absence of a clear connection between their work and judicial proceedings.[15] Nonetheless a brief review of these activities is in order, lest excessive credence be given either to claims that Sri Lanka is not capable of accountability, or that it would necessarily undermine stability or reconciliation.

In 2000, the Batalanda Commission issued a report on allegations regarding torture and abuse at the Batalanda housing estate which implicated a senior superintendent of police and leading politicians, but its recommendations were not implemented. Similarly, in 2002, a Presidential truth commission on Ethnic Violence covering 1981 to 1984 examined the causes and consequences of ethnic violence in the country. Although some analysts consider it a useful historical document, its recommendations were also not taken up, and it appears to have had little public impact.[16] When President Kumaratunga was elected in 1994, she sought to follow through on electoral promises to address past abuses, creating a number of new mechanisms to investigate disappearances and political assassinations, including that of her own husband. She created small regional commissions, which encountered resistance from the military and police, who denied knowledge of abuses.[17] Other steps towards protection of human rights included plans to have senior military officers investigate claims of disappearances in the north and east, and the creation of a Human Rights Commission under the president's direct supervision to monitor complaints of human rights violations by the

15 Kishali Pinto-Jayewardena, *Still Seeking Justice in Sri Lanka: Rule of Law, the Criminal Justice System and Commissions of Inquiry since 1977* (Bangkok: International Commission of Jurists, 2010).

16 Pinto-Jayewardena, *Still Seeking justice in Sri Lanka*, pp. 95–99; Anonymous, 'Against the Grain: Pursuing a Transitional Justice Agenda in Postwar Sri Lanka,' *International Journal of Transitional Justice*, Vol. 5, No. 1 (2011), pp. 31–51.

17 John F. Burns, 'Sri Lankans Hear Details of Decade of Slaughter,' *New York Times* (21 May 1995). Special Commissions of Inquiry, *Gazette of the Democratic Socialist Republic of Sri Lanka* (23 September 1994), pt. 2, supp. The underlying legal basis for the commissions can be found in the Commissions of Inquiry Act, *Gazette* (1948), no. 17 and Special Presidential Commissions of Inquiry Act, *Gazette* (1978), law no. 7, amended by Act, *Gazette* (1978), no. 4.

military, police, and other state bodies.[18] In September 1997, the final reports of the three regional commissions of inquiry were handed over to the president, and it was announced that their contents would be made public. In September 1997, the government publicly acknowledged that 16,000 to 17,000 people had disappeared during the crackdown on the JVP and promised to prosecute the perpetrators. One military commander in Jaffna made an unusual public promise to guard against future abuses.[19]

The reports covered political violence by both parties to the conflict around the country dating back to 1988. The commissions apparently inherited some 5,000 complaints from an earlier (1991) commission to inquiry into 'involuntary removal' of persons.[20] A key concern of human rights advocates was that they did not inquire into violence before 1988 or after the Kumaratunga administration came into power.[21] The reports

18 Gaston de Rosayro and Matthew Chance, 'Military Officers to Probe Cases of 'Disappearances,' *South China Morning Post* (16 December 1996), p. 15.

19 'Sri Lanka: Amnesty International Welcomes News that Reports of Commissions Will Be Made Public,' (4 September 1997), available at http://humanrights.tqn.com/b1AIasa372397.htm (accessed 15 May 2012); 'News in Brief: Sri Lanka's Disappeared,' *The Guardian* (4 September 1997), p. 12. John F. Burns, 'Unable to Beat Rebels, Sri Lanka Eases Stance,' *The New York Times* (5 November 1997), p. A3.

20 'Sri Lanka: Human Rights Developments,' *Human Rights Watch World Report 1999*, available at http://www.hrw.org/hrw/worldreport99/asia/srilanka.html (accessed 15 May 2012); Amnesty International, 'Sri Lanka: Time for Truth and Justice,' (April 1995), AI Index 37/04/95, pp. 13–14. This earlier commission spanned the period between January 1991 and January 1993, see Permanent Mission of Sri Lanka, 'Situation Report,' (Colombo, Sri Lanka/Geneva: Permanent Mission, 1993), p. 8, a statement of the human rights situation to the UN HRC.

21 In particular, human rights advocates were concerned about the exclusion of disappearances of Tamils from the east in 1984 to 1988 and disappearances after the government re-took Jaffna in mid-1996. 'Sri Lanka: Human Rights Developments,' available at http://www.hrw.org/hrw/worldreport99/asia/srilanka.html (accessed 15 May 2012); see also Inform, 'Lobby Document: UN Commission on Human Rights, 1995,' (Colombo, Sri Lanka: Inform, 1995), p. 3. The civil rights movement argued that the commissions should examine incidents since 1984; Inform argues that the commissions should examine events since 1979, the year that the Prevention of Terrorism Act entered into force; Civil Rights Movement, 'The Investigation of 'Disappearances' in Sri Lanka,' (Colombo, Sri Lanka: Civil Rights Movement, 1998); see also Imran Vittachi, 'That Time of Terror,' *Sunday Times* (15 March 1998), pp. 1, 10. Author's interview

were extensive, although the degree of investigation varied significantly by region.[22] Although the mandates were the same, some named names, but others did not. Thus, for example, the commission investigating disappearances in the north and east had considerably less information, largely due to the security situation at the time it began its work. In particular, in Jaffna, the LTTE stronghold, the situation was such that the commission could not go to the region and investigate complaints, but instead invited Tamils residing outside the region to come to the capital and file with the commission at the ministry of justice.[23] There was no consistency among reports regarding identification of perpetrators. Although the report for the northern and eastern provinces provided a list of victims and individuals alleged to be perpetrators, the other two commissions did not; the

with the chair of the southern commission and the island-wide commission, Manouri Muttetuwegama, 15 February 1999, Colombo.

22 The reports of the three commissions into disappearances are: *Final Report of the Commission of Inquiry into the Involuntary Removal of Persons in the Central, Northwestern and Uva Provinces, Sessional Paper No. VI* (Colombo, Sri Lanka: Department of Government Printing, 1997); *Final Report of the Commission of Inquiry into the Involuntary Removal or Disappearances of Persons in the Northern and Eastern Provinces, Sessional Paper No. VII* (Colombo, Sri Lanka: Department of Government Printing, 1997); and *Final Report of the Commission of Inquiry into Involuntary Removal or Disappearance of Persons in the Western, Southern, and Sabaragamuwa Provinces, Sessional Paper No. V* (Colombo, Sri Lanka: Department of Government Printing, 1997). Additional reports addressed a number of high-profile political killings, including that of the President's husband. See *Report of the Presidential Commission of Inquiry into the Assassination of Mr. Vijaya Kumaratunga* (Colombo, Sri Lanka: Department of Government Printing, 1996) and *Report of the Special Presidential Commission of Inquiry Regarding the Assassination of the Late Lalith Athulathmudali PC and Connected Events* (Colombo, Sri Lanka: Department of Government Publications, 1997). One observer has said that the manner of setting up the commissions was 'clumsy' and that not enough human rights experts were consulted; in addition many complainants felt let down because before some of the commissions they were not treated with compassion. Author's interview, not for attribution, Colombo, Sri Lanka, 9 February 1999.

23 *Final Report... Northern and Eastern Provinces*, p. 57. Thus, while the commission received 537 complaints it investigated only around 100, of which half were of disappearances of soldiers. To be sure, a significant number of Tamils have left Jaffna, in addition to being 'disappeared'; the population fell from 850,000 to 500,000 between 1981 and 1997, see University Teachers for Human Rights (Jaffna), *Information Bulletin* (24 August 1997), p. 1.

report for the western and southern region explicitly ruled out such a list, citing the need for confidentiality pending further investigations.[24]

Finally, the commissions did not all address the same period of time. Although the mandates for all referred to the investigation of disappearances 'at any time after January 1, 1988',[25] one report addressed disappearances through 1991, another through 1996, and one was less clear about its cut-off.[26] Nonetheless, the initial accusations by human rights advocates that the commissions would be loath to examine any abuses under the Kumaratunga administration appear to have been somewhat excessive, although the record after 1994 is spotty.

On 30 April 1998, the President established a nationwide commission whose mandate was to investigate the reports of disappearances that the previous three commissions had been unable to address or resolve.[27] Again, the commission faced heavy criticism for its limited mandate. Although it did not address complaints before January 1988, it investigated complaints that continued to be received until just prior to the dates when the previous commissions had completed their work. All told, the commissions of inquiry set up under President Kumaratunga identified about 20,000 cases of disappearances, although advocates suggest the number may be several times that.[28]

In 2006, another Presidential Commission of Inquiry (COI) was established by President Rajapaksa to investigate a series of high-profile assassinations and killings. An attendant international monitoring body, the

24 *Final Report... Northern and Eastern Provinces*, pp. 94–97; *Final Report... Western, Southern, and Sabaragamuwa Provinces*, pp. 12, 29. The latter commission submitted a list of those implicated under separate cover to the President. See Mario Gomez, *Emerging Trends in Public Law* (Colombo: Vijitha Yapa Bookshop, 1998), pp. 246–247 and 257–258.

25 The mandate is reprinted in *Final Report... Western, Southern, and Sabaragumawa Provinces*, pp. 179–181.

26 These are, respectively, *Final Report... Western, Southern and Sabaragawuma Provinces*; *Final Report... Northern and Eastern Provinces*; and *Final Report... Central, Northwestern, North Central and Uva Provinces*.

27 'By Her Excellency Chandrika Bandaranaike Kumaratunga, President of the Democratic Socialist Republic of Sri Lanka,' Ref. No. SP/6/N/214/97 (photocopy on file with current author).

28 Human Rights Watch, 'Recurring Nightmare.'

International Independent Group of Eminent Persons, was also created, but this group disbanded after finding that the commission did not meet international standards, given the conflicts of interest of several members, and the limited mandate, which did not provide for investigations into serious violations of international human rights law and international humanitarian law.[29] Critics charge that the creation of both bodies was simply a response to donor pressure rather than a sincere attempt to address abuses.[30] The commission was mandated to investigate sixteen serious incidents of human rights abuses since August 2005 and examine the adequacy of investigations to date and recommend criminal prosecutions be initiated by the Attorney-General if necessary. The COI began operations in 2007 but was not renewed in 2009; at that time it had investigated seven of the incidents, but its final report was not made public.[31] Critics, including the international experts group, raised concerns that the appointment of legal officers by the Attorney-General to assist the commission constituted a conflict of interest, given that the COI would be considering the adequacy of prior investigations by the Attorney-General's office.[32] In 2007, the President of the COI reported that some 2,000 disappearances had been reported to his office, but he also claimed that most had subsequently been 'found', a claim refuted by credible civil society organizations.[33]

The national Human Rights Commission, which was created in 1996 to inquire into complaints regarding procedures of government bodies, faced persistent criticism regarding its strength and independence.[34]

29 *Report of the Secretary-General's Panel of Experts on Accountability in Sri Lanka*, p. 7.

30 Sujith Xavier, 'Sri Lankan Presidential Commission of Inquiry (2007): Did It Amount to a Fair Hearing?' *Mexican Yearbook of International Law*, Vol. 10, (2010), (online version; not properly numbered). International Crisis Group, 'Reconciliation in Sri Lanka,' pp. 5–6.

31 Amnesty International, 'Sri Lanka: Presidential Commission of Inquiry Fails Citizens,' (17 June 2009), at http://www.amnesty.org/en/for-media/press-releases/sri-lanka-presidential-commission-inquiry-fails-citizens-20090617 (accessed 31 May 2011).

32 Xavier, 'Sri Lankan Presidential Commission of Inquiry' (2007).

33 Human Rights Watch, 'Recurring Nightmare.'

34 Parliament of the Democratic Socialist Republic of Sri Lanka, 'Human Rights Commission of Sri Lanka Act, No. 21 of 1996,' *Gazette*, pt. 2 (23 August 1996), p. 4, art. 10.

The commission was criticized by human rights activists from the outset as weak, particularly because it could address only the 'fundamental rights' enshrined in the Sri Lankan constitution, not the far broader rights enshrined in the International Convention on Civil and Political Rights, and only had the power to make recommendations, not to enforce compliance.[35] Its work has continued to be limited by the lack of cooperation by both the government and the LTTE, and in recent years, as discussed below, its independence has been undermined by executive interference.[36]

Prosecutions

A number of prosecutions for human rights abuses by the security forces took place in 1995, with the arrests of eighteen members of the security forces and seven civilian informants; ten of those arrested were members of the Special Task Force (STF), a security body in the police that performed military functions and that had acted with particular impunity. A total of twenty-two STF members were arrested in 1995 but were released on bail and soon after resumed police duties; the case has been delayed several times by the failure of the prosecution to appear at court proceedings.[37]

For a brief history of the bill, see Mario Gomez, 'Sri Lanka's New Human Rights Commission,' *Rights Link*, Vol. 1, No. 1 (1997), p. 5; Mario Gomez, 'The Sri Lankan Human Rights Commission,' *Law and Society Trust Review*, Vol. 9, No. 13 (1998), p. 31; Mario Gomez, 'Sri Lanka's New Human Rights Commission,' *Human Rights Quarterly*, Vol. 20 , No. 2 (1998), pp. 281–302.

35 Author's interview with Manouri Muttetuwegama, chair of the island-wide commission and of the previous southern commission, 15 February 1999, Colombo, Sri Lanka.

36 Sri Lanka Democracy Forum, 'Submission to the Universal Periodic Review of Sri Lanka.'

37 Amnesty International, 'Sri Lanka: Amnesty International Welcomes Government Action to Stop Death Squad Activities,' (1 September 1995), AI Index ASA 37/17/95, reports that the head of the STF was rumoured to have been suspended by the president; U.S. Department of State, *Sri Lanka Country Report on Human Rights Practices for 1997*, available at http://www.state.gov/www/global/human_rights/1997_hrp_report/srilanka.htm, p. 4 (accessed 15 May 2012).

Further prosecutions for abuses in the north against Tamils took place in 1998 and 1999. In one key case, six soldiers and a reserve police officer were convicted and sentenced to be executed for killings committed in September 1996.[38] In other cases of abuses involving the security forces, however, many of those charged remained free and in some cases remained on active duty. Five senior police officers were forced to go on leave in connection with charges of torture and extrajudicial execution at a government detention center at the Batalanda Housing Estate.[39] In February 1999, in a case involving the disappearance of thirty-two schoolboys in Embilipitiya, seven of the nine persons accused, all but one security personnel, were convicted and sentenced to about ten years in prison.[40] Although these prosecutions marked a break with earlier patterns of impunity, they were quite limited compared to the scope of abuses.[41] NGOs report continuing and extensive police involvement in abductions, for which impunity largely reigns. From 2001 onwards, most cases involving abuse by the security forces continued from year

38 'Judge's Absence Aborts Chemmani Hearing,' (26 March 1999), available at http://www.tamilnet.com/ (accessed 15 May 2012).

39 Pinto-Jayewardena, *Still Seeking Justice in Sri Lanka*; Civil Rights Movement of Sri Lanka, 'The Alleged Mass Burials at Chemmany in the North,' (Colombo, Sri Lanka: Civil Rights Movement, 1998). 'Executions Ordered for Rights Abuses,' *Chicago Tribune* (4 July 1998), p. 4. This was the disappearance of a schoolgirl, Krishanthy Kumaraswamy, and family members and a neighbour who sought to find her. 'Sri Lanka: Human Rights Developments,' available at http://www.hrw.org/hrw/worldreport99/asia/srilanka.html (accessed 15 May 2012). It should be noted that reports are inconsistent regarding the number of indicted and convicted: see V. Varathasuntharam, 'Nine Soldiers Indicted on Abduction and Murder Charges,' *The Island* (3 July 1997), and Sharmini Fernando, 'Bitter Victory: Krishanthi Kumaraswamy, The Women's Vigil, and the Verdict,' *Options*, No. 14 (1998), p. 17.

40 P.D.A.S. Gunasekera, 'Ten Years RI for Seven Accused, Two Acquitted,' *Daily News* (11 February 1999), pp. 1, 20; J. Antony, 'Seven Accused Including Ex-Principal Sentenced to 10 Years,' *The Island* (11 February 1999), p. 1. See also Gunasekera, 'Witness Describes How Torture Instrument Was Used,' *Daily News* (11 June 1996); and Gunasekera, 'First Accused Told Her that a Few Children Should Be Kidnapped, Witness Days,' *Daily News* (26 February 1996); 'Tragedy, Trauma and Finally Justice at Embilitpitiya,' *Daily News* (17 February 1999), p. 3.

41 Wasana Punyasena, 'The Facade of Accountability: Disappearances in Sri Lanka,' *Boston College Third World Law Journal*, Vol. 23, Issue 1 (2003), pp. 115–158.

to year without proceedings. However, in 2003 there were five persons sentenced to death for the extrajudicial killings of twenty-seven Tamil men in the Bindunuwema camp; twenty-three others were acquitted and the sentences of those convicted were commuted; in the same year a small number of torture victims were able to claim civil compensation. In 2004 there were two convictions for torture.[42] In 2005, convictions were secured for a number of individuals accused of murdering a judge and his bodyguards, and four defendants were acquitted in the aforementioned killings in the Bindunuwema camp. Several cases against police officers did not proceed, and the officers remained on duty. Outstanding prosecutions remained pending in 2006.[43] Although in 2007 the police inspector general acknowledged that thirty-one police officers had been arrested for human rights violations, details of dates, abuses, and subsequent proceedings were not made available.[44]

Apology

The current government has claimed to want reconciliation, while blocking all attempts at investigation and failing to acknowledge its own abuses. However, this does not mean that at some point more genuine reconciliation efforts through apologies and other measures would be impossible. In 2002 and 2004, former president Kumaratunga offered apologies for the anti-Tamil riots of 1983, which helped to spark the war, and called for reconciliation, referring to the riots as 'one of the most shameful crimes

42 *U.S. Department of State Country Reports on Human Rights Practices 2003* (25 February 2004) at http://www.state.gov. In 2004, there were no reported indictments, investigations, or prosecutions of security force personnel; see *U.S. Department of State Country Reports on Human Rights Practices 2004* (28 February 2005) at http://www.state.gov (accessed 16 June 2011).

43 *U.S. Department of State Country Reports on Human Rights Practices 2005* (8 March 2006) and *U.S. Department of State Country Reports on Human Rights Practices 2006* (6 March 2007) at http://www.state.gov (accessed 16 June 2011).

44 Human Rights Watch, 'Recurring Nightmare.'

ever perpetrated on this nation'.[45] The 2004 apology was accompanied by the offer of compensation, which was rejected by the LTTE and vanished in the return to conflict.[46]

Conflict, Accountability, and Rule of Law in Decline

Despite the range of accountability measures which occurred in the 1990s, it would be incorrect to say that Sri Lanka has experienced transitional or post-conflict justice – there was no regime change other than democratic electoral change of leadership, nor had the conflict ended when these measures were undertaken. It is notable, however, that these measures occurred alongside progressive degradation of human rights and rule of law. Even as the regime reinitiated negotiations with the LTTE and opened investigations and a number of trials, it engaged in a two-track strategy which also escalated the conflict, with a sharp rise in disappearances in 1996 and 1997 in Jaffna as a result of increased military operations.[47] President Kumaratunga consolidated greater power through the imposition of emergency regulations and the Prevention of Terrorism Act, which involved roadblocks and routine harassment and imprisonment of citizens, as well as extrajudicial killing, torture, and disappearance of civilians, particularly Tamils.[48] In 2003, Kumaratunga sparked a cabinet crisis by divesting the Information, Interior, and Defence ministers of their powers. Diplomatic efforts by both India and the United States to resolve the crisis failed, and the President dissolved

45 Krishan Francis, 'Sri Lankan President Regrets Anti-Tamil Riots that Started Civil War,' *Associated Press* (23 July 2004).

46 International Crisis Group, 'Reconciliation in Sri Lanka,' p. 5.

47 Human Rights Watch, 'Recurring Nightmare.'

48 Jayewardena, *Still Seeking Justice in Sri Lanka*, pp. 12–41; Kishali Pinto-Jayewardena, *The Rule of Law in Decline: Study on Prevalence, Determinants, and Causes of Torture and Other Forms of Cruel, Inhuman, or Degrading Treatment or Punishment in Sri Lanka* (Copenhagen: Rehabilitation and Research Centre for Torture Victims, 2009); Chandra Lekha Sriram, *Confronting Past Human Rights Violations* (London: Frank Cass, 2004), pp. 171–201.

Parliament. She called new elections in April 2004 which brought her party back to power.

Disappearances in particular rose sharply after 2005, with Human Rights Watch reporting 1,500 civilian disappearances from 2005 to 2007 alone.[49] The resumption of open hostilities in 2006 was accompanied by widespread attacks on civilians by both the government and the LTTE, and with the government's support of the Karuna faction, which splintered from the LTTE, attacks on civilians were particularly brutal.[50] Despite allegations of widespread torture, prosecutions for abuses by the security forces appear to have ended, there is no independent system to monitor or address violations, and thus security forces enjoy impunity.[51] The Human Rights Commission and the National Police Commission, two bodies which are ostensibly autonomous and which would provide oversight, have had their independence undermined by unconstitutional moves by President Kumaratunga, and then President Rajapakse, to directly appoint commissioners.[52] Despite receiving extensive communications, the Human Rights Commission ceased issuing public reports in 2006.[53] In 2006, two senior members of the Judicial Service Commission, responsible for judges of the high court, resigned 'as a matter of conscience' while independent regional NGO the Asian Human Rights Commission denounced executive interference in the judiciary and independent commissions.[54] Following an attempted assassination of the

49 Human Rights Watch, 'Recurring Nightmare: State Responsibility for "Disappearances" and Abductions in Sri Lanka,' (27 August 2008) at http://www.hrw.org (accessed 15 May 2012).

50 Human Rights Watch, 'Recurring Nightmare.' Karuna has since been made a government minister.

51 Human Rights Watch, 'Recurring Nightmare.'

52 Human Rights Watch, 'Recurring Nightmare.'

53 Human Rights Watch, 'Recurring Nightmare.'

54 Asian Human Rights Commission, 'Sri Lanka: Two Senior Judges Quit the Judicial Service Commission as a Matter of Conscience,' (3 February 2006), at http://www.humanrights.asia/news/ahrc-news/ (accessed 16 June 2011); Asian Human Rights Commission, 'SRI LANKA: Sixth Day of Mourning Against Executive Interference into the Judiciary and Other Independent Institutions,' (3 June 2006), at http://www.humanrights.asia/news/ahrc-news/ (accessed 16 June 2011).

minister of defence in 2006, emergency regulations were strengthened, allowing arrest without warrant and detention of civilians without charge for up to twelve months.[55] The monitoring committee set up in 2007 on Abductions and Disappearances has not reported on its findings, and its head has resisted discussions of disappearances in the country, claiming that Sri Lanka was unfairly being singled out. President Rajapakse has referred to disappearance figures as inaccurate and 'just numbers', claiming that these are simply people who have 'gone [on] their honeymoon without the knowledge of their household.'[56] The country has also failed to implement recommendations of the UN Human Rights Committee or of the Committee Against Torture, drawing further criticism.[57] Widespread impunity for police torture was cited by some as an indicator of the decline of the rule of law.[58]

In October 2010, the eighteenth Amendment to the Constitution was passed, eliminating restrictions on term limits of the President and replacing a constitutional council with a parliamentary council over which the president would exercise control. The constitutional council's powers, over independent commissions on bribery, police, elections, and the judiciary, were transferred to the executive presidency. This further weakened the independence of the Human Rights Commission, to which Rajapakse appointed a former inspector general of the police and a former government analyst in 2011.[59]

55 United States Department of State, *U.S. Department of State Human Rights Country Reports Sri Lanka 2006* at www.state.gov (accessed 15 May 2012).

56 Human Rights Watch, 'Recurring Nightmare.'

57 Human Rights Solidarity, 'UNHR Council/Sri Lanka: Refusing to Implement Human Rights Committee Recommendations,' (2006), at http://www.hrsolidarity.net/ (accessed 16 June 2011).

58 Sofie Rordam, 'SRI LANKA: Police Torture as an Indicator of the Constitutional Degradation of the Rule of Law,' (12 January 2011), at http://www.humanrights.asia/news/ahrc-news/ (accessed 16 June 2011).

59 Ashley LS Perera, '18th Amendment to the Constitution: A Critique,' *Sri Lanka Guardian*, (11 October 2010), at http://www.srilankaguardian.org (accessed 16 June 2011); Asian Human Rights Commission, 'SRI LANKA: Friday Forum Deeply Concerned about Recent Appointments to Human Rights Commission,' (15 June 2011), at http://www.humanrights.asia/news (accessed 16 June 2011); Joseph Perera, 'Sri Lanka

Abuses in the Final Stages of Conflict

Ongoing abuses by the government, including civilian killings, enforced disappearances, and abuses of antiterrorism and emergency legislation, intensified in the final stages of the conflict, from January to May 2009, as did abuses by the LTTE. The government was responsible for shelling hospitals filled with civilian victims, increased disappearances, and extra-judicial executions of civilians and of combatants seeking to surrender, and for blocking humanitarian assistance to civilians in the war zone, as well as trapping civilians in detention camps in very poor conditions, as extensively documented by several respected international NGOs, the U.S. and UK governments, and eventually a UN panel.[60] The UN expert report suggested that at as many as 40,000 civilians had been killed in the final stages of the conflict.[61] The International Crisis Group, an international NGO which ordinarily focuses solely upon conflict and its resolution, issued its first-ever report detailing alleged war crimes in the country and suggesting that the government's brutal approach to concluding the conflict was viewed as the 'Sri Lankan solution' by other governments engaged in protracted armed conflicts.[62] This 'solution' involves the invocation of a terrorist threat as a justification for a brutal military crackdown and apparent indifference to the consequences for the civilian population, notwithstanding international criticism.

Jettisons Constitutional Council Altogether,' *Asian Tribune* (17 June 2010), at http://www.asiantribune.com (accessed 16 June 2011).

60 Human Rights Watch, 'Uncovering Sri Lanka's War Crimes,' (21 January 2010), at http://www.hrw.org (accessed 28 February 2011); International Crisis Group, 'War Crimes in Sri Lanka,' *Asia Report No. 191*, (17 May 2010), at http://www.crisisgroup.org (accessed 28 February 2011); United States Department of State, *Report to Congress on Incidents During the Recent Conflict in Sri Lanka*, (2009), at http://www.state.gov (accessed 28 February 2011); UK House of Commons Library, 'War and Peace in Sri Lanka,' *Research Paper 09/51* (5 June 2009).

61 *Report of the Secretary-General's Panel of Experts on Accountability in Sri Lanka* (31 March 2011), p. 41.

62 International Crisis Group, 'War Crimes in Sri Lanka,' *Asia Report No. 191* (17 May 2010), at http://www.crisisgroup.org (accessed 15 January 2011).

These abuses earned criticism from UN Special Rapporteur on Extra-judicial Killings Philip Alston, particularly in relation to a leaked video showing Sri Lankan soldiers executing unarmed civilians. He called for the opening of an investigation into war crimes, prompting accusations from the government that he was biased.[63] Sri Lanka was penalized for abuses with the loss of its seat on the UN Human Rights Council in 2008.[64] However, this condemnation softened only one year later. Notwithstanding evidence of widespread abuses in the final stages of the conflict, the UN Human Rights Council, rather than condemning these or even expressing concern, passed a resolution on 27 May 2009 commending the government and ignoring widespread international calls for investigation into abuses.[65] President Rajapakse has alternately rejected allegations that there have been widespread disappearances or blamed the LTTE.[66]

The Lessons Learnt and Reconciliation Commission

In May 2009, President Rajapaksa promised that the government would investigate allegations of war crimes. The government created a domestic commission of inquiry, the Lessons Learnt and Reconciliation

63 'Deeming Sri Lanka Execution Video Authentic, UN Expert Calls for War Crimes Probe,' *UN News Centre* (7 January 2010), at http://www.un.org/apps/news/story.asp?NewsID=33423 (accessed 15 May 2012).

64 Basil Fernando, 'UN Human Rights Council Drops Sri Lanka,' *UPI Asia* (23 May 2008), at http://www.upiasia.com (accessed 28 February 2011); Sri Lanka Democracy Forum, 'Submission to the Universal Periodic Review of Sri Lanka,' (9 February 2008), at http://www.srilankademocracy.org (accessed 28 February 2011).

65 'Full Text of Resolution Adopted by the UN Human Rights Council' reprinted in the *Sunday Times* (Sri Lanka) (28 May 2009), at http://sundaytimes.lk (accessed 28 February 2011); Human Rights Watch, 'Sri Lanka: UN Rights Council Fails Victims,' (27 May 2009), at http://www.hrw.org (accessed 11 May 2011); Michael Binyon, 'A Disgraceful Vote which Discredits the UN Human Rights Council,' *The Times* (28 May 2009), at http://www.timesonline.co.uk (accessed 28 February 2011). Arguably, the state has been able to resist calls for accountability because pressure from traditional donors has been muted, and from newer donors nonexistent. Anonymous, 'Against the Grain: Pursuing a Transitional Justice Agenda in Sri Lanka,' *International Journal of Transitional Justice*, Vol. 5, No. 1 (2011), pp. 46–47.

66 Human Rights Watch, 'Recurring Nightmare.'

Commission (LLRC), in May 2010, partly in response to demands for accountability. Its mandate was to report on events between 21 February 2002 and 19 May 2009 and to identify those responsible for the breakdown of the 2002 ceasefire as well as a method for reparations. The LLRC was also tasked with identifying administrative and legislative measures needed to prevent recurrence of conflict and to promote national unity and reconciliation. According to the UN commission of experts, the LLRC did not meet international standards for an accountability process. Specifically, the UN commission found that the LLRC was compromised by conflicts of interest of various members, a failure to engage in what it termed 'genuine truth-telling' about abuses which took place in the final stages of the conflict and failure to engage in proper investigation of abuses by both sides of the conflict.[67]

Human rights advocates have strongly criticized the LLRC because it was not mandated to address and not interested in addressing accountability for serious abuses such as war crimes or crimes against humanity. Its mandate was to focus on the root causes of conflict and methods for promoting reconciliation only. The commission had no mandate to investigate allegations of international humanitarian law, nor to impose accountability. Further, the commission came under severe criticism as being subject to government interference and therefore not independent.[68] Its chair, C.R. de Silva, was the Attorney General under Rajapaksa, and was charged with implementing the Prevention of Terrorism Act and accused of tolerating and covering up police abuses. Many who sought to testify before the commission claimed that the commissioners appeared unsympathetic and uninterested, and witnesses were subject to threats and intimidation.[69]

67 *Report of the Secretary-General's Panel of Experts on Accountability in Sri Lanka*, pp. v; 'The Lessons Learnt and Reconciliation Commission' at http://www.llrc.lk (accessed 1 May 2011).

68 'Sri Lankan War Inquiry Commission Opens Amid Criticism,' *BBC News* (11 August 2010), at http://www.bbc.co.uk (accessed 21 April 2011); Human Rights Watch, 'Sri Lanka: New Evidence of Wartime Abuses,' (20 May 2010), at http://www.hrw.org (accessed 21 April 2011).

69 International Crisis Group, 'Reconciliation in Sri Lanka', pp. 24–25.

The significant turnout of individuals wishing to testify amongst the affected populations even at the flawed LLRC indicates a demand for an accounting of abuses and for accountability. Despite the LLRC's many shortcomings, large numbers of civilians did present testimony across the country, and thousands in former conflict areas in the north and east presented detailed testimony about abuses. According to Amnesty International, the commission was not prepared for the turnout, lacking adequate facilities and Tamil translation. Further, despite some reports of threats to witnesses, the commission's mandate did not include witness protection.[70]

In its hearings, which were held around the country and concluded in January 2011, the LLRC did not investigate allegations of violations of international humanitarian law; hearings in Colombo largely included government officials and others who focused exclusively on the limited topics of the mandate – the causes of conflict and modes of reconciliation. When the commission was presented with testimony of violations such as disappearances in the north, it did not investigate them further. The recommendations of the commission have offered what one expert at Amnesty International terms 'problem solving' proposals, such as technical reforms to trace the disappeared, rather than to investigate abuses or punish perpetrators.[71] An expert at the International Center for Transitional Justice characterized the commission as simply another in a long line of commissions of inquiry in Sri Lanka and elsewhere, ostensibly designed to reach the truth about past abuses, which in operation would do the reverse.[72] The report of the commission was released in mid-December 2011, amid criticism that it had sought to minimize government responsibility, although its report did identify extensive harm to civilians whom it categorized as caught in the crossfire. Independent international

70 Yolanda Foster, 'LLRC is Not a Credible Domestic Process of Accountability,' *LankaNewsWeb* (16 March 2011) at http://www.sangam.org (accessed 25 March 2011).

71 Yolanda Foster, 'LLRC is Not a Credible Domestic Process of Accountability,' *LankaNewsWeb* (16 March 2011) at http://www.sangam.org (accessed 25 March 2011).

72 Vasuki Nesiah, 'Unpacking the Truth,' (16 August 2009), at http://www.ictj.org (accessed 21 April 2011).

observers raised concerns that the report failed to apply international humanitarian law standards and relied upon testimony of government officials and of Tamil doctors detained under terrorism legislation.[73]

Options for Accountability outside Sri Lanka

The UN Panel on Sri Lanka

In June 2010, following international calls for accountability, the United Nations convened a panel of experts to investigate alleged violations of international human rights and humanitarian law in the final stages of the conflict.[74] It began work formally on 16 September, delivering its report on 12 April 2011 to the UN Secretary-General. The government of Sri Lanka sought at first to prevent the public dissemination of the report, claiming its release would damage reconciliation, and then proceeded to denigrate it, referring to the panel as a non-panel and denouncing the report as flawed and biased.[75]

The final report of the panel of experts, which was denied access to the country, found 'credible evidence' of serious violations of international humanitarian and international human rights law.[76] The report found

73 International Crisis Group, 'Statement on the Report of Sri Lanka's Lessons Learnt and Reconciliation Commission,' (22 December 2011), at http://www.crisisgroup.org/en/publication-type/media-releases/2011/asia/statement-on-the-report-of-sri-lanka-s-lessons-learnt-and-reconciliation-commission.aspx; Human Rights Watch, 'Sri Lanka: Report Fails to Advance Accountability,' (16 December 2011) at http://www.hrw.org/news/2011/12/16/sri-lanka-report-fails-advance-accountability (accessed 15 May 2012).

74 Secretary-General's Panel of Experts on Sri Lanka, call for submissions (18 October 2010), at http://www.un.org, (accessed 15 May 2012); 'Secretary-General's Panel of Experts on Sri Lanka,' at http://www.un.org/en/rights/srilanka.shtml (accessed 11 May 2011).

75 'Sri Lanka Asks UN Not to Publish War Crimes Report,' *Agence France Press* (21 April 2011) at http://www.afp.com/en/home/ (accessed 21 April 2011); 'Leaked UN Report Urges Sri Lanka War Crimes Probe,' *Agence France Press* (21 April 2011) at http://www.afp.com/en/home/ (accessed 21 April 2011); Miriam Krule, 'Sri Lankan Government Retaliates before UN War Crimes Report,' (14 April 2011), at http://www.theatlantic.com (accessed 11 May 2011).

76 *Report of the Secretary-General's Panel of Experts on Accountability in Sri Lanka* (31 March 2011); 'Ban's Sri Lanka War Crimes Panel Stuck in New York,' *The Sunday*

that tens of thousands of people had died between January and May 2009 during the final government offensive. The report identifies violations by both the government and the LTTE and indicates that if the allegations were proven, both government officials and LTTE leaders could face criminal charges. It also criticizes the domestic commission of inquiry as flawed and calls for an international mechanism.

Internationalized Criminal Justice?

Following the ICG report, there have been repeated calls for war crimes trials for Sri Lanka, including the creation of an ad hoc international criminal tribunal. Sri Lanka is not a state party to the International Criminal Court (ICC) Statute and thus would not be subject to the jurisdiction of that court in the absence of a referral by the United Nations Security Council. The UN High Commissioner for Human Rights, Navanethem Pillay, called for war crimes trials in May 2011, and was condemned by the Sri Lankan government, while at the UN Human Rights Council, Pakistan, China, Russia and others sought to halt debate about war crimes.[77] Given the resistance of two permanent, veto-wielding members of the UN Security Council to even discussing government abuses at the Human Rights Council, it is extremely unlikely that either would permit a referral to the ICC.[78] This would not of course bar the possibility of a specialized international tribunal, such as those created for Rwanda and the former Yugoslavia, or even a hybrid body, such as that created for Sierra Leone, Cambodia, and other countries, although again political will could prove problematic.[79] The prospects for international criminal

Times (Sri Lanka) (23 January 2011), at http://sundaytimes.lk (accessed 28 February 2011).

77 Tamilnet, 'UN Commissioner's Call for War-Crimes Prove Jolts Colombo,' (31 May 2011) at http://www.tamilnet.com (accessed 31 May 2011).

78 Eric Michael Liddick and John T. Gagnon, II, in 'Striving for Peace and Reconciliation in Sri Lanka: A Creative Solution to Conflict,' *War Crimes, Genocide, and Crimes Against Humanity*, Vol. 3 (2009), pp. 39–88, call for the involvement of the International Criminal Court.

79 Tamilnet, 'Time for International Criminal Tribunal on Sri Lanka,' (7 March 2010) at http://www.tamilnet.com (accessed 31 May 2011).

justice appear limited given the resistance of the government and the protection of it by powerful states such as Russia and China and the relatively limited pressure applied by the United States, the European Union, or Japan.[80]

Criminal accountability is not the only option to address abuses in Sri Lanka. Another option is civil accountability under the Alien Tort Claims Act in the United States. Such accountability has been imposed since 1980 for violations of the law of nations committed by foreigners outside the United States around the world.[81] In September 2011, a civil case was filed in a federal district court in New York under the Alien Tort Claims Act and Torture Victims Protection Act, claiming that General Shavendra Silva, the acting permanent representative of Sri Lanka to the United Nations, was responsible for torture and other crimes as a commander of the fifty-eighth division of the army in the final stages of the conflict.[82]

Implications

Clearly, at this point in time, with a government apparently uninterested in accountability and without significant pressure from powerful states, the prospects for a thorough accounting, whether through trials or a full and genuine commission of inquiry, domestically or at a formal international level, are slim. The consolidation of power in the hands of the Rajapaksa family, including through the eighteenth amendment to the

80 Charu Lata Hogg, 'Sri Lanka: Prospects for Reform and Reconciliation,' Chatham House Asia Programme Paper ASP PP 2011/06 (October 2011).

81 Chandra Lekha Sriram, *Globalizing Justice for Mass Atrocities: A Revolution in Accountability* (London: Routledge, 2005).

82 'Lawsuit Filed against Sri Lankan Army General,' (23 September 2011), at http://www.warwithoutwitness.com accessed 15 May 2012; 'Civil Lawsuit Filed against Major General Shavendra Silva,' *BBC Sinhala* (24 September 2011), at http://www.bbc.co.uk; *Vasali Devi and Seetharam Sivam v. Shavendra Silva*, U.S. District Court for the Southern District of New York; 'First Complaint for Torture, Cruel, Inhuman, Degrading Treatment, Intentional Infliction of Emotional Distress, Negligence, and Wrongful Death,' at http://www.warwithoutwitness.com (accessed 15 May 2012).

constitution, make accountability unlikely in the near term.[83] However there is clearly a demand for some form of justice in Sri Lanka, emanating from within the country as well as from international NGOs and the United Nations. Certainly the turnout to testify at the LLRC illustrates the demand, if not for legal justice, at least to be heard, on the part of many in the population, including in the north.

Perhaps the most troubling implication is for post-conflict justice more generally, as the experience of Sri Lanka illustrates the possibility that a democratic country which has held several trials and numerous commissions of inquiry for past abuses may simultaneously experience a decline in the quality of rule of law driven by executive consolidation of power. For scholars and practitioners who have sought to link accountability and rule of law in conflict-affected countries, the implications seem unfortunately evident: failures of the rule of law and constitutional reforms centralizing power may emerge alongside or despite accountability measures including both trials and commissions of inquiry, and at the same time that such consolidation of power may contribute to future constraints upon accountability, even in a country with a reasonably longstanding history of democratic rule, such as Sri Lanka. The experience of Sri Lanka suggests that, rather than promote human rights and democracy in the future, past accountability measures may do little to constrain state violence, and that the state may engage in serious international crimes well after those past accountability measures and robustly resist demands for genuine accountability for those crimes. The prospects for true peace and reconciliation in the country are, to say the least, not heartening. In the absence of a thorough domestic investigation, the argument for an international investigative mechanism, as recommended by the UN panel of experts, the International Crisis Group, and Human Rights Watch, seems the most viable next step, although prospects for such a mechanism are, at the time of this writing, unclear.[84]

83 International Crisis Group, 'Reconciliation in Sri Lanka,' p. 10.
84 Human Rights Watch, 'Sri Lanka: Report Fails to Advance Accountability.'

3 Transitional Justice Delayed in Aceh, Indonesia

Edward Aspinall and Fajran Zain

FOR ALMOST THIRTY YEARS, BETWEEN 1976 AND 2005, AN intermittent but often bitter civil war was waged in the province of Aceh, on Indonesia's northwestern periphery. The Free Aceh Movement (Gerakan Aceh Merdeka, GAM) strove to win Aceh's independence, but the Indonesian military (Tentara Nasional Indonesia, TNI) fought to prevent this outcome at all costs. In the process, violent abuses were committed on both sides, with GAM fighters trying to purge the province of Javanese and retaliating against 'traitors' who betrayed the cause, and the TNI engaging in a protracted dirty war in which many thousands of civilians fell victim to arbitrary detention, torture, extrajudicial killing and other forms of abuse.

As time passed, more and more actors began to define the conflict in human rights terms. This began in the early 1990s, when international human rights organisations first began to document reports of large-scale abuses being conducted as part of the military's so-called Military Operations Zone (*Daerah Operasi Militer*, DOM) actions.[1] After the collapse of the Suharto regime in 1998, there was a brief period of political opening in Aceh, and an array of new local activist human rights organisations sprang into being. Collaborating with Jakarta-based and international

1 Asia Watch, *Indonesia: Human Rights Abuses in Aceh* (New York: Asia Watch, 1990); Asia Watch, *Indonesia: Continuing Human Rights Violations in Aceh* (New York: Asia Watch, 1991); Amnesty International, '"Shock Therapy": Restoring Order in Aceh', 1989–1993 (London: International Secretariat, Amnesty International, 1993).

groups, they campaigned to expose military abuses in the province and to have the perpetrators punished. In the first years of Indonesia's *Reformasi* period, there were also some official investigations of past abuses, and even the first halting steps toward prosecution of military perpetrators. At the same time, a new generation of Acehnese nationalists began to define Aceh's struggle for self-determination in human rights terms, arguing that Indonesian repression justified independence, an argument that was also taken up by GAM.[2] Soon, however, such arguments were again overshadowed by a return to full-scale conflict which greatly narrowed the space for humanitarian and civil society activity and led to the return of many of the worst features of the dirty war. In 2003 the Indonesian government declared a state of 'military emergency' in Aceh, announcing that it wished to destroy GAM once and for all. This declaration became the cover for forced evacuations of villages and other harsh actions, many of which were associated with high levels of abuse against civilians.[3]

It is therefore not surprising that when a peace deal was eventually negotiated for Aceh, in Helsinki in 2005, transitional justice mechanisms featured prominently. The Helsinki Memorandum of Understanding (MoU), signed by GAM and the Indonesian Government on 15 August 2005, featured four classic elements of transitional justice: security sector reform, reparations, a truth and reconciliation commission, and a human rights court (and thus at least the possibility of prosecutions). Hopes were high among human rights activists in Aceh that the territory would begin the long-delayed process of confronting its history of abuses against civilians.

Though they are often conflated, because they frequently run together in practice, it is at least possible to conceptually distinguish between transitional justice mechanisms that are implemented in response to

2 Edward Aspinall, *Islam and Nation: Separatist Rebellion in Aceh, Indonesia* (Stanford: Stanford University Press, 2009), pp. 121–150.

3 Human Rights Watch, 'Aceh under Martial Law: Inside the Secret War', (2003), at http://hrw.org/reports/2003/indonesia1203/indonesia1203.pdf.

democratic transitions and those that occur as a part of efforts to make peace after protracted civil conflict. In democratisation cases, the human rights abuses at issue were typically perpetrated in the name of defending a society-wide authoritarian regime, and are therefore at least potentially directly relevant to all citizens. In civil war cases, especially if the conflict occurred in a small part of the country concerned, many citizens and political actors may not feel directly implicated in the abuses that occurred there, and even do not feel that they are relevant to their own experiences and interests. Both forms of transitional justice can pose particular challenges: the former can pose elemental threats to powerful political actors and be seen to threaten to derail democratic transition or consolidation; in the latter case sometimes simple indifference of key actors is the major challenge.

Viewed through this lens, Aceh faces a double burden: it has experienced both forms of transitional justice, in two separate phases. The first halting efforts to achieve justice in response to past human rights abuses were taken after 1998 as part of the democratic transition then occurring throughout Indonesia. The post-2005 and more comprehensive transitional justice efforts were a purposeful attempt to deal with Aceh's particular experiences of violence. Though these later efforts were coloured by the experiences of Indonesia's democratic transition, they potentially would deal with many abuses that occurred after the democratic transition on a national level had already taken place. As a result, transitional justice in Aceh has arguably experienced the worst aspects of both forms of transitional justice with the first round involving the political challenges of confronting a powerful military amidst an uncertain democratic transition, and the later efforts dealing with the legacies of conflict in a remote province that seemed far from the main currents of national political life, and in which much of the national political class and wider public had lost interest. To make matters even worse the Aceh-focused efforts after 2005 came as the impetus was running out of efforts at the national level to deal with the legacy of past human rights crimes committed in the name of defending the authoritarian regime.

In this chapter, we analyse progress in the key elements of Aceh's transitional justice agenda, noting that in most cases the process stalled within a couple of years of implementation, and some key initiatives have failed to get off the ground altogether. Our main focus is on the Aceh-specific measures that were taken as part of the peace process initiated by the 2005 Helsinki MoU. Since that time, the peace process and the Helsinki MoU have come to provide both the legal and the discursive framework in which almost all discussion of transitional justice occurs in Aceh. In this context, inaction has been especially great in areas where actors are expected to examine responsibility for past abuses. There has been more progress in areas where it is possible to take action without delving into the past, notably in security sector reform and reparations. The Truth and Reconciliation Commission, however, has failed to materialise so far, while there is virtually no prospect of prosecutions for past abuses. Although administrative problems have played their part in delaying the transitional justice agenda, we also point to underlying reluctance on the part of both Acehnese and national governments – where former perpetrators of abuses continue to be important actors or veto-players – to seriously confront the past. As a result, the initiative to pursue justice has to a large extent shifted to former victims and civil society actors themselves. Even among victims, however, views are mixed on the desirability of retributive measures vis-à-vis reconciliation, while the civil society organizations have found they have relatively limited political clout in post-conflict Aceh.

Background: Peace and the Transformation of Aceh

The inclusion of transitional justice mechanisms in the Helsinki peace accord was surprisingly uncontroversial. Indeed, as one of us has elsewhere observed,[4] few of the individuals directly involved in the 2005

4 Edward Aspinall, 'Peace without Justice. The Helsinki Peace Process in Aceh', (Geneva: Centre for Humanitarian Dialogue, 2008), p. 18.

Transitional Justice Mechanisms in the Memorandum of Understanding between GAM and the Government of Indonesia (GoI)

- point 2.2: 'A Human Rights Court will be established for Aceh'
- point 2.3: 'A Commission for Truth and Reconciliation will be established for Aceh by the Indonesian Commission of Truth and Reconciliation with the task of formulating and determining reconciliation measures'
- point 3.1.1: 'GoI will, in accordance with constitutional procedures, grant amnesty to all persons who have participated in GAM activities as soon as possible and not later than within 15 days of the signature of this MoU'. Point 3.1.2 held that 'political prisoners and detainees held due to the conflict' should be released within the same time frame
- point 3.2.5.c: 'All civilians who have suffered a demonstrable loss due to the conflict will receive an allocation of suitable farming land, employment or, in the case of incapacity to work, adequate social security from the authorities of Aceh'

* Several other provisions are relevant to the issue of security sector reform, including one which requires the GoI to adhere to UN covenants on civil and political rights and on economic, social and cultural rights (point 2.1), two which suggest a division between police and military responsibilities ('internal law and order' (4.10) and 'external defence' (4.11), respectively), and another which requires military personnel who commit civilian crimes to be tried in civil courts (1.4.5).

peace talks can clearly recollect how human rights and justice issues were dealt with in the negotiations, suggesting that they were simply less prominent and controversial than many of the thornier issues being discussed by the negotiators (such as the part to be played by local political parties in post-conflict Aceh). Early on in the talks, some GAM negotiators apparently spoke extensively about military abuses and called for international investigations of them. These approaches were effectively defused by Martti Ahtisaari, the former president of Finland and chief mediator, who called on the participants to focus on the future, not the past, and by the main Indonesian negotiators who reassured their GAM counterparts that Indonesia was now a democratic country and had already established transitional justice mechanisms of its own, including a new framework of human rights courts and a Truth and Reconciliation Commission. As a result, by the time of the final rounds of negotiations, these issues were so uncontroversial that the negotiators had even forgotten to include the human rights court in the text of the agreement, and it was President Ahtisaari who, during the final drafting, insisted on its inclusion.[5]

Before we look at the implementation of various elements of the transitional justice agenda in greater detail, it is important to review two important aspects of the broader context.

First is the broader Indonesian transitional justice context. The transition from war to peace in Aceh is embedded in a larger setting of transition from authoritarian rule to democracy in Indonesia. As part of this democratic transition, especially early on (i.e. 1998 to 2001) a host of initiatives were taken and institutions set up to deal with past human rights abuses and to ensure that they would not be repeated in the future. There were, for example, several investigations into past gross human rights abuses and even trials of their perpetrators. However, and accounting for much of the tension surrounding transitional justice issues in Aceh, Indonesia's transitional justice institutions have been largely ineffective, especially in dealing with gross abuses. For instance, no senior military officer has been successfully prosecuted by the new Human Rights Courts established under the 2000 Human Rights law. Some were prosecuted and convicted in relation to abuses committed in East Timor around the time of the UN-supervised poll on independence in the territory in 1999, but they were later released on appeal to the Supreme Court.

5 Aspinall, 'Peace without Justice', p. 17.

Such failures have primarily, though not entirely, been due to resistance by the TNI, which remains a powerful veto player in the Indonesian political system even if it no longer plays a determining role in day-to-day politics.[6] Indeed, it might be said that one unstated but central element of democratisation in Indonesia has been an implicit political deal by which the military eased itself out of politics in exchange for effective impunity for past abuses. Certainly, very few members of Indonesia's political elite believe that there is much purpose or benefit to be gained by pursuing military officers for past abuses, even if they agree that steps should be taken to avoid repeating these abuses in the future. Partly as a result of this factor, but also due to a host of other problems (including serious problems of judicial corruption and ineffectiveness) transitional justice in Indonesia overall must be assessed as a failure, despite the large number of initiatives. As the International Center for Transitional Justice and KontraS (*Komisi untuk Orang Hilang dan Korban Tindak Kekerasan,* Commission for Disappeared Persons and Victims of Violence) argue in a comprehensive review of Indonesia's transitional justice efforts, 'The series of successive failed mechanisms indicates systemic factors that undermine efforts to achieve truth and accountability for past crimes.'[7]

Elements of this national context have been important in Aceh. While, as we shall see, military personnel have largely withdrawn as central political players in Aceh, they remain a looming presence there, and many other political actors are careful to avoid antagonizing them needlessly or providing them with a motive to intervene once more in local affairs (especially in a context where there is constant speculation about covert operations by intelligence agencies designed to once more fan the flames of conflict). Certainly, at the time of the negotiation of the 2005 Helsinki agreement, numerous serving and retired military officers

6 Marcus Mietzner, Military Politics, Islam, and the State in Indonesia: From Turbulent Transition to Democratic Consolidation (Singapore: Institute of Southeast Asian Studies, 2009).

7 ICTJ and KontraS, Derailed: Transitional Justice in Indonesia Since the Fall of Soeharto (Jakarta: ICTJ, 2011), p. 2.

made it very clear that they did not want TNI personnel to be punished for actions they had taken as part of their 'duty' to eliminate GAM from the province, especially in circumstances in which former GAM fighters were being granted an amnesty.[8] At the same time, certain elements of the national framework have also greatly complicated transitional justice in Aceh: in particular, a TRC in Aceh is supposed to be formed as part of Indonesia's national TRC, but such an institution has been in limbo since late 2006 when the Constitutional Court ruled that the 2004 law under which it was to be established was invalid (in part because it provided for amnesty and hence legal immunity for perpetrators of gross human rights abuses).

The second element of broader context is the dramatic transformation of Aceh itself. Since the 2005 Helsinki peace agreement was signed, the level of post-conflict violence between the two sides has declined dramatically, with the consequence that Aceh is often promoted internationally as a role model of how to resolve protracted internal conflicts. Part of the reason for this success has been the climate of reconstruction and rebuilding that came in the wake of the peace deal and, even more importantly, after the devastating 26 December 2004 Indian Ocean tsunami. The recovery and reconstruction effort not only enhanced goodwill among former conflict actors, but also provided them with major economic benefits, cementing their commitment to peace.[9] For present purposes, however, the most important part of the post-conflict climate has been the dramatic political transformation experienced in Aceh. At the heart of the peace deal was a political compromise in which supporters of GAM agreed to give up their demand for independence in exchange for the chance to compete for local political power in a more autonomous Aceh that remains part of Indonesia. In December 2006, Aceh held direct local elections to choose heads of local government. Irwandi Yusuf, a former GAM propagandist, and Muhammad Nazar, a

8 Aspinall, 'Peace without Justice', p. 27.

9 Edward Aspinall, 'Combatants to Contractors: The Political Economy of Peace in Aceh', *Indonesia*, no. 87 (2009), pp. 1–34.

former pro-independence student leader, were elected as governor and deputy governor. Then and in subsequent elections, former GAM combatants were also elected to head ten of Aceh's twenty-three districts. This political transformation of GAM from a guerrilla movement into a central player in local official politics became even clearer during the 2009 legislative elections when Partai Aceh (PA), the party established as the vehicle of former adherents of the movement, won just under 50 percent of the vote for the provincial parliament. PA also dominated the election results in many district parliaments.[10] Subsequently, in 2012, the PA candidates Zaini Abdullah and Muzakkir Manaf (prominent leaders of the civilian and armed wings of GAM respectively) were elected as the governor and deputy governor of the province.

This move of the former GAM combatants to the centre of political power in Aceh has mixed results for the transitional justice agenda. On the one hand, the movement itself contains many former combatants who themselves might have good reasons to fear an open and honest accounting of past abuses against civilians, as it is widely understood (but poorly documented) that many GAM combatants perpetrated violent acts not only against their military adversaries but also against civilians. The movement has also prioritized various other issues (such as fleshing out details of the new special autonomy granted to Aceh as part of the Helsinki peace deal) above transitional justice issues. On the other hand, the movement and its allies previously made campaigning against human rights abuses in Aceh a central plank of their international campaigning and might therefore be expected to retain at least some residual sympathy for justice approaches. Certainly, both Governor Irwandi Yusuf and his deputy Muhammad Nazar, at times (especially early on in their tenure) indicated their support for a Truth and Reconciliation Commission and various other elements of the transitional justice agenda, indicating the

10 Blair Palmer, 'Peace, Patronage and Post-Conflict Elections in Aceh', in Edward Aspinall and Marcus Mietzner (eds.), *Problems of Democratisation in Indonesia: Elections, Institutions and Society* (Singapore: Institute of Southeast Asian Studies, 2010), pp. 286–306.

continuing influence of the human rights ideas they espoused when they campaigned against Indonesia and in favour of independence.

Having reviewed the broad context, we are now in a position to examine various elements of transitional justice which have become significant in Aceh.

Human Rights Court and Prosecutions[11]

In the late 1990s and early 2000s, when Indonesia made the transition to democracy and political space opened up widely – but briefly – within Aceh, the prospect of trials for perpetrators of human rights abuses seemed to become very real. There was a series of official investigations of past abuses in Aceh and, following one especially egregious massacre of civilians, a trial of military personnel took place and resulted in sentences, albeit very light ones.[12] Meanwhile, as a result of political lobbying in Jakarta, a 2000 law was passed that established special Human Rights Courts (Pengadilan HAM) throughout the country.

The Helsinki MoU picks up on this existing framework and includes a clause on the Human Rights Court that is minimalist in the extreme: 'A Human Rights Court will be established for Aceh'. Even so, this clause is potentially highly contentious in the Indonesian context, largely because the TNI has already demonstrated its hostility to, and its ability to obstruct, human rights trials in other cases around the country, especially those associated with East Timor.

Sure enough, the first public controversy about the meaning of the MoU, only one day after it was signed, concerned the interpretation of the Human Rights court clause. GAM negotiator Nur Djuli said that

11 This section is adapted from Aspinall, 'Peace without Justice'.

12 The soldiers responsible for the notorious Beutong Ateuh killings of 1999, in which they shot dead a religious teacher and more than fifty of his followers in West Aceh, were tried by a *koneksitas* (joint civil-military) court. Twenty-four low-ranking soldiers and one civilian were convicted and sentenced to terms of imprisonment of between eight and ten years. The most senior officer indicted for these killings, Lieutenant Colonel Sudjono, absconded and was never rearrested.

the court would have retroactive authority and would be able to rule on past human rights abuses.[13] National military and government leaders immediately countered, saying that this would not be the case, and that 'scratching open' the old sores left from the past would 'endanger the peace'. As then TNI Commander-in-Chief, General Endriartono Sutarto put it, 'It shouldn't be at the very moment we are resolving the problem, that we are always oriented to the past, with the result that we'll be unable to create the peace we desire.'[14] Retired General Kiki Syahnakri was even more blunt, reflecting an assessment of the MoU widely shared by serving officers: 'GAM, who have opposed the republic, get a pension. TNI soldiers who fell in battle, or whose legs had to be amputated, what do they get? They get threatened with a Human Rights Court.'[15]

Before long, it became clear that the Human Rights Court would be established as part of Indonesia's elaborate but so far largely dysfunctional national framework of human rights protection. Theoretically, national human rights mechanisms could have been used to punish human rights abusers in Aceh even prior to the Helsinki accord. Indonesia's 2000 Human Rights law provides that serious human rights crimes prior to 2000 can be tried by 'Ad Hoc Human Rights courts', which can be established for particular cases by the president in cooperation with the national parliament. Crimes taking place after the law was passed (that is, after 2000) can be tried in regular Human Rights Courts. One such court was established in Medan, North Sumatra, following a 2001 Presidential Decree and has jurisdiction over Aceh (thus fulfilling the MoU clause that a Human Rights Court be established 'for' Aceh), but to our knowledge it has not yet heard a single case. According to the 2000 law, the prosecution process begins with an investigation by Indonesia's National Human Rights Commission (Komnas HAM). If this body finds evidence

13 *Tempo Interactive*, 16 August 2005.

14 *Analisa*, 26 August 2005.

15 *Kompas*, 20 August 2005. The reference to the 'pension' presumably referred to the (meagre) reintegration funds that were to be made available to former GAM combatants.

of gross abuses, it hands its findings to the Attorney General's office for preparation of a case. In Aceh, there have been numerous Komnas HAM investigations of abuses over the years but to our knowledge the Commission has not yet handed any cases over to the Attorney General's office.

The Law for the Governing of Aceh (LoGA, the law designed to embody special autonomy and implement other aspects of the 2005 MoU), passed by the national parliament in July 2006, mandates the establishment of a Human Rights court in Aceh. It also says that such a court should be established within twelve months of the law being passed, though this had still not happened by late 2012, more than six years after the law was passed. However, the LoGA explicitly states that the court will have the authority to rule only on cases occurring *after* the passage of the law itself. This means that all the architecture outlined in the preceding paragraph remains the potential mechanism for prosecuting past human rights abuses.

Given this background, few political actors in Aceh seriously believe that prosecutions for past abuses will take place, or seriously work toward that end. Also, and as noted by one former senior official from Aceh Monitoring Mission (AMM, the international body that oversaw implementation of the peace accord in 2005 to 2006), serious human rights investigations and prosecutions were simply not part of the agenda in AMM discussions with the Indonesian government during the implementation phase: 'It will take a long time before the TNI will be prosecuted. It was and still is a complete taboo. It was simply not possible to discuss or raise it.'[16] Local legal and human rights organisations such as the Legal Aid Institute (LBH) and the Commission for Disappearances and Victims of Violence (KontraS) still campaign for such an outcome, and there are occasionally congresses or demonstrations by victims – sometimes very rowdy demonstrations – that call for prosecutions.[17] Those

16 Confidential interview, 3 October 2007, Brussels.
17 For example, *see Aceh Kita*, 2 March 2006.

involved, however, often seem to be standing up for a matter of fundamental principle without evincing optimism about the prospects. Other actors believe that human rights investigations and prosecutions would be premature and could even endanger the peace process by triggering military resistance and attempts to undermine it.

Truth and Reconciliation Commission

Given the obvious difficulties in pursuing justice through the Human Rights Court pathway, many human rights advocates at the local level have instead invested energy in pursuing the Truth and Reconciliation Commission (TRC) option. An Aceh TRC is mandated by both the 2005 MoU and the 2006 Law for the Governing of Aceh (LoGA). A law (No. 27 of 2004) providing for the establishment of a national TRC had already been passed by Indonesia's national parliament in 2004, well before the Helsinki MoU was signed. The MoU (article 2.3) states that 'A Commission for Truth and Reconciliation will be established for Aceh by the Indonesian Commission of Truth and Reconciliation', while the LoGA (article 229.2) describes the Aceh TRC as an 'inseparable part' of the national TRC. A TRC is thus clearly an accepted part of the national political agenda in Indonesia and there is therefore little doubt that an Aceh TRC eventually will be established, even if some elements of the government's security establishment have apparently privately pressed for the abandonment of the idea.

However, the legal context for the establishment of an Aceh TRC was thrown into deep confusion in late 2006 when the Constitutional Court (*Mahkamah Konstitusi*) revoked Law 27 of 2004, before President Susilo Bambang Yudhoyono had even appointed the members of the national TRC (a delay of more than two years, for which he was widely condemned by Indonesian human rights activists). The Court took this step partly because the Law provided for amnesty and hence legal immunity for perpetrators of gross human rights abuses (for instance, article 27 stated that compensation and rehabilitation of victims would occur only when an amnesty had been granted). Although many human rights advocates welcomed the Court's defence of the principle of accountability, they deeply regretted that revocation of the law delayed even further the formation of a national TRC. It also threw the formation of an Aceh TRC into doubt because of the provisions of the MoU and LoGA, which stated that such a body would be part of, or established by, the national TRC. Further complicating the picture, the LoGA also states that the Aceh TRC would be established 'by this law' and that it needed to be operating effectively within twelve months of the LoGA being passed, which occurred in July 2006.

There has thus been, since this time, an ongoing debate in Aceh about whether the provincial government should go ahead and establish a local TRC by way of *qanun* (provincial legislation), or should await action by the national government. On the one hand, advocates of a locally constituted TRC note the fading central government interest in such a process and the generally bleak situation of human rights enforcement at the national level, evidenced by paralysis on reforming the national TRC following the Constitutional Court decision. They thus argue that political conditions may be more supportive of a locally initiated process and believe that the leaders of the Aceh government might support, or be persuaded to support, such a process. And indeed, various local government officials, and local legislators, have at various times endorsed an Aceh TRC.

Others warn that a locally constituted body might be seriously compromised. Among them are local legal experts and advisers to the provincial government who have argued that the explicit wording in both the MoU and the LoGA on the question of an Aceh TRC being part of a national body would lead to great legal uncertainty if a local body were established independently. Another key issue concerns the powers of such a commission to subpoena witnesses and perpetrators, especially those from national bodies like the military and police. Presumably, a TRC established by the central government would, or at least could, depending on the political will to create such an outcome, have such powers. It is much more doubtful, indeed very unlikely, that a commission established by the provincial government in Aceh would have either the legal authority or the political weight to achieve this goal. Advocates respond that the critical functions of a local commission, even if unable to call witnesses or perpetrators, would be to constitute official acknowledgment that human rights abuses actually happened, and to provide a forum for victims to finally talk about their experiences in a formal context.[18]

By as early as late 2007, it appeared that those who counselled caution and insisted that any local TRC would have to be constituted in conjunction with a national body were winning the day. Even many of the local human rights advocates favoured national-level backing for an Aceh TRC, as did Aceh's provincial government. The national Department of Law and Human Rights announced, for its part, that a new draft bill on the TRC would be on the government's list of bills to be considered by the national legislature in 2008.[19] For several years now, national policy makers have been drafting their own version of a TRC concept paper, one that allegedly promoted 'healing' rather than emphasizing a process that might lead to legal sanctions for perpetrators. Local human rights advocates feared that such a TRC might function as a means of conferring immunity on perpetrators (though the Constitutional Court has already determined that this would be unconstitutional). They formed a body called the Coalition for Truth Recovery (*Koalisi Pengungkapan Kebenaran*, KPK) which involves human rights groups and other NGOs in Aceh and Jakarta and prepared a working paper calling for the rapid formation of a TRC.[20] This proposal advocated disclosing 'those facts that have been intentionally hidden' which may be 'critical for resolving past crimes, including the search for victims of forced disappearances and the graves of those who were killed.'[21] In part, the role of the TRC would

18 Interview with Evi Zain, director of Koalisi NGO HAM, 13 June 2012, Banda Aceh, Indonesia.

19 *Serambi Indonesia*, 27 November 2007.

20 KPK (Coalition for Truth Recovery), A Proposal for Remedy for Victims of Gross Human Rights Violations in Aceh. Working Paper, 14 June 2007.

21 KPK, A Proposal for Remedy, p. 16.

be to provide a truth-telling mechanism that could accumulate data for human rights prosecutions at a later date.

At the same time, the KPK proposal advocates forgiveness and reconciliation for local perpetrators of relatively minor crimes at the community level and encourages the use of various customary legal mechanisms for this purpose. These include payment of *sayam* and *suloeh*, material reparations paid by the guilty party for, in the first case, physical injury and, in the second, civil disputes where no physical injuries have occurred. In both cases the reparations are to be paid after a community adjudication and reconciliation process presided over by the village head and other dignitaries.[22] However, the KPK's supporters are also adamant that such mechanisms of forgiveness and community reconciliation would not apply to serious violators of human rights. Borrowing from the South African model, they argue that any TRC should:

> Clearly name those most responsible for gross human rights violations. There shall be no amnesty recommendations for those most responsible for gross human rights violations. The Commission shall work in a complementary manner with the courts for serious crimes, namely, crimes against humanity, genocide and war crimes. The Commission shall give legal immunity recommendations only to the perpetrators who have confessed their crimes during the process of reconciliation facilitated by the Commission.[23]

Despite such advocacy by the KPK and similar groups, after more than seven years of the peace process, the TRC for Aceh has not yet been formed. In practical terms, there are at least three reasons why the TRC has stalled. First, at the international level, there seems to be a widespread view that the peace process in Aceh is a success, and that conflict has more or less ended. As a result, there is disengagement by international actors who might otherwise promote transitional justice mechanisms, and reluctance to endorse measures which might undermine the peace that

22 KPK, A Proposal for Remedy, pp. 23–24.
23 KPK, A Proposal for Remedy, p. 26.

has been achieved. In a meeting with civil society activists in Aceh in late 2009, Martti Ahtisaari, the former president of Finland and chief mediator in the 2005 Aceh negotiations, argued that Aceh did not need a TRC and that such an agency might stimulate resistance which could harm the peace process.[24] His argument was that the reintegration of former combatants into civilian life was running well, democratic transition in Aceh had proceeded peacefully, and economic indicators were positive. Thus, there was no urgency to put a TRC in place. His views prompted a heated response from the floor.

Second, Jakarta continues to drag its feet and has still failed to provide a regulatory framework. Despite both the MoU and the LoGA requiring the TRC in Aceh to be established as part of a national body, the government in Jakarta has not yet placed before the national parliament a bill to replace the law invalidated by the Constitutional Court in 2006. The preparation of a national TRC bill falls under the authority of the Ministry of Human Rights and Law. Ministry staffers have long been working on the draft and have held public hearings on its content in many places, including Jakarta, Papua and Aceh. One of the hearings was conducted with local government and civil society activists in Aceh on 17 July 2009. Those attending made various criticisms and suggestions for changes to the bill, but overall they were satisfied with its general shape and could see that the bill had responded to the main weaknesses (including the issue of impunity) that had been identified by the Constitutional Court in the original law. The Ministerial team seemed receptive, and promised that it would revise the bill by the end of July 2009, prior to submitting it to parliament in August 2009. Yet in December 2009, the TRC bill did not appear on the National Legislation Program list (*prolegnas*) of bills to be discussed by the parliament in 2010. Then, on 15 October 2010, the Directorate General (*Dirjen*) for Bills Harmonization of the Law and Human Rights Ministry, submitted the TRC draft to the National Secretariat

24 Personal observation by Fajran Zain: Civil Society Consultation with President Martti Ahtisaari on Truth Commission and Reconciliation. The Pade Hotel, Banda Aceh, Indonesia, 11 December 2009.

and to the President, but not to the Minister of Law and Human Rights; on 8 March 2011, the Minister withdrew the draft. Clearly, there are obstacles within the Ministry of Law and Human Rights itself.[25] At the very least we can conclude from this that the bill is not a high priority for the government, and it is likely that the bill is running into powerful internal opposition.

Third, Aceh government players have given few signs of treating the TRC as a priority issue, either by lobbying Jakarta hard to establish a national framework, or by taking steps to establish an Aceh-based TRC. In particular, governor Irwandi Yusuf and deputy governor Muhammad Nazar were both elected in large part due to their records of staunch opposition to the central government during the conflict years. However, after they came to power, they neglected many of the campaign issues they raised during more difficult times in Aceh, including human rights. Early on in their term, they made some statements endorsing the establishment of a TRC for Aceh, but subsequently this issue largely disappeared from their public statements, and neither individual seriously urged the Indonesian government to push the National TRC bill forward. In January 2009, Irwandi refused to include a local TRC bill in the list of priority bills for the Aceh parliament in the upcoming year, despite the bill's inclusion having been endorsed by thirty members of the outgoing 2004–2009 parliament. Likewise, Zaini Abdullah and Muzakkir Manaf have given few indications that the issue is a priority for them.

At the same time, members of Aceh's civil society have continued to push for a local TRC process, with some success. They hoped to achieve their goal soon after the 2009 elections when Partai Aceh members were elected to local parliaments in great numbers across the province. Initially, members of the new Aceh parliament agreed to include a draft *qanun* (local regulation) as part of their priority list for the whole 2010 to 2014 period, but when the time came they did not list it as a priority

25 For review, see minutes meeting notes of the Law and Human Rights Ministerial office in Hotel Cemara, Jakarta, 30 May 2011.

in either 2010 or 2011 (in the Indonesian system, there is typically a great backlog of bills and only those in the regional priority list (*prolegda*) will make it onto the legislative agenda). Several prominent local parliamentarians have also publically stated that they support such a bill, including the powerful Chairman of Commission-A of the Aceh parliament, Tgk. Adnan Beuransyah of Partai Aceh. A group of prominent local politicians including the speaker of the Aceh Parliament, Hasbi Abdullah of Partai Aceh, signed a statement in December 2010 – in response to demonstrations by victims and human rights organisations – promising that parliament would discuss a TRC bill by June 2011, but this did not happen even by the end of 2011. There was a major breakthrough in mid-2012, however, when the provincial parliament agreed to establish a TRC, and discussed a draft regulation to establish such a body. The draft was based on a version provided by civil society groups, modelled on the KPK work of some years earlier. For a time, it seemed that a TRC would be formed soon, but the situation was once more thrown in doubt when leaders of the parliament in late 2012 said that they were suspending their preparation of the regulation – eliciting condemnation by human rights activists – and then, in early 2013, announced that they would pass it sometime in 2013.[26] The early optimism among some civil society activists about the prospects of an Aceh-specific TRC process has thus been replaced by periods of deep disappointment, interspersed with renewed hopefulness, given the intermittent support by the PA and provincial parliament for such a process.

In addition to having a record of very slow legislative action on any issue, we may assume there are at least two reasons the new Aceh government and parliament have dragged their feet in creating a local TRC in Aceh. First, in legal terms, the absence of national regulations as a framework for a local TRC is certainly a significant problem that would, as explained above, limit the mandate of a local commission and

26 'Pembahasan Raqan KKR Tunggu Pengesahan KKR Pusat', Atjehpost.com, 11 September 2012; '*Qanun KKR Prioritas DPRA 2013*', Atjehlink, 6 January 2013.

consequently reduce the meaning of the justice it could provide. In particular, it would limit the ability of the Commission to compel high-ranking officials from Jakarta to provide testimony. Governor Irwandi Yusuf did not spell out his objections to an Aceh-based TRC in quite these terms but stated that it was necessary to wait for national legislation because 'The conflict was not among the Acehnese people, but between the central government and Aceh'. Speaking at the fifth anniversary of the Helsinki MoU, he also indicated that a TRC would be a far too costly exercise for Aceh to afford by itself.[27] Likewise, when they announced their suspension of their bill in late 2012, parliamentarians said it would not make sense for the local TRC to be established prior to the formation of the national body.

Second, and more important perhaps, are the implications that a TRC would have for former GAM members. It is likely that unfettered truth seeking would uncover evidence of violence committed by former GAM combatants, which could discredit the former independence movement. Some former leaders of the movement are surely also aware that despite the amnesty provision in the MoU there is still a possibility their members could face trial for past crimes. It is well known that during the conflict years many GAM fighters tortured or killed suspected informants (*cuak*) and residents with ethnic Javanese backgrounds.[28] Many feel that this factor explains the reluctance by many of Aceh's new political elite to embrace truth and reconciliation mechanisms.[29] Indeed, one of us (Fajran Zain) has witnessed one Partai Aceh member, during an NGO-organised training on transitional justice and the TRC, confide to his friends that 'we should be careful with this, we could be hit'. More tellingly yet, in 2012 when the Aceh parliament deliberated the TRC

27 *Serambi Indonesia*, 18 August 2010.

28 Nashrun Marzuki, & Adi Warsidi, *Fakta Bicara: Mengungkap Pelanggaran HAM di Aceh 1989–2005* (Banda Aceh, Indonesia: Koalisi NGO HAM Aceh, 2011).

29 Scott Cunliffe, Eddie Riyadi, Raimondus Arwalembun, & Hendrik Boli Tobi, *Negotiating Peace in Indonesia: Prospects for Building Peace and Upholding Justice in Maluku and Aceh* (Jakarta: IFP Mediation Cluster of ICTJ and ELSAM, 2009). Country Case Study: Indonesia.

bill which had been initiated by civil society groups, the relevant parliamentary committee (of which PA had half the members) struck out 'non-state actors' from among the categories of perpetrators of human rights abuses to which the bill could apply, meaning that the commission would only deal with abuses for which state actors or corporations were responsible.[30]

Overall, it is hard to avoid concluding that the legal complications that have entangled the TRC have been welcomed by key international, national and Aceh actors. Underlying the foot-dragging on the TRC appears to be a shared view that setting up such a body would potentially undermine the peace process. Thus, Jakarta and Aceh have continued to trade responsibility on the issue while taking no concrete actions to establish a TRC. As we shall discuss in the next section, this situation has led some local victims and human rights organisations to initiate their own reconciliation and truth-telling processes.

Amnesty[31]

Closely related to the issues of prosecution and truth telling, but implemented far more successfully, were the amnesty provisions of the Helsinki MoU. Unlike in many transitional justice situations, in which amnesty is granted to government officials and allies who are human rights perpetrators, in the Aceh case there was a one-sided amnesty that applied only to former rebels and GAM members.

Two weeks after the MoU was signed in Helsinki, President Susilo Bambang Yudhoyono signed a Presidential Decree (No. 22 of 2005) granting a general amnesty to persons involved in GAM activities. Approximately 500 prisoners received remission and immediately released from jail on 17 August 2005. In total, more than 1,400 prisoners were amnestied and released. The amnesty typified the power configuration underpinning

30 Interview with Evi Zain, 13 June 2012, Banda Aceh, Indonesia.

31 This section is largely adapted from Aspinall, 'Peace without Justice'.

the agreement. It was granted to GAM members by the government, in a procedure approved by the constitution and which, in the eyes of government officials, was akin to a pardon for crimes against the state. It was never intended to be a general amnesty absolving all persons of responsibility for past crimes in the conflict and so was not as controversial as, for instance, the amnesty clause in the 1999 Sierra Leone peace accord.[32] During both the negotiations and the implementation of the MoU, it was never suggested by either party that the amnesty would apply to individuals from the government side. For government officials, such a provision would have been an admission of culpability that would have undermined their previous assertions that government troops had operated lawfully and within a framework for protecting human rights. That the amnesty applied only to GAM was, perhaps ironically, a sign of the government's strength.

There were, however, two major controversies concerning the amnesty. The first and most serious question was how liberally the amnesty would be applied. It soon emerged that not all persons with GAM affiliations were released from jail. It was disputed whether the amnesty should apply to GAM members imprisoned for any crime carried out on behalf of the movement, as GAM argued, or would be restricted to those imprisoned only for narrowly defined political crimes against the state. The Minister of Justice and Human Rights at the time, Hamid Awaludin, repeatedly ruled against granting amnesty to persons imprisoned for crimes such as robbery and murder, saying that it applied only to those convicted of *makar*, or treason. Accordingly, the government initially refused to release from prison more than 100 individuals associated with the rebellion who had been convicted for general or civilian crimes as diverse as murder, narcotics possession and smuggling.

The head of the AMM was empowered by the MoU (article 5.2.f) to rule on disputed cases, but it was up to the Indonesian government, as

32 Priscilla Hayner, *Negotiating Peace in Sierra Leone: Confronting the Justice Challenge*, (Geneva, Switzerland: Centre for Humanitarian Dialogue, 2007).

the sovereign power, to release prisoners from jail and annul their convictions. Moreover, although AMM leaders knew they had a 'strong card in the fact that the Head of the AMM could actually decide whether or not a person should be amnestied', they wanted to avoid using this card because they believed it 'would not have been conducive to the peace process and the mutual trust building between the parties.'[33] Eventually, the AMM brought in a Swedish judge, Christer Karphammar, to facilitate resolution of the outstanding cases by deciding on a list of the individuals to be amnestied, to which the two parties would then agree. Working with another AMM member, Karphammar emphasised quiet diplomacy, persuasion and absolute confidentiality (even secrecy) in his deliberations, coordinating with senior representatives of the two parties and with Pieter Feith, the head of the AMM. Judge Karphammar and his assistant worked through court documents and other materials. The judge based his decisions on two sets of criteria: connection of the crime to GAM's struggle and its seriousness.[34] On this second matter, the judge himself, largely guided by his own 'ethical judgment', determined that persons convicted of 'cold-blooded' crimes against civilians would not be pardoned. In fact, much of the time for assessment was spent on determining whether a prisoner's crime had been carried out on behalf of the movement.[35]

The AMM team members expended much effort to persuade Minister Hamid to broaden the amnesty beyond *makar* to incorporate other

33 Robert Hygrell, 'Case Study – Aceh Peace Process', presentation prepared for CSCAP Study Group on Preventive Diplomacy and the Future of the ASEAN Regional Forum, (Bandar Seri Begawan, 30–31 October, 2007), p. 6.

34 According to some confidential sources, the AMM and Judge Karphammar also worked on the basis of the principles of an amnesty which had been agreed upon between the parties in Helsinki prior to the negotiation of the MoU. It is not clear, however, if these principles were the same as the two named above, which were detailed by a very senior participant in the process.

35 Thus, for example, there were a number of prisoners convicted on narcotics charges who said that they had been involved in the marijuana trade to help fund GAM's struggle; some common criminals also tried to take advantage of the amnesty by claiming GAM membership.

crimes. But, in a few cases, Judge Karphammar also determined that individuals involved in serious violent crimes against civilians should not be pardoned. Assessing far more than one hundred disputed cases, the judge decided that most of those prisoners should be released and that fewer than ten should remain in prison. A few of the more difficult cases were resolved when the government granted accelerated remissions rather than amnesties. Those who remained in prison included individuals involved in the bombing of the Jakarta stock exchange in September 2000, in which ten people died, and the killer of Dayan Dawood, a respected university rector. After considerable hesitation, both Minister Hamid and the senior GAM leader Malik Mahmud approved this negotiated outcome. The MoU parties declared the amnesty issue closed on 14 August 2006, meaning that 'there were no disputed cases for the Head of AMM to decide upon'.[36]

Thus, a year after the signing of the MoU, the amnesty issue was formally closed. There was considerable bitterness and dissension in GAM ranks, however. Irwandi Yusuf, the GAM representative to the AMM (and later governor) was sidelined in the decision making and was reportedly angry with Malik Mahmud because the outcome meant that some of the movement's supporters remained behind bars. Some GAM supporters say that those remaining in prison had been sacrificed in order to disassociate the movement from their acts and to absolve the leadership of guilt. The Forum for Justice for Acehnese Political Prisoners (Forum Keadilan Tapol/Napol GAM) formed and, with family members of prisoners and some other civil society groups, it campaigned for the release of the remaining prisoners.

While the outcome of the amnesty arguably prevented a serious breach between the parties and preserved the principle that there would be no immunity for perpetrators of serious crimes, the secretive nature of the deal meant that it was not presented to the public in this way.

36 Robert Hygrell, 'Case Study – Aceh Peace Process', presentation prepared for CSCAP Study Group on Preventive Diplomacy and the Future of the ASEAN Regional Forum, (Bandar Seri Begawan, 30–31 October 2007), p. 7.

Moreover, it was anomalous in that other GAM members who had not been arrested or imprisoned before the MoU, but who may have been responsible for equally serious crimes (or who even may have ordered the very crimes for which others remained in jail), did not face investigation or prosecution. It is not clear – and not widely discussed – whether such people are considered to have been amnestied for these actions.

The second controversial issue, also not widely discussed in public, concerns the one-sided nature of the amnesty and its implications for possible future human rights investigations and legal processes. Many military officers and some government officials privately argue that it would be unjust for government troops to be investigated and, in theory at least, prosecuted before a Human Rights Court while GAM members have been amnestied. During the deliberations leading to the passage of the LoGA in early 2006, members of former President Megawati Soekarnoputri's Indonesian Democracy Party–Struggle (PDI–P) argued precisely this and proposed a general amnesty for police and army soldiers who had been posted to Aceh.[37] This proposal was not incorporated into the law. However, government or military officials sometimes make similar comments, at least privately. For instance, some officials have privately floated the idea of watering down, or even abandoning, plans for a TRC and Human Rights Court, justifying this by saying that GAM members have been amnestied while members of the security forces have not.

In fact, although this matter is far from certain legally, it appears that the amnesty granted by the Presidential Decree would not confer immunity to GAM members for crimes against civilians, even though few GAM members are likely to be aware of this. After all, it was precisely on the grounds that they had committed gross or 'cold-blooded' crimes against civilians that a small number of GAM members remained in prison. Legal experts interviewed by the author have different views on

37 *Koran Tempo*, 8 May 2006.

this matter, but the weight of opinion seems to be that the amnesty does not close the door legally on future prosecutions of GAM members for crimes against civilians, even if nobody in authority in Aceh or Jakarta has any appetite for such prosecutions at present. Therefore, the argument does not appear strong that the amnesty for former GAM supporters would justify protecting other parties, such as the military.

Reparations

The Helsinki MoU included a far-reaching provision providing a right to compensation, in the form of land, employment or social security for those unable to work, to 'all civilians who have suffered a demonstrable loss' in the conflict. This agenda of compensation was thus not linked explicitly to any wider truth-seeking or transitional justice framework. Instead, it continued a policy that had begun prior even to the signing of the MoU under which payments (*diyat*) were made to compensate members of the community who had lost family members in the conflict, without inquiring into who had killed them or under what circumstances. This policy was initiated by Azwar Abubakar, then deputy governor of Aceh, in 2002 and drew on Islamic law precepts about compensation as a means to substitute for eye-for-eye punishments in cases of criminal law. It also reflected a broader mindset in the Jakarta government and amidst sections of the local political elite that a thirst for revenge among family members of slain rebels and villagers was fuelling the conflict, as well as a frank assessment by them that legal investigations into killings of civilians by the military would be impossible.[38]

The closest Aceh has come to a policy of reparations in the years since the Helsinki MoU has been through the policies implemented by the Aceh Reintegration Agency (*Badan Reintegrasi Damai Aceh*, BRA). This body was formed in February 2006 as an ad hoc body through a President's Instruction and a Governor's Decree. Its mandate has largely focused on reintegrating former GAM combatants into society, and much

38 See Aspinall, 'Peace without Justice', pp. 25–26 for more discussion.

controversy has surrounded the ways by which it went about disbursing cash and other forms of assistance to former GAM fighters. In fact, at this point it is important to note a larger context of transitional justice activities in Aceh: the Disarmament, Demobilization and Reintegration (DDR) framework according to which many of them were carried out. Disarmament and demobilization of former GAM fighters was from the start seen as a key to the success of the peace process in Aceh (various provisions of the Helsinki MoU dealt with the issue), and numerous programs were carried out and funds expended, to achieve these goals. Space does not permit a thorough review of the various DDR activities that took place in Aceh, or their failings and successes (a useful summary is MSR 2010). It is worth noting, however, that the DDR framework has provided an overarching meta-narrative through which many other activities that in other contexts might be considered part of transitional justice have been carried out. The core guiding principle of post-conflict activities in Aceh has very much been 'reintegration' rather than 'transitional justice'.

A good example here is reparations. These have very much been seen as part of the reintegration process. Thus a large part of the work of the BRA has focused on assisting civilians who were negatively affected by the conflict. According to a World Bank report of 2010, to the end of 2009, the BRA had spent 72.2 billion rupiah (about US$7.4 million) to run its programs, with 43 billion (59.9 percent) disbursed to civilians. The money came from many different sources, including international agencies and local and central government. Various forms of economic assistance to individuals have been paid, including a continuation of *diyat* payments to family members of people who were killed in the conflict, the construction of houses to replace those destroyed (26,000 by late 2010, according to the BRA)[39] and artificial limbs and other assistance to people who were seriously injured. There was considerable policy inconsistency within the agency and major problems of implementation, and the agency itself claims that its job is far from complete; however, there is no further commitment of money from the central government.

39 *Waspada*, 25 November 2010.

BRA programs to help civilians generated considerable controversy among local academics, peace scholars, civil society activists and victims, specifically about whether such programs could truly be considered reparations, from a transitional justice perspective. The government made this claim, at least implicitly. In contrast, many activists say that reparations first require truth seeking, in order to determine who is and who is not eligible for assistance. In this perspective, the efforts so far by the BRA amount only to emergency treatment as part of the general post-conflict recovery effort. Though they are thus defensible, according to the activists, they must be seen as the beginning, not the end, of the process of compensating victims.[40]

One particular point of concern was that in the early years of its operations, BRA did not assist women who had experienced sexual or physical assault during the conflict because BRA refused to acknowledge rape cases in the absence of medical or other physical evidence.[41] It was only in 2009 that many such women were included in BRA's target lists. This change happened after various local NGOs agreed to establish a Task Force on Emergency Reparations for women who experienced sexual assault or other forms of gender-based violence during the conflict. The Task Force met the BRA management and promotes the idea of emergency reparations for victims, providing the BRA with a list of women who need such assistance.

40 This opinion was aired in many discussions or workshops in Aceh attended by one of the authors (Fajran Zain), such as the Seminar and Workshop on Truth and Peace in Aceh (23–24 September 2007), National Seminar and the Dissemination of the Initial Draft of TRC Bill (23–24 July 2008), Restrategy Workshop for the Empowerment of the Truth Seeking Coalition, KPK (4 June 2009), Public Discussion and Focus Group Discussion on Reparations in Aceh (24–25 June 2009), Socialization Agenda of the Initial Draft TRC Bill in 10 Districts (July – Aug 2009), Coordination Meeting between TRC Stakeholders Aceh and the Ministry of Law and Human Rights (17 July 2009). See also Ross Clarke, Galuh Wandita and Samsidar, *Considering Victims: The Aceh Peace Process from a Transitional Justice Perspective* (New York: International Center for Transitional Justice, 2008), pp. 32–33.

41 Samsidar, 'Kehidupan korban yang semakin sulit', in M. Nashrun & W. Adi (eds.) *Fakta Bicara: Mengungkap Pelanggaran HAM di Aceh 1989–2005*, Vol. 1 (Banda Aceh, Indonesia: Koalisi NGO HAM, 2011), pp. 209–213.

Security Sector Reform

Another part of the transitional justice agenda where there has been at best mixed progress is security sector reform. This is of course another area where progress in Aceh is strongly linked to developments in the broader Indonesian context. Certainly, since the fall of the Suharto government in 1998, an historic reorientation of the military has taken place, with the institution largely withdrawing from its former participation in day-to-day management of political affairs. However, deeper institutional reforms, such as the abolition of the military's 'territorial structure' which shadows the civilian administration at every level throughout the country, or the subordination of the institution to a truly civilian-dominated Ministry of Defence, have stalled.

In Aceh, which in the years of intense military operations seemed to be a bastion of unreformed military behaviour and ideology, there has also been significant progress. Under the terms of the Helsinki MoU, the military presence in Aceh was dramatically reduced, and the military function in the province was supposedly limited to external defence. Military checkpoints all but disappeared from Aceh's roads, the military presence is far less visible than it used to be, and the police have taken over running most security affairs. The gross human rights abuses that were almost daily fare during the conflict years have ended.

Various local programs and initiatives have also been taken to push forward the Security Sector Reform agenda. For example, a parliamentary caucus for monitoring and advocacy on the implementation of the security sector reform was established, drawing together fifty elected members of parliaments representing sixteen districts in Aceh, all of whom had participated in SSR workshops run by NGOs in 2009 and 2010.[42] Since February 2009, the International Organization for Migration (IOM) has been running a program aiming to train so-called community police (POLMAS/Polisi Masyarakat), and has established a working group to monitor and evaluate the performance and behaviour

42 Personal communication, Hendra Fadli of KontraS Aceh, 13 June 2011.

of police officers. The ultimate goals of this project are to change the behaviour of police officers, switching them from being military-minded to community-oriented and thus to alter public perceptions toward the police.

But such efforts have so far had little impact on the underlying institutional foundations or patterns of behaviour in the security sector. Military officers retain their territorial structure and their networks of intelligence operatives throughout the province, closely monitoring political affairs and the activities of former GAM combatants, even if they relatively rarely intervene, at least openly (there are constant rumours, however, of covert intelligence operations of various kinds). As in the past, military and police officials also participate in a variety of both legal and illegal business activities, though at a less intense level than during the conflict years. There have also been occasional reports of military officers interfering in local political affairs (such as when one officer angrily ordered physical punishments for civil servants in West Aceh who, in accordance with an instruction from the governor, had flown the Indonesian flag at half mast after the death of GAM founder Hasan Tiro).[43]

According to a report from the local human rights organisation KontraS Aceh (2010), there are several indications that security sector reform is stalling within Aceh. These signs include criminal behaviour by security force personnel, where the police are unable or unwilling to disclose who is responsible for various crimes or take action against them.[44] Similarly, members of the TNI, in the view of KontraS, frequently participate in activities that exceed their mandate as a professional military,

43 *Serambi Indonesia*, 5 June 2010.

44 For example, eight personnel of the Yon Armed 17/RC Laweung military unit beat up a businessman Tgk. Azhar on 5 February 2010 in Pidie, at http://www.theglobejournal.com/kategori/hukum/kontras-protes-warga-dianiaya-setelah-menabrak-anggota-tni.php; a high ranking officer tortured a journalist, Ahmadi in Simeuleu, for his report on illegal logging on 21 May 2010, at http://hankam.kompasiana.com/2010/05/21/wartawan-aceh-dianiaya-militer; members of the marine corps tortured a man named Syahrudin and forcibly dismantled his house in Aneuk Laot village, Sabang on 21 June 2010, at http://international.okezone.com/read/2010/06/21/340/345194/340/oknum-tni-al-aniaya-warga-sabang.

for instance being involved in providing security for post-tsunami reconstruction projects, or intervening in the judicial process such as following a violent incident at Alue Dua village when TNI personnel beat fourteen villagers in retribution in the aftermath of a brawl. KontraS also point out that the TNI and police were also striving to access allocations from local state budgets at both the provincial and district levels, despite the fact that such allocations are explicitly proscribed in law (as so-called vertical institutions, the security forces are supposed to be fully funded by the national budget).[45] Moreover, there has never been an official audit of military spending in Aceh, despite the frequent and longstanding allegations of participation by military officers in corruption and illegal business.

Such behaviour indicates that security sector reform has a long way to go if it is to transform Indonesia's security agencies into truly professional organisations that are fully subordinate to civilian authority. However, it should also be pointed out that they make Aceh little different from other Indonesian provinces, where petty abuses and illicit economic activity by security personnel are also rife.

Grassroots Reconciliation and Truth Seeking Initiatives

Aceh still retains a lively civil society sector, with a large number of organisations oriented specifically to human rights, most of which can trace their origins to the immediate post-Suharto period of 1998–2001. In the absence of formal government initiatives, several such local NGOs and victims' organisations, with support from national and international bodies, have tried to launch their own activities to push forward the transitional justice agenda.

In pursuing these activities, local groups have had to confront the two-sided nature of the conflict in Aceh. The conventional understanding

45 Through 2008 approximately 22 billion rupiah was granted in local budgets to such vertical institutions (Kontras Aceh, Annual Report, 2010).

of the conflict was that it pitted members of local communities, and the GAM rebels in particular, against the central government and its security agencies. In this Aceh-versus-Jakarta 'vertical' struggle, many ordinary Acehnese citizens became victims of the state's security forces. Yet at the same time, the conflict also involved considerable violence *within* Acehnese society itself, even if this is not often acknowledged today (especially by former adherents of GAM). Such violence could involve threats and retribution by GAM fighters against citizens who assisted the security forces, or in some parts of the province abusive behaviours (theft, extortion, kidnapping for ransom, etc.) by GAM fighters against ordinary citizens. It also involved violence by members of pro-government militias against individuals who were believed to be sympathetic to GAM. These conflicts within Acehnese society were especially severe in ethnically mixed parts of the province, where GAM was often understood in ethnic terms and seen as representing the ethnically Acehnese sector of the population, rather than the various minority groups, and where the conflict sometimes took on the character of a 'horizontal' conflict between ethnic communities.

During the early post-conflict years, there were many symbolic actions designed to facilitate community-level healing in the wake of such intra-community conflicts. In particular, at many events in which former GAM fighters were welcomed back to their communities, local religious leaders held *peusijeuk* ceremonies in which participants were sprinkled with water and flour and clasped hands as signs of reconciliation.[46] Most of these events did not thus involve truth telling, even if they sometimes implied that participants forgave one another for past sins. In most places, however, reconciliation efforts ended with such one-off events, such that ordinary members of the community are sometimes still required to live

46 John Braithwaite, Valerie Braithwaite, Michael Cookson and Leah Dunn, *Anomie and Violence: Non-truth and Reconciliation in Indonesian Peacebuilding* (Canberra: ANU E-Press, 2010), pp. 389–391; see also Leena Avonius, 'Reconciliation and Human Rights in Post-conflict Aceh', in Birgit Bräuchler (ed.), *Reconciling Indonesia: Grassroots Agency for Peace* (Abingdon, UK: Routledge, 2009), pp. 121–137.

side by side with individuals who once perpetrated serious abuses against them or family members.

One example of a more recent and sustained initiative to pursue grassroots reconciliation has been organised in the central highlands district of Bener Meriah by Kontra Aceh and the Peace Loving Women's Group (*Kelompok Perempuan Cinta Damai*, KPCD). This multi-ethnic district was a site of serious communal conflict and gross abuses committed by GAM, the security forces and pro-government militias during the conflict years. The reconciliation program is designed to involve all three major ethnic groups in the district – Acehnese, Gayo and Javanese – which used to be in conflict during the years of violence, to work together in livelihoods programs, such as in vegetable production, fish farming and handicrafts, as well as in discussion groups on various aspects of transitional justice. This program began in 2008. At first it targeted only the women in the three communities. Later on, it was supported by many prominent people in the area, and has extended its activities to target various other community groups as well as ordinary villagers throughout the highlands.

In an example of what John Braithwaite and colleagues have described as bottom-up reconciliation characteristic of post-conflict regions of Indonesia (which happens 'as a micro-politics massively dispersed among thousands of leaders of villages, clans, churches, mosques and sub-districts'[47]), this program appears to have achieved significant results. For example, former GAM combatants and their enemies in the pro-government militia group PETA have been working together in the same caucus in the district's local parliament, in part a product of the cooperation fostered by this and similar programs. Participants have also noted that interethnic mixing and communication have also increased, spreading from the formal settings of the program, such as in seminars, classes and trainings, to informal settings such as markets, schools or other public places.

47 Avonius, 'Reconciliation and Human Rights in Post-conflict Aceh', p. 42.

As for truth seeking, although various official inquiries and investigations of past human rights abuses were held in Aceh in the brief opening between the collapse of the Suharto government and the intensification of military operations in 2000 to 2001, since the Helsinki MoU there have been no more official investigations.[48] Given the stalling of the official TRC agenda, the only serious attempts to investigate past abuses and to allow victims to speak out about their experiences have been organised by local civil society groups. The best known such attempt was initiated by the Association of Victims of Human Rights Violations of North Aceh (KP2HAU) and was a direct response to the government's failure to establish a TRC. KP2HAU set up a series of public hearings around the time of the eleventh anniversary of the so-called Simpang KKA (KKA Junction) massacre in North Aceh, a terrible event in May 1999 when military units opened fire on a crowd of several hundred demonstrators, at a junction close to the PT Kertas Kraft Aceh (KKA) paper mill, just outside the industrial city of Lhokseumawe, North Aceh, killing at least 49 people and wounding 156 others. Those speaking out at the hearing included relatives of those killed as well as individuals who had suffered both mild and serious injuries, though in the end only five persons were willing to speak out given the lack of legal protection they could expect. Several hundred villagers and local officials witnessed their very moving

48 There were three major fact-finding commissions in 1998 to 1999. The first was sent by the national parliament and contributed to the ending of the 'military operations zone' status that (at least informally) to that time applied in Aceh. After only four days of hearings provisional findings were released which stated that at least 1,700 cases of human rights violations had occurred in Aceh, including 426 torture cases and 320 unlawful killings. The second was led by the National Human Rights Commission and involved dramatic unearthing of several mass graves. After only three days of hearings the commission released its own provisional findings that at least 781 people had been killed, 163 people were missing, 368 people had been tortured, 3,000 had been widowed, 15,000 to 20,000 had been orphaned, 98 houses had been burnt down and 102 women had been raped. A third investigation was held by the Commission on Violence in Aceh (Komisi Independen Pengusutan Tindak Kekerasan di Aceh, KIPTKA, established by Presidential Decree No. 88, 1999). This team produced a figure of at least 5,000 cases of serious human rights violations and identified five strong cases which should immediately be brought to trial.

testimony. Strikingly, those speaking mostly rejected the 'forgive and forget' discourse that is prominent when such matters are discussed by cultural and political leaders in Aceh, instead calling for trials of the perpetrators. As one of them (R, a 28-year-old female) put it: 'I will forgive them, but they have to be sent to court first'; another explained, 'I will not forgive them, until they are sentenced' (HS, female, 46). After the public hearing, representatives of the community and the local government set a stone to begin construction of a memorial.[49]

Civil society groups have taken other actions to keep the transitional justice agenda alive. Several groups have continued to document past acts of violence and other human rights abuses, in preparation for the day when a formal transitional justice process might begin. The International Center for Transitional Justice (ICTJ) assists several local NGOs (Koalisi NGO HAM, Kontras Aceh, Relawan Perempuan untuk Perdamaian [RPuK], and SPKP HAM)[50] in updating and managing relevant data using the Maltus Program so that it is available in an internationally recognized format and ready to be used for future advocacy. Some of these groups also supported an initiative by a local cultural organization, Tikar Pandan, to establish a Human Rights Museum (an initiative that attracted unwelcome attention from local security forces) and proposed the commemoration of several major human rights violations, as part of the memorialisation of victims of human rights abuses.

Another important step has been the organising of victims' group. While waiting for the establishment of the TRC, civil society groups started organising solidarity and communication between victims of

49 Information on this event is taken from direct observation by one of us (Fajran Zain). Further details are in Fabian Junge, 'Public Commemoration for Victims of the Aceh Conflict,' *Watch Indonesia! Information and Analysis*, 9 June 2010, at http://home.snafu.de/watchin/KKA_Commemoration.htm.

50 Of these organisations, Koalisi NGO HAM (Human Rights NGO Coalition) is particularly noteworthy. It was established on 7 August 1998 and supervises twenty-nine local organisations in Aceh. Its main mandate is to collect data and information regarding human rights violations in Aceh and to provide advocacy for victims and their families. It is currently investigating 1,388 cases across fourteen districts in Aceh.

abuses. About ten such groups have been established. The most active include Brotherhood Solidarity of the Victims of Human Rights Violations in Aceh (Solidaritas Persaudaraan Korban Pelangaran HAM Aceh, SPKP HAM Aceh) and Community for Missing People in Aceh (Komunitas Ureung Gadoh Aceh, KAGUNDAH), which claims about 200 members. These groups undertake various activities such as writing workshops that enable conflict survivors to record their own experiences systematically; psychosocial advocacy for conflict survivors; focus group discussions on topics such as understanding TRCs and victim-based reparation principles; and building statues to memorialize such events as the Simpang KKA tragedy. Members of these groups have also demonstrated vociferously in favour of government action on the formal TRC process, such as when several hundred members of the Aliansi Korban Pelanggaran HAM Aceh (Alliance of Human Rights Abuse Victims of Aceh) occupied the Aceh parliament building in late 2010, urging its members to pass a regulation establishing a TRC.[51]

Conclusion

Our analysis suggests that the transitional justice agenda in Aceh has been beset by two formidable challenges, both of which relate to the way by which transitional justice has been bound up in the politics of the Aceh peace process and its relationship to the wider political context. On the one hand, transitional justice in Aceh will necessarily take place in a way that is fundamentally conditioned by its Indonesian context. Yet the Aceh peace process, and hence the possibility of transitional justice, occurred at a time when the wider transitional justice process at the national level was already stalling. There are many reasons for this, most of which are beyond the scope of our discussion in this chapter, but one important factor was the continuing political influence exerted at least indirectly by the military. Everybody who counts in Indonesia's official politics knows

51 *Serambi Indonesia*, 9 December 2010.

that the military would be a major loser in any process of truth telling about the Aceh conflict, and they can see little to benefit for themselves in antagonising the military on this issue. Without a supportive national context, the Aceh transitional justice agenda has therefore stalled, just like the process at the national level.

The second challenge concerns the local context. Aceh's new rulers have been able to point to lack of action at the national level toward (re)establishing a framework for an Aceh TRC. In part, their reluctance to either press Jakarta on the issue or to bypass the centre and establish a local process is a result of a similar attitude of political pragmatism as that exhibited by national politicians: they see little to be gained from antagonising their most fearsome former rivals – and the most potentially dangerous peace spoilers – in the military, when there is so much to be gained politically and economically from securing the peace. At the same time, as already pointed out several times in this essay, former leaders and members of GAM also have reasons to suspect that a formal truth telling process would implicate them in crimes against civilians during the conflict years, crimes that do not fit easily within their narrative of an entirely 'vertical' conflict that pitted Aceh against the centre. Indeed, given the political dominance of the movement now in many parts of Aceh – and the thuggish behaviour of many of its supporters – it is even questionable whether people would feel sufficiently secure to be able to discuss former GAM abuses in formal hearings in GAM base areas. More broadly, however, many other influential voices in Aceh, including those of many religious scholars (*ulama*) have been raised to argue that the time is not ripe now, if it ever will be, for 'digging into' (*mengungkit-ungkit*) the unpalatable past.

Despite the efforts of many of Aceh's highly committed civil society organisations, the lack of strong political backing suggests there is a possibility that Aceh will become like several post-conflict societies (Mozambique is one example), where there is an ongoing peace process without truth and reconciliation.

4 Transitional Justice in Cambodia

The Coincidence of Power and Principle

Kirsten Ainley

BETWEEN 17 APRIL 1975 AND 6 JANUARY 1979, AROUND ONE quarter of the population of Cambodia died at the hands of the Party of Democratic Kampuchea (also referred to as the Communist Party of Kampuchea, or the Khmer Rouge (KR)). The catalogue of atrocity during the period of Democratic Kampuchea (the period during which the KR held power) is extensive. When the KR succeeded in their coup in April 1975, they declared a new start for the country – the calendar was reset to Year Zero, and the regime began to establish what it claimed to be a communist agrarian utopia. The results of this utopia were deadly. Somewhere between 1.6 and 1.9 million people died, most of them through starvation, disease and exhaustion that were either KR policy or foreseeable consequences of it.[1] Up to 400,000 were tortured to death at a series of prisons set up around the country or executed in purges.[2] Ethnic and racial minorities, religious leaders, professionals, educated people, government officials and people with contacts abroad were targeted in particular. Of those who did not manage to flee the country, almost 100 per cent of the Vietnamese were murdered, 50 per cent of those of Chinese descent, 40 per cent of the

1 Ben Kiernan, 'The Demography of Genocide in Southeast Asia', *Critical Asian Studies*, Vol. 35, No. 4 (2003), pp. 585–597.

2 David Chandler, *A History of Cambodia* (Boulder Colorado: Westview Publishers, 2008), p. 259.

Thai and Lao and 36 per cent of the Cham.[3] All but forty-three doctors and all but seven lawyers were killed, along with 18,000 teachers and 10,550 students.[4] In addition to the loss of such a high proportion of the Cambodian population, Cambodian society was also all but destroyed. Cities were evacuated, and people were forced to work under armed guard on collective agricultural projects with little food and no medical care. Children were used as prison guards and spies and forced or encouraged to commit acts of appalling violence. Money was abolished, schools closed and Buddhism suppressed. An offence of 'familyism' was devised to punish people who showed attachments to anything other than Angka ('the organisation', i.e. the KR party), and marriages were forced. Angka controlled all aspects of people's lives and condemned many of them to death.[5]

The regime was finally overthrown on 7 January 1979 when Vietnam intervened (with Soviet backing), captured Phnom Penh and installed the People's Republic of Kampuchea (PRK) government. The PRK was staffed for the most part by ex-Khmer Rouge cadres who had fled to Vietnam during the purges, and included Hun Sen – now prime minister of Cambodia – as foreign affairs minister of the regime. The KR were driven into refugee camps along the border with Thailand, from which they maintained significant influence in Cambodian politics until KR leader Pol Pot's death in 1998.

The damage done to Cambodian people and their society during the period of Democratic Kampuchea was deep, long-lasting and perhaps impossible to ever remedy. Yet very little has been done to attempt to hold perpetrators accountable for their actions in the period until

3 Ben Kiernan, The Pol Pot Regime: Race, Power, and Genocide in Cambodia under the Khmer Rouge, 1975–79 (New Haven: Yale University Press, 2008), p. 458.

4 Tom Fawthrop and Helen Jarvis, 'Getting Away with Genocide' (London: Pluto, 2004) pp. 14–15.

5 Chandler, *A History of Cambodia* and Kiernan, *The Pol Pot Regime* give scholarly accounts of the KR regime. Nick Dunlop, *The Lost Executioner* (London: Bloomsbury, 2005) and Haing Ngor, *Survival in the Killing Fields* (London: Robinson, 1987) are journalistic accounts.

recently. The PRK regime held the People's Revolutionary Tribunal in 1979, which, after five days of hearings, found Pol Pot and his Deputy Prime Minister for Foreign Affairs Ieng Sary guilty in absentia of genocide and sentenced them to death. The Tribunal was the first ever legal body to try or convict suspects for the crime of genocide, and did attempt to bring some form of justice to victims of the prior regime, though it was widely regarded in the West as a show trial organised by Vietnam's puppet government. Between 1979 and 1997 no further trials were held and instead amnesties were issued first in 1994 to members but not leaders of the KR and second in 1996 to Ieng Sary.[6] Only in 1997, eighteen years after the fall of the KR regime and four years after the 1993 elections which mark Cambodia's transition to some form of democracy did the Co-Prime Ministers of Cambodia request help from the United Nations (UN) to set up a tribunal to try KR leaders. Lengthy negotiations followed, and it was not until March 2003 that the international community and the Cambodian government agreed a way to try those who are alleged to have committed the greatest crimes in the KR period. The Extraordinary Chambers in the Courts of Cambodia (ECCC) were set up to try 'senior leaders of Democratic Kampuchea and those who were most responsible for the crimes and serious violations of Cambodian penal law, international humanitarian law and custom, and international conventions recognized by Cambodia, that were committed during the period from 17 April 1975 to 6 January 1979.'[7] In this chapter, which is substantially informed by research conducted at the ECCC and in Phnom Penh in 2011, I will first set out the key features of the ECCC, then document the successes and failures of the court, before broadening the analysis beyond the limited mandate of the court to look at the political context of efforts to bring justice in Cambodia, the actors and interests involved and the implications of the Cambodian case for recent accounts of the effects of trials on human rights and democracy. The Cambodian case is

6 The amnesties are discussed in more detail in the second half of the chapter.

7 Law on the Establishment of the Extraordinary Chambers, with inclusion of amendments as promulgated on 27 October 2004 (NS/RKM/1004/006).

a particularly rich one in the context of the three debates outlined in the Introduction to this volume, given that efforts to bring peace (through amnesty or pardon) were replaced, once peace was established, by efforts to bring justice (through trials), and those trials have both retributive and restorative elements. There is also a tension between top-down control (through the UN and the Cambodian government) and bottom-up influence through newly formed human rights NGOs who campaign for and around the trials.

Key Features of the ECCC

The ECCC is a genuinely hybrid court – the first of its kind – in which local and international actors, money and procedures coexist (and often clash). In many ways it can be seen as an improvement upon past international and hybrid tribunals. The Chambers are a part of the Cambodian court system rather than a stand-alone tribunal and are located in a military compound outside Phnom Penh – close to where many of the crimes took place – instead of thousands of miles away (as is the case with the International Criminal Tribunal for the former Yugoslavia and the International Criminal Tribunal for Rwanda). Unlike at the Special Court for Sierra Leone, the judges appointed by the Cambodian government at the ECCC (hereinafter 'Cambodian' or 'national') are in the majority in each Chamber vis-à-vis the judges appointed by the UN (hereinafter 'international'). There are three Cambodian judges out of five in the Pre-Trial and Trial Chambers and four out of seven in the Supreme Court Chamber, which hears appeals. But a balance has been struck between local and international influence: judges must reach a 'super majority' (or 'majority plus one') judgement on any positive decision, meaning it is not possible for the Cambodian judges alone to override concerns of the international judges or vice versa. The other organs of the court are also divided along national-international lines. There are two Co-Prosecutors (one Cambodian and one international), two Co-Investigating Judges, and two Civil Party Lead Co-Lawyers. Most major administrative functions of the court (for instance the Budget and Finance, Personnel and

Security and Safety sections) also have co-heads. Importantly for public coverage of, and involvement in, the court, and in contrast to other war crimes trials, much of the business in trials is conducted in the Cambodian national language (Khmer), and a Khmer translation of all proceedings is broadcast into the public gallery.

The funding for the ECCC is also hybrid, with the budget split into national and international components. The national component for 2012 is US$10.3 million, and the international component $35.4 million.[8] Both components are funded by voluntary contributions, with the shares from main donors up to June 2012 as follows: Japan 50 per cent; Australia 11 per cent; United States 9 per cent; Germany 6 per cent; France 6 per cent.[9] The major donors to the national component are Japan, the UN Trust Fund and the European Union, alongside the Cambodian government, which has paid around $5.12 million into the budget as well as provided the premises for the court and paid for the detention of suspects (claimed to be an in-kind contribution of $8.2 million, making the funds contributed by Cambodia overall second only to those contributed by Japan).

Finally, the law applied by the ECCC is hybrid – mostly Cambodian and therefore mostly civil, with some elements of international criminal law used when Cambodian law does not provide sufficient guidance on an issue, and some common-law practice used by international judges who find it hard to learn the civil law system. The civil law system means not just that Co-Investigating Judges rather than an Office of the Prosecutor conduct investigations for cases, but also that many more people may be parties to the case than under common law systems. Anyone with a prima facie reason to be classified as a victim can be represented in cases as a Civil Party. The ECCC is the first of the international and hybrid tribunals to allow victims of alleged crimes to participate in this way.

8 ECCC Budget 2012–13, at http://www.eccc.gov.kh/sites/default/files/ECCC%20Budget%202012-2013.pdf, accessed 24 June 2013.

9 Report: 'ECCC Financial Outlook' 30 June 2012, at http://www.eccc.gov.kh/sites/default/files/5-Financial%20Outlook%20-%2030%20June%202012.pdf, accessed 24 June 2013.

Successes of the ECCC

Perhaps the most significant and unexpected success of the ECCC is the fact that it is functioning at all. After years of negotiations, which were often at the verge of collapse, the ECCC has opened four cases. The court cannot, unfortunately, hold Pol Pot to account – he died in 1998, after having been tried by the leader of another KR faction, Ta Mok, for the murder of his second-in-command, Son Sen, and placed under house arrest in Thailand (ironic indeed that the only justice Pol Pot ever faced was from a member of his own regime – a regime which murdered almost all legal professionals in Cambodia while it held power). However, the accused persons being tried by the ECCC are of (for the most part) significant rank.

Case 001 is a single-accused case, which is now complete. After seventy-two days of evidence and the testimony of twenty-four witnesses, nine experts and twenty-two Civil Parties, Kaing Guek Eav (alias Duch), the former Chairman of the Khmer Rouge S-21 Security Center in Phnom Penh (also known as Tuol Sleng) was found guilty by the Trial Chamber on 26th July 2010 of crimes against humanity (persecution on political grounds, under which extermination, imprisonment, torture and other inhumane acts were subsumed) and grave breaches of the Geneva Conventions (willful killing, torture and inhumane treatment, willfully causing great suffering or serious injury to body or health, willfully depriving a prisoner of war or civilian of the rights of fair and regular trial, and unlawful confinement of a civilian). Around 17,000 people are estimated to have been tortured at S-21, with most of them being taken, after signing coerced confessions, to be murdered at the 'killing fields' of Choeung Ek.[10] Duch was sentenced to life imprisonment (increased by the Supreme Court Chamber from the thirty-year sentence imposed

10 The ECCC press release on the Duch verdict states, 'Although finding a minimum of 12,272 individuals to have been detained and executed at S-21 on the basis of prisoner lists, the Chamber indicated that the actual number of detainees is likely to have been considerably greater.' ECCC press release, at http://www.eccc.gov.kh/en/articles/kaing-guek-eav-convicted-crimes-against-humanity-and-grave-breaches-geneva-conventions-1949, accessed 24 June 2013.

by the Trial Chamber), and the trial is regarded as generally fair, having been conducted according to accepted standards of international due process.[11]

Case 002 is a more significant case, due to the status of its defendants. On 21 November 2011, the Trial Chamber began to hear evidence against Nuon Chea, former Deputy Secretary of the Communist Party of Kampuchea; Ieng Sary, former Deputy Prime Minister for Foreign Affairs (now deceased) and Khieu Samphan, former Head of State.[12] The defendants are charged with crimes against humanity, grave breaches of the Geneva Conventions of 1949 and genocide under international law and homicide, torture and religious persecution within the meaning of the Cambodian Penal Code from 1956. This is the centrepiece trial of the ECCC, as the accused are alleged to be the most senior surviving leaders of Democratic Kampuchea.

Cases 003 and 004 are less progressed, and may not progress at all beyond their current state (for reasons explained below). In September 2009, the international Co-Prosecutor requested the Co-Investigating Judges to initiate investigations of five additional suspects – the as-yet officially unidentified subjects of Cases 003 and 004. The accused are widely believed to be former KR military commanders Meas Muth and Sou Met (who are thought to be accused of murder, torture, unlawful detention, forced labour and persecution) in Case 003 and rumoured to be KR Secretaries (district chiefs) 'Me' Im Chaem, 'Ta' An and 'Ta' Tith in Case 004.[13]

11 Michelle Staggs Kelsall et al., 'Lessons Learned from the "Duch" Trial', Asian International Justice Initiative's KRT Trial Monitoring Group, December 2009, p. 6.

12 The fourth of the original defendants in Case 002, Ieng Thirith, former Minister of Social Affairs, has been declared unfit to stand trial at present due to her progressive degenerative Alzheimer's disease.

13 Open Society Justice Initiative, 'The Future of Cases 003 and 004 at the Extraordinary Chambers in the Courts of Cambodia', October 2012, at http://www.opensociety foundations.org/sites/default/files/eccc-report-cases3and4-100112_0.pdf, accessed 24th June 2013; KI-Media, "Charged Persons" of Case 003/004 Named in PUBLIC Documents (a Compliation), 9 April 2011, at http://www.scribd.com/doc/52628662/Charged-Persons-of-Case-003-004-Named-in-PUBLIC-Documents-a-Compilation, accessed 24 June 2013.

Beyond confounding expectations by actually staging trials, other important successes cited by ECCC staff in interviews include allowing, for the first time in the history of international criminal justice, survivors to participate as Civil Parties. Although some victims feel that they are being asked to do too much (they are being given the responsibility for reconciling when senior KR cadres are not prepared to admit they were wrong or to ask for forgiveness, and many are being shielded from prosecution instead of put in front of the court) there is a broad consensus that the inclusion of Civil Parties in war crimes trials such as this is a progressive move as it has the potential to make justice more victim-centred or restorative.[14]

Almost as significant as Civil Party participation is public access to the Duch trial. The ECCC has the largest public gallery of any war crimes tribunal, and 28,000 people observed some part of Case 001 (usually a maximum of half a day) – which court staff proudly cites as the largest ever attendance at any court case, anywhere in the world.[15] It's not entirely clear if this is indicative of public interest – Robert Petit, the first international Prosecutor at the ECCC, noted that there were long queues to attend the first days of the Duch trial, but that attendance fell off after that, and the ECCC itself paid for the majority of the attendees to be bussed in for the trial.[16] However, the numbers of attendees to some extent speaks for itself – even if people did not see much of the trial or did not understand the technical argument or the context, they did still see Duch in the dock, which many found hard to believe after the KR enjoyed more than thirty years of impunity and

14 Interviews in 'S-21 The Khmer Rouge Killing Machine' film, directed by Pithy Pan, and interviews with court staff and Civil Parties conducted by the author in Cambodia in March 2011.

15 ECCC, ECCC Surpasses Milestone of 100,000 Visitors press release, 4 January 2012, at http://www.eccc.gov.kh/en/articles/kaing-guek-eav-convicted-crimes-against-humanity-and-grave-breaches-geneva-conventions-1949, accessed 24 June 2013, and interviews with senior court officials, March 2011. The total number of public visitors to the court since February 2009 has now exceeded 110,000.

16 Remarks made at event 'The Khmer Rouge Tribunal and the Challenges of the Hybrid Model', SOAS, London, 17 June 2009.

a not inconsiderable amount of power within Cambodia. The Outreach office of the ECCC has learned from previous tribunals and invested a great deal in communicating the activities of the ECCC to the public, and international donors supported the production of 'Duch on Trial', a television show summarising and discussing developments in Case 001, which attracted up to three million viewers – 20 per cent of the Cambodian population.[17]

In the interviews of senior staff conducted by the author in 2011, public interest in justice and the ECCC was commonly declared to be a mark of success, and Cambodians have been regularly surveyed to find out their views on accountability and the court. However, the results do not tell a clear story. A nationwide survey of 1,000 Cambodians published in 2009 showed that while 80 per cent of respondents considered themselves to be victims of the KR, 85 per cent had little or no knowledge of the ECCC (despite five detainees already being in custody at the ECCC at the time of the survey, and the Duch trial about to start).[18] The majority wanted to see those responsible for what happened during the KR regime held accountable (90 per cent), to learn more about the KR period (85 per cent) and to see the KR suffer (71 per cent). Smaller majorities were in favour of the Cambodian government being in charge of the accountability process (58 per cent) and of KR leaders and officials being held accountable (51 per cent – versus 24 per cent Pol Pot; 20 per cent the KR regime as a whole; 11 per cent the five detainees at the time; KR cadres and local officials 6 per cent; foreign states who supported the KR 2 per cent).[19] Trials (49 per cent), punishment (23 per cent) and imprisonment (12 per cent) were far preferred to making those responsible speak the

17 Christopher Shay, 'Cambodia's Trial of the Century, Televised', *Time Magazine*, 11 September 2009, at http://www.genocidewatch.org/images/Cambodia_09_09_11_Cambodia_s_trial_of_the_century,_televised.pdf, accessed 24 June 2013.

18 Human Rights Center, University of California Berkeley, 'So We Will Never Forget', January 2009, at http://www.law.berkeley.edu/HRCweb/pdfs/So-We-Will-Never-Forget.pdf, accessed 24 June 2013.

19 Human Rights Center, 'So We Will Never Forget', p. 31.

truth (5 per cent), confess (5 per cent), or apologise (2.5 per cent).[20] Only 26 per cent thought the ECCC was likely to bring justice, but this has increased since the Duch trial, with a 2010 follow-up survey showing that 37 per cent believed the ECCC would bring justice.[21] Seventy-five per cent of Cambodians surveyed were aware of the ECCC in the 2010 survey, indicating the Outreach program's success, but 90 per cent could still not name the five suspects detained at the time.

A final likely success of the ECCC is the momentum it has helped to generate towards a broader societal debate. It is too early to know if it has or will deter future violence, but it has, it seems, enabled the violence of the past to be discussed more openly: the KR period is now (for the first time) a compulsory aspect of school curriculums.[22]

Problems Faced by ECCC

The ECCC faces fundamental problems as an institution, and less overwhelming problems in its conduct of trials. The most difficult aspects of its operation are due to its hybrid structure. International staff are UN employees, with UN protection, UN pay cheques and UN rights and responsibilities, which breeds resentment. Cambodian staff have to rely on the largesse of the Cambodian government rather than the UN. The high level of Cambodian involvement at the court has led to a number of corruption allegations, with reports, for instance, of Cambodian staff having to pay parts of their salaries to government officials who gave them their jobs, or to Sean Visoth, former administrative director of the ECCC.[23] A report by independent auditors in 2007 went as far as to recommend that because of the corruption in hiring practices at the tribunal,

20 Human Rights Center, 'So We Will Never Forget', p. 32.

21 Human Rights Center, University of California Berkeley, 'After the First Trial', June 2011.

22 Interview with Youk Chhang, Director of the Documentation Center of Cambodia, March 2011.

23 Elena Lesley, 'Court Staffers Confirm Corruption at Tribunal', *Phnom Penh Post*, 27 February 2009.

all Cambodian staff should be fired.[24] Interviews with international staff in 2011 revealed that many of them believe the majority of the Cambodian staff were appointed for their connections to government more than their qualifications for their jobs. The Cambodian judges are for the most part members of the Cambodian People's Party or otherwise connected to the Hun Sen regime. That said, international staff also tend to accept that the national staff at the ECCC are often very good at their jobs – many have more senior roles in the national system (which they usually retain) but appreciate the salary and status benefits that a job at the ECCC offers.[25]

Aside from controlling the staff at the court, the government has other effects. For instance, the agreement between the UN and Cambodia specified that trials should take place in Phnom Penh, but the government preferred to locate the trials out of the centre – citing reasons of security for putting the court in a military compound forty-five minutes' drive from the city. In order to square the location with the agreement, a Royal Decree was passed to change the boundaries of Phnom Penh to include the part of Chaom Chau Commune in which the compound is found.[26] This has served to make the court less accessible to ordinary Cambodians (there are very rarely Cambodians present in the public gallery who are not funded to attend, or there as Civil Parties), and it may serve to intimidate witnesses who are reminded by the military insignia around the compound of the strength and capabilities of the government, but it is relatively benign compared to other examples of government interference.

The most invidious effect that the government has had has been to intimidate national staff at the ECCC, leading to an 'unprecedented crisis of confidence [in the court] due to allegations of judicial

24 John Hall, 'Trial on Trial', *New York Times*, 11 March 2009, at http://www.nytimes.com/2009/03/10/opinion/10iht-edhall.1.20723411.html?pagewanted=all&_r=0, accessed 24 June 2013.

25 Interviews with senior court officials, March 2011.

26 See ECCC webpage 'The address of the ECCC changed', 29 July 2006, at http://www.eccc.gov.kh/en/articles/address-eccc-changed, accessed 24 June 2013.

misconduct'.[27] Prime Minister Hun Sen strongly opposes the international Co-Prosecutor's determination to see the Co-Investigating judges complete proper investigations of at least five more Khmer Rouge officials in Cases 003 and 004.[28] Hun Sen stated his views in April 2009: 'I would prefer to see this court fail than for war to come back to Cambodia . . . [t]hat is my absolute position . . . just focus on these few people [i.e. the accused in Cases 001 and 002] . . . I would pray for this court to run out of money and for the foreign judges and prosecutors to walk out. That would allow for Cambodia to finish the trial by itself'.[29] In September the same year he argued: 'If you tried [more suspects] without taking national unification and peace into consideration, and if war occurred, killing between 200,000 and 300,000 people more, who would be responsible for it? . . . I have achieved this work [peace]. I will not let anybody destroy it.'[30] And in October 2009, he is reported to have told UN Secretary General Ban Ki-Moon that the ECCC should shut down after Case 002.[31] The prime minister's position on Cases 003 and 004 seems to have had significant effects on the Cambodian staff at the court, and deep divisions have become apparent between national and international staff. In September 2009, the international Co-Prosecutor at the time, Robert Petit, requested that the office of the Co-Investigating Judges open investigations into five suspects not covered in Cases 001 and 002. His national Co-Prosecutor, Chea Leang, objected to his request.

27 Open Society Justice Initiative, 'Recent Developments at the ECCC', November 2011, p. 1.

28 Neth Pheaktra and Georgia Wilkins, 'Judges should Focus on Current KR Suspects: Government', *The Phnom Penh Post*, 12 March 2008; Open Society Justice Initiative, 'Political Interference at the Extraordinary Chambers in the Courts of Cambodia', July 2010.

29 Georgia Wilkins, 'Government Rejects Charges of Political Manipulation at ECCC', *The Phnom Penh Post*, 29 May 2009.

30 Ian MacKinnon, 'Prosecutor Wants to Indict Five More Khmer Rouge', *Financial Times*, 7 September 2009, at http://www.ft.com/cms/s/0/e6dc489e-9b98-11de-b214-00144feabdc0.html#axzz2X7iVx01o, accessed 24 June 2013.

31 Open Society Justice Initiative, 'Recent Developments at the ECCC: December 2010 Update.'

The Pre-Trial Chamber was asked to make a decision, but split along national-international lines, so could not reach a super majority. Failure to reach a decision meant that Internal Rule 71 (4) c applied – that is, action proposed by the international Co-Prosecutor had to be executed. In 2010, Co-Investigating Judge Marcel Lemonde announced that he was moving forward with the investigations despite a lack of support from the national Co-Investigating Judge, You Bunleng. However, You managed to block the investigation until Lemonde resigned. Some form of investigation was eventually conducted, and the Co-Investigating Judges (with Lemonde now replaced by Siegfried Blunk) announced on 29 April 2011 that their investigation was concluded – without having interviewed the suspects or visited alleged crime sites. Andrew Cayley, the international Co-Prosecutor, requested that the investigation be re-opened, and a day later Chea Leang, the Cambodian Co-Prosecutor, issued a statement recommending that Case 003 be closed without trial on the basis that the accused do not fall under the jurisdiction of the court.[32] On 7 June 2011 the Co-Investigating Judges rejected Cayley's request that they continue to investigate Case 003, and later the same month a number of Blunk's international staff resigned in protest at the premature closure of the Case 003 investigation. The crisis escalated further when Blunk resigned in October 2011, citing repeated statements by Cambodian government officials opposing Cases 003 and 004 that 'will be perceived as attempted interference'.[33] Swiss Judge Laurent Kasper-Ansermet was appointed by the UN to replace Blunk, but the Cambodian government refused to approve his appointment, and Kasper-Ansermet resigned in March 2012, effective May that year. According to a press release, he

32 The Cambodian public is also split over whether the court should try more than the current four detainees. A 2009 survey by the Documentation Center of Cambodia found that 52% of the 1,100 people questioned supported further indictments. See 'Indict No More', *Voice of America*, 25 March 2009, at http://www.voacambodia.com/content/a-40-2009-03-25-voa3-90171967/1356797.html, accessed 24 June 2013.

33 ECCC Press Release by the International Co-Investigating Judge, 10 October 2011, at http://www.eccc.gov.kh/sites/default/files/documents/courtdoc/2012-12-24%2016:37/E189_3_1_1.1.3_EN.pdf, accessed 24 June 2013.

'found himself in a highly hostile environment and was severely impeded in the day-to-day performance of his duties' for 'reasons which are manifestly more political and financial than strictly judicial'.[34] The breakdown of national-international relations over Cases 003 and 004 is a grave threat to the court, and the court has been condemned by NGOs and potential Civil Parties for seeming to bow to government pressure.[35]

The reputation the ECCC has for corruption and government tampering and the inefficiency of the court in bringing the cases to trial has led to severe problems generating sufficient funds for the institution to continue its work. From July 2008 until the end of 2009, amid allegations of corruption, the UN Development Program froze funding from international donors to the Cambodian side of the budget, almost bankrupting the court and causing Cambodian staff to work for several months without pay.[36] In January 2012 the Cambodian budget was again exhausted as no new funds were pledged by donors, leaving around 300 Cambodian staff unlikely to be paid for their work in the first quarter of 2012, and reports suggested that Cambodian judges had not been paid since October 2011.[37] The court is not short of funds only because of donor reticence – it is also running substantially over budget. The court was initially expected to cost around $60 million in total, and have completed its work in three years.[38] Both of those figures have been exposed as

34 Press Release by the Reserve International Co-Investigating Judge, 4 May 2012, at http://www.eccc.gov.kh/en/articles/press-release-reserve-international-co-investigating-judge, accessed 24 June 2013.

35 Sebastian Strangio, 'Limited Liability for Khmer Rouge Tribunal', *Asia Times*, 12 May 2011, at http://www.sebastianstrangio.com/2011/05/12/limited-liability-for-khmer-rouge-tribunal/, accessed 24 June 2013. In November 2011 the Open Society Initiative began to call for the UN to establish an Independent Inquiry into 'allegations of judicial misconduct, incompetence, and lack of judicial independence by the co-investigating judges' ('Recent Developments', November 2011, p. 2). There is no sign at present that the UN will heed this call.

36 Interviews with senior court officials, March 2011.

37 Bridget di Certo, 'KRT Pay Freeze Will Linger', *Phnom Penh Post*, 30 January 2012.

38 Peter Maguire, 'Cambodia's Troubled Tribunal', *New York Times*, 28 July 2010, at http://www.nytimes.com/2010/07/29/opinion/29iht-edmaguire.html, accessed 24 June 2013.

significant underestimates. The total estimated expenditure for 2006 to 2013 is now almost $240 million, and the ECCC Web site declares: 'There is still an urgent need for funding in order to continue the work of the court. We are hoping to receive ongoing funding from donor countries as well as concerned organisations, companies, foundations and individuals.'[39]

There is no sense yet of whether the court will have enough money to continue even to the end of Case 002. There is also little sense of whether it should continue, given the many needs of Cambodian people. When asked in a 2008 survey what their priorities were, Cambodians listed jobs (83 per cent), health services (20 per cent) and food (17 per cent). They felt that the government should focus on the economy (56 per cent) and building infrastructure (48 per cent) more than justice (2 per cent). Seventy-six per cent felt that the government should focus on contemporary problems rather than addressing crimes committed by the KR. Fifty-three per cent would rather spend money on something other than the ECCC.[40] Given the corruption at the court, its lack of efficiency and the low level of public support for spending so much money (despite a reasonably high appetite for accountability), it is hard to justify continuing to spend such large sums on such imperfect justice.

As well as facing significant structural problems, the court has faced problems connected to running trials. Case 001 ran relatively smoothly for months, assisted by the fact that the defendant, Duch, cooperated with the court, gave large amounts of information and expressed remorse at his actions.[41] However, on the final day of his trial, Duch announced that

39 ECCC webpage 'How is the court financed?', at http://www.eccc.gov.kh/en/faq/how-court-financed, accessed 24 June 2013 and ECCC Budget 2012–13, at http://www.eccc.gov.kh/sites/default/files/ECCC%20Budget%202012-2013.pdf, accessed 24 June 2013.

40 Human Rights Center, 'So We Will Never Forget', pp. 34–35.

41 Julia Wallace, 'The Eccentricity of Evil: A Khmer Rouge Leader Goes on Trial', *The Atlantic*, 12 April 2011, at http://www.theatlantic.com/international/archive/2011/04/the-eccentricity-of-evil-a-khmer-rouge-leader-goes-on-trial/237179/, accessed 24 June 2013.

he should be released in the name of national reconciliation, as he was not one of the senior leaders of the KR, and could not therefore be one of those most responsible. This debate over the court's personal jurisdiction, that is, over who counts as a senior leader of the KR or one of those most responsible (and whether by implication only senior leaders of the KR can be thought of as those most responsible) continues and is the main issue on which Duch's appeal was based. It is a loaded and divisive issue, as shown by the 2011 statement of the national Co-Prosecutor, which argues that defendants in Cases 003 and 004 fall outside the jurisdiction of the court.[42]

The role of victims has also presented challenges. The victim support section of the ECCC and the Trial Chamber became overwhelmed by Civil Parties in Case 001, and the situation can only get more difficult to manage. In Case 001, the ninety people entitled to act as Civil Parties were divided into four groups, each with one Cambodian and one international Co-Lawyer, meaning that witnesses could be questioned by up to eight Civil Party lawyers, as well as lawyers for the prosecution and defence. More than 2,000 people have applied for Civil Party status in Case 002, which has led to the court ordering that all Civil Parties coordinate their cases through two lead Co-Lawyers. This may be necessary for the efficient running of the case, but it also denies Civil Parties control of their own representation and reduces the restorative aspect of the justice offered.

Civil Parties have also been deeply disappointed at the lack of imagination on the part of the Trial Chamber in awarding reparations. There is

42 Press Release: Statement from the National Co-Prosecutor Regarding Case File 003, 10 May 2011, at http://www.eccc.gov.kh/sites/default/files/media/5-Press%20release%20by%20the%20National%20Prosecutor-10%20May%202011-Eng.pdf, accessed 24 June 2013. The Supreme Court Chamber found in the Duch judgment that 'the term "senior leaders of Democratic Kampuchea and those who were most responsible" refers to two categories of Khmer Rouge officials which are not dichotomous . . . Both categories are "suspects" subject to criminal prosecution before the ECCC.' Paragraph 9, Summary of Duch Appeals Judgment, at http://www.eccc.gov.kh/sites/default/files/documents/courtdoc/03022012Summary-Eng.pdf, accessed 24 June 2013. This judgment is significant in that it leaves open the possibility of prosecuting those who were not 'senior leaders', e.g. the accused in Cases 03 and 04.

no provision for the ECCC to award reparations to individuals, but there is scope to award collective or 'moral' reparations.[43] Many were suggested by Civil Parties in Case 001 – for instance, naming public buildings on behalf of victims, funding victims' visits to memorial sites, funding psychological and medical help for victims with some of the entrance money to the Tuol Sleng and Choeung Ek memorial sites and so on. However, the Trial Chamber found it outside its competence (for reasons which are unclear) to award any such reparations, and instead decided only to list the names of the Civil Parties in the final judgement. The Supreme Court Chamber clarified the position of the ECCC, but not in favour of the Civil Parties. It ruled that the court had no jurisdiction to grant requests for reparation that would require the Cambodian authorities to act to provide the reparatory measures. It further ruled that the ECCC could only order reparations the costs of which were borne by the convicted person/s. In this case, Duch was found to be indigent, thus no reparations of any significance were awarded.[44]

Finally, a problem that did not emerge in Case 001, but is likely to slow down or even prevent the completion of Case 002 is the condition of the defendants. Nuon Chea is 86 and Khieu Samphan is 82, and each has health problems. There is a genuine concern that one or both may not live to the end of the trial.

Assessing the ECCC

None of the challenges faced by the ECCC are insurmountable, and it has made some notable achievements. However, judging the success or failure of the court requires doing more than examining how the institution is performing according to its own mandate. For a transitional mechanism to be a success – for it to bring some sort of justice and some measure of reconciliation – it should identify and hold to account those most responsible for harms under the previous system. Yet, because of

43 On reparations at the ECCC see Renée Jeffery, 'Beyond Repair? Collective and Moral Reparations at the Khmer Rouge Tribunal', *Journal of Human Rights* (forthcoming).

44 Paragraphs 65–68 of Duch Appeals Judgment.

the very small number of people likely to face trial at the court, the ECCC works to offer impunity to the vast majority of those responsible for the destruction of Cambodia that started in the 1960s and whose effects are still felt now. To understand the challenges facing the ECCC and judge its contribution to a Cambodian transition, the national and international political contexts of the KR regime, the negotiations to establish the ECCC and the contemporary operation of the court must be examined.

At the start of this chapter I noted that the KR regime was in place between 1975 and 1979. The Introduction to the ECCC page on the ECCC Web site confirms this story:

> The Khmer Rouge regime took power on 17 April 1975 and was overthrown on 7 January 1979. Perhaps up to three million people perished during this period of 3 years, 8 months and 20 days. The end of Khmer Rouge period was followed by a civil war. That war finally ended in 1998, when the Khmer Rouge political and military structures were dismantled.[45]

This is factually correct, and it is the truncated narrative on which justifications for the limited scope of the ECCC rest (that the Chambers should try only the KR leadership and those most responsible for crimes committed during the four-year period), but such a narrative omits too much to be allowed to stand without challenge. A more sensitive history of the period identifies many more actors who could (and should) be held to account – many of whom were and remain keen for the ECCC to be structured and operate in ways that omit consideration of their responsibility.

Few states have been so caught up in the machinations of great power politics in the second half of the twentieth century as Cambodia. The Khmer Rouge did not arise from nowhere – the instability through which it gained sufficient support and room for manoeuvre to launch a coup was aided significantly by the U.S. bombing of North Vietnamese supply

45 ECCC webpage 'Introduction to the ECCC', at http://www.eccc.gov.kh/en/about-eccc/introduction, accessed 24 June 2013.

routes in Cambodia that started in earnest in 1969. The United States dropped a higher tonnage of bombs onto Cambodia (a neutral state) than the total of all allied bombs used in the Second World War, in a bombing campaign that is estimated to have killed around 150,000 Cambodians and forced two million from their homes and into towns and cities.[46] Between 1969 and 1973, the Khmer Rouge is estimated to have grown from a movement of 10,000 to more than 200,000 troops and militia, with their recruitment propaganda giving prominence to the effects of the U.S. bombing.[47] The KR rise was also aided, according to one of the defendants in Case 002, by U.S. support for the Lon Nol regime which the KR deposed: Khieu Samphan claims he realised that violence was necessary to transform Cambodia after the United States supported a violent coup in 1970 to install Lon Nol.[48] Soon after Lon Nol took power, he declared war on the Vietnamese and their perceived communist comrades the KR and allowed a U.S. and South Vietnamese ground invasion of Cambodia that left 11,000 dead.

The KR organised its own violent coup to depose the widely despised and extremely repressive U.S.-sponsored Lon Nol regime and embarked on its mission to create a classless society through radical revolution. But the KR did not rule alone – it relied heavily on Chinese support. Up to 15,000 Chinese technical advisors were deployed to Cambodia between 1975 and 1979.

A cooling in Sino-Vietnamese relations coupled with KR paranoia turned the regime against the Vietnamese, who had initially been thought of as sympathetic to the revolution. Border skirmishes began to break

46 Actual casualties are unknown. Kiernan estimates 150,000 (*The Pol Pot Regime*, New Haven: Yale, 2002), but some estimates are upwards of 600,000 (for instance, Christopher Hitchens, *The Trial of Henry Kissinger*, London: Verso, 2001).

47 Ben Kiernan and Taylor Owen, 'Roots of U.S. Troubles in Afghanistan: Civilian Bombing Casualties and the Cambodian Precedent', *The Asia-Pacific Journal*, 28 June 2010, at http://www.japanfocus.org/-ben-kiernan/3380#, accessed 24 June 2013. See also William Shawcross, *Sideshow: Kissinger, Nixon and the Destruction of Cambodia* (New York: Cooper Square Press, 2002).

48 'Facing Genocide' film, directed by David Aronowitsch and Staffan Lindberg.

out, and in 1979 Vietnam invaded Cambodia and deposed the KR – for reasons of realpolitik much more than humanitarianism (as reports of later Vietnamese atrocities attest). China and the United States (pursuing a détente in their relations) worked together for the first time to try to prevent the Vietnamese-installed regime from being recognised as a legitimate government.[49] Chinese advisors in Cambodia were replaced by Vietnamese, Soviet, Cuban and East European advisors – which led the U.S. and UK governments to block, well into the 1980s, NGO attempts to deliver emergency aid to the victims of the KR regime who desperately needed it.[50] In turn, the Vietnamese and Cambodians tried to block aid being sent to the refugee camps on the Thai border into which the KR (along with thousands of refugees) had been driven, and from where they regrouped and gained control of various zones. The Thai army tried to prevent the influx of refugees in part by driving many (40,000 in one incident alone) of those fleeing war back into Cambodia across mine fields. Thousands died this way – from mines, disease or dehydration.[51]

Throughout the period 1979 to 1993, the KR were supplied by China and Thailand and supported by many Western states (led by the United States and including the United Kingdom, Canada and Australia) who insisted that the KR delegation retain control of Cambodia's seat at the UN General Assembly long after the scale of atrocities committed by the KR was known.[52] From 1979: 'Not upsetting China over Cambodia became a major plank in Western governments' approach to resolving the conflict, right up to the drafting and signing of the Paris Peace Agreement twelve years later'.[53] The international community tried to starve the PRK of power, in the hope that the regime would collapse. In order to avoid this, the PRK (led by Hun Sen) started a peace and reconciliation initiative with rival factions and began calls to prosecute KR leaders

49 Fawthrop and Jarvis, *Getting Away with Genocide*, p. 25.
50 Fawthrop and Jarvis, *Getting Away with Genocide*, p. 18 and pp. 64–66.
51 Haing, Survival in the Killing Fields, p. 414; Dunlop, The Lost Executioner, p. 186.
52 Fawthrop and Jarvis, *Getting Away with Genocide*, pp. 52–70.
53 Fawthrop and Jarvis, *Getting Away with Genocide*, p. 26.

as part of the peace process. However, during the two years of peace negotiations in Paris from 1989, no Western states supported such trials. Japan proposed a commission of inquiry, but the United States resisted on the basis that it was 'likely to introduce confusion in the international peace efforts'.[54] Peace was unequivocally prioritised above justice by international actors – though the commitment of the PRK to justice is doubtful. The call for trials was driven more by a desire to discredit a rival force in the civil war as it was by ethical principle, as evidenced by the PRK's pragmatic use of amnesties in the 1990s.

Vietnam unilaterally withdrew from Cambodia in 1989, and a peace was finally brokered between the warring factions in 1991, following sustained pressure by China and the United States. The peace agreement did not include a mechanism to hold anyone accountable for past crimes, but rather acted to re-legitimise the KR within Cambodian politics by giving the KR delegation – led by Case 002 defendant Khieu Samphan – rights equal to those of other political parties. The United Nations Transitional Authority in Cambodia (UNTAC) was deployed in 1992 to organise elections. The elections (which were boycotted by the KR, who refused to participate in the new Supreme National Council) were held in May 1993, and UNTAC left only four months later, at the behest of the UN Security Council (UNSC) rather than because there were any signs that Cambodia was now at peace: '[f]or the outside world, the main objective had been achieved, namely to enable the former cold war powers to disengage from a country in which they no longer had any interest'.[55]

Hun Sen lost the 1993 elections, but forced his way into a power-sharing coalition by threatening a coup. He worked through the 1990s to defeat the KR politically, including passing the 1994 Law on Outlawing the Group of Democratic Kampuchea. The law included an amnesty clause for rank and file members of the KR, which attracted thousands of

54 Fawthrop and Jarvis, *Getting Away with Genocide*, p. 98.

55 Margot Picken, 'The Beleaguered Cambodians', *New York Review of Books*, 13 January 2011, p. 4.

defectors to the coalition's side.[56] He also engineered in 1996 a controversial Royal Pardon for his 1979 conviction and immunity from prosecution under the 1994 Law for ex-Case 002 defendant Ieng Sary in exchange for his defection along with his forces to the government.[57] These amnesties were useful in bringing peace and accruing power to the coalition, but did not provide for any alternative forms of accountability in lieu of trials, making them hard to categorise as transitional justice mechanisms at all. The 1994 Law did recognise that the KR had committed crimes (the Preamble to the Law states that: 'criminal, terrorist and genocidal acts [have] been a characteristic of the group since it captured power in April 1975 – forcible movement, abduction, killing and subsequently also robbery and banditry, laying mines, indiscriminately throughout the plains and forests, destroying public and private property, leading the killing of civilians, forcibly taking and illegally occupying national territory, and selling natural resources by violating the sovereignty of the Kingdom of Cambodia') and Article 3 noted that KR members were still liable to existing criminal law, but Article 5 gave 'members' (as opposed to 'leaders') of the political organisation of the military forces of the KR six months to 'return to live under the control of the Royal Government in the Kingdom of Cambodia without facing punishment for crimes which they have committed.'[58] No alternative form of accountability was proposed in the Law, nor any attempted prior to the establishment of the ECCC, the scope of the amnesty (for 'crimes which they have committed') was extremely broad, and no human-rights-based justification for

56 Kassie Neou and Jeffrey C. Gallup, 'Human Rights and the Cambodian Past: In Defense of Peace Before Justice', *Human Rights Dialogue*, Vol. 1, No. 8 (1997), p. 1.

57 The ECCC Trial Chamber ruled on 3 November 2011 that the 1996 amnesty and Royal Decree are inapplicable to breaches of the 1949 Geneva Conventions, genocide and crimes against humanity, reasoning that 'an emerging consensus prohibits amnesties in relations to serious international crimes, based on a duty to investigate and prosecute these crimes and to punish their perpetrators' (Trial Chamber Judgment, 3 November 2011, E51/15, paragraph 53). This decision is currently under appeal.

58 Translation of the 1994 Law is taken from Ieng Sary's Supplement to His Rule 98 Preliminary Objection (Royal Pardon and Amnesty), 27 May 2011, at http://www.cambodiatribunal.org/sites/default/files/resources/e51_10_en.pdf, accessed 24 June 2013.

the amnesty was given, nor any commitment to improving human rights included. Even though the 1994 Law stated that KR leaders would still be liable for prosecution, even this provision was overturned in negotiations with Ieng Sary in 1996. The 1994 amnesty and the 1996 pardon and amnesty that followed it were straightforwardly power-political instruments which may have led (although I am not aware of any evidence for this) to improved human rights observance due to a de-escalation of conflict, but certainly did not aim at such a result.[59]

Only in 1997, when the KR was almost a spent force, did Co-Prime Ministers Hun Sen and Norodom Ranariddh request assistance from the UN in creating a judicial forum to bring the most senior leaders of the KR to justice. In order to avoid a Chinese veto at the UNSC, the issue was brought to the UN General Assembly, who supported the efforts to hold the KR leadership accountable (the UNGA resolution in 1997 was the first time either of the UN's principal organs had acknowledged the human rights violations of the KR regime).[60] The UN Secretary General responded by appointing a 'Group of Experts' who recommended that an international criminal tribunal be established on the basis that the Cambodian legal system lacked independence, skilled practitioners and the capacity to conduct trials with due process, and also because of concerns that the KR connections of some of those in power in the country would lead to too much political interference with the court.[61] The experts recommended trials of twenty to thirty people and supported a limited temporal and subject matter jurisdiction that excluded consideration of atrocities committed before or after 1975 to 1979 or war crimes committed by other states during 1975 to 1979 in order not to 'detract

59 For further discussion of legal aspects of the amnesties, see: Ronald C. Syle, 'A Limited Amnesty? Insights from Cambodia', in F. Lessa & L. Payne (eds.) *Amnesty in the Age of Human Rights Accountability* (Cambridge: Cambridge University Press, 2012), pp. 291–314.

60 Fawthrop and Jarvis, *Getting Away with Genocide*, p. 124.

61 The Group of Experts for Cambodia, Report of the Group of Experts for Cambodia Pursuant to General Assembly Resolution 52/135, UN doc S/1999/231, A/53/850, 16 March 1999.

from the unique and extraordinary nature of the crimes committed by the leaders of Democratic Kampuchea'.[62]

Hun Sen refused to accept a solely international court (in part to keep some level of control over it, but in part because of a deep – and mutual – distrust of the UN and international actors generally). While negotiations to establish a court were underway, Hun Sen continued his policy of de-fanging the KR, this time by welcoming Case 002 defendants Khieu Samphan and Nuon Chea to Phnom Penh as defectors in December 1998 and expressing a desire to 'dig a hole and bury the past' in order to avoid war (though stopping short of offering formal amnesty).[63] In spite of the public criticism this engendered, it marked the final defeat of the KR – and a corresponding decrease in Hun Sen's appetite for an accountability mechanism, suggesting again that the threat of trials was more a tool used to end the civil war and consolidate his regime's power than supported on the basis of justice.[64] After another four years of often acrimonious talks (spurred slowly onwards by Cambodian NGOs and international actors optimistic for success after the drafting of the Rome Statute to establish the International Criminal Court), in 2002 the UN pulled out of the negotiations on the basis that the court being proposed by Cambodia was neither independent nor impartial. Eventually a group of states, led by Japan and including the UK, France and the United States (which had changed policy in 1994 after NGO and Cambodian diaspora pressure had prompted the U.S. Congress to pass the Cambodian Genocide Justice Act, which required the U.S. government to support justice efforts in Cambodia) as well as ASEAN, pushed the UN back to the negotiating table, and a final agreement was reached in 2003.[65]

This history of the context and negotiations of the ECCC demonstrates both the political and moral implications of the limited jurisdiction

62 Cited in Fawthrop and Jarvis, *Getting Away with Genocide*, p. 127.

63 Cited in Fawthrop and Jarvis, *Getting Away with Genocide*, p. 135.

64 Robert Petit. 'Lawfare and International Tribunals', *Case Western Reserve Journal of International Law*, Vol. 43 (2010), p. 195.

65 See Craig Etcheson, *After the Killing Fields* (Westport: Praeger, 2005) and Fawthrop and Jarvis, *Getting Away with Genocide*, for more detail on the negotiations.

of the court, the shifting and often self-serving motives of the actors responsible for establishing it, and the difficulties involved in judging what success might mean given the history of internal repression and outside interference in Cambodia. Unfortunately the contemporary context of the court does not make assessment any easier – and a closer examination of the motives of both Hun Sen and international actors with regards to the ECCC suggests that the court is too much an instrument of power and misguided principle rather than of justice.

The relationship of the Hun Sen government to the ECCC since its establishment has been a troubled one. To its credit, the Cambodian government pushed for a tribunal to hold KR leaders to account well before the international community was willing to support such an idea. But it has not handled the court well. There are advantages to the government if the court legitimises the current regime's narrative of rescue, reinforcing the role of Hun Sen and his senior officials in overthrowing the KR, and drawing attention away from accusations of ongoing corruption and human rights. Duncan McCargo notes, 'Putting ageing Khmer Rouge leaders on trial provides a convenient set of domestic scapegoats for the shortcomings of the current government; and by demonstrating an ability to undermine the goals of the tribunal's international backers, Hun Sen may prove able further to entrench his power base and secure his own standing.'[66] Cooperation with the UN in establishing the ECCC also helped Cambodia to secure international aid and benefits. But the court is potentially a danger to the regime. In press coverage of the ECCC, in particular with regard to government interference in Cases 003 and 004, are frequent remarks that refer to Hun Sen's past as a KR cadre who was purged from the party in 1977 and fled to Vietnam.[67] References to his past are used to suggest that he does not want the court to prosecute more than Cases 001 and 002 because he himself could be implicated. In fact,

66 Duncan McCargo, 'Politics by Other Means?', *International Affairs*, Vol. 87, No. 3 (2011), p. 617.

67 For instance, MacKinnon, 'Prosecutor Wants to Indict Five More Khmer Rouge'; Ek Madra, 'Cambodia PM rejects wider Khmer Rouge Trials', 31 March 2009, at http://www.reuters.com/article/2009/03/31/us-cambodia-rouge-idUSTRE52U1IZ20090331, accessed 24 June 2013.

he held a relatively low status (junior commander) within the KR and it is more likely that he has two concerns: that if senior ex-KR politicians or officials are implicated it will undermine his regime and disrupt his claims to have led a movement that saved Cambodians from the KR, and that the longer the ECCC continues to work, the more unwelcome interest could be generated in the role played by China – once the KR's major patron, now the largest contributor of foreign aid and foreign direct investment to Cambodia – during the 1975 to 1979 period.[68] Hun Sen publically claims to be concerned that broadening the scope of prosecutions will lead Cambodia back to civil war – a concern that incidentally also serves to justify his particular style of for-all-intents-and-purposes authoritarian government.

Hun Sen and the Cambodian People's Party govern 'with absolute power and control all institutions that could challenge their authority'.[69] Since overthrowing his Co-Prime Minister, Norodom Ranariddh, in a coup in July 1997, and winning an election in 1998 that was marred by violence and intimidation, Hun Sen has had full control over the country. His regime has been accused of severely limiting rights of expression, association and assembly, of committing numerous human rights abuses and of allowing widespread corruption.[70] As Hauter explains:

> Hun Sen and his entourage have plunged Cambodia into a kind of hell. The country has become a regime of organized pillage, a vast bazaar of plundered goods, a regional center for shady business of every kind: drugs, gambling, sex. The head of the national police, one of Hun Sen's three closest associates, owns the largest brothel in the country.[71]

Much corruption (which USAID estimates is the cause of $500 million stolen by government officials from public funds every year in Cambodia)

68 As Craig Etcheson notes, as well as not wishing the details of its support for the KR to become widely known, for China, 'prosecuting the leaders of an Asian communist revolution for the deaths of millions of people during the revolution [would] be a very bad precedent, indeed'. Etcheson, *After the Killing Fields*, p. 154.

69 Picken, 'The Beleaguered Cambodians'.

70 Picken, 'The Beleaguered Cambodians'.

71 Francois Hauter, 'Chinese Shadows', *New York Review of Books*, 11 October 2007, p. 1.

is connected to the logging industry.[72] Logging was first used by the KR to gain funds and weapons from Thailand, but is now exploited by the many Cambodian politicians who have developed stakes in the industry. In 2007 *Global Witness* reported that:

> Cambodia is run by a kleptocratic elite that generates much of its wealth via the seizure of public assets, particularly natural resources. The forest sector provides a particularly vivid illustration of this asset-stripping process at work . . . Cambodia's army, military police, police and Forest Administration (FA) are all heavily involved in illegal logging . . . Cambodia's most powerful logging syndicate is led by relatives of Prime Minister Hun Sen and other senior officials.[73]

As well as logging, the government has been criticised for land-grabbing schemes (around 20,000 residents were ejected from their land in Phnom Penh alone in 2008) and in September 2009 Hun Sen withdrew from a World Bank project aimed at settling land disputes, signalling the likelihood of further forced evictions.[74] Land grabs are often designed to clear land for Chinese exploitation, and Western donors complain that their (weak) attempts to incentivise the Cambodian government to reform are blocked or outbid by China.[75] However, Japan and large Western donors continue to donate – a record $1.1 billion in 2010 – while encouraging but not requiring reform.[76]

72 Joel Brinkley, 'Cambodia's Curse', *Foreign Affairs,* 1 March 2009, at http://www.foreignaffairs.com/articles/64833/joel-brinkley/cambodias-curse, accessed 24 June 2013.

73 Global Witness, *Cambodia's Family Trees* (London: Global Witness, 2007), p. 6. Global Witness, *Country for Sale* (London: Global Witness, 2009) documents similar corruption around oil and mineral exploitation.

74 MacKinnon, 'Prosecutor Wants to Indict Five More Khmer Rouge'.

75 In March 2006 a group of international donors promised $600 million to Cambodia, with strict anticorruption and human rights conditions. A month later, China offered $600 million of its own – no strings attached. The 2006 attempted reforms, unsurprisingly, failed. For more on China's relationship with Cambodia, see Hauter, 'Chinese Shadows' and Ian Storey, 'China's Tightening Relationship with Cambodia', The Jamestown Foundation, China Brief, 1 July 2006, at http://www.asianresearch.org/articles/2881.html, accessed 24 June 2013.

76 Robert Carmichael, 'Cambodia's Donors Pledge $1.1 Billions for Development', *Voice of America*, 2 June 2010, at http://www.voanews.com/english/news/asia/Cambodias-Donors-Pledge-11-Billion-For-Development-95519109.html, accessed 24 June 2013.

There is good reason, therefore, not to trust the motives of the Cambodian government in its dealings with the court, and not to allow the court to provide legitimacy to the regime. Yet Hun Sen has been allowed to use the ECCC very well in his own interests thus far. He can claim credit for the establishment of the ECCC and its success in Case 001 and Case 002 (assuming it runs its course) and looks likely to prevent Cases 003 and 004 from reaching the Trial Chamber. His staff are still embedded in the court, and corruption allegations have not been meaningfully confronted. If the court collapses through lack of funding or the withdrawal of the UN, he can blame the international community. And at the same time as claiming to support justice, his government continues to pursue policies that run counter to the principles of human rights and international justice that underlie the ECCC, safe in the knowledge that little effort will be made by international actors to attach conditions to the millions of dollars' worth of external aid and investment given to Hun Sen's regime each year.

It is not clear whether external actors can help bring justice to Cambodia. The UN was correct to insist during negotiations on a court which was impartial and independent, but the ECCC has turned out not to be, and neither the UN nor external donors have used the leverage open to them. Of Cambodia's \$1.5bn national budget, \$825 million was supplied by foreign donors in 2010, meaning a great deal of scope for states to pressure the Hun Sen government to stop interfering in the court.[77] Despite Cambodia's reliance on external aid, '[n]either the UN nor state donors have vocally supported the court's judicial independence in the face of bellicose government statements.'[78]

It is also unclear whether external actors really want to bring justice to Cambodia. The expanded history of the KR given in this chapter should

77 Bureau of East Asian and Pacific Affairs Fact Sheet 'U.S. Relations with Cambodia', 13 June 2012, at http://www.state.gov/r/pa/ei/bgn/2732.htm, accessed 24 June 2013.

78 'Observers Fear Khmer Rouge Court Being Wound Down', *International Justice Tribune*, 6 April 2011, at http://www.rnw.nl/international-justice/article/observers-fear-khmer-rouge-court-being-wound-down, accessed 24 June 2013.

cause us to question any narrative that posits the Hun Sen regime as 'bad' and the international community as 'good' with regards to accountability in Cambodia. McCargo identifies an 'uneasy tension' between international liberalism and local authoritarianism, suggesting that, unlike liberal states, authoritarian states may choose to do business with their defeated enemies instead of or in addition to doing justice: '[t]he Hun Sen government chose to do business with Nuon Chea and other former Khmer Rouge leaders, until it became more advantageous to embrace a policy of putting them on trial.'[79] As outlined above, the situation is rather more complex. As well as some Cambodian victims and NGOs that support the ECCC for liberal reasons (and work alongside liberal international actors), the UN and a series of powerful, occasionally liberal, states did business with the KR and are keen to forget having done so, and/or do business with Hun Sen and are keen to continue.

Now that the ECCC has reached a crisis over Cases 003 and 004, the UN must decide whether to stay involved, and confer legitimacy onto the proceedings, or withdraw, and allow either show trials or no trials of the alleged masterminds of a genocide. If international actors withdraw from the ECCC and cause it to shut down, not only will this serve the interests of the government by ending trials, it will also reinforce the view of many in the country (and not without evidence) that the international community cannot be relied upon to protect or support them.

Conclusion

It is difficult to know how to conclude, in part because ECCC proceedings are ongoing, but also because there is so little hope in the story of transitional justice in Cambodia. Amnesty for lower-level perpetrators helped to attract KR deserters to the side of the Cambodian government (which brought some level of stability, but at a high price, given the allegations of government corruption just detailed) and there have been small

79 McCargo, 'Politics by Other Means?', p. 621.

successes at the ECCC – the most significant of which are the completion of Case 001 and the progress made in Case 002. It remains a possibility that the existence of the ECCC will inspire reform in the Cambodian judiciary – currently heavily dependent upon the government for patronage and protection, widely seen as untrustworthy and corrupt and often poorly qualified.[80]

It does seem clear, however, that the Cambodian case does not support the findings of recent studies that 'prosecutions may deter human rights violations by increasing the perception of the possibility of costs of repression for individual state officials' and that 'transitional justice overall has a positive effect on the change in human rights and democracy measures'.[81] Rather than its leaders feeling vulnerable to prosecution or being socialised into observing human rights and democracy norms, Cambodia seems to be regressing in its human rights record. Kheang finds that '[s]ince 2003, Cambodia has evolved into hegemonic party authoritarianism wherein the minimum criteria for democracy – freedom of expression, freedom of assembly – have been seriously curtailed while periodic elections have been maintained.'[82] With respect to human rights measures, based on PHYSINT data which uses a range of zero to indicate no government respect for physical integrity and eight to indicate full respect, Cambodia shows a significant decline from a score of five in 2002 to two in 2007. In line with the discussion above, Kheang notes that the international community has 'settled on granting the Cambodian government its international legitimacy based on economic performance and political stability' rather than on its observance of international norms.[83]

80 Surya Subedi, 'The UN Human Rights Mandate in Cambodia', *The International Journal of Human Rights*, Vol. 15, No. 2 (2011), pp. 247–261.

81 Kathryn Sikkink, *The Justice Cascade: How Human Rights are Changing World Politics*, (New York: W.W. Norton, 2011), p. 258, and Tricia Olsen, Leigh Payne and Andrew G. Reiter, 'The Justice Balance: When Transitional Justice Improves Human Rights and Democracy', *Human Rights Quarterly*, Vol. 32, No. 4 (2010), pp. 995–996.

82 Kheang Un, 'Cambodia: Moving Away from Democracy?', *International Political Science Review*, Vol. 32, No. 5 (2011), p. 547.

83 Kheang, 'Cambodia: Moving Away from Democracy', p. 547.

The willingness of the international community to overlook the present government's disregard of human rights standards coupled with the success of interested parties in limiting the temporal and personal jurisdiction of the ECCC so severely, means that far from signalling an end to impunity in Cambodia, the ECCC has demonstrated the power of the ruling elite to limit the administration of justice to those it seeks to delegitimise.

Of course no institution will be perfect – certainly not one run in an unsettled political climate, with authority split between national and (often uncoordinated) international actors. But what we are seeing in Cambodia is not bureaucratic incompetence or the best available option (which will inevitably reflect the existing power hierarchy to some extent), but complicity in impunity. It might be argued that Cambodia would be worse off without the ECCC than with it, and there is no way to prove that this is not the case. It might also be argued that Cambodia would be better off with a fully international tribunal than a hybrid model, though this was never a political possibility. But to end the discussion with either argument is to renege on the responsibility that theorists of transitional justice have to imagine better options and think of creative ways to hold more actors more thoroughly to account. It may be that criminal accountability is impossible to achieve for many of those most instrumental in the suffering of Cambodians, but criminal mechanisms do not exhaust the possibilities for accountability. Legal and political mechanisms such as inquiries and commissions at the international level may be appropriate to try to capture the broader responsibilities alluded to above and to generate sufficient shame to deter actors from repeating their behaviour in future.[84] Certainly, those seeking to judge the ECCC should avoid accepting its limited scope and judging its successes and failures within that scope, as to do so is to miss the bigger picture, and effectively to offer impunity to many who do not deserve it. The Cambodian civil war lasted

84 See Kirsten Ainley, 'Excesses of Responsibility: The Limits of Law and the Possibilities of Politics', *Ethics and International Affairs*, Vol. 25, No. 4 (2011), pp. 407–431, for further discussion of alternatives to criminal trials.

at least from 1968, when the KR launched an armed struggle against the Cambodian government, until their final collapse in 1998 – it is this that the people are transitioning from and deserve justice for, not a conflict that ended thirty years ago.[85] And even though the civil war has ended, the repression remains. The existence of the ECCC does not seem to be stemming human rights violations in Cambodia, and is more likely instead to be bolstering the power of a government that has been allowed to control the court by external actors who cannot generate the political will to defend the rule of law.

Accountability efforts for the Cambodian genocide have fallen victim to a process in which peace was prioritised over justice, and national interest (on the part of Cambodia and an array of international actors) was prioritised over both. Leaving aside the question of whether this can be justified, it means the ECCC is in many ways a charade of accountability that does not meet the expressed needs of many of the victims of the past or the citizens of the present. It is an accountability mechanism over which many of those who should be asked to account for their actions have power. It is in the interests both of Hun Sen and the international community to limit accountability to a relatively small number of individuals. Yet it is quite probably in the interests of Cambodian victims, and all those people who may be caught up in civil strife in Cambodia in the future, for a much wider range of actors to be held accountable. This will not happen, leaving the ECCC responsible for achieving an impoverished form of justice, which is better than nothing, but not by much.

85 Etcheson, After the Killing Fields, pp. 1–11.

5 Beyond 'Pragmatism' versus 'Principle'

Ongoing Justice Debates in East Timor

Lia Kent

SINCE THE 1999 REFERENDUM FOR SELF-DETERMINATION brought the repressive twenty-four-year Indonesian occupation of East Timor to an end, multiple transitional justice mechanisms have been established to address the violence of the past. These have included two prosecutorial mechanisms: a serious crimes investigations and prosecutions process (Serious Crimes Process) based in East Timor and a Jakarta-based Ad Hoc human rights court set up by the Indonesian government; and two truth and reconciliation commissions: a Commission for Reception, Truth and Reconciliation (CAVR) established by the United Nations Transitional Administration in East Timor (UNTAET), and a bilateral East Timorese and Indonesian government-initiated Truth and Friendship Commission (CTF). Despite these efforts to 'deal with the past', no member of the Indonesian military has yet been tried for 1999-related violence, and the East Timorese leadership has progressively promoted a narrative of forgiveness, forgetting and 'moving on' from the past.

After providing a brief background to the conflict during the Indonesian occupation, this chapter traces the competing imperatives that have shaped the transitional justice agenda since the 1999 referendum and have underpinned the East Timorese leadership's increasingly anti-prosecutorial stance. In particular, I acknowledge that, in a context in which powerful members of the UN Security Council have increasingly prioritised the maintenance of relations with Indonesia over the establishment of an international criminal tribunal to prosecute senior members of its military, it is not surprising that the East Timorese leadership has implored its population to forgive and forget. In addition, I suggest that the leadership's forward-looking reconciliatory narrative has served *internal* nation-building purposes, and reflects preoccupations with building national unity and establishing political legitimacy during a fragile and formative nation-building era. Anxieties about these issues can be seen in the attempts by some East Timorese leaders to orient the justice debate towards social justice rather than retributive justice and the ongoing parliamentary discussions about amnesties and pardons for convicted East Timorese perpetrators of serious crimes.

Despite the UN's broken promises to hold those 'most responsible' to account for the violence of 1999, and the East Timorese leadership's entreaty to the population to move on, this chapter argues that it is too simplistic to characterise the transitional justice process as representing a triumph of 'pragmatism' over 'principle'. Specifically, it is apparent that new and unforseen possibilities are emerging from the CAVR and CTF reports and the activities of NGOs and local victims' groups, which may help to shift the terrain on which justice struggles are enacted. These developments indicate that transitional justice in East Timor is perhaps best described as an open-ended, political conversation without a predetermined end point, rather than a project confined to a specific 'transitional' period.

East Timor: from Colonisation to 'Transition'

East Timor, a Portuguese colony for roughly three centuries, underwent dramatic changes in the mid-1970s. Following the overthrow of the Caetano regime in Portugal, in 1974, political parties in East Timor rapidly emerged, including the radical pro-independence party FRETILIN (*Frente Revolucionária de Timor-Leste Independente*/Revolutionary Front for an independent East Timor), which had high hopes of a smooth decolonisation process. These hopes, however, were very quickly crushed due to Indonesia's expansionist ambitions. Indonesia proffered support to a small party called Apodeti, which advocated integration with Indonesia, and encouraged another party, UDT (*União Democrática Timorense*/Timorese Democratic Union), which favoured eventual independence but with continued ties to Portugal, to fight with FRETILIN. This led to a brief, but brutal, conflict between FRETILIN and UDT, sometimes referred to as the internal political conflict or civil war, during which an estimated 1,500 to 3,000 people lost their lives.[1] After winning a military victory, FRETILIN declared East Timor's independence on 28 November 1975. Nine days later, however, the new nation was invaded and occupied by Indonesian forces, an act which was immediately condemned by the UN Security Council and General Assembly.[2] In 1976, East Timor was incorporated into Indonesia as its twenty-seventh province. A tenacious resistance struggle was then waged by East Timorese opponents of the occupation over the next twenty-four years.

An estimated 100,000 to 200,000 people are believed to have lost their lives during the occupation, out of a population of less than 800,000, due to a combination of direct military assaults, illness and starvation.[3] The East Timorese population also endured other forms of violence, including

1 Parts of this chapter have appeared in a different form in Lia Kent, *The Dynamics of Transitional Justice: International Models and Local Realities in East Timor*, London: Routledge 2012; Commission for Reception Truth and Reconciliation (CAVR). *Chega!*, Dili: CAVR, 2005, part 7.2, p. 8.

2 See UN Security Council Resolution 384, 22 December 1975, and UN General Assembly Resolution 3485, 12 December 1975.

3 The CAVR estimates that approximately 100,000 people died during the occupation. See CAVR, *Chega!*, part 6. Other sources include Geoffrey Robinson, *East Timor: Crimes Against Humanity*, Report Commissioned by the OHCHR, July 2003, Geneva: Office of the High Commissioner for Human Rights, 2003, p. 16; Ben Kiernan, 'The Demography of Genocide in South-East Asia: the Death Tolls in Cambodia, 1975–79, and East Timor, 1975–80,' *Critical Asian Studies*, Vol. 35, No. 4 (2003), pp. 585–597; John Taylor, *East Timor: The Price of Freedom*, London and New York: Zed Books, 1999, pp. 84–92; Geoffrey Robinson, *If You Leave Us Here, We Will Die: How Genocide Was Stopped in East Timor*, Princeton, New Jersey: Princeton University Press, 2010, p. 51.

arbitrary imprisonment, torture, assault and rape, repeated displacement, deprivation of basic needs including food and healthcare, and ongoing restrictions on freedom of movement.[4] Within the coercive context of the occupation a great deal of violence was also committed by East Timorese people against one another. Much of this was a consequence of Indonesia's counterinsurgency strategy, a key aspect of which involved the use of East Timorese as spies and informants and their recruitment into combat battalions, paramilitary groups and civil defence forces. This strategy created a highly militarised society which undermined social bonds and cultivated fear and distrust within local communities.[5] East Timorese political parties and resistance groups were also responsible for acts of violence against the population, not only during the internal political conflict of 1974 to 1975 but throughout the occupation. In the late 1970s, for instance, under the strain of Indonesian military onslaught, FRETILIN arrested and often severely punished those perceived to be 'traitors' and 'counterrevolutionaries' within its own ranks.[6]

Despite international awareness of Indonesian atrocities, it was not until the Indonesian President Soeharto's fall from power in 1998 in the wake of the Asian Economic Crisis that real change became possible. The new President B.J. Habibie, announced his government's intention to conduct a referendum in which the people of East Timor would choose between autonomy within Indonesia and independence. The UN was put in charge of conducting the referendum and, following negotiations with the Indonesian government, the Indonesian police were entrusted with providing security. This decision proved to be poor judgement on the part of the UN as, in the lead-up to ballot day on 30 August 1999, a series of violent incidents took place in which East Timorese militia groups, backed by the Indonesian military and police forces, sought to intimidate

4 CAVR, *Chega!*, part 7.

5 Robinson, *If You Leave Us Here*; Ben Larke, '"... And the Truth Shall Set You Free": Confessional Trade-offs and Community Reconciliation in East Timor,' *Asian Journal of Social Science*, Vol. 37, No. 4 (2009), p. 654; CAVR, *Chega!*, part 4.

6 CAVR, *Chega!*, part 5, p. 19.

voters in order to persuade them of their power to wreak further havoc should they decide to vote for independence.[7]

Amid this tense environment, an incredible 98 percent of registered East Timorese turned out to vote. Within days of the announcement of the results, however, which demonstrated that an overwhelming majority of East Timorese people were in favour of independence, the territory was subjected to an intensified campaign of violence and abuse at the hands of the Indonesian military and police and their proxy local militias. More than 1,000 people were killed, houses and villages were burned and destroyed, around 400,000 people were displaced (including more than 200,000 into West Timor), and all significant government and commercial basic infrastructure was destroyed.[8] On 8 September, the UN was forced to withdraw most of its personnel from the territory due to grave concerns about security, and eventually a multinational military force known as the International Force for East Timor (INTERFET) was deployed to restore order. The UN then assumed the administration of East Timor, through the UN Transitional Administration for East Timor (UNTAET), until formal independence was declared on 20 May 2002.

The UNTAET mission represented one of the most ambitious state-building projects undertaken by the UN. Security Council resolution 1272, establishing UNTAET, gave the mission 'overall responsibility for the administration of East Timor' and the power 'to exercise all legislative and executive authority, including the administration of justice'.[9] In effect, this was the first time that the UN had exercised full sovereignty over territory independently of any parallel local authority.[10] UNTAET

7 Robinson, *If You Leave Us Here*, p. 106.

8 CAVR, *Chega!*, part 7.5, p. 48.

9 United Nations Security Council (UNSC), UNTAET Mandate, Security Council Resolution 1272 (1999) (UN Doc. S/RES/1272), at http://www.un.int/usa/sres1272.htm (accessed 19 May 2010).

10 Jarat Chopra, 'Building State Failure in East Timor,' *Development and Change*, Vol. 33, No. 5 (2002), p. 28; Simon Chesterman, 'East Timor in Transition: Self determination, State-Building and the United Nations,' *International Peacekeeping*, Vol. 9, No. 1 (2002), p. 46.

was responsible for a daunting array of tasks including: providing security and maintaining order, rehabilitating infrastructure, establishing an effective administration, assisting in the development of civil and social services, supporting capacity building for self-government and reconstructing the justice sector.[11] The World Bank, in cooperation with the Asian Development Bank, had responsibility for facilitating economic reconstruction and development, and focused on the sectors of health, education, agriculture, transport, power and water supply and private sector development. East Timor's transition to independence was expected to take two to three years.

In the immediate aftermath of the post-referendum violence, UN statements and reports were imbued with strong language about the importance of criminal prosecutions to hold the perpetrators accountable for their actions. For example, the Security Council resolution establishing INTERFET in September 1999 condemned all acts of violence and demanded that those responsible be 'brought to justice'.[12] A report of the UN High Commissioner for Human Rights, also in September, concluded that:

> To end the century and the millennium tolerating impunity for those guilty of these shocking violations would be a betrayal of everything the United Nations stands for regarding the universal promotion and protection of human rights.[13]

The demands of East Timorese political leaders and local and international human rights organisations began to coalesce around the need for an international criminal tribunal, along the lines of the tribunals established for Rwanda and the former Yugoslavia[14] to bring Indonesian

11 UNSC, UNTAET Mandate.

12 United Nations Security Council, Security Council Resolution 1264 (UN Doc. S/RES/1264), 15 September 1999.

13 United Nations Commission on Human Rights (UNHCR), Report of the High Commissioner for Human Rights on the Human Rights Situation in East Timor (E/CN.4/S-4/CRP.1), 17 September 1999, para 48.

14 International Criminal Tribunal for Rwanda (ICTR) and International Criminal Tribunal for the former Yugoslavia (ICTY).

military generals to trial.[15] These pleas were reinforced by the findings and recommendations of a UN Commission of Inquiry (COI) which visited East Timor in September 1999. The COI concluded that gross violations of human rights and breaches of humanitarian law had taken place that appeared to implicate the Indonesian military, and recommended that the UN establish an international criminal tribunal.[16] Rather than following this recommendation, however, the UN Secretary General – responding to assurances from the Indonesian government – decided that the Indonesian courts must first be given an opportunity to investigate and prosecute perpetrators in Indonesia. At the same time, he declared that he intended to strengthen UNTAET's capacity to conduct investigations and collaborate with the Indonesian processes.

The UN Secretary General's decisions led, in 2000, to the creation of the Serious Crimes Process to investigate and prosecute those who had committed 'serious crimes' during the conflict and the 1999 period.[17] Serious Crimes were defined as genocide, crimes against humanity and war crimes committed at any time, and murder, torture and sexual offences committed between 1 January and 25 October 1999. Located in East Timor's capital city, Dili, this process consisted of a Serious Crimes Investigations Unit (SCIU) and a 'hybrid' or internationalised tribunal, known as the Special Panels for Serious Crimes (the Special Panels), which was comprised of both East Timorese and international judges, and attached to the Dili District Court. This model was purported to combine the

15 See, for example, National Council for Timorese Resistance (CNRT), Resolution Commission 3 (Outcomes of the CNRT National Congress 21–30 August 2000), copy on file with author; National Council for Timorese Resistance, 'CNRT on Recent Events in West Timor; Calls for an International Tribunal, Postponement of CGI Meeting,' Media Release, 13 September 2000, at http://etan.org/news/2000b/CNRT2.htm (accessed 30 November 2009); 'Urgent Steps Needed to Establish Justice,' Letter to members of UN Security Council to Members of the United Nations Headquarters from East Timorese NGOs, 24 October 2001, at http://members.pcug.org.au/~wildwood/01octsteps.htm (accessed 10 January 2011).

16 Office of the High Commissioner for Human Rights (OHCHR), Report on the International Commission of Inquiry on East Timor to the Secretary General, January 2000 (UN Doc. S/2000/59).

17 UNTAET Regulations 2000/11 and 2000/15.

strengths of an international tribunal with the benefits of local prosecutions. It was promoted as being more meaningful to victim populations due to its proximity to the community and more effective at rebuilding the local judicial system than an international tribunal – factors which were expected to contribute to its local legitimacy.[18] A Memorandum of Understanding (MoU) between Indonesia and UNTAET was signed to ensure cooperation in the exchange of evidence, requests for witnesses and making arrests and the transfer of suspects when needed in the investigation and prosecution of serious crimes.[19] In response to international pressure, the Indonesian government announced the establishment of its own Ad Hoc human rights court in November 2000 to try, within its jurisdiction, individual perpetrators who had played a leading role in the post-referendum violence.[20]

UNTAET and East Timorese leaders were also faced with the question of what to do with the thousands of other cases of 'less serious' crimes, including looting, arson, theft and the destruction of property, committed immediately prior to and following the referendum of 1999. It was clear that the nascent domestic legal system, with its inexperienced legal actors and limited infrastructure, would not be capable of dealing with all these issues. A related preoccupation was how to ensure the safe return of some quarter of a million people who remained displaced in West Timor following the referendum. To respond to these concerns, following a consultative process, UNTAET created the *Comissão de Acolhimento, Verdade e Reconciliação* (Commission for Reception, Truth and Reconciliation/CAVR) in July 2001, as an independent statutory body.[21] This body was then formally recognised in the East Timorese constitution.

18 Suzanne Katzenstein, 'Hybrid Tribunals: Searching for Justice in East Timor,' *Harvard Human Rights Journal*, Vol. 16 (2003), pp. 245–246.

19 Republic of Indonesia and the United Nations Transitional Administration in East Timor Memorandum of Understanding between the Republic of Indonesia and the United Nations Transitional Administration in East Timor Regarding Cooperation in Legal, Judicial and Human Rights Related Matters (5–6 April 2000), at http://www.unmit.org/legal/Other-Docs/mou-id-untaet.htm (accessed 3 January 2010).

20 Indonesian Law 26/2000.

21 UNTAET Regulation 2001/10.

The CAVR had three core programs. Its truth seeking program sought to establish the 'truth' about the twenty-four-year Indonesian occupation by collecting statements from individuals throughout the nation and compiling them into its final report. The CAVR's Victim Support Unit was responsible for organising a number of national public victims' hearings on issues such as women and the conflict, forced displacement and famine, massacres and children and the conflict, during which selected individuals were given the opportunity to give public testimonies. It also organised a number of 'healing workshops' and coordinated a small urgent-reparations scheme to provide one-off payments to victims who were deemed particularly vulnerable.

The third, and perhaps most innovative of the CAVR's programs, was the Community Reconciliation Program (CRP), which aimed to encourage the 'reception' and reintegration of former militia members who had committed less serious crimes during 1999 back into their communities. Incorporating local East Timorese dispute-resolution practices, in particular a practice known as *nahe biti* (lit. stretching, rolling the mat), which typically involves a public meeting mediated by the community's customary leaders,[22] the CRP involved the convening of hearings at the *suco* (village) level overseen by panels comprising CAVR representatives and local leaders (which were obliged to include women and youth representatives). During the hearings, panel members would listen to the perpetrator of the minor crime (known as the 'deponent'), victims and other community members, before deciding on an 'Act of Reconciliation' that the deponent would be required to complete, which usually involved a form of community service. On completion of the Act, deponents received a court-approved notification that they were immune from civil or criminal prosecution for all those acts they had declared during the CRP. CRP hearings also included a role for traditional elders, and

22 *Nahe biti* is practised in many different forms throughout East Timor. It is both a process as well as a philosophy that connotes the willingness on the part of conflicting parties to sit together and resolve past mistakes in order to achieve future harmony and social stability. See Dionesio Babo-Soares, '*Nahe Biti*: Grassroots Reconciliation in East Timor,' in Elin Skaar, Siri Gloppen and Astrid Suhrke (eds.), *Roads to Reconciliation* (Lanham, MD: Lexington Books, 2005), pp. 225–246.

agreements were generally sealed with binding oaths, and often involved the sharing of betel nut, the sacrificing of a chicken or pig, a symbolic rolling up of the *biti* (mat) and a celebratory feast. Although it was developed quite separately from the Serious Crimes Process, the CRP was expected to play a complementary role. In particular, it was hoped that this program would relieve the pressure on an overburdened and underdeveloped East Timorese legal system and thus enable the courts to concentrate on the 'most serious' crimes.

At first glance it may appear that the transitional justice approach adopted after the referendum represented a balanced, coordinated and locally responsive attempt to combine prosecutions, reconciliation and truth seeking. The reality, however, was far from it. I now chart the competing political imperatives that shaped transitional justice decision making during the period of UN transitional administration of East Timor from 1999 to 2002, following formal independence in 2002, and in the wake of the so-called 'crisis' of 2006. An analysis of these dynamics highlights that decision making about 'dealing with the past' involved a fraught process of negotiation between and amongst an array of international and national actors which brought to the fore specific interests and multiple views. In this process, stability concerns, which highlighted Indonesia's economic and strategic influence in the region, came to overshadow retributive justice goals.

The Politics of Transitional Justice Decision Making since the Referendum

The UNTAET Period

Despite the UN's forceful statements after the referendum that those responsible for serious crimes must be brought to justice, it was soon apparent that this prosecutorial narrative was being shadowed by a powerful stability discourse that was emanating from some sections of the UN and some East Timorese leaders. Some voices argued that those responsible for the crimes of 1999 must be held to account, especially as some of those crimes could be characterised as 'crimes against humanity' and, as such, were subject to the principal of universal jurisdiction and should be prosecuted wherever they occur.[23] A contrasting view, however, promoted the need to strengthen diplomatic ties with Indonesia and support the democratisation efforts of then-resident Abdurrahman Wahid in order to ensure East Timor's future stability and development.[24]

The emergence of these debates and contradictory messages can be understood as reflecting the complex policy dilemmas facing East Timorese leaders and the UN in the aftermath of the referendum. At this time, the former Indonesian regime, although no longer officially present within the country, maintained a strong influence as a powerful neighbour.[25] An antagonistic Indonesia was perceived as a threat to the future security and viability of East Timor, particularly given the vulnerability of East Timor's land and sea borders and its fragile economic position. Stability concerns were also motivated by fears that too much pressure on Indonesia could threaten the repatriation of East Timorese refugees from Indonesian West Timor, some of whom were former militia leaders who, it was believed, had the capacity to cause continued instability on the West Timor border. These concerns were not hypothetical given the presence of 'armed spoilers' who were 'operating minor hit-and-run missions across the border'.[26] Given this situation, as one UNTAET official in East Timor explained in late 2000, 'Everyone here recognises that

23 See, for example, views expressed by UN Secretary General Kofi Annan in David Cohen, 'Seeking Justice on the Cheap: Is the East Timor Tribunal Really a Model for the Future?' in *Analysis from the East-West Center*, Vol. 61 (Honolulu, HI: East-West Center, 2002), pp. 2–3.

24 See, for example, views of the UN official cited in John Aglionby, 'Timorese Pay Price for Stability,' *The Guardian*, 15 November 2000, at http://www.guardian.co.uk/world/2000/nov/15/indonesia.easttimor (accessed 17 December 2009).

25 Nehal Bhuta, 'Great Expectations – East Timor and the Vicissitudes of Externalised Justice,' *Finnish Yearbook of International Law*, Vol. 12 (2001), p. 173.

26 J. Braithwaite, H. Charlesworth, and A. Soares, *Networked Governance of Freedom and Tyranny: Peace in Timor-Leste*, Canberra, ACT: ANU E-Press, 2012, p. 193.

it's in no one's interests to rock the fragile political position of President Wahid'.[27] Compounding these difficulties were the vast social, economic and infrastructural tasks facing those involved in the reconstruction of East Timor and the widespread and chronic poverty affecting much of the population. In this context, both UNTAET and the East Timorese leadership viewed the restoration and maintenance of regional peace and stability as critical to the viability and development of the new nation state.[28]

At the level of the UN Security Council, the stability discourse was also fuelled by other preoccupations, namely, the importance of maintaining Indonesia's position as a key ally of powerful Western states. The value accorded Indonesia's economic and strategic influence in the region assumed even more prominence following the terrorist acts of 11 September 2001, when Western states began to seek Indonesia's assistance in the so-called 'war on terror'.[29] These events provided impetus for the United States to resume military ties with Indonesia and to support the *Tentara Nasional Indonesia*, (TNI/National Indonesian Army) which was seen as a stabilising force within the country.[30] Thus, soon after 11 September, then-U.S. President George Bush and Indonesian President Megawati Sukarnoputri agreed to resume regular meetings between the militaries of the two countries. Thereafter, the U.S. government lifted its embargo on sales of non-lethal military items to Indonesia and provided millions of dollars for counter-terrorism measures to Jakarta.[31] Other U.S. allies were similarly focused on rebuilding strategic alliances with Indonesia, including the Australian government, which was intent on restoring the relationship following the prominent role it had taken in encouraging and supporting the East Timor referendum.[32]

27 Aglionby, 'Timorese Pay Price.'
28 Larke, "... And the Truth Shall Set You Free," p. 655.
29 Reyko Huang and Geoffrey Gunn, 'Reconciliation as State-Building in East Timor,' In *Lusotopie* (2004), p. 24.
30 Bhuta, 'Great Expectations,' p. 176; Huang and Gunn, 'Reconciliation as State-Building,' p. 24.
31 Huang and Gunn, 'Reconciliation as State-Building,' p. 24.
32 Bhuta, 'Great Expectations,' p. 176.

Amongst the East Timorese leadership (particularly Xanana Gusmão, the charismatic former resistance fighter and then-leader of the National Council of Timorese Resistance/CNRT), preoccupation with stability questions began to show itself in an increasingly prominent reconciliatory narrative. Thus, the emphatic demands made soon after the referendum for the Indonesian military to be tried began to give way to an emphasis on the importance of forging a new relationship with East Timor's former occupier.[33] These shifts undoubtedly reflected a growing awareness on the part of the leadership that the international community was turning a deaf ear to demands for the prosecution of Indonesian war criminals and a consciousness of their inability to do this alone. It was soon apparent, for example, that the UN's initial decision to rely on Indonesian cooperation with the Serious Crimes Process had been fundamentally misguided. By early 2001, the Indonesian government had begun to make it clear it was not willing to cooperate with the MoU, in which it had agreed to 'the widest possible measure of mutual assistance in investigations or court proceedings',[34] and was openly ignoring repeated requests for assistance and extradition issued by the SCIU.[35] This meant that the Serious Crimes Process was able to prosecute only suspects present in the territory of East Timor (who were overwhelmingly low-level East Timorese militia leaders) and was unable to touch those living across the border in Indonesia, among them senior members of the Indonesian military.

The absence of serious UN commitment to a retributive justice agenda was also reflected in the under-resourcing of the Serious Crimes Process. Indeed, one only needs to compare the budget for the Serious Crimes Process, which stood at U.S.$6.1 million in 2002 and U.S.$7–8 million in

33 See, for example, 'Gusmao Calls for Reconciliation in Jakarta Speech,' *Lusa*, 20 April 2001, at http://www.etan.org/et2001b/april/22-30/20gusmao.htm (accessed 7 December 2012).

34 Republic of Indonesia and the United Nations Transitional Administration in East Timor, Memorandum of Understanding, 2000, section 1.

35 Cohen, 'Seeking Justice on the Cheap,' p. 7.

2004 to 2005,[36] with that of the Extraordinary Courts in Cambodia, which were budgeted at just short of U.S.$19 million per year, the Special Court in Sierra Leone, which cost U.S.$16 million per year, and the ICTY and ICTR, which each have an annual budget of about U.S.$100 million.[37] The impact of this 'justice on the cheap'[38] (combined with poor management and planning) could be seen in a range of critical areas.[39] There were, for example, inadequate resources for translation, and it was not unusual for judges to translate for themselves or for a chain of translations to take place that greatly increased inaccuracies.[40] Witness protection was neglected, and, as Cohen observed, witnesses and victims travelling to Dili sometimes rode in the same minibus as the accused they were to testify against.[41] The Public Defenders Unit also suffered and, in its early stages, was staffed entirely by local defense lawyers, most of whom were recent law graduates with no prior litigation experience.[42] Resources for public outreach were also sorely lacking, and the fact that trials were not publicised had critical consequences for public perceptions of the Serious Crimes Process. Another limitation of the Serious Crimes Process was the narrow investigations and prosecutorial strategy adopted by the SCIU. Although it could theoretically investigate all serious crimes cases from 1975 until 1999, the SCIU focused its efforts on ten 'priority cases'

36 David Cohen, 'Justice on the Cheap Revisited: the Failure of the Serious Crimes Trials in East Timor,' Analysis from the East-West Center, No. 80 (Honolulu, HI: East-West Center, 2006), p. 5.

37 Elizabeth Stanley, *Torture, Truth and Justice: the Case of Timor-Leste*, London: Routledge, 2008, p. 173.

38 See Cohen, 'Seeking Justice on the Cheap.'

39 For detailed critiques of the Serious Crimes Process, see the following prominent studies: Cohen, 'Justice on the Cheap'; Megan Hirst and Howard Varney, 'Justice Abandoned? An Assessment of the Serious Crimes Process in East Timor,' ICTJ Occasional Paper Series, New York: International Center for Transitional Justice, 2005; Caitlin Reiger and Marieke Wierda, 'The Serious Crimes Process in Timor-Leste: In Retrospect,' ICTJ Prosecutions Case Studies Series, New York: International Center for Transitional Justice, 2006; Katzenstein, 'Hybrid Tribunals.'

40 See Stanley, 'Torture, Truth and Justice,' p. 96.

41 Cohen, 'Seeking Justice on the Cheap,' p. 5.

42 Cohen, 'Seeking Justice on the Cheap,' p. 17.

from the 1999 period, in part because of its limited resources; this left untouched the bulk of cases from the pre-1999 period.

By early 2001, it was also clear that the UN had misjudged its decision to rely on Indonesia to prosecute suspects based in its territory. Although the Indonesian government eventually established an Ad Hoc Human Rights Court to prosecute Indonesians responsible for serious crimes in East Timor during 1999, the mandate of the tribunal was limited to the events that occurred between April and September and restricted to crimes committed in Dili, Liquica and Suai. The Indonesian Attorney General then limited the scope of the tribunal even further by announcing that attention would be given to only five specific cases.[43] The promised trials were also repeatedly delayed.[44]

In the climate of competing imperatives, the CAVR fared better than the Serious Crimes Process. Through its community-based CRP, the CAVR adjudicated almost 1,400 cases of minor crimes, while the nationwide truth-seeking process collected 7,669 statements across all thirteen districts of East Timor which were incorporated into its final report.[45] These efforts were facilitated by significant donor funding, including from Japan, which contributed close to U.S.$1 million and the United Kingdom, which contributed approximately U.S.$931,300.[46] Nonetheless, despite its considerable achievements, East Timorese perceptions of this institution were influenced by the lack of progress in the prosecution of serious crimes. Studies of participants' views of the CAVR began to highlight dissatisfaction with the fact that only those perceived to be the 'small fish' had been required to atone for their acts (through the

43 Richard Burchill, 'From East Timor to Timor-Leste: A Demonstration of the Limits of International Law in the Pursuit of Justice,' in J. Doria, H.-P. Gasser and M. C. Bassiouni (eds.), *The Legal Regime of the ICC: Essays in Honour of Prof. Igor Blishchenko*, Leiden and Boston: Martinus Nijhoff, 2009, p. 282.

44 Although Indonesian officials had announced in August 2001 that court hearings would begin in October, it was then announced in October that the judges would not be named until December. (La'o Hamutuk, 'Sites of Justice-Related Efforts,' *La'o Hamutuk Bulletin*, Vol. 2 (2001), pp. 6–7.)

45 CAVR, Exec Summary, pp. 20–23.

46 CAVR, Annex 3.

community-based CRP), while those responsible for more serious crimes remained free.[47]

Post-Independence Developments

Following East Timor's formal independence, the political leadership's narrative of reconciliation-as-forgiveness became increasingly prominent. The appearance of East Timor's new President Xanana Gusmão and Indonesian President Megawati Sukarnoputri on stage together during East Timor's independence day celebrations on 19 May 2002 with their hands joined in a victory salute solidified the government's 'forward-looking' approach to building diplomatic relations with Indonesia. In his speech, Gusmão spoke of 'twenty-four years of difficult relations', which he suggested were the result of a 'historical mistake which now belongs to history and to the past'.[48] Over time this stance came to be embodied in the government's progressively more public opposition to the establishment of an international criminal tribunal. This stance was evident in the statement made by then- Foreign Minister Jose Ramos-Horta in 2004:

> The government of East Timor does not contemplate lobbying for an international tribunal to try the crimes of 1999 because we know this would undermine the existing relations between the two countries.[49]

The government's increasingly 'forward-looking' approach to building relations with Indonesia was taking shape in a context in which the UN mission was downsizing. Following independence, UNTAET was

47 See, for example, Lia Kent, 'Unfulfilled Expectations: Community Views of the Reconciliation Process,' Report for the Judicial Systems Monitoring Programme, Dili: Judicial Systems Monitoring Programme, 2004; Pierre Pigou, 'The Community Reconciliation Process of the Commission for Reception, Truth and Reconciliation,' *Evaluation Report for the UNDP*, Dili: United Nations Development Programme, 2004.

48 Gusmão quoted in Joseph Nevins, *A Not So Distant Horror: Mass Violence in East Timor*, Ithaca, Cornell University Press, 2005, p. 154.

49 Ramos-Horta, quoted in Global Policy Forum, 'East Timor Says No to UN tribunal,' *Laksama.Net*, 9 August 2004, at http://www.globalpolicy.org/intljustice/tribunals/timor/2004/0809no.htm (accessed 10 December 2009).

replaced with a 'patchwork' of smaller successor missions,[50] the first of which was the United Nations Mission of Support in East Timor (UNMISET).[51] Although some notable attempts were made to improve the functioning of the Special Panels and the management of the SCIU,[52] there was little additional commitment of resources, extension of time, or strengthening of the mandate of the Serious Crimes Process. According to the initial UNMISET 'implementation plan', investigations were to be completed by 31 December 2002 and trials completed by the end of 2003, when the mission itself was initially due to conclude.[53] Compounding the problematic nature of this plan was the fact that the flaws in the Indonesian Ad Hoc Human Rights Court established in Jakarta had by now become glaringly apparent.[54] Although twelve trials eventually took place between March 2002 and August 2003, and six defendants were found guilty in the first instance, all six were acquitted on appeal.[55]

The distancing of both the UN and the East Timorese leadership from a prosecutorial agenda was laid bare in the controversy that surrounded the indictment of General Wiranto. On 24 February 2003, the SCIU

50 Juan Federer, *The UN in East Timor: Building Timor-Leste, a Fragile State*, Darwin: Charles Darwin University Press (2005), p. 106.

51 UNMISET was initially given a one-year mandate, which was later extended until 20 May 2004 and followed by another extension until 19 May 2005. The mission was then replaced by the United Nations Office in East Timor (UNOTIL), a much smaller mission, from May 2005 to August 2006. Unlike UNTAET, UNOTIL was not a peace-keeping mission but a political mission. Following the violence of April and June 2006, the UN Security Council established a new, expanded mission, called the United Nations Integrated Mission in Timor-Leste (UNMIT), which was given a far-reaching mandate to assist the country in overcoming the consequences and underlying causes of the violence.

52 See Cohen, 'Justice on the Cheap.'

53 United Nations, Report of the Secretary General on the United Nations Transitional Administration in East Timor (UN Doc. S/2002/432), 14 April 2002.

54 For an excellent overview of the problems of the Ad Hoc Human Rights Court, see David Cohen, 'Intended to Fail: The Trials before the Ad Hoc Human Rights Court in Jakarta,' ICTJ Occasional Paper Series, New York: International Center for Transitional Justice (2003).

55 International Center for Transitional Justice and Commission for the Disappeared and Victims of Violence (ICTJ/Kontras), 'Derailed: Transitional Justice in Indonesia since the Fall of Soeharto,' Jakarta: ICTJ/Kontras (2011).

issued an indictment against General Wiranto, the Minister of Defence and Security and Commander of the Indonesian Armed Forces at the time of East Timor's referendum, charging that he was responsible under international law for the crimes against humanity of murder and deportation, under the doctrine of command responsibility.[56] In response, the Indonesian Foreign Minister, Dr Hassan Wirajuda, stated that his government would 'simply ignore' the indictment on the basis that the UN did not have a mandate to try Indonesian citizens in East Timor.[57] Shortly after this, UNMISET also attempted to absolve itself of responsibility for the indictment, declaring that it had been issued through the prosecution service of East Timor and not the UN.[58] As Stanley observes, although the UN's position was technically correct, it was disingenuous, as the UN had set up the judicial process and the SCIU was staffed by UN employees.[59] The East Timorese government responded by declaring that the indictment was the work of the UN and not of East Timor and followed this by declining offers of overseas aid for the funding and staffing of the Serious Crimes Process.[60]

Tensions mounted after the Special Panels for Serious Crimes issued its warrant on 10 May 2004 for the arrest of General Wiranto, who, by this point, was a front-runner in the election campaign for the next president of Indonesia. Not long after this, President Xanana Gusmão and Indonesian President Megawati Sukarnoputri met and agreed that

56 Hirst and Varney, 'Justice Abandoned?,' p. 25.

57 Detik Com, quoted in Susan Harris-Rimmer, *Transitional Justice and the Women of East Timor*, Unpublished PhD Thesis, Australian National University, p. 191.

58 UN News Centre (2003), Timor-Leste Not UN Indicts Indonesian General for War Crimes, UNMISET Statement, 26 February 2003, at http://www.un.org/apps/news/story.asp?NewsID=6273&Cr=timor&Cr1 (accessed 1 August 2010).

59 Elizabeth Stanley, 'The Political Economy of Transitional Justice in Timor-Leste' in K. McEvoy and L. McGregor (eds.), *Transitional Justice from Below: Grassroots Activism and the Struggle for Change* (Oxford: Hart Publishing, 2008), p. 177; see also Hirst and Varney, 'Justice Abandoned?,' p. 25.

60 Hirst and Varney, 'Justice Abandoned?,' p. 25; Katzenstein, 'Hyrid Tribunals,' pp. 268–269; S. G. Harris-Rimmer, *Gender and Transitional Justice: the Women of East Timor* (London and New York: Routledge, 2010), p. 138.

outstanding human rights issues between the countries should be resolved through a 'reconciliatory approach'.[61] These actions influenced the East Timorese General Prosecutor who had been originally supportive of the indictment. Reversing his position, he presented a motion to the Court seeking to have the indictment against Wiranto 'revised'.[62]

Not long after shelving the Wiranto indictment, the East Timorese and Indonesian governments agreed to establish their own bilateral Commission of Truth and Friendship (CTF). Following the meeting between Presidents Gusmão and Sukarnoputri in May 2004, Gusmão met with General Wiranto, hugged him as an 'act of reconciliation' and reportedly referred to him as his 'dear friend'.[63] Foreign Minister Ramos-Horta then put forward a proposal for an 'International Truth and Reconciliation Panel, which was to be composed of eminent persons from Asia.[64] The concept evolved into a proposal for the bilateral CTF which was publicly announced by the Presidents in March 2005.

The CTF was emblematic of the East Timorese leadership's promotion of a nation-building agenda that stressed moving on from the past and building diplomatic relations with Indonesia. The CTF's terms of reference explained that 'Indonesia and Timor-Leste have opted to seek truth and promote friendship as a new and unique approach rather than the prosecutorial process'.[65] They called for 'definitive closure of the issues of the past [that] would further promote bilateral relations'[66] and emphasised the need to establish 'institutional responsibilities' rather than identifying and assigning individual blame. While the CTF was empowered to seek the 'conclusive truth' about the violence of 1999 and had the power

61 Hirst and Varney, 'Justice Abandoned?,' p. 25.

62 Hirst and Varney, 'Justice Abandoned?,' p. 26.

63 Hirst and Varney, 'Justice Abandoned?,' p. 25.

64 M. Hirst, 'Too Much Friendship, Too Little Truth: Monitoring Report on the Commission of Truth and Friendship in Indonesia and Timor-Leste,' ICTJ Occasional Paper Series, New York, International Center for Transitional Justice (2008), p. 11.

65 Republic of Indonesia and the Government of Timor-Leste (RI and GOTL) Terms of Reference for the Commission of Truth and Friendship, 2005, para 10, at http://www.etan.org/et2005/march/06/10tor.htm (accessed 5 July 2010).

66 RI and GOTL, Terms of Reference, para 8.

to recommend amnesties and rehabilitation of those 'wrongly accused', it was precluded from recommending prosecutions.

The CTF was heavily criticised by local and international human rights activists from its very inception. They condemned it as a mask to hide back-door agreements between elite political leaders in Indonesia and East Timor to end all prosecutorial efforts. Truth and justice, they argued, were being traded off for 'friendship'.[67] The UN also declined to participate in the CTF, citing concerns about its amnesty provisions, in particular the lack of clear criteria for when amnesty would be recommended, including in relation to the international crimes of crimes against humanity and war crimes.[68] More specifically, critics saw the CTF as an attempt by the East Timorese government to divert attention away from the proposal of the UN Secretary General to appoint a Commission of Experts (COE) to review justice developments in East Timor, which, it was anticipated, would recommend reconsideration of the establishment of an international criminal tribunal. These suspicions were reinforced by a joint press release issued by the foreign ministers of Indonesia and Timor-Leste, which stated 'In the light of the initiative of the Heads of States of Indonesia and Timor-Leste [to establish the CTF], the said initiative of the UN Secretary-General [to appoint a COE] appears to be redundant'.[69]

67 See, for example, Timor Leste National Alliance for an International Tribunal, 'Response to the Indonesian and East Timorese Governments to Establish a Truth and Friendship Commission,' 21 December 2004, at http://etan.org/news/2004/12etngo.htm (accessed 7 December 2012).

68 Hirst, 'Too Much Friendship,' p. 16.

69 Republic of Indonesia and the Government of Timor-Leste, 'Joint Press Release of Foreign Minister of the Republic of Indonesia and the Democratic Republic of Timor Leste,' 22 December 2004, at http://www.kbri-tokyo.go.id/menue/information/press/jointpress-release-ri-timorleste.htm (accessed 5 July 2010). Nonetheless, the COE was appointed, and its report, which was officially released on 15 July 2005, provided a scathing critique of the Indonesian Ad Hoc court. It recommended that Indonesia reopen the prosecutions that had been brought before the Ad Hoc court and that, should it fail to do so within a six-month timeframe, the Security Council should create an international criminal tribunal to be located in a third state. However, despite the

The CTF's credibility in the eyes of human rights activists was further eroded once it began public hearings, which were dominated by senior Indonesian public officials, members of the TNI and former militia commanders. Observers noted that these individuals presented views that were heavily skewed towards the perspective of the institutions they represented and were rarely subjected to rigorous scrutiny by CTF commissioners.[70] Opportunities for victims to participate in public hearings were also highly circumscribed. According to observers, victims who were invited to give testimony were treated poorly, often finding themselves in rooms filled with uniformed members of the TNI who ridiculed and intimidated them.[71] The fact that few public outreach programs were undertaken by the CTF only contributed to its reputation as a 'corrupt, disingenuous truth commission'.[72]

It was soon after these developments that the CAVR's final report *Chega!* (No More!/Stop!/Enough!) was released. Tabled in East Timor's parliament in November 2005, *Chega!* presented a detailed and disturbing account of the 'widespread and systematic atrocities' committed by members of the Indonesian security forces during the occupation, which it suggested, amounted to crimes against humanity.[73] It also held the Indonesian government and security forces 'primarily responsible and accountable' for the deaths of between 100,000 and 180,000 civilians from hunger and illness as a direct result of the occupation.[74] *Chega!* also drew attention to a number of uncomfortable and controversial facts about the involvement of the international community in the twenty-four-year Indonesian occupation. For instance, it criticised the policies and practices

momentum it generated, the COE report did not lead to any dramatic change of strategy amongst UN Security Council members.

70 Hirst, 'Too Much Friendship,' pp. 32–35.

71 Hirst, 'Too Much Friendship,' pp. 32–35.

72 Leigh-Ashley Lipscomb, *Housing the Truth: The Archived Legacy of Transitional Justice in Timor-Leste*, Unpublished PhD Thesis, University of California, Berkeley (2011), p. 130.

73 CAVR, chapter 8, pp. 5–6.

74 CAVR, chapter 8, p. 6.

of a number of Western states, including Australia, the United States and the UK, for their support of the Indonesian regime. Amongst its many recommendations, *Chega!* proposed that the UN's Serious Crimes Process be continued and that the UN be prepared to institute an international criminal tribunal should Indonesia persist in the obstruction of justice.[75] It also called for the establishment of a reparations fund to assist the most vulnerable victims, which would be partially financed by contributions from governments and institutions that had provided military support to Indonesia.

Maintaining its reconciliatory stance towards Indonesia, the East Timorese leadership was critical of *Chega!*, particularly its recommendations. In his 23 January 2006 speech before the UN Security Council, President Gusmão argued that it was more important that East Timor follow the path of 'restorative justice' than pursue prosecutions, by which he meant restoring relations with Indonesia and fostering social harmony:

> I have to ask myself if it is in our national interest, which must include social harmony, to adopt a process that I am told by some friends will bring justice, and have this process go on for years, and possibly set back our democratic consolidation, that is being undertaken in Timor-Leste and Indonesia respectively? The answer that I came to, after wide consultation with the people, was that it is not.[76]

With regards to reparations, President Gusmão suggested that the international community had already made amends for their mistakes by providing significant development assistance to East Timor since 1999, and argued that demanding reparations would make the new nation seem 'ungrateful' in the eyes of the international community. In a letter, President Gusmão reassured international donors that he did not endorse the report's recommendation for reparations because of the commitment of the international community to the rebuilding of East Timor. He wrote:

75 CAVR, Part 11, p. 26.

76 Statement of Gusmão to UN Security Council 5351st meeting, the Situation in East Timor (UN Doc. S/Pv.5351), 23 January 2006.

> How can we go to the world community, one that was indifferent to our plight for too long, when it did finally help us to achieve independence and made enormous contributions exceeding $1 billion to help us cope with our emergency situation? We still need their help and should not be ungrateful for what they have contributed. They are making amends for their mistake.[77]

The decision of key members of the East Timorese leadership to distance themselves from the CAVR recommendations and establish the bilateral CTF thus represented a deepening of the leadership's reconciliatory narrative in a context of their growing awareness of their new nation's geopolitical constraints.

Post-2006 Developments

Interestingly, following the violent events of 2006 (sometimes referred to as the 2006 crisis), both the UN and the East Timorese leadership appeared to demonstrate – at least on the face of it – a willingness to reassess their transitional justice approach. The crisis, which was precipitated by the government's dismissal of around one-third of the military, who had left their barracks complaining of poor pay and conditions and ethnic prejudice, soon became a catalyst for a range of disaffected groups to express their diverse grievances.[78] By the middle of 2006, the state was 'largely paralysed'.[79] Tens of thousands of people were living in refugee camps in and around Dili, and many houses had been destroyed.[80] The crisis also brought to the fore a number of serious issues within the East

77 Gusmão, in Jeffrey Kingston 'Balancing Justice and Reconciliation in East Timor,' *Critical Asian Studies*, Vol. 38, No. 3 (2006), pp. 271–302.

78 Damian Kingsbury, and Michael Leach, 'Introduction' in Damian Kingsbury and Michael Leach (eds.), *East Timor: Beyond Independence*, Melbourne: Monash University Press, 2007, p. 6; International Crisis Group, 'Resolving East Timor's Crisis,' Asia Report no. 120, 10 October 2006.

79 Damian Grenfell, 'Reconciliation: Violence and Nation-Formation in Timor-Leste,' in Damian Grenfell and Paul James, Rethinking Insecurity, *War and Violence: Beyond Savage Globalization?*, London: Routledge, 2008, p. 181.

80 ICG, 'Resolving East Timor's Crisis.'

Timorese government regarding the increasing politicisation of the military and police, the exercise of personal power in political decision making, and the resurfacing of grievances and ideological differences within the East Timorese resistance movement, some of which harked back to the 1970s and 1980s.[81] It exposed, too, the misguided nature of the UN's assumption that East Timor could make the 'transition' to a stable, liberal democracy, within a two- to three-year period.

In response the violent acts committed during the crisis, the UN High Commissioner for Human Rights appointed a special Commission of Inquiry (COI) in June 2006. Although the crimes committed during the Indonesian occupation did not fall within its mandate, the COI's final report concluded that the violent events of 2006 were 'the expression of deep-rooted problems inherent in fragile State institutions and a weak rule of law' and called for the need for an end to the 'culture of impunity' in East Timor.[82] In response to the COI, a new expanded UN mission – the United Nations Integrated Mission in Timor-Leste (UNMIT) – was announced on 25 August, mandated, among other things, to establish a new Serious Crimes Investigation Team (SCIT) to resume investigations into serious crimes cases committed in 1999 that remained outstanding since the closure of the SCIU in 2004 and to strengthen the capacity of domestic institutions to prosecute serious crimes.[83]

For its part, the East Timorese leadership's stated willingness to address the past was evident at the swearing-in ceremony of Jose Ramos-Horta as the nation's new president on 10 July 2006, at which Ramos-Horta acknowledged that 'the extensive CAVR report is an encyclopaedia of our history, both rich in teachings and suffering. We must utilise its great teachings to better understand today's crisis and to help prevent

81 ICG, 'Resolving East Timor's Crisis,' p. 22.

82 Commission of Inquiry (COI), Report of the United Nations Independent Special Commission of Inquiry for Timor Leste (Geneva, 2 October 2006), pp. 64, 74.

83 United Nations Security Council, UN Security Council 5351st meeting, the Situation in East Timor (UN Doc. S/Pv.5351), 23 January 2006.

future crises'.[84] Gusmão's speech at the swearing-in of members of the new government in 2007 similarly made reference to the need to learn the lessons of the past in order to understand the current crisis and protect the future.[85]

Nonetheless, the renewed emphasis by the UN and East Timorese government to addressing the past gave little attention to the issue of prosecutions. Although investigations into serious crimes cases were resumed, that the UN Security Council was not wholly committed to prosecutions was made evident by the fact that the SCIT was given only investigatory, not prosecutorial, powers. Moreover, in contrast to the SCIU, the SCIT was precluded by its mandate from investigating crimes committed prior to 1999 and was given even fewer investigative resources than the SCIU.[86] All of this means that future prosecutions (and dealing with hundreds of outstanding indictments left pending following the closure of the former Serious Crimes Process) will depend on the East Timorese government's political will and the capacity and resources of the national justice sector, both of which appear to be limited.[87]

84 J. Ramos-Horta, Address by José Ramos-Horta at His Swearing-in Ceremony as Prime Minister of the Democratic Republic of Timor-Leste, Dili, 10 July 2006, at http://www.etan.org/et2006/july/15/10address.htm (accessed 8 July 2009).

85 X. Gusmão, Speech of HE Prime Minister of Timor-Leste, Kay Rala Xanana Gusmão at the Swearing-in Ceremony of the Members of the Government, Dili, 8 August 2007.

86 According to a report by the International Center for Transitional Justice, SCIT was initially staffed with ten international investigators. It was eventually able to increase this amount to thirteen by taking its own initiative to secure additional outside resources. See International Center for Transitional Justice (ICTJ), 'Impunity in Timor-Leste: Can the Serious Crimes Investigation Team Make a Difference?,' ICTJ, June 2010, p. 18. SCIT wound up it's operations in December 2012 following the end of it's mandate, having failed to complete around 60 investigations into outstanding cases of serious human rights violations. See Amnesty International, 'Annual Report 2013: State of the World's Human Rights', Amnesty International, 2013, p. 268.

87 Since the closure of the SCIU in 2005, only three serious crimes cases have come before the Dili District Court involving indictees who had returned to East Timor (ICTJ, 'Impunity in Timor-Leste, pp. 21–22). As of February 2010, the UNMIT Serious Crimes Investigating Team (SCIT) had completed 110 investigations into 396 outstanding cases inherited from the previous SCIU and had submitted a number of completed case files with recommendations for indictments to prosecutors. However, the prosecutor general

Hamstrung by geopolitical constraints, the East Timorese government continues to evince a drive towards closure, forgiveness and building diplomatic relations with Indonesia. This agenda was particularly evident in the controversial events that surrounded the Martinus Bere case, which can be seen as a litmus test of how the government would respond to indicted serious crimes defendants who returned to East Timor. This case concerned Bere, a former leader of the Laksaur militia group in Covalima, now an Indonesian citizen, who crossed the border from West Timor back into East Timor in August 2009 to attend his father's funeral. Bere had been indicted by the SCIU in 2003 for his role in the Suai church massacre in 1999 and charged with crimes against humanity. Recognised by members of his former local community, he was arrested by the police and transferred to Becora prison to await trial. Soon after this, the Indonesian foreign minister reportedly demanded the intervention of President Ramos-Horta and Prime Minister Gusmão to release Bere.[88] His release occurred on 30 August, the tenth anniversary of the referendum, allegedly in order to ensure that Indonesian Foreign Minister Hassan Wirajuda would participate in the anniversary celebrations. In his speech to the nation, Ramos-Horta declared that 'there will be no international tribunal', asked the UN to disband the newly constituted SCIT and called for an amnesty of all crimes committed between 1974 and 2009.[89] The release of Bere was widely criticised by international and national human rights activists as representing political interference in the judicial process and abrogation of the Constitution.

had not issued any new indictments. See United Nations, Report of the Secretary-General on the United Nations Integrated Mission in Timor-Leste for the Period from 24 September 2009 to 20 January 2010 (UN Doc. S/2010/85), 12 February 2010, para 76.

88 The Centre for International Governance Innovation (CIGI), 'Security Sector Reform Monitor: Timor-Leste,' SSRM January 2011, No. 4, Waterloo, Ontario, Canada.

89 See Jose Ramos-Horta, 'The Dreams Shall Never Die, We Must Keep the Faith, the Struggle Goes on,' speech marking the tenth anniversary of the United Nations-sponsored 'Popular Consultation' on the status of East Timor on 30 August 1999, Dili, 30 August 2009, at http://www.laohamutuk.org/Justice/99/JRHSpeech30Aug2009.htm (accessed 10 February 2012).

Internal Nation Building and Reconciliation Imperatives

While an analysis of the significance of the Indonesia relationship goes some of the way to explaining the East Timorese leadership's retreat from a prosecutorial agenda, there is, however, more to it than this. I want to now turn to a discussion of the ongoing attempts by members of the East Timorese leadership (in particular Gusmão and Ramos-Horta) to introduce bills granting amnesties and pardons to East Timorese perpetrators of serious crimes. These attempts indicate that the leadership's forward-looking reconciliatory narrative can be understood, in part, as a reflection of perceived internal nation-building imperatives. In particular, the continuing debates about these issues underscore the extent to which there are deeply embedded anxieties about building national unity and establishing political legitimacy during a formative, chaotic and fluid period of nation building.

The first attempt to pass a law on amnesties and pardons occurred during the lead-up to independence, in early May 2002, when Gusmão introduced a draft bill on these matters to the Constituent Assembly, the precursor to the National Parliament.[90] Given it was so close to independence, the Constituent Assembly declined to debate the law, which was reintroduced into Parliament five days after independence.[91] Sweeping in its scope, the law proposed an amnesty for all crimes before September 1999 committed by East Timorese who were coerced into joining militia groups, provided the crimes were not 'violent or bloody'[92] and, in addition, conferred an amnesty on all FALINTIL fighters for past criminal conduct, provided that the conduct did not amount to war crimes, crimes against humanity or genocide.[93] Despite being passed by the Council of Ministers on 25 May 2002, the law was promptly withdrawn after strong

90 B. Wilson, *Smoke and Mirrors: the Development of the East Timorese Police 1999–2009*, Unpublished PhD Thesis, The Australian National University, 2010, p. 119.

91 Wilson, *Smoke and Mirrors*, p. 119.

92 This rather vague term was not defined, but presumably referred to cases of murder.

93 Bhuta, 'Great Expectations,' p. 175; Wilson, *Smoke and Mirrors*, p. 119.

criticism from many sectors, including national and international human rights NGOs, UNTAET and East Timorese lawyers.[94] It was soon followed by another draft law on 'Amnesty and Other Clemency Measures', which appeared in 2004, in the lead-up to the anniversary of independence (and around the time of the SCIU's indictment of General Wiranto), the preamble of which stressed the importance of forgiving even those who have committed so-called 'serious crimes'.[95]

More recently, on 4 June 2007, immediately prior to the elections, Parliament approved the law on 'Truth and Measures of Clemency for Diverse Offences', which included provision for amnesties for crimes committed between April 2006 and April 2007. This was widely regarded as an attempt by the then FRETILIN government to ensure that various members of the political elite (including the former Minister of the Interior, Rogério Lobato, who had been recommended for prosecution due to his role in the 2006 crisis), would either be pardoned or their cases abandoned.[96] However, following a referral by President José Ramos-Horta, the Court of Appeal declared the law unconstitutional.[97] Soon afterwards, on 20 May 2008, the anniversary of East Timor's independence, Ramos-Horta issued a Presidential Decree granting full or partial pardons to ninety-four prisoners, more than half the total prison population,[98] including nine former militia members who had received sentences for committing serious crimes during 1999. Among those pardoned was Joni Marques, who had been convicted by the Special Panels for crimes against humanity and originally given a thirty-three-year prison sentence. Another was former Lobato who, at that point, had been convicted of distributing weapons to civilians during the 'crisis' of 2006. Then, in 2009, in the context of the Martinus Bere controversy and the tenth

94 Bhuta, 'Great Expectations,' p. 175.

95 Wilson, *Smoke and Mirrors*, pp. 118–119.

96 Wilson, *Smoke and Mirrors*, p. 120; Judicial Systems Monitoring Programme, 'Justice Update,' Report by the Judicial Systems Monitoring Programme, Dili, June 2007.

97 United Nations Integrated Mission in Timor-Leste (UNMIT) 'Human Rights Developments in Timor-Leste August 2006–August 2007,' Report by Human Rights and Transitional Justice Section of UNMIT, Dili: United Nations, 2007, p. 5.

98 CIGI, 'Security Sector Reform,' p. 13.

anniversary of East Timor's independence, the President called for an amnesty for all crimes committed between 1974 and 2009.[99]

In order to build consensus for their agenda of amnesties and pardons, political leaders (in particular Gusmão and Ramos-Horta) have invoked popular narratives of resistance, collective struggle and national unity. These stories portray the East Timorese people as the 'little people' who, having engaged in a united and heroic twenty-four-year nationalist struggle against the Indonesian occupiers until they finally triumphed, should not turn against one another. Relatedly, East Timorese militia who committed violence during the 1999 referendum are sometimes depicted as not being fully responsible for their actions. This narrative was apparent in President Ramos-Horta's defence of his pardoning of Joni Marques on the grounds of 'fairness' in 2008:

> This militia [has] already served eight years. Can you imagine? There is no Indonesian military on trial or in prison and East Timor, showing great heroism of its judicial system, keeps an idiot, an unfortunate guy, in prison.[100]

Political leaders have also sought to make meaning from the population's experiences of suffering and pain by transforming them into willing sacrifices for the nation. For example, Gusmão has indicated that he does not wish to refer to those who suffered as victims, preferring the term 'heroes'. As he stated in response to the CAVR report:

> In times of sacrifice we rose to be heroes. Today, in times of peace, we are regarded as victims! Our people, the heroic and forsaken people of Timor-Leste, do not deserve to be treated with so blatant a disrespect.[101]

99 International Crisis Group, 'Timor-Leste: Reconciliation and Return from Indonesia,' Asia Briefing No. 122, 18 April 2011, Dili/Brussels, p. 16.

100 Ramos-Horta, quoted in Stephanie March, 'Horta Pushes Amnesty Laws,' Dili, Australian Associated Press, 13 July 2008, at http://www.etan.org/et2008/7july/19/13horta.htm (accessed 27 July 2010).

101 X. Gusmão, Address by the H.E. The President of the Republic Kay Rala Xanana Gusmão on the Occasion of the Presentation of the Final Report of the Commission, Reception and Reconciliation, CAVR, Dili, 31 October 2005.

Leaders have also sought to redefine justice as 'social justice' rather than 'retributive justice' in an effort to convince the population that improving their living standards is of more value than a narrow focus on the judiciary, trials, punishment and prison. This narrative emerged soon after the referendum when Gusmão began to publicly question the resources that were being spent on imprisoning East Timorese militia, suggesting that these funds would be more effectively channelled into development:

> These men, they will go to trial, they will go to prison. Who will pay for their daily life in prison? The money that you pay in taxation, instead of going to teachers and nurses, will go to prisoners. Do you accept this?[102]

Although no amnesty law has yet been promulgated, the fact that these laws have been continually 'on the table' since 2002[103] and that significant numbers of pardons have been granted to those convicted of serious crimes during 1999 and the crisis of 2006, points to deep-seated anxieties amongst the political elite about the fragility of national cohesion during a formative period of nation building. As discussed earlier, there were very real concerns in the aftermath of the referendum about defusing tensions along the East Timor/West Timor border. The leadership's forward-looking, reconciliatory narratives also display an awareness of deep divisions and resentments within the East Timorese population. These divisions emerged within the coercive circumstances of the Indonesian occupation, when many had 'collaborated' with the occupiers, and some had committed violence against their fellow East Timorese, not only as militia in 1999, but as members of paramilitary groups, civil defence forces, the military and police. These narratives also evoke the spectre of East Timorese 'disunity' during the brief internal conflict between FRETILIN

102 Gusmão, quoted in 'Interview: What Happens Next? Independence Leader and Presidential Hopeful Xanana Gusmão Talks with TIME about East Timor's Challenges,' *TIME Asia*, 3 September 2001, at http://members.pcug.org.au/~wildwood/01augnext.htm (accessed 10 February 2010).

103 Wilson, *Smoke and Mirrors*, p. 118.

and UDT in 1974 and 1975 and the leadership's anxieties about shining a torch on the violence committed by the resistance movement during the occupation. Former Falintil fighters remain a powerful constituency in present-day East Timor, and those who had perpetrated war crimes had signaled to their leaders after the referendum that they expected them to stand by them.[104] That Gusmão is aware of these complexities is evident in the following statement:

> When people call for justice they must understand there are no clear lines. Where do you begin? In 1974? In 1999? To take the path of justice there is no beginning and no end, and we all stay stuck in the past.[105]

Given their own role in the violence of the past, key political leaders also have a collective vested interest in not stirring up discussion of these difficult and sensitive truths.

Unexpected Possibilities: Recent Transitional Justice Developments and Civil Society Initiatives

For a complex blend of reasons, then, transitional justice developments in East Timor have been marked by the increasingly prominent eschewing of a prosecutorial agenda by both the UN and the East Timorese leadership. Factors such as the perceived necessity to both powerful Western states and the East Timorese leadership of maintaining diplomatic relations with Indonesia, and internal reconciliation and nation-building imperatives, have shaped this trajectory. Despite the lack of high level prosecutions, it is too simplistic, I suggest, to characterise the transitional justice process as representing a triumph of 'pragmatism' over 'principle'. Indeed, although it has been deeply enmeshed in international, regional and domestic politics, the transitional justice process has nonetheless

104 Braithwaite, Charlesworth, and Soares, 'Networked Governance,' p. 194.
105 Gusmão, quoted in G. Phan, *A Hero's Journey*, documentary film, East Timor, Luxlucis, 2006.

fostered some new and unexpected possibilities which may help to move the current debate beyond the 'prosecutions' versus 'stability' impasse and to develop a broader vision of justice.

One possibility relates to the release of the final report of bilateral CTF, *Per Memoriam ad Spem* (*Through Memory to Hope*) in 2008. Despite the scepticism of many observers, this report was not the whitewash that many were anticipating. Handed over to Indonesian President Susilo Bambang Yudhoyono and East Timorese President José Ramos-Horta at a ceremony in Bali on 15 July 2008, the CTF report concurs with many of the CAVR's findings that crimes against humanity did occur in 1999 and that the TNI was principally responsible for those crimes.[106] Moreover, it concludes that these crimes were not an aberration, but resulted from entrenched policies and practices within the Indonesian security sector.[107] In addition, although it does not make explicit recommendations for a reparations scheme, it does recommend a number of measures – including the creation of a documentation and conflict resolution centre and the establishment of a commission for 'the disappeared' to recover information about the fate of disappeared persons – that could be seen to constitute 'reparations' in a collective sense.[108] Significantly, by not recommending amnesties, clearing names or claiming a 'conclusive truth', the CTF report leaves open the possibility of future prosecutions and also presents evidence that could be used to implicate senior Indonesian officials.[109] Given the East Timorese and Indonesian Presidents' explicit endorsement of the CTF, the final report may well have more chance than the CAVR of influencing the approach of both governments to dealing with the past.

106 Commission of Truth and Friendship (CTF), 'Per Memoriam Ad Spem (From Memory to Hope),' Final Report of the Commission for Truth and Friendship, Indonesia/East Timor, March 2008, chapter 8.

107 CTF, 2008, p. 283; see also Megan Hirst, 'An Unfinished Truth: An Analysis of the Commission of Truth and Friendship's Final Report on the 1999 Atrocities in East Timor,' ICTJ Occasional Paper Series (New York: International Center for Transitional Justice, 2009), p. 6.

108 CTF, 2009, pp. 300–303; see also Hirst, 'An Unfinished Truth,' p. 28.

109 See Hirst, 'An Unfinished Truth,' p. 6.

Further possibilities may emerge following the East Timorese parliament's belated decision to adopt a resolution on the CAVR and CTF reports on 14 December 2009, which occurred after repeated delays. The resolution, which owed much to the advocacy efforts of individual members of parliament and human rights NGOs, authorised a parliamentary committee to prepare concrete steps to implement the recommendations of the two reports. In response, the committee prepared two draft laws. The first law proposes the establishment of an 'Institute for Memory'[110] which would implement agreed recommendations of the CAVR and CTF, including establishing a human rights documentation centre and promoting the search for missing persons. The second law proposes a reparations program[111] to provide a range of symbolic and material reparations to individuals deemed to be 'vulnerable victims'. Although it is important not to read too much into these developments, especially as parliamentary debate on these laws has been repeatedly stalled, the fact is that a painfully slow process of negotiation has begun about these issues amongst elected representatives.[112] The CTF report has also provided the basis for the establishment of a Joint Ministerial Commission that is facilitating high level cooperation between the Indonesian and East Timorese governments, including discussions of the CTF recommendations. While some issues, such as the fate of missing persons, remain off-limits due to their sensitivity, some progress has been made on the less controversial topics of border demarcation, more lenient visa conditions for East Timorese students studying in Indonesia, and pensions for East Timorese who were employed as Indonesian civil servants.

Among the most interesting transitional justice possibilities are those emerging from the activities of East Timorese NGOs and local victims' groups. East Timor has an active civil society sector, particularly in human rights advocacy. Since the referendum, activists have rallied behind the popular slogan, 'No reconciliation without justice'. Predominantly based

110 Draft Law Establishing the Public Memory Institute, No. 2.

111 Draft Framework of the National Reparations Program, No. 2.

112 Both the laws were originally scheduled for debate in September 2010. The laws were then delayed for debate until February 2011, and now have been delayed indefinitely.

in East Timor's capital, Dili, and politicised during the Indonesian occupation, human rights activists are perhaps best described as 'transnationalised local actors'[113] who promote the globalised discourse of human rights and have links to international human rights organisations such as Amnesty International and Human Rights Watch. Although these connections have enabled activists to build international support for their cause, they have not always been an advantage in the domestic political context where East Timor's political elite has too easily been able to dismiss their campaigns as lacking popular support.[114]

In the first few years after the referendum, East Timorese activists were fairly narrowly focused on lobbying for an international criminal tribunal. This, it was commonly argued, was what 'victims want'. Activists were prominent critics of the UN Serious Crimes Process and the Jakarta-based Ad Hoc human rights court. They were initially wary of the CAVR due to concerns that the commission may sap donor resources which would be better directed to building a more effective criminal justice system.[115] As previously discussed, activists were even more sceptical of the CTF based on their conviction that it was established to close off discussions of the past and avoid calls for an international tribunal.

Since the public release of the CAVR and CTF reports in 2006 and 2008, however, NGO criticism has softened, as activists have begun to see the potential of both reports as advocacy and educational tools. They have lobbied the national parliament to debate and implement the recommendations of *Chega!* and the CTF report. Alliances between East Timorese and Indonesian activists are also being forged on the basis of a

113 James Ferguson and Akhil Gupta, 'Spatializing States: Toward an Ethnography of Neoliberal Governmentality,' *American Ethnologist*, Vol. 29, No. 4 (2002), p. 995.

114 For example, Horta, while president, claimed that in his trips around the country no one raised the issue of prosecutions, instead asking for better roads, jobs and food. See 'Interview Given by President Ramos-Horta to TVTL, 23 September 2009,' cited in International Crisis Group, 'Timor-Leste: Reconciliation and Return from Indonesia,' Asia Briefing No. 122, Dili/Brussels: International Crisis Group, 2011, p. 16.

115 See, for example, La'o Hamutuk, 'Sites of Justice-Related Efforts.'

mutual interest in lobbying their respective parliaments to implement the CTF recommendations and prosecute senior members of the Indonesian military.

In the years since the referendum, the justice narratives promoted by East Timorese human rights activists have also begun to broaden. Although campaigns for an international tribunal continue, there appears to be a growing recognition that a single-minded focus on prosecutions may not address the multifaceted needs of East Timorese survivors. Issues such as reparations and the need for a Commission for Missing Persons are increasingly part of the agenda. Both issues, it could be argued, are of immense significance to ordinary East Timorese people, many of whom continue to live in impoverished conditions and hold deep spiritual beliefs about the importance of honouring and respecting the dead, including by conducting the necessary rituals to facilitate the safe travel of the soul of the dead to the sacred world.[116] This broadening of priorities is encapsulated by the reflections of the former director of the East Timorese women's rights NGO, FOKUPERS[117], on working with widows groups. As Manuela Long Pereira explains:

> When we speak to women survivors about justice they also say their daily lives are important. They want to send their children to school, they want to know where their husbands bodies are . . . Some say that if we don't help their lives it is just the same.[118]

NGOs have also begun to direct more attention to strengthening victims groups in both Dili and the rural areas. Reflecting a growing awareness amongst NGO leaders that they cannot 'speak for' all victims and a belief that that more voices from the grassroots will challenge the leadership's insistence that people are not interested in justice, NGOs organised the first National Victims Congress in 2009. The Congress, which brought

116 Simon Robins, 'An Assessment of the Needs of Families of the Missing in Timor-Leste,' Report for the Post War Reconstruction and Development Unit, February 2010, York: University of York, 2010, p. 11.

117 Women's Communication Forum.

118 Interview with Manuela Long Pereira, Dili, 2 July 2008.

together victims from around the country to Dili, led to the formation of a national Victims' Network, aimed at strengthening advocacy work in relation to justice, reconciliation and reparations. Nonetheless, given the intensive role NGOs have played in the establishment and cultivation of this network, the extent to which it will become truly 'grassroots' one remains to be seen.

Beyond their advocacy efforts, NGOs are also assisting local communities to document their own stories about the past and to conduct commemorations of past massacres. For example, they have helped the local community in Liquica to construct a small monument of an angel at the site of the Liquica church massacre of 6 April 1999, when up to sixty people were killed by the Besih Merah Putih (Red and White Iron) militia group while they were seeking refuge in the church. A mass is now held here each year to commemorate the massacre. They have also assisted local groups to organise commemorations of massacres that occurred earlier in the occupation, such as the 2008 ceremony that took place in Kraras, Viqueque district, to remember a series of brutal killings that occurred in 1983 to quash local uprisings against the Indonesian military. While these NGO initiatives are in part aimed at demonstrating to the national leadership that ordinary people do not wish to 'forgive and forget', in order to bolster the campaign for an international tribunal, they may also have local significance. For instance, in a context in which many East Timorese have been unable to recover the remains of their loved ones and in which, as previously noted, there are strong spiritual beliefs about the power exercised by the dead over the lives of their descendants, these initiatives may enable families to develop appropriate rituals to put the spirits of the dead to rest. Given the way in which the violence of the Indonesian occupation permeated everyday life, and contributed to the fragmentation of relationships and the militarisation of society, these initiatives may also help to rebuild bonds of social solidarity within local communities and families. While not without their own politics and power dynamics, local practices of memorialisation and commemoration also have the potential to tell different kinds of stories from those promoted by national elites, stories of ordinary survival, for example, rather than narratives of triumph and heroism.

Conclusion

On one reading, the trajectory of transitional justice developments in East Timor can be seen as an example of how 'pragmatism' can override 'principle' when it comes to the pursuit of prosecutions of the powerful. It is apparent that the political priorities of Western states have overridden the principle of 'universal jurisdiction' which denotes that crimes against humanity, war crimes and genocide, should be punished wherever they occur. Despite multiple attempts at truth seeking, criminal prosecution and reconciliation, no Indonesian official has successfully been prosecuted for any crime committed in 1999, and, at this point in time, it seems highly unlikely that the UN Security Council will revisit the option of an international criminal tribunal. Conscious of its geopolitical constraints as a poor nation with limited influence on the international stage, and with its own internal nation-building dilemmas, the East Timorese leadership's emerging narrative of reconciliation is an understandable response.

Yet, this chapter has suggested that this is not the whole story. Beyond the issue of prosecutions, transitional justice mechanisms – in particular the final reports of the CAVR and CTF – have helped to foster some new and unforeseen possibilities. It is too early to say what bilateral negotiations between East Timorese and Indonesian political leaders in the wake of the CTF and parliamentary discussions of the CAVR and CTF reports will achieve, but suffice it to say, a space for ongoing political dialogue about these issues has been created. These reports have also helped to broaden the justice priorities of civil society groups and have been embraced by activists as useful lobbying tools. As the voices of a more diverse group of victims become heard in the justice debate, and engaged in practices of memorialisation, story-telling, commemoration and advocacy the trajectory of transitional justice developments may further be reshaped.

Transitional justice is often conceptualised as a time-bound process that is confined to a specific transitional period. Underpinned by a notion of 'breaking with the past', transitional justice discourse implies a definitive sense of 'now' and 'then'. East Timor's experiences suggest that it is important to take an open-ended, and altogether more political, view of transitional justice. What the ongoing discussions amongst the East Timorese and Indonesian political elite, and the activities of civil society and victims groups, suggest, is that there has been no 'rupture' with the past as such and that the process of remembering and responding to the past continues, grounded in past relationships and experiences, and present realities. 'Dealing with the past', that is, is a dynamic, fluid and ongoing process, without a predetermined outcome. This process continues to be fundamentally shaped and constrained by East Timor's geopolitical constraints and the new nation's unequal position within the international community. It is also being shaped by an array of different actors, among them, members of the UN Security Council, East Timorese political leaders and opposition party members, NGOs, and local victims groups. Although these actors have vastly different levels of political power and agency, there is, nonetheless, the potential for these interactions to both progress and deepen the transitional justice conversation.

6 Reconciliation and the Rule of Law in the Solomon Islands

Renée Jeffery

'[L]aw and order is here but peace is not in our hearts.'[1]

In late 1998 the Melanesia archipelago state of the Solomon Islands was plunged into a period of chaos and violent civil conflict precipitated by a complex web of grievances, injustices, ethnic tensions, and economic insecurities. Known colloquially as 'the Tensions', the low-intensity conflict dragged on until the middle of 2003, leaving an estimated 200 people dead and more than 20,000 displaced from their homes.[2] Although in comparison to other civil conflicts in the region the events in the Solomon Islands claimed relatively few lives, they were, nonetheless, marked by the protracted, systematic, and consistent violation of human rights. In addition to the kidnapping and murder of local and international civilians, including missionaries and peace envoys, the Tensions saw rampant

1 Parts of this chapter have previously appeared in Renee Jeffery, 'Enduring Tensions: Transitional Justice in the Asia-Pacific', *Pacific Review* (available on pre-view, 2013); Statement of Solomon Islander, Honiara, November 2005, quoted in Anna Powles, 'Mission Creep: Statebuilding from Honiara to Dili', *Security Challenges*, Vol. 2, No. 2 (2006), p. 11.

2 Aileen Thomson, 'Truth and Reconciliation in the Solomon Islands', *The Human Rights Brief*, Center for Human Rights and Humanitarian Law, April 16, 2010, at http://hrbrief.org/2010/04/truth-and-reconciliation-in-the-solomon-islands/ (accessed May 2, 2011); John Braithwaite, Sinclair Dinnen, Matthew Allen, Valerie Braithwaite, and Hilary Charlesworth, *Pillars and Shadows: Statebuilding as Peacebuilding in Solomon Islands* (Canberra: ANU E Press, 2010), p. 20.

torture and the entrenchment of gender-based violence, including the widespread rape of women and girls.[3]

Following a request made by the then-Solomon Islands Prime Minister, Sir Allan Kemakeza, for assistance to quell the increasing insecurity and instability in his country, on July 24, 2003, the Australian-led Regional Assistance Mission to the Solomon Islands (RAMSI) arrived in the capital, Honiara. Operating under a pidgin name, Operation Helpem Fren, RAMSI's overwhelming display of force quickly brought 'the miracle . . . that Solomon Islanders had been praying for', the restoration of law and order and the cessation of overt violence.[4] Alongside the standard expectation of an intervening force to '[e]nsure the safety and security of the Solomon Islands', RAMSI was also mandated to institute significant reforms and improvements in the 'machinery of government', economic governance, and law and justice, the so-called 'three pillars' of the mission.[5] In particular, what made RAMSI unusual among interventions of its type was its 'unusually strong rule-of-law agenda' which, in the immediate phase, demanded the restoration of the Solomon Islands' '"barely functioning" criminal justice system.'[6] Its initial success in doing so is unquestionable: less than four months after arriving in the Solomon Islands, RAMSI had facilitated the arrests of some 1,340 individuals, many of whom were accused of committing serious offences including murder and other human rights violations.[7]

3 International Australia, 'Solomon Islands Truth and Reconciliation Commission a Historic Opportunity', March 8, 2010, at http://www.amnesty.org.au/news/comments/22663/ (accessed May 2, 2011).

4 Mary-Louise O'Callaghan, 'RAMSI – the Way Ahead' in Sinclair Dinnen and Stewart Firth (eds.), *Politics and Statebuilding in Solomon Islands* (Canberra: ANU E Press, 2008), p. 186.

5 Regional Assistance Mission to Solomon Islands, 'What is RAMSI?', at http://www.ramsi.org/about/what-is-ramsi.html (accessed May 2, 2011); Michael G. Morgan and Abby McLeod, 'Have We Failed Our Neighbour?', *Australian Journal of International Affairs*, Vol. 60, No. 3 (2006), p. 418.

6 Braithwaite et al., *Pillars and Shadows*, p. 3; Michael Fullilove, 'RAMSI and State Building in Solomon Islands', *Defender*, Vol. 23, No. 1 (2006), p. 33.

7 Tarcisius Tara Kabutaulaka, 'Australian Foreign Policy and the RAMSI Intervention in Solomon Islands', *The Contemporary Pacific*, Vol. 17, No. 2 (2005), p. 279.

Although RAMSI's actions brought with them the initial impression of swift justice for human rights violations, as time dragged on, defendants remained in remand, and the criminal justice system became bogged down by the large number of complex cases before it. Questions emerged over whether RAMSI had in fact contributed to a new set of tensions between the rule of law approach it had implemented and the reconciliation approach favoured by large sectors of the community. Indeed, amongst the defining features of the Solomon Islands case is the fact that no formal transitional justice processes has been planned or implemented: neither during the lengthy peace process that brought the conflict to an end nor in the immediate aftermath of hostilities was an explicit transitional justice process or set of mechanisms developed or instituted.[8] Rather, in what was a relatively organic process, particular interest groups devised and implemented various mechanisms designed to bring accountability for human rights violations. These fell into two broad groups. Conceiving justice through the prism of its liberal state-building mandate, RAMSI's rule of law approach was, and remains, a top-down approach that favours the strengthening of key state institutions, including those associated with law and order, and the pursuit of accountability through criminal trials. By contrast, the reconciliation approach is a bottom-up method of post-conflict justice that favours local, grass-roots, traditional, and indigenous justice processes. In the case of the Solomon Islands, these localized practices and processes were routinely implemented by community groups, women's organizations, and the churches throughout the peace process and the post-conflict recovery period.

Although these two approaches have technically operated independently in the Solomon Islands, proponents of each have accused the other of hampering their justice efforts. Thus, while supporters of

8 Hilary Charlesworth, 'Building Democracy and Justice After Conflict', Occasional Paper 2/2007, the Cunningham Lecture, the Academy of the Social Sciences in Australia, Canberra, 2007, p. 9, at http://www.assa.edu.au/Publications/OP/op22007.pdf (accessed May 2, 2011).

prosecutions and punishment have argued that forgiveness and reconciliation processes circumvent justice and limit or even eliminate the possibility of achieving accountability for past human rights violations, proponents of reconciliation maintain that RAMSI's law and justice approach is impeding reconciliation efforts.[9] In particular, supporters of reconciliation argue that the adversarial nature of the criminal justice system results in the suppression of truth rather than its recovery and stymied attempts to address and resolve the tensions that fuelled the violence.

At the heart of disagreements over how justice ought to be administered in this case is the very notion of justice itself and, in particular, what constitutes accountability for human rights violations. Also at play is a fundamental set of relationships between peace and justice, state and society, and local and international justice processes. With this in mind, this chapter examines the interactions of the law and order and reconciliation approaches pursued in the case of the Solomon Islands and assesses the extent to which they have, individually, and in concert with one another, achieved accountability for human rights violations. It also considers the extent to which the Solomon Islands' Truth and Reconciliation Commission has successfully bridged the justice divide.

The Conflict

Since the 2003 publication of the Australian Strategic Policy Institute's (ASPI) 2003 report, *Our Failing Neighbour,* the first line of which proclaimed that 'Solomon Islands . . . is a failing state', the label of 'failed

9 Interestingly, this latter view is also shared by at least one of the defence lawyers who represented individuals at the 'Tension Trials'. See Kenneth Hall Averre, 'The Tension Trials: A Defence Lawyer's Perspective of Post Conflict Intervention in Solomon Islands', State, Society and Governance in Melanesia Working Paper, Number 2008/3, Canberra: Australian National University, p. 10; Jack Maebuta and Rebecca Spence with Iris Wielders and Michael O'Loughlin, 'Attempts at Building Peace in the Solomon Islands: Disconnected Layers', *Reflecting on Peace Practice Project, Cumulative Impact Case Study* (Cambridge, MA: Collaborative Learning Projects, 2009), p. 22.

state' has been routinely attached to the Solomon Islands.[10] This is not surprising, given its lack of security, crippled economy, ineffective government, and chronic underdevelopment. Despite this, however, the Solomon Islands' descent into civil war is not a simple case of state failure or even of a 'fragile state.'[11] Rather, conflict in the Solomon Islands was precipitated by an 'intricate knot of fragilities' borne of its 'history and culture', a complex web of grievances, perceived and real injustices, and a range of underlying and proximate causes that eventually erupted into open violence.[12]

Underlying Factors

Three main factors underlie the conflict that took place in the Solomon Islands: first, the misfit between state and society that came with the establishment of the Solomon Islands as a state; second, economic mismanagement by the Solomon Islands Government leading to a loss of state natural resource revenues and resulting in uneven development, and; third, 'ethnic' tensions between Guales and Malaitans over land on the main islands of Guadalcanal.

The Solomon Islands was made a British protectorate in 1893, and, although it became an independent state in 1978, its constitution as a state sits uneasily with its traditional social structure.[13] As Braithwaite et al. note, 'The state today is still not central to most of the day-to-day existence of the overwhelming majority of the population who live in villages distant from towns.'[14] Rather the *wantok*, 'the local version of what

10 Elsina Wainwright, *Our Failing Neighbour: Australia and the Future of Solomon Islands*, Australia Strategic Policy Institute Report (Barton: ASPI, 2003), pp. 3, 6.

11 Braithwaite et al., *Pillars and Shadows*, p. 1.

12 Braithwaite et al., *Pillars and Shadows*, p. 1.

13 Judith Bennett, 'Roots of Conflict in Solomon Islands Though Much is Taken, Much Abides: Legacies of Tradition and Colonialism', State, Society and Governance in Melanesia Discussion Paper 2002/5, Australian National University, Research School of Pacific and Asian Studies, pp. 2, 7.

14 Braithwaite et al., *Pillars and Shadows*, p. 13.

anthropologists call a segmentary lineage or descent group', remains the fundamental unit of association for most Solomon Islanders.[15] However, the state is not simply seen as a benign irrelevance. Although many 'educated people may understand the benefits of being one nation, the vast majority of Solomon Islanders see it as a threat to their resources, their cultural identity and culture, their environment and the basis of their sustained community living.'[16] Thus, although the Solomon Islands formally follows the Westminster model of political representation, this structure exists in tension with 'the patchwork of semi-autonomous micro-polities' that comprise the state.[17]

This sense that the local community and not the state can be trusted to secure Solomon Islanders' livelihoods has only been exacerbated by the 'failure of successive governments to implement effective or just policies and strategies to develop the country's human and natural resources.'[18] Disputes over natural resource revenues, particularly associated with the issuing of logging licences to Asian-based companies but also related to the mining industry, have only served to heighten the sense of many Solomon Islanders that they are not receiving a fair distribution of their nation's resources. In addition, the government's inability to adequately address disputes over conflicting land tenure systems gave rise to further tensions, particularly between Malaitan immigrants and the residents of Guadalcanal.

15 Francis Fukuyama, 'State Building in Solomon Islands', *Pacific Economic Bulletin*, Vol. 23, No. 3 (2008), p. 18.

16 Ruth Liloqula, 'Understanding Conflict in Solomon Islands: A Practical Means to Peacemaking', State, Society and Governance in Melanesia Discussion Paper 2000/7, Australian National University, Research School of Pacific and Asian Studies, p. 3.

17 Hegarty et al., 'Rebuilding State and Nation in Solomon Islands', p. 5; Jaap Timmer, '*Kastom* and Theocracy: a Reflection on Governance from the Uttermost Past of the World', in Sinclair Dinnen and Stewart Firth (eds.), *Politics and Statebuilding in Solomon Islands* (Canberra: ANU E Press, 2008), p. 195; J.C. Corrin Care, 'The Search for a More Appropriate Form of Government in Solomon Islands' in B.A. Hocking (ed.), *Unfinished Constitutional Business? Rethinking Indigenous Self-determination* (Canberra: Aboriginal Studies Press, 2005), pp. 159–169.

18 Liloqula, 'Understanding Conflict in Solomon Islands', p. 5.

During World War II, large numbers of Malaitans moved to Guadalcanal to take up jobs with the U.S. military which had established a base there following its defeat of the Japanese in the Battle of Guadalcanal. Grievances between the Guales and the Malaitans who remained on Guadalcanal after the end of the war emerged over issues of uneven development, the inheritance of land, and respect. As Braithwaite et al. note, 'The people of Guadalcanal came to view Malaitans as disrespectful guests on their land' and became increasingly concerned that different land inheritance customs were resulting in the loss of lands customarily held by the people of Guadalcanal.[19] In response, Guale militants began evicting Malaitans from Guadalcanal, causing resentment from the Malaitans who 'viewed this as uncompensated eviction from lands they had paid to share.'[20] With this, the underlying elements of what has often been called 'ethnic tension' in the Solomon Islands were exposed, although, as Judith Bennett cautions, this description is not always accurate for 'sometimes the "ethnicity" of those involved [was] so uncertain' that interrogators were forced to employ language tests to ascertain which particular group combatants were from.[21] Further exacerbating the situation was a government that favoured Malaitan interests over those of the people of Guadalcanal and that 'had given in to some quite large compensation demands from Malaitans who alleged insult and violence by non-Malaitans.' For many Guales, this was simply unjust.

The Outbreak of Violence

The Solomon Islands conflict proceeded in two main phases. The first phase was the insurgency of the Isatabu Freedom Movement (IFM), formerly the Guadalcanal Revolutionary Army (GRA), during which 'young men from the impoverished Weather Coast region of Guadalcanal, with the active involvement of political leaders such as Guadalcanal Premier, Ezekiel Alebua' began 'driving settlers from Malaita off

19 Braithwaite et al., *Pillars and Shadows*, pp. 18–19.
20 Braithwaite et al., *Pillars and Shadows*, p. 19.
21 Bennett, 'Roots of Conflict in Solomon Islands', p. 11.

the island of Guadalcanal.'[22] The IFM, as we will see, 'was a loose coalition of militant groups focused on different local grievances' and, as such, did not operate as a coherent party during the many years of peace negotiations that followed the outbreak of violence.[23] During the second phase of the conflict, from late 1999 on, the Malaita Eagle Force, initially established 'to defend Malaitan interests against the Guale rebels' became operational.[24] With the police force 'fractured along ethnic lines', the Malaitan-dominated paramilitary wing of the Royal Solomon Islands Police joined the MEF in staging a de facto coup in June 2000.[25] This resulted in the forced resignation of Prime Minister Bart Ulufa'alu on June 5, 2000. Shortly after, in an overt attempt at political compromise, Manasseh Sogavare was appointed Prime Minister on account of the fact that he was neither Guale nor Malaitan. By December 2001, however, he had been replaced by Sir Allan Kemakeza, who instigated the intervention by RAMSI in 2003.

Throughout this period, fighting continued, with '[s]ome dreadful atrocities' committed between 1998 and 2003. In addition to widespread accounts of kidnappings and the beheadings of IFM members by the MEF, '[r]apes and murders, executions and mutilations occurred on both sides.'[26] As Clive Moore writes: 'Men were held and made to watch their wives and daughters being pack-raped. Innocent people became involved just because they were in the wrong place at the wrong time.'[27]

The Townsville Peace Agreement

The peace process that finally brought the Solomon Islands conflict to an end was long, arduous and marked by numerous false starts. The

22 Braithwaite et al., *Pillars and Shadows*, p. 21.

23 Braithwaite et al., *Pillars and Shadows*, p. 24.

24 Braithwaite et al., *Pillars and Shadows*, p. 21.

25 Sinclair Dinnen, 'Dilemmas of Intervention and the Building of State and Nation', in Sinclair Dinnen and Stewart Firth (eds.), *Politics and Statebuilding in Solomon Islands* (Canberra: ANU E Press, 2008), p. 12.

26 Clive Moore, 'The RAMSI Intervention in the Solomon Islands Crisis', *The Journal of Pacific Studies*, Vol. 28, No. 1 (2005), pp. 61–62.

27 Moore, 'The RAMSI Intervention in the Solomon Islands Crisis', p. 62.

Townsville Peace Agreement (TPA), finally reached on October 15, 2000, makes mention of this by listing the previous attempts made by the Solomon Islands Government to bring an end to the conflict: the Honiara Peace Accord (June 28, 1999), the Panatina Agreement (August 12, 1999), the Marau Communique (July 15, 1999), the Memorandum of Understanding between the SIG and the GPG (June 13, 1999), the Buala Peace Communique (May 5, 2000), and the Auki Communique (May 12, 2000).[28] Not mentioned in the Townsville Agreement was a Commonwealth Ministerial Action Group meeting (June 11, 2000), peace negotiations held on the HMAS *Tobruk* (July 2000) which 'fell apart when other IFM leaders said they could not sign' because the notorious rebel leader Harold Keke 'would not sign the cease-fire', and the National Peace Conference held on the New Zealand Navy ship *Te Kaha* (August 25 to 27, 2000) at which the first official calls for the establishment of a truth and reconciliation commission were made.[29] Indeed, the months leading up to the Townsville negotiations were marked, not only by numerous attempts to find a resolution to the conflict but some of the 'bloodiest engagements of the IFM-MEF conflict.'[30] During this time, Keke became 'the decisive spoiler of the peace', launching violent attacks and even hijacking a Solomon Islands Airlines airplane.[31]

In addition to securing a cease-fire, the Townsville Peace Agreement included three provisions of particular relevance to the pursuit of justice for human rights violations. First, it included a weapons amnesty, which provided anyone who relinquished their weapon with 'immunity from prosecution in respect of the stealing or possession of that weapon (or any of a similar kind) at any date after the 1st January, 1998', as well as a general amnesty.[32] The general amnesty for '[m]embers, leaders and other civilian advisors associated with the MEF, IFM, and any

28 The Townsville Peace Agreement, October 15, 2000, Preamble, at http://www.commerce.gov.sb/Gov/Peace_Agreement.htm (accessed May 2, 2011).

29 Braithwaite et al., *Pillars and Shadows*, p. 37; Fraenkel, *The Manipulation of Custom*, p. 96.

30 Braithwaite et al., *Pillars and Shadows*, p. 37.

31 Braithwaite et al., *Pillars and Shadows*, p. 37.

32 Townsville Peace Agreement, 2.3.1.

Police, Prison Service or RRU or PFF officers who participated in military operations during the course of the ethnic crisis' provided immunity for criminal acts perpetrated in connection with the Tensions, including 'killing in combat conditions or in connection with the armed conflict on Guadalcanal.'[33] However, as the IFM was not a signatory to the TPA, its members could not benefit from this amnesty provision.

Second, the TPA also made provisions for the location, identification, and recovery of the remains of those killed during the conflict. Third, it also included provisions for post-conflict reconciliation but stopped short of providing for the establishment of a truth and reconciliation commission flagged during earlier peace negotiations. Instead, it suggested that reconciliation be pursued through 'face-to-face dialogue . . . at community, village, family, individual and organizational levels' and be coupled with 'public display[s] of forgiveness and confession to be organized by the SIG.'[34] In addition, the TPA also provided for the establishment of a Peace and Reconciliation Committee 'to programme and coordinate efforts to achieve full community based reconciliation and forgiveness throughout Solomon Islands' which eventually resulted in the establishment of the Ministry of National Unity, Reconciliation, and Peace.[35]

The TPA enjoyed only limited success. While the International Peace Monitoring Team established to monitor the implementation of the agreement, along with the National Peace Council, a key player in the peace process, managed to facilitate the collection of a large number of weapons, most of those surrendered were old World War II and home-made weapons, leaving the majority of the high-powered weapons seized during the conflict at large.[36] In order to facilitate the further surrender of weapons, the Solomon Islands Government instituted Amnesty Acts in 2000 and 2001 which, like the amnesty provision included in the TPA,

33 Townsville Peace Agreement, 2.3.2.ii(b).

34 Townsville Peace Agreement, 5.1.(a)(b).

35 Townsville Peace Agreement, 5.2.(a).

36 Braithwaite et al., *Pillars and Shadows*, p. 39; Fraenkel, *The Manipulation of Custom*, pp. 102, 142.

controversially included immunity from prosecution for offences such as murder. Significantly, however, the amnesties did 'not apply to any criminal acts done in violation of international humanitarian laws, [or] human rights violations or abuses.'[37] This limitation, it is thought, was included to 'allay potential international concerns that the Acts had been drafted so as to provide amnesty for grave breaches of the Geneva Conventions that had been allegedly committed by the IFM and the MEF.'[38] However, as the precise constitution of 'human rights violations' was never specified, precisely which crimes are excluded by the amnesty remains unclear. In any case, very few applications for amnesty were made and, in the end, only two amnesties were ever granted in accordance with the 2000 and 2001 acts.

Most problematic for the TPA was, however, Harold Keke's refusal to lay down arms. Having split from the IFM and formed the Guadalcanal Liberation Front, Keke continued to rule parts of the Weather Coast of Guadalcanal. During 2002 and the early months of 2003, 'Keke and his followers threatened and murdered more than twenty people in the areas they controlled.'[39] In the first half of 2003 an Australian Seventh Day Adventist missionary was beheaded, six members of the Melanesian Brotherhood were murdered, and the retired police commissioner, Sir Frederick Soaki, was shot dead in Auki, Malaita.[40] The Melanesian Brotherhood had played a significant role in attempting to broker peace during the Tensions, with members at one stage actually

37 Solomon Islands Amnesty Act 2001, 3.5.

38 James Watson, 'A Model Pacific Solution? A Study of the Deployment of the Regional Assistance Mission to Solomon Islands', Working Paper No. 126 (Canberra: Land Warfare Studies Centre, 2005), p. 13. Amnesty International, for one, alleges that war crimes were committed during the Solomon Islands conflict. see Amnesty International Report on Solomon Islands, 2002, p. 10.

39 Tarcisius Tara Kabutaulaka, 'Solomon Islands', *The Contemporary Pacific*, Vol. 16, No. 2 (2004), p. 396.

40 U.S. Department of State, 'Solomon Islands', Country Reports on Human Rights Practices, Bureau of Democracy, Human Rights, and Labor (February 25, 2004), p. 2, at http://www.state.gov/g/drl/rls/hrrpt/2003/27789.htm (accessed May 2, 2011).

'camping between enemy lines' to prevent further violence.[41] In April 2003, six members attempted to deliver a letter to Harold Keke from the Anglican Archbishop, who had offered to act 'as go between in peace talks between Keke and the government.'[42] Accused of being government spies, two of the Brothers were shot and killed by Keke's men on April 24. The remaining four were held captive overnight and interrogated before being 'escorted to the beach . . . and shot beside a grave that had been dug earlier on for them by the GLF.'[43] As Kabutaulaka thus notes, in the period after the signing of the Townsville Peace Agreement, the 'Solomon Islands remained in a state of "latent peace" – a situation where there was fear for the potential for violence in society' to erupt once more.[44]

In response, the Solomon Islands Government launched a so-called joint operation in an attempt to capture Keke. This was a disaster. Not only were members of the joint operation accused of committing human rights violations themselves, but Keke and his militants began retaliating against villagers they believed were supporting the joint operation:[45] 'They demanded allegiances from villagers and if villagers refused to give it, would torture and kill them and even burn villages to the ground.'[46] This most notorious instance of this took place in the village of Marasa.

41 Br Richard Carter, in Stephen Crittenden, Interview with Father Peter Hosking, 'Melanesian Brotherhood murders', *The Religion Report, Radio National*, 21 July 2004; accessed at http://www.abc.net/au/rn/talks/8.30/relrpt/stories/s1156154.htm, 2 May 2011.

42 Hosking, in Crittenden, 'Melanesian Brotherhood Murders'.

43 *K v. Regina*, High Court of the Solomon Islands, Criminal Case Number 368–05 (September 16, 2005), at http://www.paclii.org/sb/cases/SBHC/2005/150.html (accessed May 2, 2011).

44 Kabutaulaka, 'Solomon Islands', p. 396.

45 Some members of the joint operation were eventually charged and prosecuted for murder, robbery, and attempting to cause grievous bodily harm. See *Gabriele Havimei, James Kili, Wawari Malolo, Nicholas Na'agi, and John Taloi v Regina*, High Court of the Solomon Islands, Criminal Case No. 464 of 2005, at http://www.paclii.org/sb/cases/SBHC/2005/26.html (accessed May 2, 2011).

46 Stephen Crittenden, 'Interview with Father Peter Hosking, "Melanesian Brotherhood Murders"', *The Religion Report, Radio National*, July 21, 2004, at http://www.abc.net/au/rn/talks/8.30/relrpt/stories/s1156154.htm (accessed May 2, 2011).

The incident at Marasa is, without question, one of the most gruesome atrocities committed during the Solomon Islands Tensions. For three days from June 16, 2003, members of the GLF held 400 villagers hostage on the beach 'to punish villagers for allegedly aiding a government operations force.'[47] Father Lionel Longarata, an Anglican priest, was tied to a canoe and, along with the rest of the villagers, forced to witness the unspeakable torture and eventual murder of two boys selected for killing. As Longarata stated in his testimony to the Solomon Islands Truth and Reconciliation Commission some seven years later:

> They were bashed, butted with their rifle, and stoned, streams of blood running down from their faces, they were tied both hands at their back and were ordered to dance while blood ran from their bodies, eventually on the beach the younger one died on the spot, then elder one tried to escape but he could not do it, they continuously to butt him with the bottom of their rifles, they stoned him and he fall, whilst on the ground one of them with a machete cut his back open, all this happened while everyone was watching, young and old, women and children witnessed everything, after being killed their bodied were dragged further down the beach to where the sun was shining and the heat of the great gravel of Marasa heated their bodied, they finished with they did and looked around and saw me . . . and they said I will be the next victim, they came towards me gun pointed me with both of my hands tied on my back and I was pushed down to stay between the 2 dead bodies, after two hours the bodies were taken away and then buried in a shallow grave.[48]

In the end Longarata's life was spared, but the village was burnt to the ground. Just one month later RAMSI arrived and brought an end to the violence.

47 'Ex-Solomons Militants Guilty of Murders', *NineMSN*, April 19, 2007, at http://news.ninemsn.com.au/world/228333/ex-solomons-militants-guilty-of-murders (accessed May 2, 2011); Fraenkel, *The Manipulation of Custom*, p. 157.

48 Testimony of Fr. Lionel Longarata, TRC Visale Public Hearing Day One, June 23, 2010, at http://solomonislands-trc.com/public-hearing-sessions/visale-public-hearing-session-one.html (accessed May 2, 2011).

Transitional Justice

Although a number of transitional justice mechanisms were mentioned in the Townsville Peace Agreement, the provisions were far too vague to provide any real basis on which to formulate a formal transitional justice process for the Solomon Islands. As a result, the development of a formal transitional justice program for the Solomon Islands has never been seriously discussed at official levels, nor has any coherent process been devised. Rather, those aspects of transitional justice that have been implemented have appeared on an ad hoc basis, as the by-product of other post-conflict state-building exercises or as part of customary conflict resolution practices. As such, they have largely fallen into one of the two approaches outlined above, focusing on either the rule of law or reconciliation.

The Rule of Law

The Facilitation of International Assistance Act 2003 passed by the Solomon Islands government to authorize the international intervention came into force on July 21, 2003. Three days later RAMSI arrived. By the end of its first week the administration of RAMSI had decided to focus its initial efforts on three issues: seizing weapons, ending ongoing fighting on the Weather Coast, and arresting Harold Keke.[49] In the end, Keke surrendered peacefully in August 2003, following talks with the head of the international mission, Nick Warner, and was taken into custody to await trial. He was not the only former militia to face incarceration.

In the early months of the RAMSI mission, large numbers of militia members and police officers were arrested and charged with a range of offences including 'very serious charges.'[50] This took place in accordance with RAMSI's underlying philosophy which held that the fastest way to restore security in the Solomon Islands was to get the guns and the

49 Watson, 'A Model Pacific Solution?', p. 19.
50 Braithwaite et al., *Pillars and Shadows*, p. 55.

militia off the streets. In practical terms, it seems that many RAMSI officers 'saw it as de facto policy . . . to charge leading militants with something reasonably plausible to get them locked up on remand while they more carefully sought to build evidence against them.'[51] Predictably, this practice saw RAMSI face criticism for apparently breaching the terms of the amnesties included in the TPA and in the SIG Amnesty Acts of 2000 and 2001. In the end, however, RAMSI officials decided that as they could not reliably determine who ought to qualify for amnesty – because they could not, as per the terms of the amnesties, reliably establish that suspects had returned 'all weapons and ammunition and stolen property in [their] possession and in [their] custody' – 'all allegations of criminal behaviour would be investigated.'[52] Thus, by Christmas at the end of the first year of RAMSI's intervention, just five months after its arrival, 'most of the militant leaders were under arrest.'[53]

However, with RAMSI's initial success in restoring law and order and in detaining a large number of militants came a further challenge. Once arrested, suspects needed to be processed through a criminal justice system which, at the time, 'barely functioned.'[54] Indeed, such was its state of disrepair that until the arrival of RAMSI, the Solomon Islands government had done 'little to investigate or prosecute persons responsible for killings and other abuses, contributing to a pervasive climate of impunity.'[55] In accordance with its state-building mission, RAMSI officials maintained that the best, and indeed, only viable way to bring an end to that climate of impunity was to strengthen the criminal justice system to allow it to undertake criminal trials.

In 2005 what became known as the 'Tension Trials' began in accordance with Solomon Islands domestic law. The first was the high profile case of Harold Keke, Ronnie Cawa, and Francis Lela who were charged

51 Braithwaite et al., *Pillars and Shadows*, p. 50.
52 Watson, 'A Model Pacific Solution?', p. 31; Solomon Islands Amnesty Act, 2001, 3.
53 Braithwaite et al., *Pillars and Shadows*, p. 52.
54 U.S. Department of State, 'Solomon Islands', p. 4.
55 U.S. Department of State, 'Solomon Islands', p. 4.

with the murder of Fr. Augustine Geve, a former cabinet minister and Member of Parliament for South Guadalcanal. Under section 202(a) of the Solomon Islands Penal Code, all three were found guilty of murder in either the first or second degree and given mandatory life sentences.[56] On October 28, 2005, the High Court handed down its judgment in the case of the Melanesian Brothers for which Ronny Cawa, Owen Isa, and Joses Kejoa were charged with six counts of murder.[57] Although Isa and Kejoa drew on the defence of compulsion/duress defined under Section 16 of the Penal Code to argue that they were not criminally responsible for the murders, the Court found that the accused 'must have known' that the GLF was engaged in the 'ruthless execution . . . [of] anyone they considered an enemy.' As the men had not made efforts to leave the GLF, the Court argued that the defence of compulsion/duress was not available to them, found all three guilty of murder, and sentenced them to life imprisonment. Finally, in April 2007, the High Court found four individuals guilty of murder, wrongful confinement, arson, and membership of an unlawful society in relation to the Marasa beach atrocities. Another six individuals were found guilty of manslaughter over the killings of the two boys.[58]

Although these high-profile cases went ahead relatively quickly, the criminal justice system found itself swamped with a large number of complicated cases. While many had hoped that most 'would be open and shut and that convictions would follow as night follows day,' this was not the case, and many individuals ended up spending lengthy periods in remand before being tried and, in some cases, acquitted.[59] Indeed, the

56 *Regina v. Keke*, Judgment, 2005: 24, 26, 27.

57 *Regina v. Ronny Cawa, Owen Isa, and Joses Kejoa*, High Court of Solomon Islands, Criminal Case No. 320 of 2004 (Judgment October 28, 2005), at http://www/paclii.org/sb/cases/SBHC/2005/18.html (accessed May 2, 2011).

58 *Roddy Seko v. Regina*, High Court of Solomon Islands, Criminal Case No. 350 of 2005, at http://www.paclii.org/sb/cases/SBHC/2005/100.html (accessed May 2, 2011).

59 Averre, 'The Tension Trials', p. 4; RAMSI now reports that remand times have been reduced to an average of five months. See http://www.ramsi.org/our-work/law-and-justice/justice.html (accessed May 2, 2011).

justice system was caught in a bind. As the Deputy Special Coordinator of RAMSI, Paul Ash acknowledged, on one hand, 'no-one is comfortable with delays in the delivery of justice.' On the other, however, '[t]here is no room for short cuts where justice is concerned – either for defendants or for the victims of crime.'[60]

At the same time, while few, if any other post-conflict peace-building operations have been more successful in securing convictions, particularly among senior militants, RAMSI has faced significant criticisms. In particular, in a Parliamentary Inquiry, RAMSI was accused of 'pursuing selective justice' in focusing its efforts on capturing and prosecuting ten most wanted figures.[61] As its critics noted, this meant that other 'big fish', including prominent political and business leaders, were allowed to get away with serious crimes.[62] In addition, some of those charged and imprisoned or held on remand argued that they were political prisoners (although external reports such as the 2005 U.S. State Department's annual human rights country reports have consistently stated that there are no political prisoners in the Solomon Islands). Explicitly referring to the laws of war, these detainees have maintained that they did not act criminally in killing enemy soldiers in battle.[63] That said, the murder charges they have faced have all involved the killing of civilians.

Reconciliation

In contrast to the rule of law approach pursued through RAMSI's state-building program, a grass-roots, community-led reconciliation movement has been well underway in the Solomon Islands. Gathering pace in the

60 Paul Ash, Address to the Rotary Club, Honiara, March 13, 2007, at http://www.ramsi.org/Media/docs/070313-Deputy-Special-Coordinator-Paul-Ash – Address-to-Rotary-Honiara-2265a572–63c2–430c-aedb-8edcbf90c9fb-0.pdf (accessed May 2, 2011).

61 Parliamentary Inquiry, *Parliamentary Inquiry into the Facilitation of International Assistance Notice 2003 and RAMSI Intervention*, Chairman, Hon. Peter Boyers (Honiara: Parliament of Solomon Islands, 2009), p. 135.

62 Braithwaite et al., *Pillars and Shadows*, p. 138; Kabutaulaka, 'Solomon Islands', p. 427.

63 Braithwaite et al., *Pillars and Shadows*, p. 138.

years of the Tensions prior to the signing of the TPA, its various members have continued to pursue justice for the victims of wrongs in the post-conflict era. These reconciliation processes have largely emerged as the result of three sets of influences: *kastom*, religion, and women's organizations.

The foundations of the reconciliation approach to post-conflict justice in the Solomon Islands are found in *kastom*, or the culture and traditions, of its different peoples. In line with other Pacific societies, Solomon Islanders 'have long-established methods of dispute resolution' based on the complex interactions between *wantoks*, kinship lines, clans, status, and social relations.[64] Reconciliation is traditionally conceived as 'a process that encourages the restoration of relationships' through the acknowledgment of wrong, the attribution of accountability, the tendering of apologies and the provision of an 'opportunity to forgive.'[65] It does not necessarily attempt to 'restore society to the position before the dispute began' but rather aims to 'transform' society and 'move [it] forward.' What is more, these processes are ongoing. Customary methods of dispute resolution have 'no concept of a fixed adjudication' and, as such, 'deals can be renegotiated when the circumstances change.'[66]

To a great extent this reflects the fact that *kastom* is not fixed or static but can be remoulded, redefined, redesigned, and manipulated to deal with 'new and unfamiliar circumstances.'[67] This has been most prominently illustrated in recent years with regard to the role that compensation plays in customary reconciliation processes in the Solomon Islands. According to *kastom*, justice means 'compensation for both sides' of a dispute.[68] Indeed, '[i]n the traditional context, reconciliation and compensation are inseparable when it comes to brokering peace'; it is literally the payment of compensation that renders a conflict over.[69] Traditionally,

64 Moore, 'The RAMSI Intervention in the Solomon Islands Crisis', p. 63.
65 Kabutaulaka in Moore, 'The RAMSI intervention', p. 64.
66 Moore, 'The RAMSI Intervention in the Solomon Islands Crisis', p. 63.
67 Fraenkel, *The Manipulation of Custom*, p. 11.
68 Braithwaite et al., *Pillars and Shadows*, p. 46.
69 Maebuta and Spence, 'Attempts at Building Peace in the Solomon Islands', p. 15.

compensation associated with reconciliation ceremonies has been in the form of pigs and shell money although, more recently and, in particular in urban areas, it has come to be conceived in more financial terms. As one Solomon Islander explained, 'When compensation is paid, in shell money or whatever, then the two sides are joined together again. Both sides are satisfied and nobody is angry afterwards.'[70]

Just as *kastom* is not fixed in the Solomon Islands, so too is its relationship with Christianity. This relationship has developed over time to the point where they are now largely inseparable. Thus, contrary to the common assumption that Christianity, introduced by outsiders, competes with traditional values and customs, *kastom* has adapted to embrace Christianity, and the version of Christianity practiced by many Solomon Islanders has become infused with interpretations of religious teachings specific to the Solomons.[71] Thus, as mentioned above, traditional notions of reconciliation include distinctly Christian practices such as forgiveness and conceive them in explicitly Christian terms.[72]

Indeed, the role that Christianity has played in driving the reconciliation agenda in the Solomon Islands has been considerable. Throughout the peace negotiations and in the years that followed the TPA, the Christian Churches of the Solomon Islands played a key role in promoting and facilitating reconciliation processes. The Melanesian Brothers, in particular, 'played significant roles as mediators' and peacekeepers, some paying for their peacemaking efforts with their lives.[73] On local and community levels, the 'Christian churches have been leaders in holding reconciliation services' and promoting ethnic reconciliation ceremonies.[74] On a broader

70 Fifi'I quoted in Nick Goodenough, 'Reconciliation and the Criminal Process in the Solomon Islands', *Journal of South Pacific Law*, Vol. 10, No. 1 (2006), at http://www.paclii.org/journals/fjSPL/vol10/3.shtml (accessed May 2, 2011).

71 See Timmer, '*Kastom* and Theocracy.'

72 For an interesting comparison of forgiveness in traditional justice in the Solomon Islands and Uganda see Renée Jeffery, 'Forgiveness, Amnesty, and Justice: The Case of the Lord's Resistance Army in Northern Uganda', *Cooperation and Conflict*, Vol. 46, No. 1 (2011), pp. 78–95.

73 Braithewaite et al., *Pillars and Shadows*, p. 31.

74 Moore, 'The RAMSI Intervention', p. 63.

level, the establishment of the Solomon Islands Truth and Reconciliation Commission was largely the result of lobbying and research conducted by the Solomon Islands Christian Association (SICA). Commissioned to investigate the best way to address the injustices of the past, its Peace Committee (the SICA PC), recommended a TRC modelled on the South African TRC. Its proposal was eventually accepted by Cabinet, which formed a reference group to draft the TRC Bill that was finally passed by the Solomon Islands Parliament on August 28, 2008.[75]

However, some of the most significant reconciliations have taken place as part of Prison Fellowship International's Sycamore Tree Program, a five- to eight-week in-prison program that 'brings together unrelated victims and offenders' to 'consider concepts of responsibility, confession, repentance, forgiveness, amends, and reconciliation in the context of crime and justice.'[76] This program is widely attributed with facilitating numerous reconciliations between prisoners including between former Prime Minister Alebua who 'was shot in the head, losing an eye, and through the elbow'[77] and Ronnie Cawa, Harold Keke's 'right-hand man who did much of his killing.' Outside the confines of the prison, the Sycamore Tree Program has also engaged in 'community mediation in former conflict areas, especially on Malaita' and held several peace and reconciliation conferences in Honiara.[78]

Reconciliation has also been driven by women's groups such as the Catholic Daughters of Mary Immaculate Sisters, the Reconciliation and Peace Committee, and the Honiara Women for Peace Group. The main aim of Women for Peace 'is to convince the warring parties to lay down

75 'Creation of the TRC', Solomon Islands Truth and Reconciliation Commission, at http://solomonislands-trc.com/about-us/creation-of-the-trc/ (accessed May 2, 2011).

76 'Sycamore Tree Project', Prison Fellowship International, at http://www.pfi.org/cjr/stp (accessed May 2, 2011).

77 Braithwaite et al., *Pillars and Shadows*, p. 84.

78 Braithwaite et al., *Pillars and Shadows*, pp. 83–84; 'Sycamore Tree Project Opens in Honiara', *One Television*, October 12, 2010, at http://www.onetelevision.com.sb/index.php%3F;option=com_content%26;view=article%26;id=13651:sycamore-tree-project-conference-opens-in-honiara%26;catid=82:community-interest%26;Itemid=459 (accessed May 2, 2011).

their arms to enable the restoration of peace, the return of law and order, and the renewal of good governance and democracy in Solomon Islands.'[79] The group works to achieve this through a range of activities including meetings with militants, their leaders, the 'highest decision-making bodies', police officers, and the displaced; organizing basket exchanges between the women of Honiara and women in the rest of Guadalcanal to promote goodwill between the women of Guadalcanal; holding prayer meetings; and organizing peace conferences.[80] In addition, the Women for Peace Group 'was also present at the ceasefire talks between the Government, the MEF and the IFM', its members being 'able to mingle with the militants and leaders in any way they could, such as by welcoming people and serving tea' and, in doing so, 'share their views and opinions on matters under discussion.'[81] Indeed, the role played by women in the peace negotiation processes is especially prominent in the case of the Solomon Islands, Oxfam reporting that:

> If it wasn't for the women of Solomon Islands the armed conflict wouldn't have ended. They went beyond their own safety and security to go out there to the camps to talk to their warring boys to stop fighting.[82]

As Moore notes, the women's groups were first to enter the militants' bunkers to attempt to negotiate peace, and before long, 'Stories emerged of men from both sides in the conflict leaving their bunkers and meeting together with the brave women, hugging and crying, honestly showing

79 Alice Aruhe'eta Pollard, 'Understanding Conflict in Solomon Islands: A Practical Means to Peacemaking', State, Society and Governance in Melanesia Discussion Paper 2000/7, Australian National University, Research School of Pacific and Asian Studies, p. 10.

80 Pollard, 'Understanding Conflict in Solomon Islands', pp. 11–12, notes: 'A Honiara woman's basket would contain items such as rice, taiyo (canned tuna), noodles, soup, kerosene, matches, salt and sugar, while a Guadalcanal woman's basket would contain food such as potatoes, cassava, vegetables, fruits and betel nut.'

81 Pollard, 'Understanding Conflict in Solomon Islands', p. 12.

82 Quoted in Braithwaite et al., *Pillars and Shadows*, p. 31.

fear of the conflict in which they were enmeshed.'[83] This, as Alice Aruhe'eta Pollard explains, is a traditional conflict resolution role for women.[84]

Tensions

Although these two approaches to transitional justice have operated in parallel with each other in the post-conflict context of the Solomon Islands, significant tensions have emerged between them. Most prominently, many people view the pursuit of prosecution and punishment for the perpetrators of serious crimes committed during the Tensions as hampering attempts at reconciliation.[85] While significant reconciliation processes have taken place within Rove prison, the incarceration of so many militants runs the risk of preventing 'reconciliation processes outside the prison walls.'[86] There are two main reasons for this. First, because of security restrictions placed on the number of relatives who have been permitted to attend reconciliation ceremonies conducted at the prison, reconciliation remains largely interpersonal. As Alebua stated at the completion of his reconciliation ceremony with Ronnie Cawa, 'There is peace in my heart after the reconciliation, but not peace in the heart of my tribe.'[87] As such, some argue that RAMSI's '[e]mphasis on law and order and the resultant court and prison sentences has interrupted necessary and ongoing reconciliation processes at the inter- and intra-community levels.'[88] As Averre explains, '[t]he initially non-programmatic, ad-hoc and reactionary approach taken to support the law and justice sector resulted in a narrow prosecutorial focus' that did not pay adequate attention to the 'holistic impact of arrests and prosecutions on the community and reconciliation' until it was far too late. By then, 'entrenched,

83 Moore quoted in Braithwaite et al., *Pillars and Shadows*, p. 31.
84 Pollard, 'Understanding Conflict in Solomon Islands', p. 9.
85 Averre, 'The Tension Trials', p. 10.
86 Averre, 'The Tension Trials', p. 10.
87 In Braithwaite et al., *Pillars and Shadows*, pp. 84–85.
88 Maebuta and Spence, 'Attempts at Peacebuilding in the Solomon Islands', p. 22.

polarized positions on truth and reconciliation' had been established.[89] Second, Averre also suggests that 'whilst charges are outstanding there is unlikely to be any acceptance of culpability for what occurred' and, as such, the adversarial nature of the criminal justice system inhibits the recovery of truth.[90] Averre thus argues that 'a stronger reconciliation at the national level' might have been achieved had the criminal justice process been mixed with a truth and reconciliation process.

However, criticisms of this suggestion have come from two different sources, one predictable, the other not. Somewhat surprising is the position of non-governmental organizations, such as Prison Fellowship International, which maintain that reconciliation should remain exclusively a community-based activity. To this end, the Sycamore Tree Project makes a deliberate effort to keep 'the government out of their reconciliation work' because project leaders believe that when the government becomes involved, reconciliation becomes strongly associated with financial compensation.[91] This monetarization of compensation has come to be seen, not simply as a form of conflict resolution, but as a conflict driver; in a very real sense, for many Solomon Islanders, violence now pays. As a result, some now argue that reconciliation ought to remain the exclusive preserve of local communities.

More predictably, RAMSI officials have routinely argued that issues of reconciliation 'fall outside the mission's mandate and can be addressed only by local stakeholders.'[92] They have maintained that RAMSI's role 'is to create the 'space' for conflict reconciliation to take place.'[93] In response to a June 2006 report by the Review Taskforce sponsored by the Solomon Islands Government which, in part, criticized RAMSI for failing to address the causes of the conflict, Special Coordinator James Batley stated:

89 Averre, 'The Tension Trials', pp. 21–22.
90 Averre, 'The Tension Trials', p. 10.
91 Braithwaite et al., *Pillars and Shadows*, p. 84.
92 Dinnen, 'Dilemmas of Intervention', p. 16.
93 Powles, 'Mission Creep', p. 10.

> RAMSI's position has always been that one of its key roles is to help create a stable environment in which Solomon Islanders themselves can take forward the task of peace and reconciliation, at their own pace, in accordance with their own customs and traditions.[94]

This is not, however, to say that RAMSI or those involved in conducting the Tension Trials are wholly dismissive of traditional and customary forms of justice. As part of its law and justice mission, RAMSI has said that it aims to 'ensure that the legal system also recognizes the traditional justice systems that have been used for many centuries in Solomon Islands.'[95] Rather, what it seems to suggest is that although RAMSI is open to the idea of incorporating traditional justice mechanisms within the rule of law approach, hybridization has not yet occurred. Recognition of the importance of traditional reconciliation has also come from within the justice sector. In the case of John Leveti Randy, a member of the GLF tried on charges of arson and membership of an unlawful society over the Marasa Village atrocities, Justice Palmer noted that:

> some sorts of reconciliation ceremony have been conducted within the community. That is also good and is noted. But again this is inevitable, for any community to survive and to rebuild there must be forgiveness, true forgiveness from the heart, for that is an essential ingredient to reconciliation. At least that opens the way forward for the Accused on his release to be accepted back into the community as a changed reformed person.[96]

Of course, in thus arguing, Justice Palmer was not suggesting that forgiveness and reconciliation ought to replace processes of criminal justice but rather that they both have important roles to play. In raising the issue of forgiveness, however, he touched on what has become a very sensitive

94 In Powles, 'Mission Creep', pp. 10–11; 'Taskforce: Cause of Solomons Conflict Not Addressed', *Solomon Star*, June 15, 2006, at http://pidp.org/archive/2006/June/06-16-07.htm (accessed 1 July 2013).

95 RAMSI, 'Law and Justice', at http://www.ramsi.org/our-work/law-and-justice/justice.html (accessed May 2, 2011).

96 *Randy v. Regina*, Judgment.

issue in the Solomon Islands and one that has come to the fore with the establishment of the Truth and Reconciliation Commission.

The Truth and Reconciliation Commission

On April 29, 2009, Archbishop Desmond Tutu, one of the key architects of the South African Truth and Reconciliation Commission, launched a Truth and Reconciliation Commission (TRC) for the Solomon Islands. In accordance with the TRC Act, passed by the Solomon Islands Government on August 28, 2008, it is a hybrid commission, presided over by three commissioners from the Solomon Islands and two international commissioners (currently one from Peru and one from Fiji). The mandate of the TRC is threefold: to investigate and report on human rights violations that took place during the Tensions; to provide 'opportunities for affected parties . . . to tell their story' through a range of mechanisms, and to recommend 'policy options or measures that may prevent future repetition of similar events.'[97] To these ends, the planned activities of the TRC have included:

- fifty closed hearings and seven public hearings, five held in the regions and two in Honiara, one of which was a thematic hearing addressing issues faced by women and youth;
- attempting to take 5,000 statements about 'Who did what to whom, when and where' of which 50 percent must be provided by women;
- conducting and supervising 'the exhumation of bodies . . . in agreement with the Director of Public Prosecutions';
- carrying out 'a mapping exercise of reconciliation activities that have already being [sic] implemented';
- facilitating additional activities designed to 'complement existing reconciliation activities' including 'apologies from all actors; the

97 'Mandate of the Commission', Solomon Islands Truth and Reconciliation Commission, at http://solomonislands-trc.com/about-us/mandate-of-the-commission.html (accessed May 2, 2011).

inclusion of traditional and religious ceremonies in the process; and the organization of social and recreational ceremonies'; and,

- holding twenty-eight regional and six national discussions on reconciliation between victims and perpetrators.[98]

However, the TRC not only represents the Solomon Islands' most concerted effort to confront its violent past to date but an attempt to reconcile the seemingly incompatible approaches to transitional justice that had previously been pursued in the post-conflict context. It has attempted to do this in two inter-related ways: first, by overcoming the problem of silence associated with the criminal justice system, and; second, by pursuing truth and reconciliation but not at the expense of attributing accountability or responsibility to the perpetrators of serious crimes.

Truth

Amongst the key intentions of the TRC was to facilitate the recovery of truth, a key element of justice allegedly hampered by the pursuit of the rule of law approach in the criminal justice system. To achieve this, the TRC was given the power to issue summonses and subpoenas, and to refer those who failed to respond to a summons or subpoena to the High Court as being in contempt of court. To compel witnesses to tell the truth, the TRC was also granted the power to refer those who failed to truthfully or faithfully answer its questions or who intentionally provided misleading information to the High Court for prosecution.[99]

As the Chairman of the TRC, the Reverend Samuel Ata, noted at the end of the first day of public hearings in Honiara on March 9, 2010, 'The aim of this public hearing is to put an end to the silence.'[100] In

98 Solomon Islands Truth and Reconciliation Commission Activities, at http://www.solomonislands-trc.com/about-us/activities (accessed May 2, 2011).

99 TRC Act, article 8.

100 Reverend Samuel Ata, Chairman of the Solomon Islands Truth and Reconciliation Commission in 'Solomon Islands: Public Hearings Fuel Hopes for Reconciliation', United Nations Development Programme, March 9, 2010, at http://content.undp.org/

doing so he highlighted a theme common to truth commissions the world over that was to be reiterated throughout the Solomon Islands truth and reconciliation process. Indeed, some months later, in the Western Province town of Gizo, Ata explained to those assembled at one of the seven TRC public hearings that the purpose of the hearings was to 'put an end to the silence so that entire society will begin to listen and accept' its recent history. He continued to explain that the TRC

> offers a space and solemn moment to the victims, give them opportunity to share the harsh history which they suffered and for the country to offer them the long denied recognition. It is also a moment for which the people of this nation are given the opportunity to listen with respect and compassion and above all retrieve the memories of those who were killed, to hear the pain of those who were humiliated and abused in countless ways and to restore the dignity of victims.[101]

However, Ata also made it clear that the purpose of the TRC was not simply to meet the rights and needs of the victims of human rights violations but to offer 'the Perpetrators the chance to recognize and gain their humanity' and contribute to uncovering the truth about the past. 'Giving testimony to our pain, and paying respectful attention to one another' Ata argued, 'will . . . begin to close old wounds and finally set the foundation for reconcile peaceful and eternal life together as a nation.'[102]

Accountability

At the same time however, what makes the TRC especially significant is its explicit attempt to incorporate elements of the rule of law within its reconciliation approach. In particular, the TRC is mandated to 'look

go/newsroom/2010/march/first-trc-hearing-brings-relief-and-hopes-for-reconciliation .en (accessed May 2, 2011).

101 Reverend Samuel Ata, Chairman of the Solomon Islands Truth and Reconciliation Commission, Public Hearing at Gizo, Day One, Session, One, July 13, 2010, at http://solomonislands-trc.com/public-hearing-sessions/gizo-public-hearing-session-two.html (accessed May 2, 2011).

102 Ata, Public Hearing at Gizo, July 13, 2010.

at issues of **accountability and responsibility** for human rights violations and other abuses that occurred during the Tensions. This includes the question of whether human rights violations were the result of deliberate planning, policy, or authorization by any government, group or individual.'[103]

Unlike the South African TRC on which it was modelled, the Solomon Islands TRC does not have the power to grant amnesties in exchange for truth. The TRC Act 2008 thus declares, 'For the avoidance of doubt [that] any facts or information disclosed or statements made pursuant to this Act or the findings or recommendations of the Commission shall not in any manner be construed as.... qualifying or entitling any person to any amnesty or further amnesty except amnesty or immunity granted in terms of the Amnesty Acts 2000 or 2001.'[104] Of course, as mentioned above, the application of these existing amnesties was extremely restrictive and in the end only a couple of people were actually granted immunity.

What is more, although witness statements are 'inadmissible against the person in any action, suit, or proceeding', witnesses are granted the usual right not to incriminate themselves or members of their immediate family, and 'facts or information disclosed or statements made' cannot be considered 'admissible evidence in any proceeding before a court of law', the TRC is authorized to recommend criminal proceedings.[105] This leaves open the possibility that on the basis of the evidence heard at the TRC it will, in its final report, refer a new set of matters to the High Court for prosecution.

Although the TRC Act was passed unanimously, the provisions allowing for the TRC to recommend further prosecutions is not universally supported in the Solomon Islands. In particular, in July 2009, before the TRC had begun its hearings, the Solomon Islands Minister for National Unity, Reconciliation and Peace, Sam Iduri, proposed the introduction of

103 'Mandate of the Commission'. Bold in original.

104 Solomon Islands Truth and Reconciliation Act 2008, No. 5 of 2008, article 20(b), at http://www.paclii.org/sb/legis/num_act/tarca2008371/ (accessed May 2, 2011).

105 Solomon Islands TRC Act, article 7, 5(1), 20(f).

a 'Forgiveness Bill' to provide amnesty for perpetrators giving evidence before the TRC.[106] Although many proponents of forgiveness are at pains to stress that forgiveness and amnesty are distinct practices, the connection forged here is not unusual. Not only is amnesty defined in *Black's Law Dictionary* as 'A sovereign act of forgiveness for past acts, granted by a government to all persons (or to certain classes of persons) who have been guilty of crime or delict, generally political offences – treason, sedition, rebellion, draft evasion – and often conditioned upon their return to obedience and duty within a prescribed time', but numerous other states have conceived amnesties explicitly in terms of forgiveness.[107]

However, like many that have gone before it in other countries and contexts, the proposed Bill has faced criticism from a number of quarters. In particular, the Chairman of Transparency International, Australia, Bob Pollard, has argued that 'forgiveness is something that can only be given by the victim to the offender' and, as such, there is no way 'to legislate for forgiveness.' In addition, he has suggested that offering amnesties to the perpetrators of serious crimes 'could actually offend those who suffered during the civil war' and, in doing so, suggested that the Forgiveness Bill may even 'set the country's healing process back.'[108]

In contrast to Pollard however, the Solomon Islands Western Province Premier, George Solingo Lilo, has argued that 'there will be no nation building and reconciliation and our people will forever remain blemished

106 'Solomon Islands Government Plans Forgiveness Bill', *Solomon Star*, (July 20, 2009), at http://www.islandsbusiness.com/news/index_dynamic/containerNameToReplace=MiddleMiddle/focusModuleID=130/focusContentID=16058/tableName=mediaRelease/overideSkinName=newsArticle-full.tpl (accessed May 2, 2011).

107 *Black's Law Dictionary*, B. Garner and H. Black (eds.), 8th ed. (St. Paul, MN: Thomson/West, 2006). See for example, Guatemala's 1996 Amnesty Law, Angola's 1994 Lusaka Protocol, and El Salvador's 1993 Amnesty Act; Mallinder, *Amnesty, Human Rights and Political Transitions*, pp. 4, 37; Alfonso Anzueto, 'War Crimes Amnesty Approved, One of the Last Obstacles to Peace', *Associated Press* (December 18, 1996); Lusaka Protocol, annex 6. Stephen J. Pope, 'The Convergence of Forgiveness and Justice: Lessons from El Salvador', *Theological Studies*, Vol. 64, No. 3 (2003), p. 815.

108 ('Transparency Solomon Islands Criticises Proposed Bill': 27 July, 2009).

if we fail to forgive each other and forget the past.' Although he does not explicitly mention the proposed Forgiveness Bill, he alludes to the question of granting amnesties to the perpetrators of serious crimes when he acknowledges the difficulty of the task faced by the TRC in attempting to 'reconcile discordant elements and make them cling together in one society'. Lilo argues that the members of the TRC 'may have to put themselves in the position of those perpetrators of these gross human rights violations, who genuinely demonstrates remorse and regret and were willing to ask for forgiveness and help our society move forward.'[109] Despite continued opposition from some quarters, the Solomon Islands Government still plans to put forward the Forgiveness Bill although that has not, as yet, taken place.[110]

Nonetheless, in the absence of legislation formally connecting forgiveness to amnesty, throughout the TRC's five regional public hearings in 2010 talk of forgiveness was abundant. Indeed, most people who testified before the Commission either offered forgiveness to those who had perpetrated crimes against them or appealed to the perpetrators to come forward so they could discuss what had happened and be forgiven.[111] While some offers of forgiveness pertained to loss of livelihoods, threats, intimidation, and arson, others involved far more serious offences, including violent assaults, torture, and murder. For example, in his testimony Mathew Amali Toma told of how, when fleeing from GRA militants with his children, including a baby in his arms, he was stopped by a GRA commando who ordered one of the militants to shoot him. When the gun failed to go off, the militants began attacking him with a hook knife used for harvesting palm oil. Still holding the baby, he managed to run to safety with his children who had witnessed the attack. Toma finished

109 ('Forgive and forget': 2 February 2010).

110 'Forgiveness Bill Disrespectful: Wale', *Solomon Times Online*, November 5, 2011, at http://www.solomontimes.com/news.aspx?nxID=5670 (accessed May 2, 2011).

111 See, for example, Testimonies of Gabriel Tuke, Elizabeth Takaingo, and Nelson Siama Vatora, Gizo TRC Public Hearing Session One, July 13, 2010, at http://solomonislands-trc.com/public-hearing-sessions/gizo-public-hearing-session-two.html (accessed May 2, 2011).

his testimony by stating, 'I would like to call on the militants who had attempted to take my life that time with their guns and knives, I call on them anywhere they are now or if they are listening I want you to know that I have forgiven you all.'[112]

While in some instances victims offered unconditional, unilateral forgiveness that was not premised on an acknowledgement of wrong, many of those who gave testimony before the TRC expressed a desire to see justice done before forgiveness was granted. Justice in this context may amount to accountability in the form of truth telling or the offering of reparations or compensation but has, at its heart, the perpetrators' acceptance of responsibility for the injustice they committed. One of the most prominent supporters of forgiveness, Lionel Longarata – the priest tied to the canoe during the Marasa beach atrocity – explains, forgiveness itself is not a problem for the people of the Solomon Islands. It is, he says, 'just a matter of following our custom procedures towards forgiveness.'[113] As Peter Hosking remarked, however, for Longarata, 'reconciliation is only possible where there is appropriate justice and truth.'[114] Indeed, as Longarata explained:

> The people of Marasa are just waiting for the relatives of those who burnt down our homes and kill our two young men, come over and pay some kind of reparations . . . a little compensation to mark they are sorry for what they are done. When they have done that, then people will forgive them. It's just a normal way for Melanesians, and of course the people of the Weathercoast of Guadalcanal.[115]

With the TRC's final report and recommendations still pending and the Forgiveness Bill before the Solomon Islands Parliament in limbo, what remains to be seen is whether further prosecutions are, in fact, pursued

112 Testimony of Mathew Amali Toma, Malaita Public Hearing Day 2, Session 3, at http://solomonislands-trc.com/public-hearing-sessions/malaita-public-hearing-session-three.html (accessed May 2, 2011).

113 Longarata, 'Melanesian Brotherhood Murders'.

114 Hosking, 'Melanesian Brotherhood Murders'.

115 Longarata, 'Melanesian Brotherhood Murders'.

or whether the TRC represents the Solomon Islands' last bite of the transitional justice cherry.

Conclusion

In the case of the Solomon Islands, transitional justice has been pursued on an ad hoc basis with little integration of the various mechanisms employed and minimal coordination between the parties responsible for delivering them. Inadvertently, however, this has resulted in the implementation of what Olsen, Payne, and Reiter have recently argued is the optimal combination of transitional justice mechanisms: trials, amnesties, and truth commissions.[116] Amnesties were successfully employed to achieve a peace-settlement even though, in the end, very few individuals actually benefitted from them. Criminal trials not only brought accountability for human rights violations to the Solomon Islands but drew a firm line in the sand, making it clear to all that criminal behaviour would be tolerated no longer. And the Solomon Islands TRC has sought the pursuit of truth for the victims of the Tensions. Together, these mechanisms have brought undeniable improvements in human rights to the Solomon Islands. Widespread human rights violations have ceased, and the perpetrators of crimes are held accountable in a functioning criminal justice system.

Despite these successes, however, several notes of caution must be sounded. First, although the Solomon Islands has successfully implemented an amnesty, trial, and truth commission process, these elements have not always sat well together. In this case, the combination of amnesties and trials has brought with it the impression and, arguably, the reality that RAMSI and the Solomon Islands' criminal justice system reneged on the amnesty deals brokered to facilitate a ceasefire. While they have largely gotten away with doing so in this case, it is difficult to

116 Tricia D. Olsen, Leigh A. Layne, and Andrew G. Reiter, 'The Justice Balance: When Transitional Justice Improves Human Rights and Democracy', *Human Rights Quarterly*, Vol. 32 (2010), pp. 980–1007.

advocate this course of action more broadly. What is more, the potential for trials to result from the TRC has proved a divisive issue. Thus, although its final recommendations remain outstanding, at this stage it seems that the TRC has not bridged the justice divide but rather helped to reify the two positions.

Second, although the Tensions have ostensibly come to an end, peace is very uneasy in the Solomon Islands. Improvements achieved thus far for human rights, justice, and peace will all be in vain if the underlying causes of the conflict, particularly disputes over the land tenure system, chronic deprivation, and underdevelopment, are not adequately addressed. Thus, while justice must remain a key priority of post-conflict peace building in the Solomon Islands, its ultimate ability to affect real change over the longer term to some extent rests on the broader success of the peace-building operation underway.

7 Transitional Justice in South Korea

Hun Joon Kim

KOREA'S RECENT HISTORY HAS BEEN MARKED BY AN EX-tremely dynamic process, with multiple political transitions: Japanese colonialism (1910–1945), the U.S. military occupation (1945–1948), the Korean War (1950–1953), the dictatorship of Rhee Syng-man (1948–1960), a short-lived democracy (1960–1961), a military coup and subsequent dictatorship by Park Chung-hee (1961–1979), the assassination of Park and the brief moment of the Seoul Spring (1979), another coup by Chun Doo-hwan and Roh Tae-woo and the authoritarian rule under Chun (1980–1988), and finally, democratization in 1987.[1]

Since democratization in 1987, various transitional justice measures have been adopted in order to address the vast array of past human rights violations. Criminal prosecutions, truth commissions, and reparations have been used, with the latter being the most frequently and consistently employed choice. Nevertheless, research on South Korea has lagged noticeably behind that for other countries. Apart from a handful of articles and monographs on the 1980 Gwangju massacre,[2] there are

1 For Korean names, the surname is written first followed by the hyphenated given name (e.g. Rhe Syng-man).

2 Gi-Wook Shin and Kyung Moon Hwang (eds.), *Contentious Kwangju: The May 18th Uprising in Korea's Past and Present* (Lanham, MD: Rowman & Littlefield, 2003); In-Sup Han, "Kwangju and Beyond: Coping with Past State Atrocities in South Korea,"

few English-language articles on this aspect of South Korea.[3] Even within Korean academia, there has not yet been a thorough study of this issue,[4] partly because these processes have occurred fairly recently, and also because most of these massacres have been a result of still ideologically controversial conflicts.[5]

The purpose of this chapter is to provide both a comprehensive analysis of state violence and transitional justice in South Korea and an in-depth analysis of its achievements and problems, focusing on the truth commission process. In the first section, I provide an overview of the repressive past in Korea between the beginning of Japanese colonialism in 1910 and democratization in June 1987. Given the understudied nature of the case, I provide a comprehensive overview of state violence over the last century to stimulate academic study of South Korea. Figure 1 summarizes the history and political transitions in South Korea from 1910 to 2012. In the next section, I examine how these human rights violations have been addressed using various policy measures. I then examine both the achievements and problems associated with the process. I conclude with a few observations on recent changes and possible further policy implications.

Human Rights Quarterly, Vol. 27, No. 3 (2005); George N. Katsiaficas and Kan-Chae Na, *South Korean Democracy: Legacy of the Gwangju Uprising* (New York, NY: Routledge, 2006).

3 For rare exceptions, see Gi-Wook Shin, Soon-Won Park, and Daqing Yang (eds.), *Rethinking Historical Injustice and Reconciliation in Northeast Asia: The Korean Experience* (London, UK: Routledge, 2007); Kuk Cho, "Transitional Justice in Korea: Legally Coping with Past Wrongs after Democratization," *Pacific Rim Law & Policy Journal*, Vol. 16, No. 3 (2007).

4 For rare exceptions, see Deuk-jung Kim, " *Ppalgaengi"-ui Tansaeng: Yeosun Sageon-gua Bangong Gukga-ui Hyeongseong [The Birth of the "Reds": The Yeosun Events and the Formation of Anticommunist State]* (Seoul: Seonin, 2009); Dong Choon Kim, *Jeonjaeng-gua Sahoe [War and Society]* (Seoul: Dolbaegae, 2000); Jung-seok Seo, *Cho Bong-am-gua 1950-nyeondae (ha) [Cho Bong-am and 1950s, Vol. 2]* (Seoul: Yeoksa Bipyeong, 1999).

5 Dong-Choon Kim, "The Long Road toward Truth and Reconciliation," *Critical Asian Studies*, Vol. 42, No. 4 (2010), p. 550.

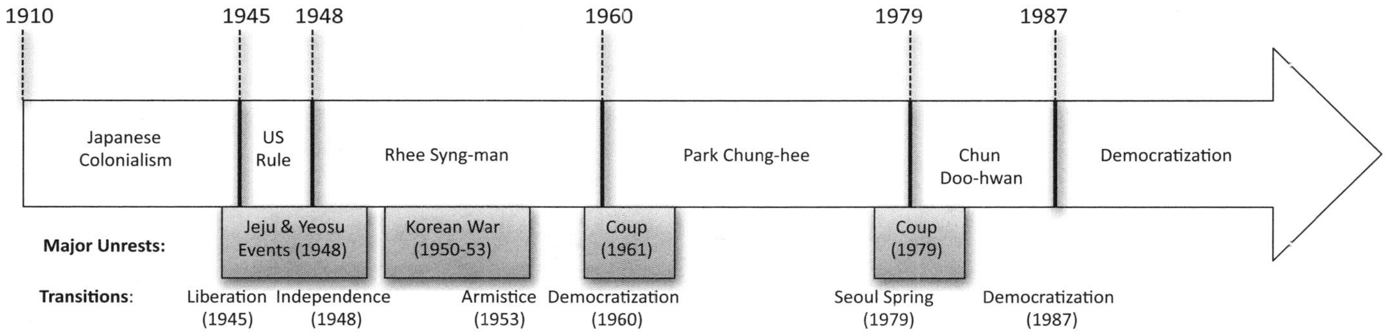

Figure 1. History and political transitions in South Korea, 1910–2012

The Repressive Past

Japanese Colonialism

The thirty-five years of Japanese colonialism in South Korea's history were marked by coercive sociopolitical repression and economic exploitation. The colonial authorities relied heavily on coercion, terror, and surveillance to rule the Korean population.[6] For instance, the 1919 independence movement was met with brutal reprisals, which left 7,500 people killed, 15,000 injured, and 45,000 arrested.[7] The colonial authorities also used an assimilation policy aimed at effacing Korean identity and incorporating Koreans as second-class citizens.[8] Throughout this process, the Japanese authority widely used Korean collaborators. Historians invented the idea that the Koreans and the Japanese share a common ancestry in order to facilitate assimilation and even to conscript Koreans into the Japanese army.[9] Koreans suffered the most after the outbreak of the second Sino-Japanese War in 1937, when the country became a reservoir of human and other resources for the Japanese military and industry. Some 140,000 Korean men and women were victims of forced labor, and thousands of women were forced to work as sex slaves – known as "comfort women" – for the Japanese military.[10]

Under U.S. Occupation

All these atrocities suddenly came to an end when the Japanese emperor surrendered to the Allied Forces in 1945. The U.S. Army arrived and

6 Michael E. Robinson, *Korea's Twentieth-Century Odyssey*, 6th ed. (Honolulu, HI: University of Hawaii Press, 2007), p. 43.
7 Robinson, *Korea's Twentieth-Century Odyssey*, p. 48.
8 Gi-Wook Shin, *Ethnic Nationalism in Korea: Genealogy, Politics, and Legacy* (Stanford, CA: Stanford University Press, 2006), pp. 42–45.
9 Shin, *Ethnic Nationalism in Korea*, p. 45.
10 Robinson, *Korea's Twentieth-Century Odyssey*, pp. 97–98.

soon set up a military government, which ruled until the establishment of the South Korean government in 1948.[11] The occupational forces pursued three major policies: first, to suppress grass-roots state-building efforts, revive the colonial state apparatus, and fill it with former officials; second, to ban the Communist Party and suppress any progressive social movements; and third, to favor the rightist groups in the course of pursuing important socioeconomic policies such as redistribution of vested land and industries, and delayed and partial land reforms.[12] Public distress and frustration with these policies exploded in two nationwide resistances in 1946: the September strike and the October uprising.[13]

In 1948, two armed uprisings took place in the southern part of the country: the Jeju 4.3 events and the Yeosu Suncheon military revolt.[14] Both started as armed protests by communists and ended with the mass killings of civilians by the police, military, and rightist youth groups in the course of brutal suppression. First, on April 3, 1948, around 320 communist insurgents attacked police substations in Jeju, the largest island and one of nine provinces in South Korea. The armed uprisings and the counterinsurgency strategy led to a prolonged confrontation of guerrilla warfare until 1954. The warfare intensified after the creation of the separate governments in August 1948, when the nascent government, backed by the U.S. military forces, decided to end the war quickly. The conflict resulted in an estimated 25,000 to 30,000 deaths, or 10 percent of the

11 Bonnie B.C. Oh (ed.), *Korea under the American Military Government, 1945–1948* (Westport, CN: Praeger, 2002).

12 Se Kyoon Kim, "Minjung Movement in Early Liberation Years," in Research Institute for Korean Politics (ed.), *Modern Korean Politics 1945–1948* (Seoul: Seoul National University, 1993), pp. 74–75; Chan-Pyo Park, "The American Military Government and the Framework for Democracy in South Korea," in Bonnie B.C. Oh (ed.), *Korea under the American Military Government, 1945–1948* (Westport, CN: Praeger, 2002).

13 Bruce Cumings, *The Origins of the Korean War, Volume II: The Roaring of the Cataract, 1947–1950* (Ithaca, NY: Cornell University Press, 2004), p. 237.

14 In Korea, major historic events are remembered by their date of occurrence. For example, the Korean War, which broke out on June 25, 1950, is referred to as "the 6.25 (War)." Within this tradition, the armed conflicts in Jeju are commonly referred to as the Jeju 4.3 events.

total population of Jeju province in 1947.[15] Of all the individual cases, 80 percent of civilian deaths were committed by state agents and only 13 percent by the insurgents.[16]

To make matters worse, the 14th Regiment in Yeosu and Suncheon in South Jeolla province, scheduled to depart for Jeju for a counterinsurgency operation, mutinied in 1948. Around 2,000 armed forces under the leadership of Ji Chang-su revolted and took two cities and their surrounding areas, which they held for eight days. In the course of operation, the military arrested and detained anyone suspected of being communist insurgents, and executed them on the spot. Scholars and a local research organization estimate that around 10,000 civilians were killed, with 95 percent of individual cases attributed to the military.[17]

The Korean War

The Korean War, which pitted communist North Korea against South Korea, backed by the U.S. military, resulted in around 640,000 combat deaths and injuries, and was accompanied by the highest number of civilian massacres in South Korea's history.[18] Nationwide systematic killings of civilians were committed by all parties to the conflict. For example, 700 villagers in Geochang were murdered by the South Korean 9th Regiment in 1951; 400 refugees were killed in Nogunri by the U.S. 7th Cavalry Regiment in 1950; and there were numerous cases of mass killings of civilians committed by the North Korean army in occupied territories.

Of the three types of massacre, the violence of the South Korean government against its own people in the early phase of the war is the most appalling, in terms of both its nature and the number of victims. In order

15 Jeju Commission, *Jeju Sasam Sageon Jinsang Josa Bogoseo [Report of the Truth About the Jeju 4.3 Events]* (Seoul: Jeju Commission, 2003).

16 Jeju Commission, *Jeju Sasam Sageon Jinsang Josa Bogoseo.*

17 Kim, *"Ppalgaengi"-ui Tansaeng: Yeosun Sageon-gua Bangong Gukga-ui Hyeongseong [The Birth of the "Reds": The Yeosun Events and the Formation of Anticommunist State]*, p. 353.

18 Robinson, *Korea's Twentieth-Century Odyssey*, p. 114.

to avoid disruption and insurgency in the noncombat zone in the South, the police and military arrested anyone who was suspected of being a communist supporter or related to communists. From June to August 1950, at least 300,000 alleged communists disappeared.[19] Testimonies of survivors and witnesses confirm that most of them were either executed in unfrequented mountains or buried at sea.[20] In addition, many prison inmates nationwide were immediately executed at the outbreak of the war, and many alleged communist collaborators in the occupied territories were executed by the South Korean government upon recovery.[21]

The Rhee Syng-man dictatorship, which was responsible for all previous civilian massacres, lasted until 1960, when it was overturned by student-led demonstrations.[22] By means of an illegally adopted constitutional amendment in 1954, Rhee served three terms as president for about twelve years, engaging in "ultra-anticommunist policy," suppressing basic civil and political rights, censoring opposition, and regarding any criticism of the regime as a breach of the National Security Act of 1948.[23] Communism was viewed as the main enemy of the state, and deterring both internal and external communist threats was the top policy priority. Alleged communists were purged from the police, the military, the congress, and the public administration, and many were executed.[24] The demands of victims to bring up past abuses were suppressed, with the government and authorities claiming that those killed had either been communists or aligned with the communists.[25]

19 Jung Seok Seo, *Cho Bongam gua 1950 [Cho Bong Am and 1950s, Vol. 2]* (Seoul: Yoksa Bipyung, 1999).

20 See generally, Gi-jin Kim, *Kkeutnaji Aneun Jeonjaeng, Gukmin Bodo Yeonmaeng [Unfinished War: Civilian Massacres during the Korean War]* (Seoul: Yeoksa Bipyeong, 2002).

21 Kim, *Jeonjaeng-gua Sahoe [War and Society]*.

22 Robinson, *Korea's Twentieth-Century Odyssey*, pp. 125–127.

23 Robinson, *Korea's Twentieth-Century Odyssey*, p. 122.

24 Gregory Henderson, *Korea: Politics of the Vortex* (Cambridge: Harvard University Press, 1968), pp. 162–163.

25 Byung-joon Jung, "Attempts to Settle the Past during the April Popular Struggle," *Korea Journal*, Vol. 42, No. 3 (2002), p. 99.

The Military and Authoritarian Regimes

The new democratic state set its priority as protecting basic civil and political rights and promoting human rights. Fledgling democracy lasted for only a year, however: people's discontent grew as they experienced economic decline and social disorder as a result of political instability.[26] In May 1961, a group of military elites headed by Park Chung-hee staged a coup and took over the government. Park skillfully maintained his rule by justifying his extraordinary seizure and exercise of power on the grounds of anticommunism, national security, nationalism, and economic development.

The Anticommunism Act of 1961, which was more draconian than the existing National Security Act, declared any criticism or challenge to the regime to be an act of communism.[27] Despite continuous challenges to his rule by dissidents and political opponents, elites and the public generally acquiesced to the dictatorship and accepted Park's claims of political legitimacy. Urban middle-class and working-class citizens temporarily accepted the dictatorship for the sake of "the historic modernization mission of the time."[28] Many agreed with the government's stance that Korean society did not have the luxury of choosing both economic development and liberal democracy.[29]

However, support for Park declined rapidly after a constitutional amendment of 1969 that allowed him to run for a third term. After a close win against Kim Dae-jung, Park staged a self-coup in 1972 by dissolving the legislative and judiciary branches and creating an extremely powerful presidency.[30] Opposition leaders and students were arrested, tortured, and disappeared. Prominent political dissents and opponents

26 John Kie-chiang Oh, *Korean Politics: The Quest for Democratization and Economic Development* (Ithaca, NY: Cornell University Press, 1999), p. 44.

27 Won Soon Park, *Gukgaboanbeop Yeongu 1: Gukgaboanbeop Byeoncheonsa [A Study of National Security Act 1]* (Seoul: Yoksa Bipyung, 1994), p. 194.

28 Shin, *Ethnic Nationalism in Korea: Genealogy, Politics, and Legacy*, p. 103.

29 Jang Jip Choi, "Political Cleavages in South Korea," in Hagen Koo (ed.), *State and Society in Contemporary Korea* (Ithaca, NY: Cornell University Press, 1993).

30 Oh, *Korean Politics: The Quest for Democratization and Economic Development*, pp. 59–60.

like Choi Jong-gil and Jang Jun-ha were found dead. Kim Dae-jung was kidnapped by the secret service and almost drowned in the Pacific Ocean. Students, intellectuals, workers, and churches started to vocally oppose Park's rule. The protests started in Busan and Masan and were on the brink of exploding into a national uprising. However, all these movements suddenly stopped when Park was assassinated by a close subordinate in 1979.

The brief moment of democracy known as the Seoul Spring was followed by another military coup, staged by a clique of army officers led by Chun Doo-hwan and Roh Tae-woo. The most violent challenge to yet another military rule occurred in May 1980, in Gwangju in South Jeolla province. Student demonstrations soon turned into a massive student-worker-citizen uprising, and the military opened fire against civilians. The widespread calls for democracy were attributed to just a few troublemakers who were sympathetic to the communist North, and the demonstration was suppressed with brute force, leaving 5,060 victims, including 154 deaths, 70 disappearances, 3,028 injuries, and 1,628 arrests, tortures, and detentions.[31]

Under the Chun regime, numerous national and local media were closed down and merged into a small number of media for more convenient control. At the same time, a nationwide sweeping arrest of gangsters and ex-convicts took place in the name of "the purification of society."[32] Many civilians were arrested and fell victim to suspicious death, disappearance, torture, and forced labor. More specifically, many student and labor activists were mysteriously found dead in the course of their mandatory military service.

After ruling for seven years, Chun started to pave the way for a long-term seizure of power by amending the constitution to favor his re-election.[33] The constitutional amendment and the torturing to death

31 May 18 Memorial Foundation, at http://www.518.org (accessed May 28, 2012).

32 Uk Heo and Terence Roehrig, *South Korea since 1980* (New York: Cambridge University Press, 2010), p. 35.

33 Oh, *Korean Politics: The Quest for Democratization and Economic Development*, p. 91.

of a university student united civil society against Chun. Pro-democracy demonstrations initiated by students and opposition leaders spread to the public, including workers, farmers, churches, and the urban middle class.[34] Due to public pressure, Roh Tae-woo, Chun's proclaimed successor, agreed to hold direct presidential elections in 1987, and Roh himself was elected president in December 1987.[35] The Roh administration was marked by a transitional period from authoritarianism to democracy. Despite the formal transition to democracy, however, the police, military, and intelligence agencies were just as powerful and obtrusive as during the Chun regime.[36]

Transitional Justice

Addressing Abuses under Japanese Colonialism

A special commission was instituted in 1948 to investigate and punish collaborators during Japanese colonialism.[37] The commission was composed of ten members headed by Kim Sang-deok, a respected figure in the national independence movement. The commission had ten regional offices and its own enforcement unit, special prosecutorial office, and special court.[38] The special court was headed by Chief Justice Kim Byeong-ro and consisted of sixteen judges who had the authority to sentence

34 Sunhyuk Kim, *The Politics of Democratization in Korea: The Role of Civil Society* (Pittsburgh, PA: University of Pittsburgh Press, 2000), pp. 91–92.

35 Roh was elected president with 36.6 percent of total votes because opposing power was not able to achieve a united candidacy and instead split between Kim Young-sam (28 percent) and Kim Dae-jung (27 percent). Heo and Roehrig, *South Korea since 1980*, pp. 40–41.

36 Si-Uk Nam, *Hanguk Bosu Seryeok Yeongu [A Study of Conservatives in Korea]* (Seoul: Cheong Media, 2011), p. 471.

37 The Special Act for the Punishment of the Anti-Nation Activities (Law No. 3 of 1948).

38 For more details, *see* Jong Heo, *Banmin Teukui Jojik-gua Hwaldong [The Organization and Activities of the Special Committee for Investigation of the Pro-Japanese Collaborators]* (Seoul: Seonin, 2003); Kang-Soo Lee, *Banmin Teukui Yeongu [A Study of the Special Committee for Investigation of the Pro-Japanese Collaborators]* (Seoul: Nanam, 2003).

collaborators to death for crimes of treason.[39] The collaborators were arrested and investigated by the commission, then handed over to the prosecutorial office and the court for a trial. Within four months, the commission had arrested 263 suspected collaborators and announced a list of 1,000 more persons for further investigation.[40]

However, the commission was doomed to fail because of its most vocal opponent, President Rhee Syng-man.[41] The Rhee administration was composed of colonial elites who survived under the protection of the U.S. occupation.[42] Rhee and his supporters openly accused commissioners of being communists who threatened national security by instigating social dissension out of hatred and vengeance.[43] The police, with the tacit consent of President Rhee, even raided the commission, injuring many and destroying documents.[44] The commission investigated 688 cases, indicted 293, tried 78, and convicted 19 – all of whom were released shortly thereafter.[45]

Pro-Japanese collaborator issues returned to the agenda with the inauguration of President Roh Moo-hyun in 2003. Tensions with Japan intensified over the issues of reparations for the victims of sex slavery and forced labor, a territorial dispute over Dokdo, the slanted content of Japanese history textbooks, and the Japanese prime minister's visit to the Yasukuni Shrine. Another commission was set up in 2005 with eleven members headed by Seong Dae-gyeong, a history professor.[46] The

39 The Special Act for the Punishment of the Anti-Nation Activities, article 1.

40 Heo, *Banmin Teukui Jojik-gua Hwaldong [The Organization and Activities of the Special Committee for Investigation of the Pro-Japanese Collaborators]*, p. 271.

41 Heo, *Banmin Teukui Jojik-gua Hwaldong.*

42 For instance, Rhee even refused to remove identified collaborators, such as Roh Deok-sul, an infamous police detective during the colonialism, from his administration.

43 Heo, *Banmin Teukui Jojik-gua Hwaldong [The Organization and Activities of the Special Committee for Investigation of the Pro-Japanese Collaborators]*, p. 331.

44 Heo, *Banmin Teukui Jojik-gua Hwaldong*, p. 351.

45 Heo, *Banmin Teukui Jojik-gua Hwaldong*, pp. 297–300.

46 The Committees for the Investigation of Anti-Nation Activities under the Japanese Colonialism was established by the Special Act for the Investigation of Anti-Nation Activities under the Japanese Colonialism (Law No. 7203 of 2004).

commission had exactly the same mandate as the 1948 commission, but with much less power – it did not have any authority to subpoena witnesses or arrest suspects, and had no adjudication power.[47] The commission published a report in 2009 revealing the names of 1,006 collaborators.[48]

At the same time, two commissions were created in order to address the related issues of Japanese colonialism. In 2004, a commission was set up to investigate the victims of forced labor.[49] The commission – with eleven members, headed by Jeon Gi-ho, a professor of labor economics specializing in the colonial era – has so far received 142,527 applications and is still working at the time of this writing.[50] In 2006, another commission was set up to investigate the properties of collaborators.[51] The commission – with nine members headed by Kim Chang-guk, a prominent lawyer – investigated 462 collaborators and confiscated the property of 168 of them.[52]

Addressing Abuses under U.S. Occupation

Because the Jeju and Yeosu Suncheon events started as communist uprisings, addressing these events was extremely difficult under anticommunist

47 The Special Act for the Investigation of Anti-Nation Activities under the Japanese Colonialism, article 4.

48 The Committees for the Investigation of Anti-Nation Activities under the Japanese Colonialism, *Chinil Banminjok Haengwi Jinsang Gyumyeong Bogoseo [Report of the Anti-Nation Activities under the Japanese Colonialism]*, 4 vols. (Seoul: The Committees for the Investigation of Anti-Nation Activities under the Japanese Colonialism, 2009).

49 The Special Committee for the Investigation of Forced Labor under the Japanese Colonialism was created by the Special Act for the Investigation of Forced Labor under the Japanese Colonialism (Law No. 7174 of 2004).

50 The Special Committee for the Investigation of Forced Labor under the Japanese Colonialism, at http://www.jiwon.go.kr (accessed May 25, 2012).

51 The Committee for the Investigation of the Properties of Pro-Japanese Collaborators was set up by the Special Act for the Reversion of the Properties of Pro-Japanese Collaborators (Law No. 7769 of 2005).

52 The Committee for the Investigation of the Properties of Pro-Japanese Collaborators, *Decisions (on the Reversion of the Pro-Japanese Collaborators' Properties to the State)*, 3 vols. (Seoul: The Committee for the Investigation of the Properties of Pro-Japanese Collaborators, 2010).

regimes. Victims and their families had to remain silent because any actions to address civilian deaths were deemed a breach of the National Security Act and the Anticommunism Act.[53] The National Commission for the Investigation of the Truth about the Jeju 4.3 Events (Jeju Commission) was established in 2000 to investigate and reveal the truth, to identify victims, and to restore the honor of the victims of the Jeju 4.3 events.[54] The special act mandated the commission to finish its investigation in two years and to prepare a report within six months of the end of the investigation.[55] The commission spent two-and-a-half years collecting 10,594 documents and conducting interviews with 503 victim survivors, police and military personnel, scholars, lawyers, and politicians.[56] The special act granted the commission the right to request confidential government files and to conduct interviews with victims and relevant witnesses.[57]

The report documented four categories of human rights violations: civilian massacre, disappearances, torture cases, and suffering related to guilt by association.[58] The report confirmed systematic massacres by the military and police and found evidence of indiscriminate and sweeping arrests, torture, illegal detention, and summary executions. The report included the suffering of the victims' relatives, who received unfair treatment in employment, promotion, and international travel under the military regimes. By March 2011, the commission reported that 15,100 victims had been identified, among whom 10,729 (71 percent) had been killed,

53 Jeju Commission, *Jeju Sasam Sageon Jinsang Josa Bogoseo [Report of the Truth About the Jeju 4.3 Events].*

54 The Special Act for the Investigation of the Jeju 4.3 Events and Restoration of the Honor of Victims (Law No. 6117 of 2000).

55 The Special Act for the Investigation of the Jeju 4.3 Events and Restoration of the Honor of Victims, articles 6 and 7.

56 Jeju Commission, *Jeju Sasam Sageon Jinsang Josa Bogoseo [Report of the Truth About the Jeju 4.3 Events]*, pp. 46, 52.

57 The Special Act for the Investigation of the Jeju 4.3 Events and Restoration of the Honor of Victims, articles 5 and 6.

58 See generally, Jeju Commission, *Jeju Sasam Sageon Jinsang Josa Bogoseo [Report of the Truth About the Jeju 4.3 Events].*

3,920 (26 percent) disappeared, 207 (1.4 percent) injured, and 244 (1.6 percent) imprisoned.[59] The commission also announced 31,255 family members of the victims.[60]

It took another ten years to address the civilian deaths of the Yeosu Suncheon revolt. The Truth and Reconciliation Commission, Republic of Korea (TRCK), received individual applications from victims and announced state responsibility for 1,340 civilian deaths.[61] The commission also made a statement that this number underrepresented the total number of victims, because in many cases whole families had been exterminated with no one left to apply for victimhood.[62] The commission also reported that although the revolt was suppressed within a week, sporadic guerrilla warfare and counterinsurgency operations continued for about two years, causing frequent civilian deaths.[63]

Addressing civilian massacres during the Korean War

The first attempt to address civilian massacres during the Korean War came after 700 villagers in Geochang, South Gyeongsang province, were murdered by the Korean army in 1951.[64] Immediately, the special investigation commission composed of lawmakers and government ministers was set up, and a special military tribunal was opened.[65] Three army officers were convicted of murder and cover-up, but all were pardoned by President Rhee Syng-man.[66] Families of victims could not even collect the remains of the dead for three long years and were constantly under surveillance and threat. Because of the Geochang case, which set

59 Jeju Commission, at http://www.jeju43.go.kr/english/ (accessed May 28, 2012).

60 Jeju Commission, at http://www.jeju43.go.kr/english/ (accessed May 28, 2012).

61 Truth and Reconciliation Commission Republic of Korea, *Jinsil Hwahae Wiweonhoe Jonghap Bogoseo [The Final Report of the Truth and Reconciliation Commission, Republic of Korea]*, 4 vols., vol. 3. Mass Sacrifice of Civilian (Seoul: Truth and Reconciliation Commission, Republic of Korea, 2010), pp. 93–94.

62 Truth and Reconciliation Commission Republic of Korea, pp. 93–94.

63 Truth and Reconciliation Commission Republic of Korea, pp. 93–94.

64 Seo, *Cho Bong-am-gua 1950-nyeondae (ha) [Cho Bong-am and 1950s, Vol. 2]*, pp. 683–684.

65 Seo, *Cho Bong-am-gua 1950-nyeondae (ha)*, pp. 683–684.

66 Seo, *Cho Bong-am-gua 1950-nyeondae (ha)*, p. 685.

precedent, victims of other severe massacres nationwide remained silent under the Rhee regime.

The second attempt came after Rhee's resignation in 1960. Families of victims nationwide formed associations to represent their demands, and this led to the institution of the special congressional commission in 1960.[67] The commission comprised nine lawmakers headed by Choi Cheon. The purpose of the commission was to conduct preliminary fact-finding for further legislation.[68] Although expectations were high, a cursory nationwide investigation ended in just two weeks without further developments. The failure of the commission was mainly due to the timing of its institution. Although Rhee Syng-man stepped down, the Fourth National Assembly, created under Rhee, still consisted of many members who were responsible for the massacres.[69] The head of the commission, for example, had been the police director of the most heavily affected area at the time of the war.[70]

Even worse, these initial efforts encountered a severe backlash with the military coup of Park Chung-hee in 1961. Many who led the victims' association were arrested and sentenced to death or life imprisonment.[71] Any evidence of massacres such as monuments or mass graves was destroyed by the military police.[72] The coup marked the beginning of thirty-two years of consecutive military and authoritarian regimes, and all discourses or attempts to bring justice to past atrocities were completely suppressed.

An important breakthrough came with the inauguration of the first civilian president, Kim Young-sam, in 1993. President Kim's constituency was Gyeongsang province, and he promised to investigate the Geochang

67 Jung, "Attempts to Settle the Past during the April Popular Struggle," p. 104.

68 Jung, "Attempts to Settle the Past during the April Popular Struggle," p. 104.

69 Jung, "Attempts to Settle the Past during the April Popular Struggle," p. 104.

70 Jeju Commission, *Jeju Sasam Sageon Jinsang Josa Bogoseo [Report of the Truth About the Jeju 4.3 Events]*, p. 192.

71 Truth and Reconciliation Commission Republic of Korea, *Jinsil Hwahae Wiweonhoe Jonghap Bogoseo [The Final Report of the Truth and Reconciliation Commission, Republic of Korea]*, 4 vols., vol. 4. Human Rights Violations (Seoul: Truth and Reconciliation Commission, Republic of Korea, 2010), pp. 77–82.

72 Truth and Reconciliation Commission Republic of Korea, pp. 77–82.

massacre.[73] In 1997, a special commission was set up to investigate the massacre and identify victims.[74] The commission acknowledged the responsibility of the military and identified 548 victims and 785 family members.[75] However, no further actions were taken beyond this investigation, except for a few subsequent commemoration projects. Families of victims brought a series of lawsuits against the government for monetary compensation, but they ended without success in 2008.[76]

Interestingly, although the special act was designed to address other cases, the commission's work had not reached beyond the Geochang case. Victims who had been hit hard by the backlash after the coup in 1961 were extremely cautious and slow to raise their voices under the Kim administration.[77] There was a reason for this. Although elected as the first civilian president, Kim gained power by a merger of his party with the old ruling party. Thus, it took another decade for victims and families to create the National Association of the Bereaved Families of the Korean War in 2000. With their fervent activism and the support of President Roh Moo-hyun, the TRCK was created in 2005.[78]

The TRCK had the mandate to investigate and reveal the truth about human rights violations and a few other past events.[79] Although victims of the Korean War massacres led the movement to establish the TRCK, the ruling party had to include additional categories of investigation in the

73 Goechang Massacre Management Office, *Geochang Sageon Chumo Gongwon Joseong Sageon Jaryojip [The Document Archive preparing the Creation of the Memorial Park of the Geochang Event]* (Geochang: Goechang Massacre Management Office, 2005), p. 34.

74 The Commission for the Recovery of the Honor of Victims of the Geochang Events and Others was set up by the Special Act on the Recovering of the Honor of Victims of the Geochang Event and Others (Law No. 5148 of 1996).

75 The Commission for the Recovery of the Honor of Victims of the Geochang Events and Others, at http://case.geochang.go.kr/main/ (accessed May 25, 2012).

76 In 2004, the National Assembly passed a special law designed to make individual reparations to the victims, but the prime minister (an acting president while President Roh Moo-hyun awaited the Constitutional Court's decision on the validity of his impeachment) vetoed the bill.

77 Jung, "Attempts to Settle the Past during the April Popular Struggle," p. 110.

78 The Framework Act on Clearing up Past Events for Truth and Reconciliation.

79 The Framework Act on Clearing up Past Events for Truth and Reconciliation, article 2.

course of negotiation with the opposition party. Thus, the Framework Act stipulated five main categories of investigation: domestic independence movements under Japanese colonial rule; overseas independence movements or cases that enhanced the national prestige; civilian massacres; human rights violations by the state; and human rights violations perpetrated by the enemies of the state.[80] The commission was mandated to investigate, at the request of the victims and their family members, individual cases of human rights violations.

Since 2006, the TRCK has published seven interim reports twice a year. The final report was released in December 2010. The commission attributed 82 percent of the 9,609 petitions regarding wartime massacres to state agents (the police, the military, and rightist groups associated with the state) and only 18 percent to the North Korean military and leftist groups.[81] The commission identified several patterns of massacres: nationwide preventive detentions and summary executions of former communists and their supporters immediately after the outbreak of war; retaliation against alleged communist collaborators with the North Korean occupational force; killings of civilians during the rooting-out of communist guerrillas during and after the war in the southern provinces of Jeolla and Gyeongsang; and killings of civilians by indiscriminate U.S. bombings.[82]

Addressing Human Rights Violations under Authoritarian Regimes

Two kinds of human rights abuses under the military and authoritarian regimes drew national attention after democratization: first, massive

80 Truth and Reconciliation Commission Republic of Korea, *Jinsil Hwahae Wiweonhoe Jonghap Bogoseo [The Final Report of the Truth and Reconciliation Commission, Republic of Korea]*, 4 vols., I. Wiweonhoe-eui Yeonhyeok-gua Hwaldong & Jonghap Gweongo [I. The History and Activities of the Commission & Policy Recommendation] (Seoul: Truth and Reconciliation Commission, Republic of Korea, 2010), p. 58.

81 Truth and Reconciliation Commission Republic of Korea, vol. 3, Mass Sacrifice of Civilian, p. 32.

82 Truth and Reconciliation Commission Republic of Korea, vol. 3, Mass Sacrifice of Civilian, p. 32.

deaths and injuries of protestors in 1980 Gwangju; and second, systematic deaths and disappearance of opposition leaders and activists. Soon after Chun Doo-hwan stepped down, a nationwide focus was given to the Gwangju massacre, for which Chun and then-incumbent Roh Tae-woo bore responsibility. The first initiative came from President Roh, who set up a presidential advisory commission to promote reconciliation after democratization.[83] The commission officially acknowledged that the Gwangju uprising was a pro-democracy movement but opposed any forms of punishment or truth seeking in order not to disrupt national unity.[84] In response, lawmakers set up the congressional commission and held seventeen hearings by summoning 67 relevant persons, including Chun.[85] It was the first time in South Korean history that a former president had been brought into a public hearing and questioned.

Despite the sensation, the congressional commission suffered innate limitations, partly due to the lack of power to enforce reluctant perpetrators to testify in public and partly due to the lack of political will of Roh and his ruling party.[86] The cases were not transferred to the court for further prosecutions, but the reparations law was enacted in 1990.[87] This marked the first national legislation stipulating reparations to the victims of state violence. A total of US$175 million in individual reparations were made to 4,537 victims.[88]

However, demands for truth and justice constantly increased under the Kim Young-sam administration, and human rights lawyers filed several lawsuits against Chun and Roh, as well as their subordinates, on

83 Truth and Reconciliation Commission Republic of Korea, vol. 1, The History and Activities of the Commission & Policy Recommendation, pp. 4–5.

84 Truth and Reconciliation Commission Republic of Korea, vol. 1, The History and Activities of the Commission & Policy Recommendation, pp. 4–5.

85 Truth and Reconciliation Commission Republic of Korea, vol. 1, The History and Activities of the Commission & Policy Recommendation, pp. 4–5.

86 Cho, "Transitional Justice in Korea: Legally Coping with Past Wrongs after Democratization," p. 581.

87 The Special Act for the Reparations for the Persons Concerned with the Gwangju Democratic Movement (Law No. 4266 of 1990).

88 Han, "Kwangju and Beyond: Coping with Past State Atrocities in South Korea."

the charge of murder and other offenses.[89] After intensive investigation, the Seoul district prosecutorial office acknowledged the crime of general murder in the course of suppressing Gwangju protestors in May 1980.[90] The office nevertheless decided not to prosecute the case, claiming that acts of the military coup of December 12, 1979, and the hard-line suppression of protestors were highly political decisions, which did not fall under its legal jurisdiction.

Both elites and the public vehemently protested against the decision and, at the same time, information about hidden assets of Roh was disclosed.[91] President Kim Young-sam, who was initially against the criminal prosecutions of two former presidents, finally supported the special act, which removed the statute of limitations and provided an opportunity for retrial of those who had been falsely convicted.[92] Both Chun and Roh, along with the fourteen other generals, were convicted but later pardoned by President Kim Young-sam, with the consent of the then-president-elect Kim Dae-jung, as a token of forgiveness and reconciliation.[93]

Another widespread abuse of state power – the deaths and disappearances of students, activists, and politicians – received attention under President Kim Dae-jung. The Presidential Commission on Suspicious Deaths (Suspicious Death Commission) was created in 2000 and served two terms until 2004.[94] The commission was set up to investigate and find the causes of deaths suspected to have been carried out directly and indirectly by government agents. The commission aimed to find the causes of

89 Cho, "Transitional Justice in Korea: Legally Coping with Past Wrongs after Democratization," p. 581.

90 Cho, "Transitional Justice in Korea: Legally Coping with Past Wrongs after Democratization," p. 582.

91 Cho, "Transitional Justice in Korea: Legally Coping with Past Wrongs after Democratization," p. 582.

92 The Special Act Concerning the May 18 Gwangju Democratic Movement (Law No. 5029 of 1995).

93 Truth and Reconciliation Commission Republic of Korea, vol. 1, The History and Activities of the Commission & Policy Recommendation, pp. 5–6.

94 The Presidential Truth Commission on Suspicious Deaths was created by the Special Act on the Investigation of Suspicious Deaths (Law No. 6170 of 2000).

suspicious deaths, especially in cases where suicide or accidental deaths were falsely alleged. In 2002, the commission concluded its first term, but because many cases were left unresolved, it began a second term in 2003.

In addition, between 2004 and 2005, the police, the Ministry of Defense, and the National Intelligence Service (formerly known as Korean Central Intelligence Agency) established an internal commission to investigate past human rights violations.[95] In 2005, the TRCK also investigated remaining cases of suspicious deaths and disappearances. In 2006, a special commission was set up to investigate suspicious deaths that had occurred within military ranks.[96]

Assessment of Transitional Justice in South Korea

South Korea used criminal prosecutions, truth commissions, and reparations to address past abuse of state power. Truth commissions stand out as the most frequently used option, with at least ten commissions. Since most truth-seeking efforts have been made in a period of less than ten years, it is too early to make a strong statement about the impact of these efforts. However, three of them – the Jeju Commission, the Suspicious Deaths Commission, and TRCK – stand out as prominent cases in terms of their extensive mandates, the number of reported victims, the authorities and resources of the commissions, the social debates and controversies these commissions created, and the media attention these commissions drew throughout their truth-seeking and reporting process. In this section, I explore both the achievements and problems of the transitional justice process in South Korea, focusing on the truth commission experience.

Achievements

Truth commissions in South Korea have revealed the systematic and gruesome nature of the abuse of state power. New documents and testimonies

95 Truth and Reconciliation Commission Republic of Korea, vol. 1, The History and Activities of the Commission & Policy Recommendation, pp. 12–15.

96 The Truth Commission on Military Suspicious Deaths was created by the Special Act for the Investigation of the Military Suspicious Deaths (Law No. 7626 of 2005).

were discovered and previously unknown aspects of civil massacres revealed. For instance, the Jeju Commission revealed that 80 percent of victims were killed by state agents.[97] Most victims were in their teens and twenties, but 12 percent were civilians under the age of 10 (5.8 percent) or over the age of 60 (6.1 percent).[98] The percentage of children and aged victims clearly indicates the indiscriminate nature of the killings. The TRCK also confirmed civilian massacres during the Korean War, such as the nationwide preventive detentions and summary executions of former communists immediately after the outbreak of war.[99]

These civilian massacres have not been entirely unknown in South Korean society. After democratization, individual scholars, local newspapers, associations for victims, and local activists and research organizations have continuously published reports and carried out awareness campaigns. Truth commissions and official reports have given an official status to the facts of civilian massacres and confirmed information that was previously private by establishing the facts in a public forum. Rumors and conjecture about civilian massacres during the war are no longer simply opinion or anti-government agitation: the facts are now established in several official government documentations.

Truth commissions not only revealed the truth of individual cases, but also revealed the systemic nature of state abuses. For example, the Suspicious Deaths Commission confirmed systemic human rights violations under the authoritarian regimes and further identified two key causes of suspicious deaths.[100] First, state power was misused to protect and prolong the regime rather than to serve the public good. Second, government bodies responsible for monitoring and protecting the citizens' basic

97 Jeju Commission, *Jeju Sasam Sageon Jinsang Josa Bogoseo [Report of the Truth About the Jeju 4.3 Events]*.

98 Ibid., p. 370.

99 See generally, Truth and Reconciliation Commission Republic of Korea, vol. 3, Mass Sacrifice of Civilian.

100 The Presidential Commission on Suspicious Deaths, *Uimunsa Jinsang Gyumyeong Wiwonhoe-eui Hwaldong-gua Gweongo: 2-Cha (2003.7–2004.6) [The Activities and Recommendations of the Presidential Commission on Suspicious Deaths: Second Term (July 2003–June 2004)]*(Seoul: The Presidential Commission on Suspicious Deaths, 2004), p. 28.

political and civil rights not only failed to fulfill their mission, but also acquiesced to government abuses and were even involved in concealing, distorting, and manipulating the truth related to suspicious deaths.

With the release of the report, truth commissions also released various policy recommendations, and this resulted in some visible achievements and policy changes. The Jeju Commission suggested seven policy recommendations: that the government issue an apology, declare a memorial day, use the report to educate students and the general public, establish a memorial park, provide essential living expenses to bereaved families, support excavations of mass graves, and continuously support further investigation and commemoration projects.[101] Similarly, the TRCK came up with three comprehensive recommendations in 2009.[102] It recommended that the government enact a special law to make reparations to the victims, establish a permanent research foundation to continue the investigative work and promote reconciliation, continue to unearth mass-murder sites, and collect and properly bury the remains of victims.

In quite a few cases, official apologies were issued. For example, in the Jeju case, President Roh Moo-hyun made an official apology immediately after the release of the report, which marked the first apology issued by the head of state regarding past abuses of state power.[103] Moreover, Roh visited Jeju on April 3, 2006, participated in a memorial service for the victims, and issued another apology for the events. The TRCK also recommended that the government apologize – as of 2010, fifty-two official apologies have been issued to individual victims.[104] Most

101 Jeju Commission, *Jeju Sasam Sageon Jinsang Josa Bogoseo [Report of the Truth About the Jeju 4.3 Events].*

102 Truth and Reconciliation Commission Republic of Korea, vol. 1, The History and Activities of the Commission & Policy Recommendation, p. 211.

103 Jeju Commission, *Hwahae-wa Sangsaeng: Jeju 4.3 Wiweonhoe Hwaldong Baekseo [Reconciliation and Coexistence: The White Paper on the Activities of the Jeju Commission]* (Seoul: Jeju Commission, 2008), p. 117.

104 Truth and Reconciliation Commission Republic of Korea, vol. 1, The History and Activities of the Commission & Policy Recommendation, p. 203.

apologies were issued by the local police chief and low-ranking military commanders, but in one case President Roh issued an apology to Ulsan victims.[105]

Official governmental records, history textbooks, and major encyclopedia entries now reflect these changes by incorporating the findings of the commissions.[106] Politicians and public officials are more cautious, and use terms and vocabularies reflecting a more balanced and neutral understanding of what happened in the past. Simple denial or ignoring of the past abuses is no longer a valid or legitimate response. A recent incident that occurred in the course of the National Assembly election illustrates the power of commission activities. The ruling Saenuri Party nominated Lee Young-jo as a candidate for Gangnam district, the party's traditional stronghold. After a few days, however, the party had to withdraw its nomination over the controversies triggered by Lee's use of terms like "rebellion" or "revolt" when referring to the Jeju 4.3 events and the Gwangju democratic movement.[107]

In addition, although still far away from being perfect, several victims cleared themselves of the past false convictions. The TRCK recommended retrials in forty-two cases, with eighteen victims having cleared their names of false convictions.[108] Several individual victims filed lawsuits against the government for reparations, and some of them have been successful in receiving awards of large damages. In the Jeju case, a minimum level of monetary subsidy was selectively given to the victims

105 Truth and Reconciliation Commission Republic of Korea, *Jinsil Hwahae Wiweonhoe Jonghap Bogoseo*, p. 107.

106 Jeju Commission, *Hwahae-wa Sangsaeng: Jeju 4.3 Wiweonhoe Hwaldong Baekseo [Reconciliation and Coexistence: The White Paper on the Activities of the Jeju Commission]*, pp. 114–115.

107 Lee Young Jo was a university professor and head of the Truth and Reconciliation Commission, Republic of Korea under the Lee Myung-bak administration. Although he served as the head of the commission, the commission's activity went downhill under his leadership. He was blamed for hurriedly closing down the commission, although it could have worked two more years.

108 Truth and Reconciliation Commission Republic of Korea, vol. 1, The History and Activities of the Commission & Policy Recommendation, p. 192.

and their family members who had been suffering economic hardship and physical and mental illness.[109]

Memorials have been built, and museums are now full of remains, documents, art, and sculptures containing the collective memory of the dark past. For instance, the Jeju Commission has been engaged in three key commemoration projects. The earliest commemoration project was mainly focused on creating a memorial park and museum. At the same time, the commission launched a long-term excavation project in 2006 to discover mass graves and find the remains of victims.[110] By 2010, eight out of 151 mass graves had been unearthed, with the remains of more than 400 victims discovered so far.[111] Similarly, the TRCK launched the exhumation of thirty-nine mass graves in 2007, and the remains of the dead provided sufficient evidence of indiscriminate killings to draw national and international media attention.

Problems

Nevertheless, the truth-seeking process was neither smooth nor without side effects. Earlier truth commissions – a special commission to investigate the Japanese collaborators in 1948 and a congressional commission to investigate the civilian deaths during the Korean War in 1960 – ended in failure. Premature truth-seeking efforts made under the weak and insecure democracy were often bogged down by endless ideological and political debates. The congressional commission showed that, when truth commissions are established immediately after transition, those who were involved – directly or indirectly – in the past abuses can still exert influence over the commission's activities or even participate in the commission.

109 Jeju Commission, *Hwahae-wa Sangsaeng: Jeju 4.3 Wiweonhoe Hwaldong Baekseo [Reconciliation and Coexistence: The White Paper on the Activities of the Jeju Commission]*, p. 115.

110 Jeju Commission, *Hwahae-wa Sangsaeng*, pp. 115–116.

111 Jeju Commission, *Hwahae-wa Sangsaeng*, pp. 275–176.

Failed commission activities have two dangerous consequences. First, once a commission has been set up and disbanded without any substantial results – like the special commission in 1948 – there is a danger that this failed experience will seriously undermine future efforts. The fact that it took almost forty-five years to re-establish a commission to address the same issue provides us with an important lesson. A failed attempt allows the perpetrators to falsely claim that the matter has already been investigated. In other words, past investigations – even if incomplete, can be used as an excuse not to pursue a full-scale and thorough investigation in the future. A failed attempt can also give the public the mistaken impression that a full investigation has been carried out, and there is actually not much to be revealed.

Second, the South Korean case shows that failed attempts could bring about a serious counteroffensive if the regime relapses to autocracy. Earlier attempts in 1960 were met with severe repression, as with the coup of Park Chung-hee in 1961. Leaders of the victims movement were arrested and sentenced to long prison terms or even death. In many places, evidence of the massacres was destroyed by the local and military police. In Daegu, for instance, a massacre site was buried deep underwater through the construction of a reservoir.[112] Police even desecrated mass graveyards, destroyed monuments, and dug up and burned the remains of the dead.[113] Identical incidents occurred nationwide, providing undeniable evidence that the order came from the top.

Late and more recent truth commissions had different problems. For example, both the Jeju Commission and the TRCK were mandated to investigate fifty-year-old atrocities, and this led to two additional difficulties. First, most of the key witnesses were already dead or were too old to give testimony, and most of the key documents had been either destroyed or lost by the time of investigation. Second, both commissions met with

112 Kim, *Kkeutnaji Aneun Jeonjaeng, Gukmin Bodo Yeonmaeng [Unfinished War: Civilian Massacres during the Korean War]*, p. 282.

113 Kim, *Kkeutnaji Aneun Jeonjaeng*, p. 282.

strong resistance from the conservative and anticommunist element of society – especially from the military and police as for more than fifty years the anticommunist regimes had effectively suppressed the truth, painted the victims as communists, and justified the crimes of the military and police.

The challenge from the conservative groups existed before, during, and after the commission's activities, and in both commissions attack came from both inside and outside. For example, the opponents – mainly retired military and police personnel and conservative elites and organizations – attempted to frustrate the activities and accomplishments of the Jeju Commission. The opponents made appeals to the Constitutional Court against the special act in 2000, the official report, and the presidential apology in 2004.[114] Although the court dismissed them all, these appeals still had a negative and constraining effect on the activities of the commission.

The TRCK also suffered conservative resistance in the course of its activities, especially during its term under the conservative Lee Myung bak administration. The effectiveness of the TRCK's work was particularly compromised, it is said, by President Lee's nomination of a new chairperson and other commissioners who were less enthusiastic about the commission's activities. Not only the military and police, but also state officials, became uncooperative with TRCK requests for the documents.[115] The TRCK also had its budget for the last year cut significantly by the government[116] and, although the TRCK had a right to

114 Jeju Commission, *Hwahae-wa Sangsaeng: Jeju 4.3 Wiweonhoe Hwaldong Baekseo [Reconciliation and Coexistence: The White Paper on the Activities of the Jeju Commission]*, pp. 123–125. For the Constitutional Court's decisions, see 2009 Hun-Ma 238 (2001); 2000 Hun-Ma 509 (2003); and 2004 Hun-Ma 577 (2004).

115 Dong-choon Kim and Mark Selden, "South Korea's Embattled Truth and Reconciliation Commission," Japan Focus, at http://www.japanfocus.org/-Kim-Dong_choon/3313 (accessed May 9, 2012).

116 "Budget cut for Truth and Reconciliation Commission," *The Dong-A Ilbo*, November 21, 2009.

request an extension of its mandate for up to two years, its new chairperson hurriedly closed it down.[117]

Truth commissions also have an innate weakness because they are mostly created as a result of political compromise between the conservative party, representing the military and police, and the progressive party, representing victims and activists.[118] The conservative party tried hard to weaken the TRCK in the first place, first by failing to give it sufficient investigative powers, and second by expanding its scope of investigation beyond its ability and resources.[119] In the Jeju case, although victims and activists demanded that the commission be granted more power to enhance its effectiveness – such as the power to search and seize, to issue warrants or to request retrials – none of these was adopted in the final bill. Both commissions were empowered to request access to government files but did not have any enforcement power when government branches or organizations rejected such requests.[120] Both commissions had the power to request interviews with witnesses, but they did not have any strong enforcement mechanism – other than issuing fines – to summon witnesses when they refused to cooperate. Opponents and supporters alike have questioned whether all these truth-seeking projects could have been carried out effectively, given the limited budgetary and human resources available. Even proponents of these processes have worried that the multiplicity and breadth of truth-seeking efforts might cause public fatigue with transitional justice mechanisms, or that it could precipitate a severe backlash by opponents of these efforts.[121]

117 "Lee Team Unveils Blueprint for Slimline Government," *The Chosun Ilbo*, January 17, 2008; Sang-Hun Cho, "Time Presses on Koreans Digging Up a Dark Past," *The New York Times*, September 4, 2009.
118 Kim, "The Long Road toward Truth and Reconciliation," p. 548.
119 Kim, "The Long Road toward Truth and Reconciliation," p. 548.
120 Kim, "The Long Road toward Truth and Reconciliation," p. 548.
121 Woong Jae Jung, "Interview with Kim Dong Choon," *Weolgan Mal*, September 2008.

Conclusion

By 2012, the major activities of various truth commissions had reached an effective end, leaving a multitude of policy recommendations behind for implementation. As many scholars and practitioners have already noted, it is extremely unlikely that another truth commission will be established in the near future.[122] The prospect is even more discouraging since Park Geun-hye, a leader of the conservative Saenuri Party and daughter of Park Chung-hee (who regarded the TRCK's finding as a "personal offensive" against her),[123] won the presidential election in December 2012. Most of Park's supporters in conservative political groups believe the activities of the TRCK are little more than "score-settling" by leftists.[124]

However, the future is still bright when we consider that the work of any truth commission does not end with the mere completion of its mandate. Rather, it is simply another beginning, as we have seen in many international and domestic examples. Civil society and academia can continue the legacy of truth commissions; one way is to create a permanent institution. A truth commission is only a temporary organization; its work and legacy can and must be continued in a permanent institution. Through a research and memorial foundation, other critical projects – such as a reparation or excavation program – can be initiated. The research and memorial foundation can better lay the foundations for the long-term goals of reconciliation and the achievement of historical, political, and legal justice.[125]

The Jeju Commission has already set up the Jeju 4.3 Peace Foundation to promote peace and human rights by both maintaining the Jeju 4.3

122 Hye Ryeong Kwon, "A Critical Evaluation on Treatment of Illegal Rulings by Truth and Reconciliation Commission – Citing Illegal Rulings Based on Unconstitutional Law," *Heonbeophak Yeongu [Studies on Constitutional Law]* Vol. 16, No. 2 (2010), p. 421.

123 Myo-ja Ser and Il-hyun Baek, "Park Calls Release of Judges' Names a Political Attack," *The Joongang Ilbo*, February 1, 2007.

124 Sang-Hun Choe, "South Korea Reviews Its Dark Past, but the Pace Is Slow," *The New York Times*, March 11, 2007.

125 Kim and Selden, "South Korea's Embattled Truth and Reconciliation Commission."

Museum and Memorial Park and conducting additional investigations.[126] For the TRCK, the Framework Act provides an explicit legal ground to establish a permanent research foundation.[127] The creation of the permanent foundation is still possible for two reasons: first, there is a group of activists, researchers, and victims who strongly believe that the work of the TRCK remains unfinished;[128] and second, South Korean scholars – particularly in the field of history – are paying more and more attention to contemporary history due to the work of various commissions. Topics once forbidden in academia are now relatively freely discussed among a new generation of scholars. As long as victims and civil society continue to demand truth and justice, and sympathetic scholars seek to find the truth, the future is bright.

126 Jeju Commission, *Hwahae-wa Sangsaeng: Jeju 4.3 Wiweonhoe Hwaldong Baekseo [Reconciliation and Coexistence: The White Paper on the Activities of the Jeju Commission]*, p. 311.

127 The Framework Act for Clearing Up Past Events, article 40.

128 Kim and Selden, "South Korea's Embattled Truth and Reconciliation Commission."

Conclusion

Hun Joon Kim and Renée Jeffery

TO DATE, SCHOLARSHIP CONCERNED WITH THE PRACTICES and processes of transitional justice has largely overlooked or ignored the Asia-Pacific region. It has, instead, favoured the study of transitions and the patterns of accountability and impunity for human rights violations that accompanied them, in Latin America, Africa and Europe. Yet, as we have seen in this book, the practices and processes of transitional justice are being implemented in the Asia-Pacific region as states and other actors grapple with the question of how best to address human rights violations committed in the past. In such a light, this book has sought to answer three sets of questions about the experience of transitional justice in the Asia-Pacific. First, which transitional justice practices have states in the Asia-Pacific adopted to address past atrocities? What factors influenced the decision to implement particular mechanisms, in isolation and in conjunction with other practices? What were the processes according to which these chosen practices were adopted? Second, what problems were associated with the implementation of particular transitional justice mechanisms or, indeed, decisions not to employ other practices? Did particular controversies emerge from the implementation of particular transitional justice practices? Did they give rise to public and scholarly debates about how best to address past human rights violations? Third and finally, what have been the outcomes associated with the implementation of transitional justice practices in the

Asia-Pacific, for peace, democracy and human rights? What have transitional justice mechanisms achieved, both independently and in combination with other mechanisms, in the transitional and post-transitional states in which they have been adopted? In terms of outcomes, what have been the limitations associated with the particular combinations of transitional justice mechanisms chosen in the cases of the Asia-Pacific?

To answer these questions we adopted a two-pronged approach. First, we sought to situate the study of transitional justice practices and processes in the Asia-Pacific within a global context. To this end, Payne and Sikkink's chapter (Chapter 1) provided our starting point by explaining the emergence, diffusion and impact of transitional justice measures on a global level, and then isolating particular trends associated with each of these phenomena in the Asia-Pacific. Second, the following chapters provided in-depth case studies of six transitional and post-transitional states in the Asia-Pacific, drawing on the theoretical findings presented in Payne and Sikkink's chapter but delving further into the nuances and particularities of the situations at hand. Each of the cases selected for inclusion in the volume has recently embraced the practice of transitional justice. Together they have implemented a range of different mechanisms and attempted several different combinations of transitional justice measures. While some have been reasonably effective, others have proved more disappointing.

This concluding chapter summarises our key findings and outlines the theoretical contributions that they make to the broader study of transitional justice. It focuses on three key areas of transitional justice research. Returning to the 'three debates' outlined in our Introduction, the first section considers how these debates might be further developed or modified to better account for practices and processes of transitional justice implemented in the Asia-Pacific. In the second section, we examine what the experience of transitional justice in the Asia-Pacific tells us about the emergence and diffusion of transitional justice measures more generally. Third, we then turn to examine what the cases of the Asia-Pacific tell us about the impact of transitional justice measures although, in doing so, we are mindful of the fact that it may simply be too early to evaluate the outcomes of some very recent practices and processes. The remainder of this conclusion then canvasses the practical implications of our findings, in general and for those states now experiencing the so-called 'fourth wave of democratisation' in the Middle East and North Africa.

The Three Debates and the Asia-Pacific

Until now, the scope and variety of transitional justice mechanisms employed in the Asia-Pacific region has been scarcely recognised by scholars of transitional justice. Until recently, the fact that at least a dozen commission-like bodies have been established in South Korea had passed without comment in the field. Similarly, the case of Sri Lanka, where numerous inquiries into abuses and disappearances, and even some limited prosecutions, have taken place, has received relatively little attention. Even less attention has been afforded on a global level to the adoption of major transitional justice initiatives in the small island states of the Pacific, such as the Solomon Islands. Indeed, as Payne and Sikkink note in Chapter 1, in global terms the experience of transitional justice in the Asia-Pacific has been underrepresented in cross-national comparative studies. In part this is due to the fact that many of the practices and processes undertaken in the region are of relatively recent genesis (for example the Solomon Island's ongoing TRC started in 2009), have occurred in sub-state regions of Asia-Pacific states (for example, the cases of Aceh in Indonesia, or Bougainville in Papua New Guinea), or have taken place in small Pacific Island states with populations too small to be captured in most global datasets.[1] Thus, although the Asia-Pacific experience has begun to be documented in some recent global databases, much of the data included in them appears to under-represent the reality of transitional justice in the region, the quality of

1 Payne and Sikkink, this volume.

information included for each state is decidedly uneven, and in-depth analyses of transitional justice cases in the region remain limited.[2] The case studies in this volume thus provide crucial insights into the Asia-Pacific experience. What is more, they have the potential to inform our understanding of the three key debates of transitional justice scholarship: prosecution versus pardon, retributive versus restorative justice, and bottom-up versus top-down approaches.

First, the experience of transitional justice in the Asia-Pacific confirms the idea, highlighted most prominently by the Latin American and African cases, that the 'culture of impunity' often possesses a strong hold over transitional states. In the Asia-Pacific, as in the rest of the world, this seems to be most acute in the period immediately after a transition has taken place. At first sight, the cases of the Asia-Pacific thus appear to largely conform to the 'pardon' side of the 'prosecute versus pardon' equation. Aceh, the Solomon Islands and East Timor all established formal amnesty laws to help facilitate their transitions to democracy and peace. Although Cambodia offered several amnesties targeted at particular individuals for specific political reasons, for an extended period post-transition it largely chose not to address the past, just as South Korea had done, thus resulting in what might be called de facto amnesties for perpetrators of human rights violations.

As we have seen in this volume, however, the practice of impunity did not endure in many states of the Asia-Pacific. Both endogenous and exogenous factors help to explain how demands for accountability came to challenge the culture of impunity in these cases. In the case of South Korea, the resilience and persistence of victims and civil society groups

2 Hunjoon Kim, Geoff Dancy, and Eric Wiebelhaus-Brahm, 'The Turn to Truth: Trends in Truth Commission Experimentation,' *Journal of Human Rights*, Vol. 9, No. 1 (2010); Hunjoon Kim and Kathryn Sikkink, 'Explaining the Deterrence Effect of Human Rights Prosecutions for Transitional Countries,' *International Studies Quarterly*, Vol. 54, No. 4 (2010); Tricia D. Olsen, Leigh A. Payne, and Andrew G. Reiter, *Transitional Justice in Balance: Comparing Processes, Weighing Efficacy*, Washington, D.C.: United States Institute of Peace, 2010; Renée Jeffery, *The Persistence of Amnesties in World Politics*, Philadelphia: University of Pennsylvania Press, forthcoming.

ensured that the question of its past never faded from the national agenda. By relentlessly demanding truth and justice for atrocities that had taken place fifty years earlier, victims and civil society activists were rewarded with criminal prosecutions, truth commissions and reparations. At the same time, the international expansion of new accountability norms and human rights standards were brought to bear on the cases of East Timor, Cambodia and the Solomon Islands where amnesties were limited and side-stepped, paving the way for prosecutions to take place. Thus, in each of these cases, the pervasive 'culture of impunity' has been overcome, to varying degrees, by the 'norm of accountability'. Here, as in other regions of the world, we are thus seeing the collapse of the 'prosecute versus pardon' dichotomy as states are pursuing both amnesties and prosecutions, concurrently or consecutively, as part of their transitional justice processes.

However, second, what we have also seen in the cases of the Asia-Pacific examined in this volume is that accountability has not always been exclusively conceived in terms of retributive justice in states wishing to overcome their cultures of impunity. Rather, several states employed restorative measures such as truth commissions and customary justice practices, in isolation or in combination with retributive measures. Although the demand for retribution and, in some cases even revenge, certainly exists in each of these transitional societies, in none of the cases examined in this volume was simple retribution pursued in isolation from other measures. Perhaps the closest to a purely retributive approach is the case of Cambodia where an old and anomalous amnesty was overcome to allow Case 002 to be heard before the ECCC. Even here, however, this characterisation is dubious: not only does the ECCC include provisions for providing reparative justice to the victims of the Khmer Rouge, but it has been accompanied by civil society-led restorative justice processes. Thus, only on the level of 'official' or 'formal' processes might the Cambodian case be conceived as an instance of retributive justice.

In a more obvious sense, the prevalence of truth commissions in the Asia-Pacific illustrates the primacy of restorative justice in the region.

Commissions of inquiry have taken place in Sri Lanka, South Korea, the Solomon Islands, and East Timor, taking the form of truth commissions in the latter three cases. In each of these cases, purposeful decisions were made not to pursue criminal prosecutions for particular types or categories of crimes. What is more, the case of the Solomon Islands is particularly instructive in illustrating the strategic adoption of a truth commission as an official 'third way' between criminal prosecutions and local, unofficial reconciliation processes. Although each of these truth commissions was different in its mandate and function, all sought to reflect the on-the-ground realities of the states in which they operated and overtly aimed to contribute to the provision of restorative justice.

Finally, the cases of the Asia-Pacific clearly show that both top-down and bottom-up approaches are at work in the region. On one hand, truth commissions adopted in South Korea and Sri Lanka were purely bottom-up measures with almost no outside intervention. At the same time, customary and indigenous justice practices have been undertaken in the cases of the Solomon Islands, East Timor and Cambodia. In particular, indigenous approaches like *nahe biti* and the use of *kastom* have played an important role in addressing the past in the cases of East Timor and the Solomon Islands. What distinguishes these two types of grass-roots-led initiatives is that unlike local, customary and indigenous justice practices, the former have been transformed into official, state-sanctioned practices.

On the other hand, however, the cases of Cambodia, East Timor and the Solomon Islands have also seen the imposition of top-down measures. The ECCC in Cambodia as well as the truth commissions and trials undertaken in East Timor and the Solomon Islands have all been established with funding, expertise and ideas provided by outside actors. That said, in each of these cases, the ultimate success of the transitional justice mechanisms instituted rests in the hands of local powers and local people. In Cambodia the ECCC future depends, more or less, on how the ongoing power games between the Hun Sen government, civil society activists and the court itself is played out, whereas the success of the Solomon Islands' TRC rests on local participation and how it is managed by the government. Thus, in many cases, top-down and bottom-up approaches to transitional justice have been mutually dependent upon one another and, in some instances, have even become fused.

The cases of the Asia-Pacific thus exhibit several key trends in the implementation of transitional justice practices which together bring into question and even serve to reorient the three debates that have marked the field to date. As many scholars and practitioners have noted, impunity for past human rights violations is certainly waning in the Asia-Pacific. With increasing numbers of states introducing transitional justice measures, achieving accountability for human rights crimes is more likely now than ever before in the region. Where accountability is concerned, however, the states of the Asia-Pacific have demonstrated some degree of reluctance in implementing backward-looking retributive measures, preferring instead to focus on the future-oriented restoration of post-transitional societies. Of the five elements of accountability we laid out in the Introduction, the notion of accountability as restoration was used most frequently in the cases examined, while accountability as retribution proved the least popular understanding of the term.

These trends suggest that the use of more synthetic and holistic accountability models is a feature of transitional justice in the Asia-Pacific. These models may include criminal prosecutions, amnesties and truth commissions, as Payne and Sikkink note, but may also include a range of other measures not ordinarily included in analyses of transitional justice processes. As the cases examined in this book reveal, holistic approaches to accountability often include new and innovative measures such as civil society involvement in criminal trials (as in the case of the ECCC in Cambodia), or much older traditional and customary practices (as in the cases of Aceh, East Timor and the Solomon Islands) in combination with trials and/or truth commissions. Moreover, in several cases, interesting local initiatives have taken place in the midst of and even been co-opted into national initiatives. Further research into the dynamics between local and national transitional justice initiatives is still required. To this end, the cases of Aceh, Indonesia and South

Korea might provide the basis for an interesting and fruitful comparative study examining the ways in which local processes can be hampered or obstructed by developments at the national level, and how local initiatives can drive the national accountability process.

The Adoption and Diffusion of Accountability Measures in the Asia-Pacific

The cases of the Asia-Pacific we have examined in this book contribute to our understanding of the adoption and diffusion of transitional justice practices and processes in two main ways. First, our in-depth case studies allow us to evaluate the particular contexts in which states adopt multiple transitional justice mechanisms and the means and combinations by which they do so. Second, our cases also provide insights into the ways in which innovation drives both the development of new transitional justice practices and the reinvention and modification of past traditional practices.

Where the first contribution is concerned, the Solomon Islands provides a good example of the sequential adoption of multiple transitional justice measures. Here an amnesty was used in an attempt to procure a peace-settlement, followed by trials and, finally, a truth commission. The use of multiple measures in this case was less the result of a planned, integrated transitional justice process, than of trial and error. Trials were implemented to address the impunity afforded by amnesties, and the truth commission has sought to mitigate the negative effects of the trials. That is, dysfunctional outcomes produced by previous measures led to the adoption of the next mechanism in what became the sequenced process.[3] The practice of sequencing transitional justice mechanisms in response to the failings of past measures also took place in the cases of Sri Lanka and South Korea. Here, however, the same measure was adopted multiple times as part of repeated attempts to achieve the same

3 Jeffery, this volume.

end. Thus, in South Korea and Sri Lanka, new truth commissions and commissions of inquiry were established in these country's attempts to overcome the limitations of their past truth-seeking efforts.[4]

By contrast, although the case of East Timor saw the same set of transitional justice mechanisms implemented as were employed in the Solomon Islands, here they were used almost all at once. Trials and truth commissions were thus employed at the same time and used in conjunction with traditional and customary practices. Combining both the sequenced and concurrent adoption of accountability measures, alongside its reiterated truth commissions, South Korea also saw the prosecutions of two former presidents and the award of a pardon.

What the cases of the Asia-Pacific examined in this book thus demonstrate is that different patterns of adopting multiple transitional justice measures lead to different emphases being placed on particular practices and mechanisms. For example, in the case of the Solomon Islands, the establishment of a truth commission has been prioritised over and above pursuing further trials or, indeed, granting new amnesties. Similarly, although South Korea has used both mechanisms, truth commissions have been far more central to its transitional justice efforts than trials have been. In both these cases, as well as the case of East Timor, dissatisfaction with retributive measures has been a significant factor in determining the relative weight of importance placed on prosecutions and truth commissions. Thus, while previous studies of holistic approaches to transitional justice have cogently elucidated the preliminary fact that different measures are often adopted within one transitional or post-transitional country, our study goes one step further to demonstrate that differing weights of importance can be applied to different accountability measures for different reasons. What is more, while previous studies of the holistic approach have tended to emphasise which combinations of transitional justice measures are most prolific and, indeed, effective, the cases of the Asia-Pacific demonstrate that considerable variation

4 Kim, this volume; Sriram, this volume.

exists even among states that implement the same combination of mechanisms. Indeed, as Kent observed with relation to the case of East Timor, the precise combination of mechanisms chosen is not always informed by a desire to see the best possible anticipated outcomes. Rather, she wrote:

> The establishment and operation of East Timor's transitional justice process . . . was not a balanced, coordinated and locally responsive attempt to combine prosecutions, reconciliations, and truth-seeking . . . it involved a fraught process of negotiation between and among an array of international and national actors which brought to the fore specific interests and multiple views about the best way to deal with the past.[5]

Until recently, the various justice measures available to transitional and post-transitional societies have been largely conceived as constituting a menu from which states can choose the options that best fit their intended ends. However, the experience of the Asia-Pacific suggests that this is not quite accurate or, indeed appropriate, for two main reasons. First, it is not necessarily the case that all transitional justice options are available to states in any given situation. Rather, the mechanisms available and the choices states make are informed by contextual particularities and practical constraints. As we have seen, sometimes a 'decision' to adopt a certain accountability measure is not so much a matter of choice as of needing to deal with political pressures and limitations. What is more, as the experiences of many of the Asia-Pacific cases examined in this volume reveal, choice of mechanism often represents a compromise between ideals and reality, or between ethics and politics.

The role that politics and, in particular, power plays in processes of transitional justice is not a new concern for scholars or practitioners interested in the pursuit of accountability in the aftermath of human rights violations. Many scholars have pointed out that the balance of power between old and new elites is an important factor for explaining the

5 Kent, this volume.

adoption of amnesties, trials and truth commissions.[6] At the same time, scholars have also drawn attention to the roles played by international actors in transitional justice contexts and debated whether it is appropriate for international organisations and regional and international powers to demand that transitional and post-transitional states adopt certain accountability measures. Our contributors observed that, in the cases of Sri Lanka, Cambodia, the Solomon Islands and East Timor, donors exerted significant pressure on the transitional justice processes in which they were involved. In some cases this pressure has been manifested in the adoption of the idea of human rights as a global norm by civil society groups and domestic populations and resulted in further pressure for accountability measures being brought to bear on transitional states.

A close examination of the Asia-Pacific cases, however, suggests that two other forms of power have been at play. The first is a form of structural power which shapes the conditions of war and peace and influences or even determines the behaviour of states. In the Asia-Pacific, the international power structures of the Cold War, particularly when coupled with the process of decolonisation, saw the ruthless suppression of communist movements. Supported covertly and, at times, overtly, by the United States, several military and authoritarian rulers responsible for brutal crackdowns found themselves sustained under the international order of the Cold War. For example, human rights violations during the period of effective U.S. military control in South Korea left thousands of civilians dead.[7] Similarly, as Ainley has pointed out, the Khmer Rouge's atrocities were made possible in part by the United States' global strategy in the region, and in part by the protection Khmer Rouge was afforded by China.[8] With the end of the Cold War the dissolution of this set of power arrangements thus allowed for a new era of democratic uprisings

6 Samuel P. Huntington, *The Third Wave: Democratization in the Late Twentieth Century*, Norman, OK: University of Oklahoma Press, 1991; Elin Skaar, 'Truth Commissions, Trials – or Nothing? Policy Options in Democratic Transitions,' *Third World Quarterly*, Vol. 20, No. 6 (1999), 1109–1128.

7 Kim, this volume.

8 Ainley, this volume.

and a move towards holding individuals accountable for human rights violations.

However, as the case studies examined in this book reveal, the impact of international power structures has not been uniform throughout the region. Rather, it has interacted with and been filtered through particular regional and sub-regional power structures. Indeed, the role that regional powers play in influencing the adoption and choice, or obstruction of accountability measures, remains an underdeveloped area of transitional justice research. As the cases of the Solomon Islands, Aceh, East Timor and Sri Lanka demonstrate, however, regional powers may play significant roles in enabling and constraining transitional justice processes. As Ainley notes in Chapter 4, regional political relations between Cambodia, Vietnam, Thailand and China affected both the ability of the Khmer Rouge to perpetrate its atrocities and, after its defeat, the transitional justice process.[9] Similarly, in Chapter 2, Sriram explains the role that India has played in obstructing the accountability process in Sri Lanka, and Kent notes in Chapter 5 the interplay between international and regional power structures in the case of East Timor.[10] In this case, as Kent explains, the transitional justice process was complicated by the international status of Indonesia and, in particular, the support it received from the United States under the umbrella of the 'War on Terror.'[11]

Second, the case studies examined in this volume also provide interesting insights into the role that innovation plays in developing transitional justice processes and practices. Innovation, in this context, may entail the invention of new transitional justice mechanisms or the reinvention or adaptation of existing, traditional or customary practices. The practices of *nahe biti* in East Timor, *sayam* and *suloeh* in Aceh and reconciliation in accordance with *kastom* in the Solomon Islands all constitute forms of customary practice modified to suit the demands of contemporary transitional justice processes. Two interesting and, indeed, important questions

9 Ainley, this volume.
10 Sriram, this volume.
11 Kent, this volume.

arise from our observations of these practices. First, what drives and produces these types of innovations in transitional and post-transitional contexts? And second, how do new and customary accountability measures interact with other mechanisms more typically associated with transitional justice, such as criminal prosecutions and truth commissions?

Although further research is required to answer these questions, the case studies examined in this volume have provided some possible explanations for the use of innovative measures in the Asia-Pacific. First, as several of the cases suggest, innovation was driven, at least in part, by dissatisfaction or frustration with typical accountability measures. In the case of East Timor, delays and debates over the seriousness of particular crimes led to the development of customary measures designed to facilitate societal restoration and reconciliation.[12] Similarly, in the Solomon Islands, the perceived limitations of the adversarial criminal justice system inspired the adaptation and development of customary inter-personal and communal reconciliation ceremonies.[13] Second, the cases examined in this volume also reveal that in most cases local actors, victims, activists and sometimes religious leaders were primarily responsible for coming up with new ideas about how to address the wrongs of the past. In the cases of Aceh, East Timor and the Solomon Islands, their passion and fervent activism led to new customary developments and, in the case of the Solomon Islands, the institution of an official transitional justice mechanism, the truth commission. In the case of East Timor, NGOs and local victims' groups were the main drivers of innovation.[14] At the same time, the roles played by religious organisations and leaders have also been noteworthy in several cases in the region. In this vein, Jeffery pointed out the role played by Christianity and Christian groups in the Solomon Islands, Kent highlighted the role of traditional religion in East Timor, and Aspinall and Zain noted the role played by religious leaders

12 Kent, this volume.
13 Jeffery, this volume.
14 Kent, this volume.

in *peusijeuk* ceremonies.[15] Third, and finally, one of the key features of these types of innovations is their flexibility. For example, in the Solomon Islands, *kastom* is not fixed or static but has been remoulded, redefined and redesigned to deal with 'new and unfamiliar circumstances.'[16] The flexibility and malleability of traditions such as this appears to have played a role in their adoption, in isolation and in combination with other measures, in post-conflict societies.

The Impact of Accountability Measures in the Asia-Pacific

Drawing on cross-national analyses, in their chapter, Payne and Sikkink present three arguments concerning the impact of transitional justice measures. First, both Payne and Sikkink argue that transitional justice measures, especially the criminal prosecution of former state officials for human rights violations, are associated with improvements in respect for human rights. This, they argue, provides some evidence supporting the deterrence and normative socialisation approaches. Second, however, while Payne agrees with Sikkink that human rights trials are associated with positive outcomes for human rights, she adds a caveat to her argument: prosecutions have a positive impact on human rights when they are combined with amnesties. In what she and her co-authors have termed the 'justice balance', the most positive outcomes for human rights, democracy and peace are produced by two particular combinations of transitional justice mechanisms: trials and amnesties; and trials, amnesties and truth commissions. Third, and finally, Sikkink and Payne reach different conclusions concerning the independent effects of truth commissions. While Sikkink, in her collaboration with Kim, has found that truth commissions are associated with improvements in human rights, Payne and her co-authors have found that they are not.

15 Jeffery, this volume; Kent, this volume; Aspinall and Zain, this volume.
16 Jeffery, this volume.

The Overall Impact of Transitional Justice in the Asia-Pacific

When we consider the overall impact that transitional justice processes and practices have had on human rights, peace and democracy in the Asia-Pacific, Payne and Sikkink's large-*N* studies produce somewhat different results to the case studies included in this volume. Rather than confirming that transitional justice has a simple, positive effect, the assessments provided by our case study authors are decidedly more mixed. Here contributors have made two different sets of judgments, about the level of accountability for past human rights violations achieved, and about the effects of transitional justice mechanisms on human rights, democracy and peace. In the first instance, a range of different outcomes were observed. While South Korea and the Solomon Islands fared reasonably well in terms of achieving accountability, Sri Lanka and Aceh performed poorly. East Timor and Cambodia experienced mixed results, with some limited accountability achieved and, inevitably, disappointment expressed over those limitations. In the cases of Cambodia and the Solomon Islands, any success in achieving accountability has been tempered by the significant problems associated with the criminal justice processes undertaken. In the Solomon Islands the process faced criticism for its selectiveness and adversarial nature, while in Cambodia the sense that the ECCC is 'generally fair, having been conducted according to accepted standards of international due process' has been accompanied by concerns over corruption, government tampering and a lack of adequate funding.[17]

When it comes to the outcomes achieved by the transitional justice processes and practices implemented in the Asia-Pacific cases, for human rights, peace and democracy, it is unclear whether a correlation exists between levels of accountability and outcomes. On one hand, in the cases of South Korea, the Solomon Islands and Sri Lanka, relationships between accountability and outcomes seem apparent. While substantial

17 Ainley, this volume.

improvements in human rights, democracy and/or peace have followed transitional justice measures in the Solomon Islands and South Korea, 'the quality of democracy, human rights, and rule of law have been progressively degraded' in Sri Lanka, where little accountability has been achieved.[18] On the other hand, however, Aceh has enjoyed improvements in human rights, democracy and peace without significant accountability for past human rights violations. What is more, even where relationships between accountability and positive outcomes have been identified, contributors were cautious in explicitly stating that the transitional justice process had been a success.

What explains this cautious assessment of the success of transitional justice processes and practices in the region provided by our case studies? There are three possible explanations for this. First, as the majority of transitional justice measures undertaken in the region are relatively recent, it may be too early to discern or analyse their effects. Most large-scale global analyses of transitional justice mechanisms and their effects employ datasets stretching back to the 1970s and are thus able to capture the long-term outcomes associated with particular approaches. Indeed, most assessments of the outcomes produced by transitional justice processes measure impact five and ten years after the event. Of the cases examined in this volume, Cambodia and the Solomon Islands still have transitional justice processes underway with the ECCC and TRC respectively, while less than ten years have elapsed since either a transition or the last use of a transitional justice mechanism in Sri Lanka, Aceh, East Timor and South Korea. It thus seems that time will tell whether the approaches employed by the states of the Asia-Pacific will ultimately bring benefits for peace, democracy and human rights.

Second, the discrepancy we have identified between the assessments of the outcomes of transitional justice processes between Payne and Sikkink's analysis and those of our case study contributors may also be the result of the different methods used. In particular, it may be the case that

18 Sriram, this volume.

impact is a more complicated social phenomenon than can be accurately measured and operationalised with indices such as the Political Terror Scale, the CIRI Personal Integrity Rights index, or the Polity IV democracy score. Third, and finally, there is also the issue of what constitutes 'success'. How successful does a transitional justice practice or process have to be before we will declare it a success? Here the assessments provided by our authors highlight the difficulties associated with making judgments of success and failure. On the one hand, it seems remiss to overlook any advances for human rights, peace and democracy achieved by implementing a transitional justice process. After all, any improvement constitutes some degree of success. On the other hand, however, is the concern that any declaration of success will overshadow problems that remain without redress, marginalise negative outcomes that have worsened some areas of concern, and foster complacency regarding the pursuit of accountability. As with the pursuit of transitional justice, 'balance' seems to be the key here.

Accountability-with-Stability

What insights into the accountability-with-stability theory do the cases examined in this volume provide? In brute empirical terms, the Asia-Pacific has exhibited the same upward trends in the use of trials and of amnesties that has been observed on a global level. While trials were used in four of the six cases examined, all six employed an amnesty at some point prior to, during or after their transition. What is more, three states, the Solomon Islands, East Timor and South Korea used a combination of all three major transitional justice mechanisms, trials, amnesties and truth commissions. That is, four of the six cases under consideration (East Timor, Cambodia, the Solomon Islands and South Korea) implemented one of what Payne and her co-authors identify as the two optimal combinations of transitional justice measures. As we have already seen, however, when we delve below the surface of these combinations, the outcomes they have achieved are not entirely clear.

Although multiple transitional justice mechanisms were used in most of our cases, our authors revealed that the relationships between and dynamics created by particular combinations of measures are highly complicated. In the cases of Aceh, Indonesia and the Solomon Islands, amnesty provisions included in the Helsinki MoU and the Townsville Peace Agreement, respectively, helped to 'end civil conflict and permitted the transition to peace', thus contributing to stability.[19] However, in Aceh the amnesty has directly blocked the pursuit of criminal trials and the issue of impunity has proved to be an obstacle to the establishment of a truth and reconciliation commission. By contrast, in the Solomon Islands, amnesties were side-stepped in order to allow prosecutions to take place, trials have been followed by a TRC, and the issue of amnesty is once again on the agenda as some wish to round out the transitional justice process with one final grant of impunity. In the case of Cambodia, the 1996 Royal Pardon was, according to Ainley, 'useful in bringing peace.'[20] For more than a decade it blocked accountability, before being overcome in the pre-trial hearings of Case 002 at the ECCC. In East Timor, amnesties and trials were pursued concurrently, on a selective basis, while establishing a connection between amnesties and other measures is difficult for the case of Sri Lanka.

The patterns according to which the states of the Asia-Pacific implemented different combinations of transitional justice mechanisms raise two key questions about the idea of accountability-with-stability. Is the decision to follow amnesties with prosecutions evidence of 'a functional relationship' between various transitional justice measures, or does it signify the triumph of accountability over the culture of impunity? And, do amnesties, through their contribution to stability or other effects, facilitate the pursuit of accountability in the future? With regard to the first question, the cases examined in this volume appear to suggest that both may be the case. In the cases of East Timor, Cambodia and the Solomon

19 Aspinall and Zain, this volume.
20 Ainley, this volume.

Islands, some sort of at least minimally functional relationship was forged between the work performed by amnesties and that of prosecutions. Yet, in the latter two cases, the addition of criminal trials to the transitional justice process also marked a sort of triumph (if limited and minimal) of accountability over impunity.

With this, the second question thus comes into play. Two possible pathways can be identified. The first is relatively simple: amnesties help create peace and stability and, in those conditions, the pursuit of prosecutions (sometimes some years later) is made possible without jeopardising the transition that has taken place. The second relates to Sikkink's normative socialisation argument. Payne and Sikkink thus argue that 'amnesty laws and accountability efforts set in motion dramatic and public debates, establishing a new justice norm to replace the prior culture of amnesty.' What is more, they also add that 'some evidence suggests that where amnesties exist, mobilisation to undermine them leads to trials, a pathway to accountability and deterrence that is less likely where no amnesty law exists to condemn domestically and internationally.'[21] Precisely which, if either, of these pathways has been at play in the cases of the Asia-Pacific remains unclear at present. Amnesty laws implemented in Aceh, the Solomon Islands, Cambodia and East Timor have certainly given rise to debates about their legitimacy, effectiveness and appropriateness, but we have not yet found evidence that these debates further facilitated the adoption of accountability measures. In Aceh, trials have not followed criticisms of its amnesty law, while in the Solomon Islands and Cambodia decisions to prosecute perpetrators of human rights violations appear to have been made independently of pre-existing amnesties and concerns over their legitimacy. Interestingly, in the cases considered in this volume, more heated debates about transitional justice measures tended to centre on the conduct, effectiveness and outcomes of holding trials.

21 Payne and Sikkink, this volume.

The Effects of Truth Commissions

Of the cases examined in this volume, four – East Timor, the Solomon Islands, South Korea and Sri Lanka – have held truth commissions. Again, a range of outcomes can be identified. Notwithstanding the limitations he notes, Kim generally views the truth commissions in South Korea as being successful for revealing the dark past, restoring the honour of victims, and making major policy recommendations.[22] Jeffery also sees a truth commission in the Solomon Islands as possibly proving to be an effective 'third way' after the two more extreme options of amnesties and trials were exhausted. She argues that the truth commission 'not only represents the Solomon Islands' most concerted effort to confront its violent past to date but an attempt to reconcile the seemingly incompatible approaches to transitional justice that were previously pursued in the post-conflict context.'[23] However, as the TRC is still in operation, it remains to be seen whether this potential will be realised.

By contrast, both Sriram and Kent were more cautious in positively evaluating the functions and effects of truth commissions established in Sri Lanka and East Timor, respectively, with both highlighting complications that arose due to domestic and international factors. Sriram thus argues that some truth commissions which were 'ostensibly designed to reach the truth about past abuses,' when in operation actually did 'the reverse.'[24] We are thus left with a somewhat unsatisfactory conclusion when it comes to the effect of truth commissions: from the case studies examined in this book it remains unclear whether truth commissions have or indeed will have a positive or negative impact on the future conditions of human rights. Again, this may be in part due to the short period of time that has elapsed since many of these commissions were established, or it may be that our small set of cases is not representative of any particular trend.

22 Kim, this volume.
23 Jeffery, this volume.
24 Sriram, this volume.

Policy Implications

What kind of policy implications do our findings have for future cases of transitional justice, not only for countries in the Asia-Pacific still awaiting transitions to democracy and/or to peace, but also for those countries experiencing the so-called 'fourth wave of democratisation' in the Middle East and North Africa? Without wanting to head down the dangerous path of prescribing particular courses of action or make vast generalisations (for, as we have seen, the pursuit of transitional justice is highly contextual), two main implications are apparent.

First, the cases of the Asia-Pacific help to illustrate the fact that although the world has experienced a rise in norms associated with human rights and accountability, the culture of impunity is still strong. It is thus not particularly surprising that demands for accountability in the wake of the Arab Spring have been met with sustained resistance. In some ways, contemporary scholarly debates about the effectiveness of transitional justice measures play into the hands of those who wish to avoid justice. Offering up claims that particular measures are a waste of money or are ineffective, backward-looking approaches often tip the scale against accountability. Yet, at the same time, we cannot shy away from developing a deeper, more nuanced and comprehensive understanding of the effects of transitional justice, for this is essential to ensuring optimal outcomes for peace, democracy and human rights are achieved for future transitional states.

Second, although the culture of impunity is still strong and considerable internal resistance to accountability exists, in four of the six cases we examined, accountability eventually overcame impunity. Even in the two cases in which accountability has not been forthcoming, Aceh and Sri Lanka, demands for truth and justice continue to be voiced.[25] As the cases of delayed accountability in the region demonstrate, however, it is not necessarily the case that impunity will always endure. If the

25 Aspinall, this volume; Sriram, this volume.

precondition of stable, consolidated democracy is met, then strong and resilient activism in the region may well see belated accountability for human rights violations achieved. So long as that remains a possibility, the future for transitional and post-transitional states in the Asia-Pacific and, indeed, the world, may not be so dark after all.

Bibliography

Ainley, Kirsten. 'Excesses of Responsibility: The Limits of Law and the Possibilities of Politics,' *Ethics and International Affairs*, Vol. 25, No. 4 (2011), pp. 407–431.

Akhavan, Payam. 'Justice in the Hague, Peace in the Former Yugoslavia? A Commentary on the United Nations War Crimes Tribunal,' *Human Rights Quarterly*, Vol. 20, No. 4 (1998), pp. 249–458.

Amnesty International, '"Shock Therapy": Restoring Order in Aceh, 1989–1993,' London: International Secretariat, Amnesty International, 1993.

Amnesty International, 'Sri Lanka: Amnesty International Welcomes Government Action to Stop Death Squad Activities,' (1 September 1995) AI Index ASA 37/17/95.

Amnesty International, 'Sri Lanka: Presidential Commission of Inquiry fails Citizens' (17 June 2009), at http://www.amnesty.org/en/for-media/press-releases/sri-lanka-presidential-commission-inquiry-fails-citizens-20090617 (accessed 31 May 2011).

Amnesty International, 'Sri Lanka: Time for Truth and Justice' (April 1995), AI Index 37/04/95.

Anonymous, 'Against the Grain: Pursuing a Transitional Justice Agenda in Postwar Sri Lanka,' *International Journal of Transitional Justice*, Vol. 5 (2011), pp. 31–51.

Anonymous, 'Human Rights in Peace Negotiations,' *Human Rights Quarterly*, Vol. 18, No. 2 (1996), pp. 249–258.

Arthur, Paige. 'How "Transitions" Reshaped Human Rights: A Conceptual History of Transitional Justice,' *Human Rights Quarterly*, Vol. 31, No. 2 (2009), pp. 329–331.

Asia Watch, *Indonesia: Continuing Human Rights Violations in Aceh*, New York: Asia Watch, 1991.

Asia Watch, *Indonesia: Human Rights Abuses in Aceh*, New York: Asia Watch, 1990.

Asian Human Rights Commission, 'SRI LANKA: Friday Forum Deeply Concerned about Recent Appointments to Human Rights Commission' (15 June 2011), at http://www.humanrights.asia/news (accessed 16 June 2011).

Asian Human Rights Commission, 'SRI LANKA: Sixth Day of Mourning against Executive Interference into the Judiciary and Other Independent Institutions' (3 June 2006), at http://www.humanrights.asia/news/ahrc-news/ (accessed 16 June 2011).

Asian Human Rights Commission, 'SRI LANKA: Two Senior Judges Quit the Judicial Service Commission as a Matter of Conscience' (3 February 2006), at http://www.humanrights.asia/news/ahrc-news/ (accessed 16 June 2011).

Aspinall, Edward, *Peace without Justice. The Helsinki Peace Process in Aceh*, Geneva: Centre for Humanitarian Dialogue, 2008.

Aspinall, Edward, 'Combatants to Contractors: The Political Economy of Peace in Aceh,' *Indonesia*, Vol. 87 (2009), pp. 1–34.

Aspinall, Edward, *Islam and Nation: Separatist Rebellion in Aceh, Indonesia*, Stanford: Stanford University Press, 2009.

Ata, Reverend Samuel, Chairman of the Solomon Islands Truth and Reconciliation Commission in 'Solomon Islands: Public Hearings Fuel Hopes for Reconciliation,' United Nations Development Programme (9 March 2010), at http://content.undp.org/go/newsroom/2010/march/first-trc-hearing-brings-relief-and-hopes-for-reconciliation.en (accessed 2 May 2011).

Ata, Reverend Samuel, Chairman of the Solomon Islands Truth and Reconciliation Commission, Public Hearing at Gizo, Day One, Session, One (13 July 2010), at http://solomonislands-trc.com/public-hearing-sessions/gizo-public-hearing-session-two.html (accessed 2 May 2011).

Austin, Dennis, *Democracy and Violence in India and Sri Lanka*, London: Chatham House, 1995.

Averre, Kenneth Hall, 'The Tension Trials: A Defence Lawyer's Perspective of Post Conflict Intervention in Solomon Islands,' State, Society and Governance in Melanesia Working Paper, Number 2008/3, Canberra: The Australian National University, 2008.

Avonius, Leena, 'Reconciliation and Human Rights in Post-conflict Aceh,' in Birgit Bräuchler (ed.), *Reconciling Indonesia: Grassroots Agency for Peace*, Abingdon: Routledge, 2009, pp. 121–137.

Babo-Soares, Dionesio, 'Nahe Biti: Grassroots Reconciliation in East Timor,' in Elin Skaar, Siri Gloppen, and Astrid Suhrke (eds.), *Roads to Reconciliation*, Lanham, MD: Lexington Books, 2005, pp. 225–246.

Backer, David, 'Civil Society and Transitional Justice: Possibilities, Patterns, and Prospects,' *Journal of Human Rights*, Vol. 2, No. 3 (2003), pp. 297–313.

Barnett, Michael, Hunjoon Kim, Madalene O'Donnell, and Laura Sitea, 'Peacebuilding: What Is in a Name?' *Global Governance*, Vol. 13 (2007), pp. 35–58.

Bass, Gary J., 'War Crimes Tribunals,' in Keith E. Whittington, R. Daniel Keleman, and Gregory A. Calderia (eds.), *The Oxford Handbook of Law and Politics*, Oxford: Oxford University Press, 2008, pp. 229–244.

Bass, Gary Jonathan, *Stay the Hand of Vengeance: The Politics of War Crimes Tribunals*, Princeton, NJ: Princeton University Press, 2000.

Bassiouni, M. Cherif, 'International Crimes: *Jus Cogens* and *Obligatio Erga Omnes*,' *Law and Contemporary Problems*, Vol. 59, No. 4 (1996), pp. 63–74.

Bassiouni, M. Cherif, 'The Universal Model: The International Criminal Court,' in M. Cherif Bassiouni (ed.), *Post-Conflict Justice*, Ardsley, NY: Transnational, 2002, pp. 813–825.

Bell, Christine, 'Transitional Justice, Interdisciplinarity and the State of the "Field" or "Non-Field",' *International Journal of Transitional Justice*, Vol. 3, No. 1 (2009), pp. 5–27.

Bennett, Judith, 'Roots of Conflict in Solomon Islands: Though Much Is Taken, Much Abides: Legacies of Tradition and Colonialism,' State, Society and Governance in Melanesia Discussion Paper 2002/5, Australian National University, Research School of Pacific and Asian Studies, 2002.

Bhuta, Nehal, 'Great Expectations – East Timor and the Vicissitudes of Externalised Justice,' *Finnish Yearbook of International Law*, Vol. 12 (2001), pp. 165–189.

Bose, Sumantra, *States, Nations, Sovereignty*, New Delhi: Sage Publications, 1994.

Braithwaite, J. H. Charlesworth and A. Soares, *Networked Governance of Freedom and Tyranny: Peace in Timor-Leste*, Canberra: ANU E-Press, 2012.

Braithwaite, John, Valerie Braithwaite, Michael Cookson, and Leah Dunn, *Anomie and Violence: Non-Truth and Reconciliation in Indonesian Peacebuilding*, Canberra: ANU E-Press, 2010.

Braithwaite, John, Sinclair Dinnen, Matthew Allen, Valerie Braithwaite, and Hilary Charlesworth, *Pillars and Shadows: Statebuilding as Peacebuilding in Solomon Islands*, Canberra: ANU E-Press, 2010.

Brinkley, Joel. 'Cambodia's Curse,' *Foreign Affairs*, Vol. 88, No. 2 (2009).

Buergenthal, Thomas. 'The United Nations Truth Commission for El Salvador,' *Vanderbilt Journal of Transnational Law*, Vol. 27, No. 3 (1994), pp. 497–544.

Burchill, Richard. 'From East Timor to Timor-Leste: A Demonstration of the Limits of International Law in the Pursuit of Justice,' in J. Doria, H. P. Gasser and M. C. Bassiouni (eds.), *The Legal Regime of the ICC: Essays in Honour of Prof. Igor Blishchenko*, Leiden and Boston: Martinus Nijhoff, 2009, pp. 255–296.

Burgess, Patrick. 'De Facto Amnesty? The Example of Post-Soeharto Indonesia,' in Francesca Lessa and Leigh A. Payne (eds.), *Amnesty in the Age of Human Rights Accountability: Comparative and International Perspectives*, Cambridge: Cambridge University Press, 2012, pp. 263–290.

Care, J. C. Corrin. 'The Search for a More Appropriate Form of Government in Solomon Islands,' in B.A. Hocking (ed.), *Unfinished Constitutional Business? Rethinking Indigenous Self-determination*, Canberra: Aboriginal Studies Press, 2005, pp. 159–169.

Carranza, Ruben. 'Plunder and Pain: Should Transitional Justice Engage with Corruption and Economic Crimes?,' *International Journal of Transitional Justice*, Vol. 2, No. 3 (2008), pp. 310–330.

Chandler, David. *A History of Cambodia*, Boulder, CO: Westview Publishers, 2008.

Charlesworth, Hilary. 'Building Democracy and Justice After Conflict,' Occasional Paper 2/2007, The Cunningham Lecture, The Academy of the Social Sciences in Australia, Canberra, 2007, p. 9, at http://www.assa.edu.au/Publications/OP/op22007.pdf (accessed 2 May 2011).

Chesterman, Simon. 'East Timor in Transition: Self Determination, State-Building and the United Nations,' *International Peacekeeping*, Vol. 9, No. 1 (2002), pp. 45–76.

Cho, Kuk. 'Transitional Justice in Korea: Legally Coping with Past Wrongs after Democratization,' *Pacific Rim Law & Policy Journal*, Vol. 16, No. 3 (2007), pp. 579–611.

Choi, Jang Jip. 'Political Cleavages in South Korea,' in Hagen Koo (ed.), *State and Society in Contemporary Korea*, Ithaca, NY: Cornell University Press, 1993.

Chopra, Jarat. 'Building State Failure in East Timor,' *Development and Change*, Vol. 33, No. 5 (2002), pp. 979–1000.

Ciorciari, John D. 'Introduction,' in *The Khmer Rouge Tribunal*, Phnom Penh: Documentation Center of Cambodia, 2006, pp. 11–27.

Civil Rights Movement, 'The Investigation of "Disappearances" in Sri Lanka,' Colombo: Civil Rights Movement, 1998.

Civil Rights Movement of Sri Lanka, 'The Alleged Mass Burials at Chemmany in the North,' Colombo: Civil Rights Movement, July 1998.

Clarke, Ross, Galuh Wandita, and Samsidar, *Considering Victims: The Aceh Peace Process from a Transitional Justice Perspective*, New York: International Center for Transitional Justice, 2008.

Cohen, David. 'Seeking Justice on the Cheap: Is the East Timor Tribunal Really a Model for the Future?' Analysis from the East-West Center, Vol. 61, Honolulu, East-West Center, 2002.

Cohen, David. 'Intended to Fail: The Trials before the Ad Hoc Human Rights Court in Jakarta,' ICTJ Occasional Paper Series, New York, International Center for Transitional Justice, 2003.

Cohen, David. 'Justice on the Cheap Revisited: the Failure of the Serious Crimes Trials in East Timor,' Analysis from the East-West Center, Vol. 80, Honolulu, East-West Center, 2006.

Commission of Inquiry (COI). Report of the United Nations Independent Special Commission of Inquiry for Timor Leste (Geneva, 2 October 2006).

Commission of Truth and Friendship (CTF). 'Per Memoriam Ad Spem (From Memory to Hope),' *Final Report of the Commission for Truth and Friendship*, (Indonesia/East Timor, March 2008).

Cumings, Bruce. *The Origins of the Korean War, Volume II: The Roaring of the Cataract, 1947–1950*, Ithaca, NY: Cornell University Press, 2004.

Cunliffe, S., E. Riyadi, R. Arwalembun, and H. B. Tobi. *Negotiating Peace in Indonesia: Prospects for Building Peace and Upholding Justice in Maluku and Aceh*, IFP Mediation Cluster of ICTJ and ELSAM, 2009.

D'Amato, Anthony. 'Peace vs. Accountability in Bosnia,' *American Journal of International Law*, Vol. 88, No. 3 (1994), pp. 500–506.

Dancy, Geoff and Kathryn Sikkink, 'Ratification and Human Rights Prosecutions: Toward a Transnational Theory of Treaty Compliance,' *New York*

University Journal of International Law and Politics, Vol. 44, No. 3 (2012), pp. 751–790.

de Greiff, Pablo. 'Repairing the Past: Compensation for Victims of Human Rights Violations' in Pablo de Greiff (ed.), *Handbook of Reparations*, Oxford: Oxford University Press, 2006.

Dinnen, Sinclair. 'Dilemmas of Intervention and the Building of State and Nation' in Sinclair Dinnen and Stewart Firth (eds.), *Politics and Statebuilding in Solomon Islands*, Canberra: ANU E-Press, 2008.

Dinnen, Sinclair, Abby McLeod, and Gordon Peake, 'Police-Building in Weak States: Australian Approaches in Papua New Guinea and Solomon Islands,' *Civil Wars*, Vol. 8, No. 2 (2006), pp. 87–108.

Downs, George W., David M. Rocke, and Peter N. Barsoom. 'Is the Good News About Compliance Good News About Cooperation?,' *International Organization*, Vol. 50, No. 3 (1996), pp. 379–406.

Doyle, Michael. 'Three Pillars of the Liberal Peace,' *American Political Science Review*, Vol. 99, No. 2 (2005), pp. 463–466.

Drexler, Elizabeth. 'The Failure of International Justice in East Timor and Indonesia' in Alexander Laban Hinton (ed.), *Transitional Justice: Global Mechanisms and Local Realities after Genocide and Mass Violence*, New Brunswick: Rutgers University Press, 2011, pp. 49–66.

Dugard, John. 'Dealing with Crimes of a Past Regime: Is Amnesty Still an Option?,' *Leiden Journal of International Law*, Vol. 12 (1999), pp. 1001–1015.

Dunlop, Nick. *The Lost Executioner*, London: Bloomsbury, 2005.

East Timor Commission for Reception Truth and Reconciliation (CAVR). *Chega!*, Dili, East Timor: CAVR, 2005.

Elster, Jon. *Closing the Books: Transitional Justice in Historical Perspective*, Cambridge: Cambridge University Press, 2004.

Ensalaco, Mark. 'Truth Commission for Chile and El Salvador: A Report and Assessment,' *Human Rights Quarterly*, Vol. 16, No. 4 (1994), pp. 656–675.

Etcheson, Craig. *After the Killing Fields*, Westport: Praeger, 2005.

Extraordinary Chambers in the Courts of Cambodia (ECCC). Appeals Judgment, Case 001, at: http://www.eccc.gov.kh/sites/default/files/documents/courtdoc/03022012Summary-Eng.pdf (accessed 13 June 2013).

Extraordinary Chambers in the Courts of Cambodia. Law on the Establishment of the Extraordinary Chambers in the Courts of Cambodia, with inclusion of amendments as promulgated on 27 October 2004 (NS/RKM/1004/006).

Extraordinary Chambers in the Courts of Cambodia Press Release: Statement from the National Co-Prosecutor Regarding Case File 003, May 10, 2011, at http://www.eccc.gov.kh/sites/default/files/media/5-Press%20release%20by%20the%20National%20Prosecutor-10%20May%202011-Eng.pdf.

Extraordinary Chambers in the Courts of Cambodia Budget 2012–2013, at: http://www.eccc.gov.kh/en/about-eccc/finances/eccc-budget-2012-2013.

Fawthrop, Tom and Helen Jarvis. *Getting Away with Genocide? Elusive Justice and the Khmer Rouge Tribunal*, London: Pluto Press, 2004.

Federer, Juan. *The UN in East Timor: Building Timor-Leste, a Fragile State*, Darwin: Charles Darwin University Press, 2005.

Ferguson, James and Akhil Gupta, 'Spatializing States: Toward an Ethnography of Neoliberal Governmentality,' *American Ethnologist*, Vol. 29, No. 4 (2002), pp. 981–1002.

Fernando, Sharmini. 'Bitter Victory: Krishanthi Kumaraswamy, The Women's Vigil, and the Verdict,' *Options*, Vol. 14 (1998).

Fletcher, Laurel E. and Harvey M. Weinstein, 'Violence and Social Repair: Rethinking the Contribution of Justice to Reconciliation,' *Human Rights Quarterly*, Vol. 24, No. 3 (2002), pp. 573–639.

Forsythe, David. *Human Rights in International Relations*, Cambridge: Cambridge University Press, 2006.

Freeman, Mark. *Truth Commissions and Procedural Fairness*, Cambridge: Cambridge University Press, 2006.

Freeman, Mark. *Necessary Evils: Amnesties and the Search for Justice*, Cambridge and New York: Cambridge University Press, 2009.

Fukuyama, Francis. 'State Building in Solomon Islands,' *Pacific Economic Bulletin*, Vol. 23, No. 3 (2008), pp. 154–159..

Fullilove, Michael. 'RAMSI and State Building in Solomon Islands,' *Defender* (2006), pp. 31–35.

Gaer, Felice D. 'UN-Anonymous: Reflection on Human Rights in Peace Negotiations,' *Human Rights Quarterly*, Vol. 19, No. 1 (1997), pp. 1–8.

Galaway, Burt and Joe Hudson. 'Introduction' to Burt Galaway and Joe Hudson (eds.), *Restorative Justice: International Perspectives*, Monsey, NY: Kugler, 1996.

Global Policy Forum, 'East Timor Says No to UN Tribunal,' *Laksama.Net*, 9 August 2004, at http://www.globalpolicy.org/intljustice/tribunals/timor/2004/0809no.htm (accessed 10 December 2009).

Global Witness. *Cambodia's Family Trees*, London: Global Witness, 2007.

Global Witness. *Country for Sale*, London: Global Witness, 2009.

Goldsmith, Jack and Stephen D. Krasner, 'The Limits of Idealism,' *Daedalus*, Vol. 132, No. 1 (2003), pp. 47–63.

Gomez, Mario. 'Sri Lanka's New Human Rights Commission,' *Human Rights Quarterly*, Vol. 20, No. 2 (1998), pp. 281–302.

Gomez, Mario. 'Sri Lanka's New Human Rights Commission,' *Rights Link*, Vol. 1, issue 1 (1997).

Gomez, Mario. 'The Sri Lankan Human Rights Commission,' *Law and Society Trust Review*, Vol. 9, No. 13 (1998).

Gomez, Mario. *Emerging Trends in Public Law*, Colombo: Vijitha Yapa Bookshop, 1998.

Goodenough, Nick. 'Reconciliation and the Criminal Process in the Solomon Islands,' *Journal of South Pacific Law*, Vol. 10, No. 1 (2006), at http://www.paclii.org/journals/fjSPL/vol10/3.shtml (accessed 2 May 2011).

Goodman, Ryan and Derek Jinks. 'How to Influence States: Socialization and International Human Rights Law,' *Duke Law Journal*, Vol. 54, No. 3 (2004), pp. 621–703.

Grenfell, Damian. 'Reconciliation: Violence and Nation-Formation in Timor-Leste,' in Damian Grenfell and Paul James (eds.), *Rethinking Insecurity, War and Violence: Beyond Savage Globalization?*, London: Routledge, 2008.

Han, In-Sup. 'Kwangju and Beyond: Coping with Past State Atrocities in South Korea,' *Human Rights Quarterly*, Vol. 27, No. 3 (2005), pp. 998–1045.

Harris-Rimmer, S. G. *Gender and Transitional Justice: the Women of East Timor*, London and New York: Routledge, 2010.

Harris-Rimmer, Susan. *Transitional Justice and the Women of East Timor*, Unpublished PhD Thesis, Australian National University.

Hayner, Priscilla. *Negotiating Peace in Sierra Leone: Confronting the Justice Challenge*, Geneva, Switzerland: Centre for Humanitarian Dialogue, 2007.

Henderson, Gregory. *Korea: Politics of the Vortex*, Cambridge: Harvard University Press, 1968.

Henkin, Alice H. 'State Crimes: Punishment or Pardon (Conference Report),' in Neil J. Kritz (ed.), *Transitional Justice: How Emerging Democracies Reckon with Former Regimes*, Vol. 1: General Considerations, pp. 184–188.

Heo, Uk and Terence Roehrig. *South Korea since 1980*, New York: Cambridge University Press, 2010.

High Court of the Solomon Islands. *Havimei, Gabriele, James Kili, Wawari Malolo, Nicholas Na'agi, and John Taloi v. Regina*, Criminal Case No 464 of 2005, at http://www.paclii.org/sb/cases/SBHC/2005/26.html (accessed 2 May 2011).

Hinton, Alexander Laban. 'Introduction: Toward an Anthropology of Transitional Justice' in Alexander Laban Hinton (ed.), *Transitional Justice: Global Mechanisms and Local Realities after Genocide and Mass Violence*, New Brunswick: Rutgers University Press, 2011.

Hirst, Megan. 'Too Much Friendship, Too Little Truth: Monitoring Report on the Commission of Truth and Friendship in Indonesia and Timor-Leste,' ICTJ Occasional Paper Series, New York: International Center for Transitional Justice, 2008.

Hirst, Megan. 'An Unfinished Truth: An Analysis of the Commission of Truth and Friendship's Final Report on the 1999 Atrocities in East Timor,' ICTJ Occasional Paper Series, New York: International Center for Transitional Justice, 2009.

Hirst, Megan and Howard Varney. 'Justice Abandoned? An Assessment of the Serious Crimes Process in East Timor,' ICTJ Occasional Paper Series, New York: International Center for Transitional Justice, 2005.

Hogg, Charu Lata. 'Sri Lanka: Prospects for Reform and Reconciliation,' Chatham House Asia Programme Paper ASP PP 2011/06 (October 2011).

Huang, Reyko and Geoffrey Gunn. 'Reconciliation as State-Building in East Timor,' *Lusotopie*, Vol. 12 (2004), pp. 19–38.

Human Rights Center, University of California, Berkeley. 'So We Will Never Forget,' January 2009, at http://www.law.berkeley.edu/HRCweb/pdfs/So-We-Will-Never-Forget.pdf (accessed 13 June 2013).

Human Rights Solidarity. 'UNHRCouncil/Sri Lanka: Refusing to Implement Human Rights Committee Recommendations,' (2006), at http://www.hrsolidarity.net/mainfile.php/2006vol16no02/2515/ (accessed 16 June 2011).

Human Rights Watch. 'Sri Lanka: Human Rights Developments,' Human Rights Watch World Report 1999, at http://www.hrw.org/hrw/worldreport99/asia/srilanka.html.

Human Rights Watch. 'Aceh under Martial Law: Inside the Secret War,' 2003 http://www.hrw.org/reports/2003/12/17/aceh-under-martial-law-inside-secret-war (accessed 13 June 2013).

Human Rights Watch. 'Recurring Nightmare: State Responsibility for "Disappearances" and Abductions in Sri Lanka,' 27 August 2008, at http://www.hrw.org/reports/2008/08/27/recurring-nightmare (accessed 13 June 2013).

Human Rights Watch,'Sri Lanka: UN Rights Council Fails Victims,' 27 May 2009, at http://www.hrw.org/news/2009/05/27/sri-lanka-un-rights-council-fails-victims (accessed 11 May 2011).

Human Rights Watch, 'Uncovering Sri Lanka's War Crimes,' 21 January 2010, at http://www.hrw.org/news/2010/01/22/uncovering-sri-lankas-war-crimes (accessed 28 February 2011).

Human Rights Watch. 'Sri Lanka: New Evidence of Wartime Abuses,' 20 May 2010, at http://www.hrw.org/news/2010/05/20/sri-lanka-new-evidence-wartime-abuses (accessed 21 April 2011).

Human Rights Watch. 'Sri Lanka: Report Fails to Advance Accountability,' 16 December 2011, at http://www.hrw.org/news/2011/12/16/sri-lanka-report-fails-advance-accountability (accessed 13 June 2013).

Huntington, Samuel P. *The Third Wave: Democratization in the Late Twentieth Century*, Norman: University of Oklahoma Press, 1991.

Hygrell, Robert. 'Case Study – Aceh Peace Process,' presentation prepared for *CSCAP Study Group on Preventive Diplomacy and the Future of the ASEAN Regional Forum*, Bandar Seri Begawan, 30–31 October, 2007.

Inform. 'Lobby Document: UN Commission on Human Rights, 1995,' Colombo: Inform, 1995, p. 3.

International Center for Transitional Justice (ICTJ). 'Impunity in Timor-Leste: Can the Serious Crimes Investigation Team Make a Difference?' ICTJ, June 2010.

International Crisis Group. 'Resolving East Timor's Crisis,' Asia Report No. 120, 10 October 2006.

International Crisis Group. 'War Crimes in Sri Lanka,' Asia Report No. 191, 17 May 2010, at http://www.crisisgroup.org/en/regions/asia/south-asia/sri-lanka/191-war-crimes-in-sri-lanka.aspx (accessed 15 January 2011).

International Crisis Group. 'Timor-Leste: Reconciliation and Return from Indonesia,' Asia Briefing No. 122, Dili, East Timor and Brussels, 18 April 2011.

International Crisis Group. 'Reconciliation in Sri Lanka: Harder than Ever,' Asia Report No. 209, 18 July 2011, pp. 17–18, at http://www.wsws.org/articles/2004/aug2004/sril-a06.shtml.

International Crisis Group. 'Statement on the Report of Sri Lanka's Lessons Learnt and Reconciliation Commission,' 22 December 2011, at http://www.crisisgroup.org/en/publication-type/media-releases/2011/asia/statement-on-the-report-of-sri-lanka-s-lessons-learnt-and-reconciliation-commission.aspx (accessed 13 June 2013).

Interviews in 'S-21 The Khmer Rouge Killing Machine' film, directed by Pithy Pan.

Interviews with court staff and civil parties conducted by Kirsten Ainley in Cambodia, March 2011.

Jeffery, Renée. 'Forgiveness, Amnesty, and Justice: The Case of the Lord's Resistance Army in Northern Uganda,' *Cooperation and Conflict*, Vol. 46, No. 1 (2011), pp. 78–95.

Jeffery, Renée. 'When Is An Apology Not An Apology? Contrition Chic and Japan's (Un)Apologetic Politics,' *Australian Journal of International Affairs*, Vol. 65, No. 5 (2011), pp. 607–617.

Jeffery, Renée. 'Amnesty and Accountability: The Price of Peace in Aceh,' *International Journal of Transitional Justice*, Vol. 6, No. 1 (2012), pp. 60–82.

Jeffery, Renée. 'Beyond Repair? Collective and Moral Reparations at the Khmer Rouge Tribunal,' *Journal of Human Rights* (forthcoming).

Jeffery, Renée. *The Persistence of Amnesties in World Politics*, Philadelphia: University of Pennsylvania Press (forthcoming).

Jeju Commission, *Jeju Sasam Sageon Jinsang Josa Bogoseo [Report of the Truth About the Jeju 4.3 Events]* Seoul: Jeju Commission, 2003.

Jelin, Elizabeth. *State Repression and the Labors of Memory*, Minneapolis: University of Minnesota Press, 2003.

Jung, Byung-joon. 'Attempts to Settle the Past during the April Popular Struggle,' *Korea Journal*, Vol. 42, No. 3 (2002), pp. 88–111.

Kabutaulaka, Tarcisius Tara. 'Solomon Islands,' *The Contemporary Pacific*, Vol. 16, No. 2 (2004), pp. 393–401.

Kabutaulaka, Tarcisius Tara. 'Australian Foreign Policy and the RAMSI Intervention in Solomon Islands,' *The Contemporary Pacific*, Vol. 17, No. 2 (2005), pp. 283–308.

Katsiaficas, George N. and Kan-Chae Na. *South Korean Democracy: Legacy of the Gwangju Uprising*, New York: Routledge, 2006.

Katzenstein, Suzanne. 'Hybrid Tribunals: Searching for Justice in East Timor,' *Harvard Human Rights Journal*, Vol. 16 (2003), pp. 245–246.

Kemper, Steven. 'J.R. Jayewardene, Righteousness, and Realpolitik,' in Jonathan Spencer (ed.), *Sri Lanka: History and the Roots of Conflict*, London: Routledge, 1990.

Kent, Lia. 'Unfulfilled Expectations: Community Views of the Reconciliation Process,' Report for the Judicial Systems Monitoring Programme, Dili, East Timor: Judicial Systems Monitoring Programme, 2004.

Keohane, Robert and Ruth Grant. 'Accountability and Abuses of Power in World Politics,' *American Political Science Review*, Vol. 99, No. 1 (2005), pp. 29–43.

Kerr, Rachel and Erin Mobekk. *Peace and Justice: Seeking Accountability after War*, Cambridge: Polity, 2007.

Kiernan, Ben and Taylor Owen. 'Roots of U.S. Troubles in Afghanistan: Civilian Bombing Casualties and the Cambodian Precedent,' *The Asia-Pacific Journal*, 28 June 2010, at http://www.japanfocus.org/-ben-kiernan/3380 (accessed 13 June 2013).

Kiernan, Ben. 'The Demography of Genocide in South-East Asia: the Death Tolls in Cambodia, 1975–79, and East Timor, 1975–80,' *Critical Asian Studies*, Vol. 35, No. 4 (2003), pp. 585–597.

Kiernan, Ben. *The Pol Pot Regime: Race, Power, and Genocide in Cambodia under the Khmer Rouge, 1975–79*, New Haven: Yale University Press, 2008.

Kim, Deuk-jung. *'Ppalgaengi'-ui Tansaeng: Yeosun Sageon-gua Bangong Gukga-ui Hyeongseong [The Birth of the "Reds": The Yeosun Events and the Formation of Anticommunist State]*, Seoul: Seonin, 2009.

Kim, Dong Choon. *Jeonjaeng-gua Sahoe [War and Society]*, Seoul: Dolbaegae, 2000.

Kim, Dong-Choon. 'The Long Road toward Truth and Reconciliation,' *Critical Asian Studies*, Vol. 42, No. 4 (2010), pp. 525–552.

Kim, Gi-jin. *Kkeutnaji Aneun Jeonjaeng, Gukmin Bodo Yeonmaeng [Unfinished War: Civilian Massacres during the Korean War]*, Seoul: Yeoksa Bipyeong, 2002.

Kim, Hun Joon. 'Why and When Do Countries Seek to Address Past Human Rights Violations after Transition? An Event History Analysis of 100 Countries Covering 1980–2004,' presentation, Annual Meeting of the International Studies Association, Chicago, Ill., 28 February–3 March 2007.

Kim, Hun Joon. *Expansion of Transitional Justice Measures: A Comparative Analysis of Its Causes*, PhD thesis, University of Minnesota (2009).

Kim, Hun Joon, Geoff Dancy, and Eric Wiebelhaus-Brahm. 'The Turn to Truth: Trends in Truth Commission Experimentation,' *Journal of Human Rights*, Vol. 9, No. 1 (2010), pp. 45–64.

Kim, Hun Joon and Kathryn Sikkink. 'Explaining the Deterrence Effect of Human Rights Prosecutions for Transitional Countries,' *International Studies Quarterly*, Vol. 54, No. 4 (2010), pp. 939–963.

Kim, Hun Joon and Kathryn Sikkink. 'How Do Human Rights Prosecutions Improve Human Rights after Transition?,' *Interdisciplinary Journal of Human Rights Law*, Vol. 7 (2012–2013) (forthcoming).

Kim, Se Kyoon. 'Minjung Movement in Early Liberation Years,' in Research Institute for Korean Politics (ed.), *Modern Korean Politics 1945–1948*, Seoul: Seoul National University, 1993.

Kim, Sunhyuk. *The Politics of Democratization in Korea: The Role of Civil Society*, Pittsburgh, PA: University of Pittsburgh Press, 2000.

Kingsbury, Damian and Michael Leach. 'Introduction,' in Damian Kingsbury and Michael Leach (eds.), *East Timor: Beyond Independence*, Melbourne: Monash University Press, 2007.

Kingston, Jeffrey. 'Balancing Justice and Reconciliation in East Timor,' *Critical Asian Studies*, Vol. 38, No. 3 (2006), pp. 271–302.

Kiss, Elizabeth. 'Moral Ambition Within and Beyond Political Constraints: Reflections on Restorative Justice,' in Robert I. Rotberg and Dennis Thompson (eds.), *Truth v. Justice: The Morality of Truth Commissions*, Princeton: Princeton University Press, 2000.

KPK (Coalition for Truth Recovery). A Proposal for Remedy for Victims of Gross Human Rights Violations in Aceh, Working Paper, 14 June 2007.

Kritz, Neil J. (ed.), *Transitional Justice: How Emerging Democracies Reckon with Former Regimes*, Washington D.C.: United States Institute of Peace, 1995.

Kumara, Sarath. 'Sri Lankan President Offers Empty Apology for 1983 Pogrom,' (6 August 2004), at http://www.wsws.org/articles/2004/aug2004/sril-a06.shtml (accessed 13 June 2013).

Larke, Ben. '". . . And the Truth Shall Set you Free": Confessional Trade-offs and Community Reconciliation in East Timor,' *Asian Journal of Social Science*, Vol. 37, No. 4 (2009), pp. 646–676.

Lederach, John Paul. *Building Peace: Sustainable Reconciliation in Divided Societies*, Tokyo: UNU Press, 1994.

Lessa, Francesca and Leigh A. Payne (eds.), *Amnesty in the Age of Human Rights Accountability: Comparative and International Perspectives*, Cambridge: Cambridge University Press, 2012.

Liddick, Eric Michael and John T. Gagnon, II. 'Striving for Peace and Reconciliation in Sri Lanka: A Creative Solution to Conflict,' *War Crimes, Genocide, and Crimes Against Humanity*, Vol. 3 (2009), pp. 39–88.

Liloquila, Ruth. 'Understanding Conflict in Solomon Islands: A Practical Means to Peacemaking,' State, Society and Governance in Melanesia

Discussion Paper 2000/7, Australian National University, Research School of Pacific and Asian Studies.

Lipscomb, Leigh-Ashley. *Housing the Truth: The Archived Legacy of Transitional Justice in Timor-Leste*, unpublished PhD thesis, University of California, Berkeley, 2011.

Lutz, Ellen and Caitlin Reiger (eds.), *Prosecuting Heads of State*, New York: Cambridge University Press, 2009.

Lutz, Ellen and Kathryn Sikkink. 'The Justice Cascade: The Evolution and Impact of Foreign Human Rights Trials in Latin America,' *Chicago Journal of International Law*, Vol. 2, No. 1 (2001), pp. 1–34.

MacGinty, Roger. 'Indigenous Peace-Making Versus the Liberal Peace,' *Cooperation and Conflict*, Vol. 43, No. 2 (2008), pp. 139–163.

Maebuta, Jack and Rebecca Spence with Iris Wielders and Michael O'Loughlin. 'Attempts at Building Peace in the Solomon Islands: Disconnected Layers,' Reflecting on Peace Practice Project, Cumulative Impact Case Study, Cambridge, MA: Collaborative Learning Projects, 2009.

Mani, Rama. *Beyond Retribution: Seeking Justice in the Shadows of War*, Cambridge: Polity, 2002.

Marzuki, A. & N. Warsidi, *Fakta Bicara: Mengungkap Pelanggaran HAM di Aceh 1989–2005* Banda Aceh, Indonesia: Koalisi NGO HAM Aceh, 2011.

Matsueda, Ross L., Derek A. Kreager, and David Huizinga, 'Deterring Delinquents: A Rational Choice Model of Theft and Violence,' *American Sociological Review*, Vol. 71, No. 1 (2006), pp. 95–122.

Matthews, Bruce. 'Devolution of Power in Sri Lanka,' *The Round Table: The Commonwealth Journal of International Affairs*, Vol. 76, No. 301 (1987), pp. 74–92.

McCargo, Duncan. 'Politics by Other Means?,' *International Affairs*, Vol. 87, No. 3 (2011), pp. 613–627.

McCarthy, Bill. 'New Economics of Sociological Criminology,' *Annual Review of Sociology*, Vol. 28 (2002), pp. 417–442.

McEvoy, Kieran. 'Letting Go of Legalism: Developing a "Thicker" Version of Transitional Justice' in Kieran McEvoy and Lorna McGrgor (eds.), *Transitional Justice from Below: Grassroots Activism and the Struggle for Change*, Oxford: Hart Publishing, 2008.

McEvoy, Kieran, Harry Mika, and Barbara Hudson. 'Introduction: Practice, Performance, and Prospects for Restorative Justice,' *British Journal of Criminology*, Vol. 42, No. 3 (2002), pp. 469–475.

Meernik, James D., Angela Nichols, and Kimi L. King. 'The Impact of International Tribunals and Domestic Trials on Peace and Human Rights after Civil War,' *International Studies Perspectives*, Vol. 11, No. 4 (2010), pp. 309–334.

Méndez, Juan E. 'Accountability for Past Abuses,' *Human Rights Quarterly*, Vol. 19, No. 2 (1997), pp. 255–282.

Mesquita, Bruce Bueno de and Lawrence E. Cohen. 'Self-Interest, Equity, and Crime Control: A Game-Theoretic Analysis of Criminal Decision Making,' *Criminology*, Vol. 33, No. 4 (1995), pp. 483–518.

Mietzner, Marcus. *Military Politics, Islam, and the State in Indonesia: From Turbulent Transition to Democratic Consolidation*, Singapore: Institute of Southeast Asian Studies, 2009.

Moore, Clive. 'The RAMSI Intervention in the Solomon Islands Crisis,' *The Journal of Pacific Studies*, Vol. 28, No. 1 (2005), pp. 56–77.

Morgan, Michael G. and Abby McLeod. 'Have We Failed our Neighbour?,' *Australian Journal of International Affairs*, Vol. 60, No. 3 (2006), pp. 412–428.

Morris, Allison. 'Critiquing the Critics: A Brief Response to Critics of Restorative Justice,' *British Journal of Criminology*, Vol. 42, No. 3 (2002), pp. 596–615.

Nagin, Daniel S. 'Criminal Deterrence Research at the Outset of the Twenty-First Century,' *Crime and Justice*, Vol. 23 (1998), pp. 1–42.

Nagy, Rosemary. 'Traditional Justice and Legal Pluralism in Transitional Context: The Case of Rwanda's Gacaca Courts' in Joanna R. Quinn (ed.), *Reconciliation(s): Transitional Justice in Postconflict Societies*, Montreal: McGill-Queens University Press, 2009.

Nam, Si-Uk. *Hanguk Bosu Seryeok Yeongu [A Study of Conservatives in Korea]* Seoul: Cheong Media, 2011.

Neier, Aryeh. 'What Should be Done About the Guilty?', *New York Review of Books*, Vol. 37, No.1 (1990), pp. 32–35.

Neou, Kassie and Jeffrey C. Gallup. 'Human Rights and the Cambodian Past: In Defense of Peace Before Justice,' *Human Rights Dialogue*, Vol. 1, No. 8 (1997), pp. 9–11.

Nesiah, Vasuki. 'Unpacking the Truth,' *Sunday Island Oline*, 16 August 2009, at http://www.island.lk/2009/08/16/features5.html (accessed 13 June 2013).

Nevins, Joseph. *A Not So Distant Horror: Mass Violence in East Timor*, Ithaca, NY: Cornell University Press, 2005.

Ngor, Haing. *Survival in the Killing Fields*, London: Robinson, 1987.

O'Callaghan, Mary-Louise. 'RAMSI – the Way Ahead' in Sinclair Dinnen and Stewart Firth (eds.), *Politics and Statebuilding in Solomon Islands*, Canberra: ANU E-Press, 2008.

O'Donnell, Guillermo A. and Philippe C. Schmitter. *Transitions from Authoritarian Rule: Conclusions about Uncertain Democracies*, Baltimore: Johns Hopkins University Press, 1986.

Oh, Bonnie B. C. (ed.). *Korea under the American Military Government, 1945~1948*, Westport, CN: Praeger, 2002.

Oh, John Kie-chiang. *Korean Politics: The Quest for Democratization and Economic Development*, Ithaca, NY: Cornell University Press, 1999.

Olsen, Tricia D., Leigh A. Payne, and Andrew G. Reiter. *Transitional Justice in Balance: Comparing Processes, Weighing Efficacy*, Washington D.C.: United States Institute of Peace, 2010.

Olsen, Tricia D., Leigh A. Layne, and Andrew G. Reiter. 'The Justice Balance: When Transitional Justice Improves Human Rights and Democracy,' *Human Rights Quarterly*, Vol. 32, No. 4 (2010), pp. 980–1007.

Olsen, Tricia D., Leigh A. Payne, and Andrew G. Reiter. 'Conclusion: Amnesty in the Age of Accountability,' in Francesca Lessa and Leigh A. Payne (eds.), *Amnesty in the Age of Human Rights Accountability: Comparative and International Perspectives*, Cambridge and New York: Cambridge University Press, 2012.

Orentlicher, Diane F. 'Settling Accounts: The Duty to Prosecute Human Rights Violations of a Prior Regime,' *Yale Law Journal*, Vol. 100, No. 8 (1991), pp. 2537–2615.

Palmer, Blair. 'Peace, Patronage and Post-Conflict Elections in Aceh,' in Edward Aspinall and Marcus Mietzner (eds.), *Problems of Democratisation in Indonesia: Elections, Institutions and Society*, Singapore: Institute of Southeast Asian Studies, 2010, pp. 286–306.

Park, Won Soon. *Gukgaboanbeop Yeongu 1: Gukgaboanbeop Byeoncheonsa [A Study of National Security Act 1]*, Seoul: Yoksa Bipyung, 1994.

Parliament of Solomon Islands. Parliamentary Inquiry into the Facilitation of International Assistance Notice 2003 and RAMSI Intervention, Chairman, Hon. Peter Boyers, Honiara, 2009.

Pasqualucci, Jo M. 'Victim Reparations in the Inter-American Human Rights System: A Critical Assessment of Current Practice and Procedure,' *Michigan Journal of International Law*, Vol. 18 (1996–1997), pp. 1–58.

Permanent Mission of Sri Lanka, 'Situation Report,' Colombo and Geneva: Permanent Mission, 1993.

Petit, Robert. 'Lawfare and International Tribunals,' *Case Western Reserve Journal of International Law*, Vol. 43, Nos. 1–2 (2010), pp. 189–198.

Picken, Margot. 'The Beleaguered Cambodians,' *New York Review of Books*, 13 January 2011, p. 4.

Pigou, Pierre. 'The Community Reconciliation Process of the Commission for Reception, Truth and Reconciliation,' *Evaluation Report for the UNDP*, Dili, East Timor: United Nations Development Programme, 2004.

Pinto-Jayewardena, Kishali. *The Rule of Law in Decline: Study on Prevalence, Determinants, and Causes of Torture and Other Forms of Cruel, Inhuman, or Degrading Treatment or Punishment in Sri Lanka*, Copenhagen: Rehabilitation and Research Centre for Torture Victims, 2009.

Pinto-Jayewardena, Kishali. *Still Seeking Justice in Sri Lanka: Rule of Law, The Criminal Justice System and Commissions of Inquiry since 1977*, Bangkok: International Commission of Jurists, 2010.

Pollard, Alice Aruhe'eta. 'Understanding Conflict in Solomon Islands: A Practical Means to Peacemaking,' State, Society and Governance in Melanesia Discussion Paper 2000/7, Australian National University, Research School of Pacific and Asian Studies.

Powles, Anna. 'Mission Creep: Statebuilding from Honiara to Dili,' *Security Challenges*, Vol. 2, No. 2 (2006), pp. 9–14.

Punyasena, Wasana. 'The Facade of Accountability: Disappearances in Sri Lanka,' *Boston College Third World Law Journal*, Vol. 23, No. 1 (2003), pp. 115–158.

Quinn, Joanna R. 'What of Reconciliation? Traditional Mechanisms of Acknowledgment in Uganda' in Joanna R. Quinn (ed.), *Reconciliation(s): Transitional Justice in Postconflict Societies*, Montreal: McGill-Queen's University Press, 2009, pp. 174–206.

Ratner, Steven R. and Jason S. Abrams. *Accountability for Human Rights Atrocities in International Law: Beyond the Nuremberg Legacy*, New York: Oxford University Press, 2001.

Reiger, Caitlin and Marieke Wierda. The Serious Crimes Process in Timor-Leste: In Retrospect, ICTJ Prosecutions Case Studies Series, New York: International Center for Transitional Justice, 2006.

Redress Trust. 'Comments and Recommendations to the Secretary-General's Panel of Experts on the Issue of Accountability with Regard to Alleged Violations of International Human Rights and Humanitarian Law during the Final Stages of the Conflict in Sri Lanka,' (15 December 2010), at http://www.redress.org.

Report of the Secretary-General's Panel of Experts on Accountability in Sri Lanka (31 March 2011).

Republic of Indonesia and the Government of Timor- Leste. Terms of Reference for the Commission of Truth and Friendship (2005), at http://www.etan.org/et2005/march/06/10tor.htm (accessed 5 July 2010).

Republic of Indonesia and the United Nations Transitional Administration in East Timor. Memorandum of Understanding between the Republic of Indonesia and the United Nations Transitional Administration in East Timor regarding Cooperation in Legal, Judicial and Human Rights Related Matters (5–6 April 2000), at http://www.unmit.org/legal/Other-Docs/mou-id-untaet.htm (accessed 3 January 2010).

Richmond, Oliver P. 'A Genealogy of Peace and Conflict Theory' in Oliver P. Richmond (ed.), *Palgrave Advances in Peacebuilding: Critical Developments and Approaches*, Basingstoke: Palgrave Macmillan, 2010.

Richmond, Oliver P. 'De-romanticising the Local, De-mystifying the International: Hybridity in Timor Leste and the Solomon Islands,' *The Pacific Review*, Vol. 24, No. 1 (2011), pp. 115–136.

Risse, Thomas, Stephen C. Ropp, and Kathryn Sikkink (eds.), *The Power of Human Rights: International Norms and Domestic Change*, Cambridge: Cambridge University Press, 1999.

Robins, Simon. 'An Assessment of the Needs of Families of the Missing in Timor-Leste,' Report for the Post War Reconstruction and Development Unit, February 2010, York: University of York, 2010.

Robinson, Darryl. 'Serving the Interests of Justice: Amnesties, Truth Commissions and the International Criminal Court,' *European Journal of International Law*, Vol. 14, No. 3 (2003), pp. 481–505.

Robinson, Geoffrey. *East Timor: Crimes Against Humanity*, report commissioned by the OHCHR, Geneva: Office of the High Commissioner for Human Rights, 2003.

Robinson, Geoffrey. *If You Leave Us Here, We Will Die: How Genocide Was Stopped in East Timor*, Princeton, New Jersey: Princeton University Press, 2010.

Robinson, Michael E. *Korea's Twentieth-Century Odyssey*, 6th ed. Honolulu, HI: University of Hawaii Press, 2007.

Roht-Arriaza, Naomi. 'State Responsibility to Investigate and Prosecute Grave Human Rights Violations in International Law,' *California Law Review*, Vol. 78, No. 2 (1990), pp. 449–514.

Roht-Arriaza, Naomi (ed.). *Impunity and Human Rights in International Law and Practice*, New York: Oxford University Press, 1995.

Roht-Arriaza, Naomi. 'Civil Society Processes of Accountability' in M. Cherif Bassiouni (ed.), *Post-Conflict Justice*, Ardsley, NY: Transnational Publishers, 2002.

Roht-Arriaza, Naomi. 'The New Landscape of Transitional Justice' in Naomi Roht-Arriaza and Javier Mariezcurrena (eds.), *Transitional Justice in the Twenty-First Century: Beyond Truth versus Justice*, Cambridge: Cambridge University Press, 2006.

Rordam, Sofie. 'Sri Lanka: Police Torture as an Indicator of the Constitutional Degradation of the Rule of Law,' Human Rights (12 January 2011), at http://www.humanrights.asia/news/ahrc-news/ (accessed 16 June 2011).

Sadat, Leila Nadya. 'Redefining Universal Jurisdiction,' *New England Law Review*, Vol. 35 (2000–2001), pp. 241–263.

Samsidar, 'Kehidupan korban yang semakin sulit,' in M. Nashrun & W. Adi (eds.) *Fakta Bicara: Mengungkap Pelanggaran HAM di Aceh 1989–2005*, Vol. 1, Banda Aceh, Indonesia: Koalisi NGO HAM (2011), pp. 209–213.

Scharf, Michael. 'The Letter of the Law: The Scope of the International Legal Obligation to Prosecute Human Rights Crimes,' *Law and Contemporary Problems*, Vol. 59, No. 4 (1996), pp. 41–61.

Scheffer, David. 'International Judicial Intervention,' *Foreign Policy*, Vol. 102 (1996), pp. 34–51.

Seibert-Fohr, Anja. 'The Relevance of the Rome Statute of the International Criminal Court for Amnesties and Truth Commissions,' *Max Planck Yearbook of Unbited Nations Law*, Vol. 7 (2004), pp. 553–590.

Seo, Jung-seok. *Cho Bongam gua 1950 [Cho Bong Am and 1950s, Vol. 2]*, Seoul: Yoksa Bipyung, 1999.

Shaw, Rosalind. 'Rethinking Truth and Reconciliation Commissions: Lessons from Sierra Leone,' United States Institute of Peace Special Report 130 (2005).

Shawcross, William. 'Sideshow: Kissinger, Nixon and the Destruction of Cambodia,' New York: Cooper Square Press, 2002.

Shin, Gi-Wook. *Ethnic Nationalism in Korea: Genealogy, Politics, and Legacy*, Studies of the Walter H. Shorenstein Asia-Pacific Research Center, Stanford, CA: Stanford University Press, 2006.

Shin, Gi-Wook and Kyung Moon Hwang (eds.), *Contentious Kwangju: The May 18th Uprising in Korea's Past and Present*, Lanham, MD: Rowman & Littlefield, 2003.

Shin, Gi-Wook, Woon-Won Park, and Daqing Yang (eds.), *Rethinking Historical Injustice and Reconciliation in Northeast Asia: The Korean Experience*, New York: Routledge, 2007.

Sikkink, Kathryn. *The Justice Cascade: How Human Rights Prosecutions Are Changing the World*, New York: Norton, 2011.

Sikkink, Kathryn and Carrie Booth Walling. 'The Impact of Human Rights Trials in Latin America,' *Journal of Peace Research*, Vol. 44, No. 4 (2007), pp. 427–445.

Singer, Marshall R. 'Sri Lanka's Ethnic Conflict: Have Bombs Shattered Hopes for Peace?,' *Asian Survey*, Vol. 36, No. 11 (1996), pp. 1146–1155.

Skaar, Elin. 'Truth Commissions, Trials – or Nothing? Policy Options in Democratic Transitions,' *Third World Quarterly*, Vol. 20, No. 6 (1999), pp. 1109–1128.

Slye, Ronald C. 'A Limited Amnesty? Insights from Cambodia' in F. Lessa & L. Payne (eds.), *Amnesty in the Age of Human Rights Accountability*, Cambridge: Cambridge University Press, 2012, pp. 291–314.

Snyder, Jack and Leslie Vinjamuri, 'Trials and Errors: Principle and Pragmatism in Strategies of International Justice,' *International Security* Vol. 28, No. 3 (2003), pp. 5–44.

Sohn, Louis B. and R. R. Baxter, 'Responsibility of States for Injuries to the Economic Interests of Aliens', *American Journal of International Law*, Vol. 55 (1961), pp. 545–546.

Solomon, Richard H. 'Preface' to Neil J. Kritz (ed.), *Transitional Justice: How Emerging Democracies Reckon with Former Regimes*, Vol. 3, Washington D.C.: United States Institute for Peace, 1995.

Solomon Islands Truth and Reconciliation Act. No. 5 of 2008, article 20(b), at http://www.paclii.org/sb/legis/num_act/tarca2008371/ (accessed 2 May 2011).

Sri Lanka. Report of the Presidential Commission of Inquiry into the Assassination of Mr. Vijaya Kumaratunga, Colombo, Sri Lanka: Department of Government Printing, 1996.

Sri Lanka. Final Report of the Commission of Inquiry into Involuntary Removal or Disappearance of Persons in the Western, Southern, and Sabaragamuwa Provinces, Sessional Paper No. V, Colombo, Sri Lanka: Department of Government Printing, 1997.

Sri Lanka. Final Report of the Commission of Inquiry into the Involuntary Removal of Persons in the Central, Northwestern and Uva Provinces,

Sessional Paper No. VI, Colombo, Sri Lanka: Department of Government Printing, 1997.

Sri Lanka. *Final Report of the Commission of Inquiry into the Involuntary Removal or Disappearances of Persons in the Northern and Eastern Provinces*, Sessional Paper No. VII, Colombo, Sri Lanka: Department of Government Printing, 1997.

Sri Lanka. *Report of the Special Presidential Commission of Inquiry Regarding the Assassination of the late Lalith Athulathmudali PC and Connected Events*, Colombo, Sri Lanka: Department of Government Publications, 1997.

Sri Lanka Democracy Forum. 'Submission to the Universal Periodic Review of Sri Lanka,' (9 February 2008), at http://www.srilankademocracy.org/files/SLDFUPRSubmission08February2008.pdf (accessed 28 February 2011).

Sriram, Chandra Lekha. 'Revolutions in Accountability: New Approaches to Past Abuses,' *American University International Law Review*, Vol. 19, No. 2 (2003), pp. 310–429.

Sriram, Chandra Lekha. *Confronting Past Human Rights Violations*, London: Frank Cass, 2004.

Sriram, Chandra Lekha. *Globalizing Justice for Mass Atrocities: A Revolution in Accountability*, London: Routledge, 2005.

Sriram, Chandra Lekha. 'Transitional Justice and Peacebuilding,' in Chandra Lekha Sriram and Suren Pillay (eds.), *Peace versus Justice? The Dilemma of Transitional Justice in Africa*, Scottsville: University of KwaZulu-Natal Press, 2009.

Staggs Kelsall, Michelle et al., 'Lessons Learned from the 'Duch' Trial,' Asian International Justice Initiative's KRT Trial Monitoring Group, December 2009.

Stanley, Elizabeth. *Torture, Truth and Justice: the Case of Timor-Leste*, London: Routledge, 2008.

Stanley, Elizabeth. 'The Political Economy of Transitional Justice in Timor-Leste,' in K. McEvoy and L. McGregor (eds.), *Transitional Justice from Below: Grassroots Activism and the Struggle for Change*, Oxford: Hart Publishing, 2008.

Subedi, Surya. 'The UN Human Rights Mandate in Cambodia,' *The International Journal of Human Rights*, Vol. 15, No. 2 (2011), pp. 247–261.

Subotic, Jelena. *Hijacked Justice: Dealing with the Past in the Balkans*, Ithaca: Cornell University Press, 2009.

Tambiah, SJ. *Sri Lanka: Ethnic Fratricide and the Dismantling of Democracy*, Chicago: University of Chicago Press, 1991.

Taylor, John. *East Timor: The Price of Freedom*, London and New York: Zed Books, 1999.

Teitel, Ruti G. 'Transitional Justice Genealogy,' *Harvard Human Rights Journal*, Vol. 16 (2003), pp. 69–94.

Testimony of Fr. Lionel Longarata, TRC Visale Public Hearing Day One, 23 June 2010, at http://solomonislands-trc.com/public-hearing-sessions/visale-public-hearing-session-one.html (accessed 2 May 2011).

The Centre for International Governance Innovation (CIGI). Security Sector Reform Monitor: Timor-Leste (SSRM January 2011, No. 4), Waterloo, Ontario, Canada, 2011.

The Group of Experts for Cambodia. Report of the Group of Experts for Cambodia Pursuant to General Assembly Resolution 52/135 (UN Doc. S/1999/231, A/53/850) (16 March 1999).

The Townsville Peace Agreement. Preamble, 15 October 2000, at http://www.commerce.gov.sb/Gov/Peace_Agreement.htm (accessed 2 May 2011).

Thomson, Aileen. 'Truth and Reconciliation in the Solomon Islands,' *The Human Rights Brief*, Center for Human Rights and Humanitarian Law, 16 April 2010, at http://hrbrief.org/2010/04/truth-and-reconciliation-in-the-solomon-islands/ (accessed 2 May 2011).

Timmer, Jaap. 'Kastom and Theocracy: a Reflection on Governance from the Uttermost Past of the World,' in Sinclair Dinnen and Stewart Firth (eds.), *Politics and Statebuilding in Solomon Islands*, Canberra: ANU E-Press, 2008.

Transitional Justice Database Project, at http://sites.google.com/sites/transitionaljusticedatabase/home (accessed 20 May 2011).

Truth and Reconciliation Commission Republic of Korea. Mass Sacrifice of Civilian, in *Jinsil Hwahae Wiweonhoe Jonghap Bogoseo [The Final Report of the Truth and Reconciliation Commission, Republic of Korea]*, 4 vols., Vol. 3. Seoul: Truth and Reconciliation Commission, Republic of Korea, 2010.

Tutu, Desmond. *No Future without Forgiveness*, New York: Doubleday, 1999.

UK House of Commons Library. 'War and Peace in Sri Lanka,' *Research Paper 09/51* (5 June 2009).

Un, Kheang. 'Cambodia: Moving Away from Democracy?,' *International Political Science Review*, Vol. 32, No. 5 (2011), pp. 546–562.

United Nations. Report of the High Commissioner for Human Rights on the Human Rights Situation in East Timor (UN Doc. E/CN.4/S-4/CRP.1) (17 September 1999).

United Nations. Report on the International Commission of Inquiry on East Timor to the Secretary General, Office of the High Commissioner for Human Rights (UN Doc. S/2000/59) (January 2000).

United Nations. Human Development Report 2000, at http://hdr.undp.org/en/media/hdr_2000_ch5.pdf (accessed 3 March 2011).

United Nations. Report of the Secretary General on the United Nations Transitional Administration in East Timor (UN Doc. S/2002/432) (14 April 2002), at http://daccess-dds-ny.un.org/doc/UNDOC/GEN/N02/327/74/IMG/N0232774.pdf?OpenElement (accessed 13 June 2013).

United Nations. Report of the Secretary-General on The Rule of Law and Transitional Justice in Conflict and Post-Conflict Societies (UN Doc. S/2004/616) (23 August 2004), at http://daccess-dds-ny.un.org/doc/UNDOC/GEN/N04/395/29/PDF/N0439529.pdf?OpenElement (accessed 6 June 2011).

United Nations. Report of the Independent Expert to Update the Set of Principles to Combat Impunity, Diane Orentlicher on Promotion and Protection of Human Rights (UN Doc. E/CN.4/2005/102) (2005).

United Nations. Rule-of-Law Tools for Post-Conflict States: Truth Commissions, Office of the High Commissioner for Human Rights (OHCHR). (UN Doc. HR/PUB/06/1) (2006), at http://www.ohchr.org/Documents/Publications/RuleoflawTruthCommissionsen.pdf (accessed 13 June 2013).

United Nations. Analytical Study of the HC – Human Rights and Transitional Justice – Addendum, Office of the High Commissioner for Human Rights (OHCHR). (UN Doc. A/HRC/12/19) (2009).

United Nations. Report of the Secretary-General on the United Nations Integrated Mission in Timor-Leste for the period from 24 September 2009 to 20 January 2010 (UN Doc. S/2010/85) (12 February 2010).

United Nations Security Council (UNSC). UNTAET Mandate, Security Council Resolution 1272 (UN Doc. S/RES/1272) (1999), at http://daccess-dds-ny.un.org/doc/UNDOC/GEN/N99/312/77/PDF/N9931277.pdf?Open Element (accessed 19 May 2010).

United Nations Security Council (UNSC). Security Council Resolution 1264 (UN Doc. S/RES/1264) (15 September 1999), at http://daccess-dds-ny.un.org/doc/UNDOC/GEN/N99/264/81/PDF/N9926481.pdf?OpenElement (accessed 13 June 2013).

United Nations Security Council (UNSC). UN Security Council 5351st meeting, the Situation in East Timor (UN Doc. S/Pv.5351) (23 January 2006), at http://www.un.org/ga/search/view_doc.asp?symbol=S/PV.5351 (accessed 13 June 2013).

United States Department of State. Sri Lanka Country Report on Human Rights Practices for 1997, at http://www.state.gov/www/global/human_rights/1997_hrp_report/srilanka.htm.

United States Department of State. 'Solomon Islands,' Country Reports on Human Rights Practices, Bureau of Democracy, Human Rights, and Labor (25 February 2004), p. 2, at http://www.state.gov/g/drl/rls/hrrpt/2003/27789.htm (accessed 2 May 2011).

United States Department of State. Report to Congress on Incidents During the Recent Conflict in Sri Lanka (2009), at http://www.state.gov/documents/organization/131025.pdf (accessed 28 February 2011).

Varathasuntharam, V. 'Nine Soldiers Indicted on Abduction and Murder Charges,' *The Island* (3 July 1997).

Villa-Vicencio, Charles. 'Why Perpetrators Should Not Always Be Prosecuted: Where the International Criminal Court and Truth Commissions Meet,' *Emory Law Journal*, Vol. 49, No. 1 (2000), pp. 205–222.

Vinjamuri, Leslie and Jack Snyder. 'Advocacy and Scholarship in the Study of International War Crimes Tribunals and Transitional Justice,' *Annual Review of Political Science*, Vol. 7, No. 1 (2004), pp. 345–362.

Wainwright, Elsina. *Our Failing Neighbour: Australia and the Future of Solomon Islands*, Australia Strategic Policy Institute Report, Barton: ASPI, 2003.

Watson, James. 'A Model Pacific Solution? A Study of the Deployment of the Regional Assistance Mission to Solomon Islands,' Working Paper No. 126, Canberra: Land Warfare Studies Centre, 2005.

Weissbrodt, David and Paul W. Fraser. 'Report of the Chilean National Commission on Truth and Reconciliation,' *Human Rights Quarterly*, Vol. 14, No. 4 (1992), pp. 610–622.

Xavier, Sujith. 'Sri Lankan Presidential Commission of Inquiry (2007): Did It Amount to a Fair Hearing?,' *Mexican Yearbook of International Law*, Vol. 10 (2010), at http://biblio.juridicas.unam.mx/estrev/derint/cont/10/cmt/cmt14.htm (accessed 13 June 2013).

Zehr, Howard. 'Restorative Justice: The Concept,' *Corrections Today*, Vol. 59, No. 7 (1997), pp. 68–70.

Index